SOLIDARITY FOR SALE

SOLIDARITY FOR SALE

HOW CORRUPTION DESTROYED THE LABOR MOVEMENT

AND UNDERMINED AMERICA'S PROMISE

ROBERT FITCH

PublicAffairs

NEW YORK

Published in the United States by PublicAffairs™, a member of the Perseus Books Group.

BOOK DESIGN AND COMPOSITION BY JENNY DOSSIN.

Library of Congress Cataloging-in-Publication Data

Fitch, Robert, 1938–

Solidarity for sale : how corruption destroyed the labor movement and undermined America's promise / Robert Fitch.—1st ed.

p.   cm.

Includes index.

ISBN–13 978–1–891620–72–0

ISBN–10 1–891620–72-X

1. Labor unions—Corrupt practices—United States. 2. Organized crime—United States. 3. Labor movement—United States—History. 4. Labor leaders—United States—History. I. Title.

HD6490.C642U535 2006

331.8'0973—dc22

2005049219

FIRST EDITION

10 9 8 7 6 5 4 3 2 1

For Jack Schierenbeck:
valued mentor, loyal friend, fearless journalist

CONTENTS

PREFACE

"*Mokita*" is the term used by the Trobriand Islanders of Papua New Guinea for a truth that everybody knows but no one talks about.[1] Corruption is *mokita* in the AFL-CIO. For generations, in the construction, longshore, hospitality, and teamster unions, mobsters have had more influence than the members in choosing the leaders; pension funds are stolen; and bribes smooth the way for contractors to replace union members with lower-paid non-union workers. To control union wrongdoing, the Justice Department routinely resorts to the federal Racketeer Influenced and Corrupt Organizations (RICO) Act, treating labor unions as criminal enterprises. In defense, union leaders provide politicians huge contributions—essentially for Get Out of Jail Free cards.

Even though, as a Harris Poll released just before Labor Day 2005 showed, most *union* households disapprove of American unions, the main reason for their disapproval is never openly discussed in union media or addressed at union conventions.[2] "Sure, unions are flawed," the defenders of American unions will concede when pressed. "They have people in them. So what do you expect? But they're like democracy: a flawed solution that is preferable to any of its competitors."

But it's misleading to blame the pervasive corruption of American unions on human nature or on the nature of unionism. You don't find gangsters running European unions.

Nor does blaming the values of American business culture get us far. Even the leftists who ostentatiously reject those values somehow wind up living by them when they become American union leaders.

Corruption flows rather from the retarded development of American unions, which still haven't broken out of nineteenth-century models of labor organization. The classic aim of the American union is still to monopolize a territory; the means—an exclusive bargaining contract; the result—20,000 local unions that inevitably behave more like semiautonomous fiefdoms than like a genuine labor movement pursuing the common good for working people.

Despite the way corruption cripples every vital union function—from organizing to mounting strikes to safeguarding pension money—even many dedicated unionists believe that any open discussion of the corruption problem would undermine the movement. Most progressives inside the AFL-CIO deeply resent critics of union corruption. Yet I believe well-meaning insiders who close their eyes to the significance of corruption can and must be challenged, because for years, as a union member and later as a union staffer, I was one of them.

In the beginning, at least, my blindness could be attributed to youth. I was fifteen when I joined Local 5 of the Laborers. The ordinary members of the local couldn't figure out what I was doing in the Chicago Heights, Illinois, based organization. Most members were Italian or black. I was Jewish, and I'd been wearing big thick glasses from the time I was five. "Cookie," a giant black fellow ditch digger, immediately dubbed me "The Professor." Although he watched my back, he rode me constantly. I would retort that he was welcome to reign as the Lord of the Ditches, but I was going to college.

One late summer afternoon just before the 4:30 quitting time, I was digging away in a rowhouse project, just south of Chicago Heights and a few miles west of the Indiana border. I noticed a small cloud of dust on the flat horizon. It kept getting bigger and bigger, until the cloud produced a big black Buick that pulled up to my ditch. Two men in suits got out. They were business agents from Local 5. Towering over me, as I stood clutching my shovel, the shorter one insisted, "You gotta pay your initiation fee." I'd just been paid, so I reached into my back pocket, took out my sweat-soaked wallet, and handed over the cash. While I don't remember getting a receipt, I do distinctly recall being politely thanked. Then the two suits drove away in the Buick.

I forgot about my brief encounter with the Local 5 officials until many years later. In 1986, I was just beginning a career in the labor movement when Chicago was shaken by the news of one of the most brutal of the more than 1,000 gangland murders in the city's history. The bodies of Anthony "The Ant" Spilotro and his brother Michael, both members of the

Chicago Outfit, had been found buried in a shallow grave in an Indiana cornfield. They'd been beaten with shovels and then buried alive. The revolting and terrifying "batting practice" scene is reprised near the end of Martin Scorsese's *Casino*.

Federal authorities found the bodies and the man who supervised the operation. He was Albert Tocco, the boss of the Chicago Heights crew that ran Local 5. His wife, Betty, gave him up by leading authorities to where the bodies were buried, and Tocco eventually received a 200-year sentence. According to testimony provided in 1997 at the trusteeship hearings into mob control of the Chicago Laborers District Council, Tocco had help from Local 5 officials: Nicholas "Nickie" Guzzino and Dominick "Tootsie" Palermo. They wielded the shovels.[3]

It still gives me a shiver to think about the Spilotros' burial by union business agents. But had I known about it at the time, I don't think it would have affected my decision to become a business agent myself. Some years before the Indiana massacre, I'd made good on my boast to Cookie. I'd graduated from college and earned enough academic credentials from the University of California, Berkeley, to become an academic gypsy. After bouncing back and forth between low-rung positions at Cornell and New York University, I began to get union staff jobs through the left-wing job network. By 1990, I'd moved up to consulting for a small Tribeca-based municipal union run by leftists. My job was to produce a very ambitious economic development proposal: a Henry George–style land reform, taxing Wall Street, reviving manufacturing, and bringing back the New York City port.

To get support beyond the handful of leftist unions that tacitly supported the economic program, I argued that we ought to try to reach out to the International Longshoremen's Association. "Who has a more direct stake in the revival of the port than the longshoremen's union?" I reasoned. And Lou Valentino, political director and former business manager of Brooklyn's Local 1814, seemed like the go-to guy. Lou was running for a city council seat from south Brooklyn. My boss agreed to write him a small check—$500 from our campaign funds. I even got permission to put the money in Valentino's hands myself.

Feeling like a player in New York City electoral politics, I walked the dozen or so blocks from Borough Hall down Court Street to the old headquarters of Local 1814. I was brought up short when above the doorway into the union hall, I read the inscription "The Anthony Anastasio Memorial Hall." I knew that name from New York City history. Most notoriously, Anthony shared the surname with his brother Albert—a founder of the Gambino crime family and the boss of Murder Inc.[4] For an instant I wondered if I should turn around. But it was too late. Besides, what would I tell my boss? I entered the building and asked a secretary, "Where's Lou?" "He's upstairs," the secretary replied. I walked up a single flight to find him all alone in a bare room just a few days before the election. He was shouting hoarsely into a telephone, "Get me half a dozen Puerto Ricans and put them on a flatbed truck." Although distracted, Lou seemed glad to get the check I'd handed him.

Practically the next day, Wayne Barrett, the principal investigative reporter for the *Village Voice,* wrote a feature story explaining who Lou Valentino really was: a Gambino crime family associate. Valentino had testified at the 1979 trial of Anthony Scotto, a Gambino captain and Lou's predecessor as Local 1814 boss. On the witness stand, Valentino acknowledged that Scotto had ordered him to take $50,000 in cash from Anthony Anastasio and give it to Mario Cuomo's 1977 mayoral campaign.[5]

Cash contributions over $100 are illegal. Valentino, who had been the favorite, lost the city council race. But instead of feeling foolish that I'd tried to help elect a mob associate, I remember feeling let down by Barrett. Here we in the labor movement were trying to do something progressive in the economic development field, and we were being undermined, in the left-wing press, by corruption charges.[6]

Perhaps if my union client hadn't decided to can me, I'd still be developing vast plans for urban economic reform, rationalizing alliances with the mob, and fulminating against muckraking radical journalists. But returning to academia, and freelancing for the *Voice* myself, gave me a second chance to reflect on the low moral horizon of the American labor movement.

Even our classic fallback excuse for union corruption—that big corporations are just as bad or worse—started to wear thin. So what if they are? We don't rely on tobacco companies or HMOs to produce social justice or fight inequality. Because our expectations are low, corporate executives can hurt us only once. But because unions are supposed to stand for something besides the worship of the golden calf, union leaders can actually hurt us twice: first with the blow to our wallets, and then with the blow to our hearts.

The refusal to probe seriously the sources of organized labor's failure shows that liberals and progressives don't take their own political vocation seriously. A half century ago, in *American Capitalism*, liberal economist John Kenneth Galbraith identified organized labor as the key institution in the constellation of countervailing powers needed to check corporate power and prevent a drift back to the politics of the Coolidge-Hoover era.[7]

It's true that U.S. labor did put together a couple of very good years (1935–1937). But for most of the last hundred years or so it's been stagnation and decline. Yet the stance of progressives toward official labor in this country, like the attitude of many Chicago fans toward their beloved Cubbies, seems to be, "Well, anyone can have a bad century." When pressed, labor's progressive supporters will blame Bush, mean bosses, bad labor laws, globalization—anything but take an unflinching look at what's gone wrong internally.

Last year's epochal split in the AFL-CIO foreshadowed what may be the end of the line for the American model of labor. Evidently, the Federation had been on the skids for more than a generation. But in the summer of 2005, the full extent of its ugly disarray became obvious to the broader American public. At the end of July, in Chicago, on the fiftieth anniversary of its founding, after two years of ankle-biting argument, the Federation finally split into two warring factions. Supposedly at issue were questions of how best to make the labor movement grow, but it was over turf and dues money that the labor chiefs had taken to cursing each other at executive committee meetings.

Less than a month later, the newly divided movement faced its first crisis. Northwest Airlines insisted on cutting the pay of mechanics and ground workers by 20 percent, and more than half would lose their jobs. When the workers struck, Northwest brought in replacement workers. For a moment, the strikers and their families held their breath, wondering how official labor would react. Then the shrunken AFL-CIO and the dissident Change to Win coalition stunned practically everyone by uniting to support the company. In exchange for not striking, one union, the International Machinists Association, was awarded the jobs of the striking workers.

It was dispiriting to see big labor siding with a corporate Goliath intent on breaking a union. It was dismaying to realize that labor had split for no principled reason. But turmoil on the tarmacs and the specter of the usually placid labor chiefs calling each other "hypocrite" and worse in public at least had one advantage. Completely overshadowed and overlooked was the Justice Department's RICO complaint earlier in July against the International Longshoremen's Association. The government charged that the nearly 60,000-member organization had been run by the Genovese and Gambino crime families for half a century. It was the usual story of extortion, robbery, bribery, and even murder.[8]

There was no comment from either faction on the Justice Department's action. What could AFL-CIO president John Sweeney say? The ILA belonged to his faction. What could Andy Stern or James Hoffa—leaders of the dissident faction—say? The Change to Win coalition was generally portrayed as the progressive alternative to Sweeney's AFL-CIO Old Guard. But the fact that it contained three of the four historically most mob-dominated unions went widely unreported.

Of course, because many unions are corrupt doesn't mean they're monolithically so. There are thousands of union staffers, and even top officials, who are trying to do their own jobs honestly. They refuse bribes, earn relatively modest salaries, and pass up the leased Lincoln Town Cars and the junkets to Honolulu or Las Vegas. But the honest officials aren't willing to commit career suicide by criticizing corruption—unless it's the corruption of a rival. If the odds of getting thrown out of the labor movement for taking a bribe are pretty steep, it's odds-on you'll get fired if you criticize bribe taking.

Still, the point of this book is not to show that American unions are corrupt. That's obvious to anyone who reads the daily paper. The real argument is about how they've become corrupt, what difference it has made, and why America can't let it stand.

Working people are never going to make sacrifices or run risks for institutions they don't trust. And they are never going to trust institutions that refuse to come clean about themselves. This book is animated by a belief that American working people really want to know why the movement that's been organized in their name has come to so little after so many years and such great sacrifices. It's also based on a faith that today's workers can stand the truth and will act on it.

ACKNOWLEDGMENTS

All writers incur obligations to people who help them. But an independent writer on organized labor relies on many helpers he can publicly acknowledge only at the risk of getting them fired. And in the case of others, who run no risk, it's especially important to stress the usual caveat that my gratitude doesn't imply their responsibility for or agreement with what I've written.

I'm grateful to the late Herbert Hill, the neglected conscience of organized labor on issues of race and corruption. At the end of his life, I benefited from his advice and encouragement. Staughton Lynd has demonstrated for me how a life of engagement with and analysis of organized labor is possible if one is not always inside it. I am also grateful that he gave me a chance to develop the argument of this book in his journal, *Impact.* I owe a similar debt to rabbi Michael Lerner, who opened up *Tikkun* to my labor journalism—and who prodded me to understand the nonmaterial dimensions of labor struggles. Among academics, my greatest debts are to Derek Bok, whose *Harvard Law Review* article on comparative labor law was brought to my attention by Dan Lazare; Sidney Fine, whose *Without Blare of Trumpets* matchlessly illuminates the early history of the ironworkers; and to David Brian Robertson, whose *Capital, Labor, and the State* shows what side the AFL was really on in the battle for Progressive Era reform. At the *Village Voice,* I benefited from the editorial assistance of Richard Goldstein, Andy Hsiao, and Bill Bastone—who have all moved on.

Also I would like to acknowledge some of those who shared their knowledge and experience as academic colleagues, union activists, scholars of the labor movement, and the criminal justice system: James McNamara, Ron Fino, Louise Furio, Chris White, Ken Boehme, Greg Butler, Steve Bronner, Roy Commer, Pete Di Nuzzo, Tom Dawes, Yin Chang, Wing Lam,

Joey Giardina, Jim Haughton, Steve Kindred, Ken Crowe, Leon Olson, Manny Ness, Jim McGough, Steve Manos, Terence Julien, Gary Wall, Paul Pamias, Carlos Guzman, Dominick Bentivegna, James B. Jacobs, Mike Moroney, Loren Goldner, John Ziv, Jessica Steiner, and Jon Fitch.

Finally, I would like to express sincere thanks to those I've worked with at my publisher, PublicAffairs. Melissa Raymond cheerfully struggled to decipher a handwriting which I myself can't even read. Editor David Patterson handled numerous revisions with a sense of humor and patience. And publisher Peter Osnos instilled in me just the right combination of hope and fear to keep me going for five years—from conception to delivery.

My biggest obligation remains to Martin Gottlieb. No Marty, no book. He's served as my agent, editor, and teacher. A fine investigative journalist, he has also displayed an unrivaled mastery of editorial skills—for synthesis and detail, for sympathy and criticism. Listening to him clarify what I was driving at served as an inspiration. I only hope I've captured it for the reader with the lucidity he explained it to the writer.

PART 1
What's Wrong With Corruption?

CHAPTER ONE

The Curse on the House of Labor ·

he Sheraton Bal Harbour, where the American Federation of Labor–Congress of Industrial Organizations (AFL-CIO) Executive Council held its 2004 meeting, is an enviable spot to be in late winter. The resort is nestled on ten acres of tropical gardens and sandy beaches in Bal Harbour, just north of Miami. There's a lagoon-style pool with waterfalls and waterslides. In the spa, guests can choose from half a dozen types of body wraps, including the Water Lily After Sun Soothing Wrap and the Desert Heat Clay Wrap. Certainly for AFL-CIO President John Sweeney, the portly, soft-handed, seventy-year-old former IBM market researcher, there were far worse places to be. The members of the old New York City janitors union he once ran would be heaving thirty-pound bags of garbage in the cold March winds into piles for the morning sanitation pickups. Still, Sweeney must have had many reasons to feel uneasy in the shade of the majestic royal palm trees that ringed the pool.

For one thing, nearly nine years before, when he was first elected as the AFL-CIO's "New Voice" president, Sweeney had pledged to give up Bal Harbour. The media, he noted, portrayed the meetings "as symbols of the labor federation's complacency—often with photos of older men lounging at poolside." Sweeney pledged that organized labor would henceforth be meeting at the sites of major organizing drives.[1]

The total, sweeping failure of Sweeney's organizing drives had been made plain just weeks earlier, when the Bureau of Labor Statistics announced that private sector union membership had hit the lowest rate since official figures were compiled: 8.2 percent. There were almost a million fewer union members than when Sweeney took office. These figures were especially derisory given Sweeney's early prediction that the AFL-CIO would add a million members a year through its organizing efforts. In 2003, National Labor Relations elections added a net of only 30,000 members.

Sweeney had already suffered public humiliations earlier in the year, in Iowa's Democratic presidential caucuses in January. Labor's two candidates, Vermont governor Howard Dean and former House majority leader Dick Gephardt, finished third and fourth—dooming their candidacies and ensuring that the Federation would have no leverage over the eventual winner.

Then, just the week before the Bal Harbour meeting, the biggest strike of Sweeney's presidency was settled on humiliating terms. Fifty-nine thousand grocery workers from seven southern California locals would return to work after four months only to accept wages and benefits that were worse than those originally offered. Leaders of the largest locals tussled publicly over the microphone at a major rally. Then they squabbled so long over who would get face time on the evening news that the network canceled them. When Sweeney's AFL-CIO intervened to organize a major Wall Street rally, only 250 people showed up.

Weakness invites attack. Sweeney faced a challenge from Andy Stern, his former aide, who was president of the Federation's largest union—the 1.8 million–member Service Employees International Union (SEIU). Stern assailed the Federation's record on organizing. If it didn't agree to a restructuring, he hinted, he'd split the AFL-CIO. With no irony intended, Stern called his movement the New Unity Partnership.

All these issues would be debated in the light of the sparkling Miami sun. But there was another problem—arguably the most widely perceived and the most fundamental—that dared not speak its name. Corruption was an issue that neither Sweeney nor Stern nor any of the Council's executive committee members would ever publicly discuss—not in the thousands of union newspapers, nor on the myriad union Web sites, nor even in the dozens of academic labor studies programs in universities around the country. It was inadmissible, undebatable, simply unmentionable— taboo.

Just as the rulers of the House of Atreus never told their subjects about the curse levied by the gods that led to five generations of family crimes and mayhem, so the leaders of the House of Labor pledged themselves to silence. There could be no recognition that they had been beset by five generations of racketeering, Mafia rule, bribery and extortion, job selling, benefit fund theft, and simple thievery, going back to the days of the early-twentieth-century labor czars.

Of course, not all fifty-four members of the Executive Council were corrupt. But silence undermined even the guiltless leaders, those who forswore kickbacks and managed to survive on their six-figure salaries, because although corruption itself was unmentionable, it was most often at the root of the mentionable problems. Understood properly, corruption could reveal why American union leaders couldn't organize, win strikes, keep their hands off pension and benefit funds, offer a progressive political agenda, keep labor standards from falling, or reform themselves.

Unlike the House of Atreus, organized labor's curse wasn't the fault of the gods. Corruption had been built into the labor movement from its very inception. Andy Stern, the rebel SEIU leader, hinted obliquely in this direction when he referred balefully to AFL-CIO's "structure"—its loose collection of affiliates and the primacy of its autonomous locals. Stern would allow that the structure produced a weak labor movement, but he refused to probe the structure deeply enough. Ultimately, the source of the Federation's crisis lay in its deepest foundations—the corrupt relations between the members and the leaders.

These foundations are often obscured by ideology. The meaning and nature of corruption have been bent and twisted to fit right- and left-wing agendas. Corruption is properly understood as the private use of public office. When union corruption appears in the press, it's usually because of illegal acts, such as the outright pilfering of union assets or collusion with the boss selling the members' jobs or giving away their benefits. But a lot of corruption is legal—hiring your relatives, taking excessive salaries, hiring-hall favoritism.

Typically, pro-business conservatives stretch the definition of corruption too far by applying it to the actions of unions they don't like—militant strikes or violent political demonstrations, for example. Such actions may be illegal, and they may even be wrong, but they aren't corrupt: no one is exploiting the union for a private purpose.

While the political right seeks to widen the notion of corruption too far, the populist left would narrow it too much. For some leftist critics, only the actions of union officials can count as corrupt. The members are eternal victims.

Exempting the membership entirely means that corruption can't ever be understood as what it patently is: systemic. Corruption in American unions isn't a matter of isolated felonious acts by individuals or permeation from outside by American culture. The U.S. labor movement relies on its own internal system for producing corruption. Some fraction of the membership is involved just as much as the leadership. That's why it has lasted so long.

Organized labor's governance resembles the ancient fiefdoms. Like feudalism, the union system is local, territorial, and based on ties of mutual dependence and protection. Those who produce the revenue—union dues and manorial rents alike—are tied to the territory. Just as serfs couldn't switch manors, workers stay in their locals unless they want to give up their jobs. Just as the serfs paid feudal dues for the right to work the land, workers pay union dues for the right to stay on the job.

Power in the system rests on reciprocal ties between leaders and favored or connected members. Together they are able jointly to exploit the union's job control power. The most favored get union office, and the less favored get staff jobs or positions as stewards and foremen. In Teamsters Local 282, Sammy "the Bull" Gravano's old local, "working teamster foreman" jobs pay six figures—and you don't have to bounce around in the cab of a truck all day long. Foreman jobs are tied to the fortunes of the leaders who give them out. A client turning on his boss, even if the boss is charged with a felony, means giving up a comfortable livelihood.

Together patrons and clients transform unionism into a special interest—a faction that thrives at the expense of the common good. At the hard core may be the officers who use loyalty to create immunity. Those who rely on the officers for jobs are loath to give them up. But the leaders' long reach into the pockets of the disfavored members could hardly exist without sinews that connect them to a substantial fraction of the membership.

The kings of the House of Atreus, Menelaus and Agamemnon, couldn't talk about the crimes of their ancestors because they owed their rule to them. It was the same for the rulers of unions like the Teamsters, the Laborers, and the United Food and Commercial Workers.

No wonder the favorite movie of Jimmy Hoffa's son Jim was *The Lion King*. Young Hoffa, a graduate of the University of Michigan Law School, had won the presidency following the 1998 expulsion-for-life of Teamsters president Ron Carey. Now Hoffa occupied the office of his father in the "Marble Palace"—the glittering, five-story white headquarters that stands in the shadows of the nation's Capitol building—that had been built in 1995 by Hoffa's immediate predecessor, right before he went off to prison. The new Hoffa was a head taller and a few steps slower than his famous father, whose abduction in 1975 by organized crime probably stands out as the signal event in postwar U.S. labor history. But Hoffa Jr.'s closest allies were chiefly the sons of his father's allies—who had been Midwestern crime family associates.[2]

To exorcise these unpleasant perceptions, Hoffa Jr. hired Ed Stier, a former U.S. attorney, to head an internal anticorruption task force. Stier tried to probe alleged second-generation Chicago mob ties, but then he accused Hoffa of stonewalling the investigation. His report alleged that several Chicago locals were still run by mobsters. The scams were traditional—kickbacks to allow companies to hire non-union drivers and kickbacks from members to get favored jobs.[3] Mobsters even communicated with union critics in traditional "Chicago Outfit" style—a .44 caliber bullet in an envelope meant "Stop passing out leaflets." In case recipient John Pavlak, who wrote a leaflet in 2001 criticizing Dominic Romanazzi, the boss of Local 330, somehow missed the symbolism, the envelope also contained a written message: "You are dead."[4]

According to Stier and his team of internal investigators, Romanazzi was in frequent contact with the Outfit. He received calls at union headquarters from nine different wiseguys. "The people who called me were nephews or sons of mobsters. They were not mobsters," explained Romanazzi to the *Chicago Tribune*. Allegedly, Romanazzi was sent by the Outfit to get Hoffa to stop Stier's investigation. Whether it was Romanazzi or someone else who convinced Hoffa, he did take Stier off the case.[5]

The latest head of the Laborers International Union of North America (LIUNA) was another junior—Terence M. O'Sullivan, the son of Terence J. O'Sullivan. Like Hoffa Jr., O'Sullivan Jr. was born on the labor union equivalent of third base. His father, O'Sullivan Sr., was a mob associate who'd been the Laborers' secretary-treasurer. So was the man O'Sullivan

Jr. had served for so long as a personal aide and had finally replaced— Arthur Coia Jr., a longtime mob associate who in 1999 finally got taken down on federal tax charges.

Coia Jr. had stepped into the union's no. 2 job on the death of his father, Arthur Coia Sr. His ascension signaled the beginning of a Coia dynasty, which succeeded the half-century reign of the Chicago-based Fosco dynasty. Now the Coias in turn were being replaced by the O'Sullivans.

Genealogy casts a dim light on LIUNA's effort to present O'Sullivan Jr.'s replacement of Coia Jr. as a movement toward union reform. Going back to the 1970s, the two families had a history of working together: the Coias—junior and senior—and the senior O'Sullivan had all been co-indictees in the same benefit fund fraud case involving eastern and Chicago crime families.[6]

Of all the AFL-CIO affiliates, though, it is the United Food and Commercial Workers (UFCW), the AFL-CIO's largest private sector union, that seemed to have the densest and most ingrained patterns of nepotism. UFCW had at least a dozen ongoing father-son—and even father-son-grandson—dynasties from California to Long Island. One of the most notorious had belonged to the Talarico family. Sam Talarico, a UFCW founder, was succeeded as its no. 2 official by his son Joseph, who may have set some kind of record for family loyalty. Joseph placed more than forty relatives on the payroll of his Utica local. In 1998, the dynasty fell when Joseph went to prison for embezzling nearly $1 million—including funds to pay for his hair transplant.[7]

The New Jersey UFCW locals had been Genovese crime family territory going back to the 1950s. The family controlled the two big grocery and meatcutters locals through associates—the Kaplans, the Randos, and the Niccollais, some of whose descendants are still running the locals today.

In the 1970s, the big central Jersey UFCW locals formed the spear point of a Genovese effort to gain a foothold in the banking and soap industries. Local 1262 in Clifton was the lead local in the Genovese scheme to take over a dozen banks by using pension funds as bait. The enterprise failed, and the local's president, Frank Rando, pleaded guilty. Frank's brother, Ramon Rando, is now the no. 2 official in Local 464a, earning $348,000 a year.[8]

UFCW Local 464a, just a few miles away in Little River, was another

Genovese stronghold. Control over the local figured prominently in a mob plot to sell dirty soap to grocery stores in New Jersey and Westchester County. The Genovese family's soap was marketed as "Ecolo G" for its alleged ecological properties. It was a hard sell because the FDA had declared that it contained an eye irritant. To hook store managers, Genovese-controlled union officials offered a break on their Local 464a members' contractual wages and benefits. When A&P executives balked at the deal, their stores were hit with explosions and arson. Two executives were murdered. After the executions, the Genovese boss in charge of the operation was heard on tape saying, "When is A&P gonna get the message?"[9]

But because release of the tapes generated pretrial publicity, nearly everyone charged, mob guys and union officials alike, got off.

Failure to convict anyone for the murder of the A&P executives led to a federal investigation seeking to determine whether organized crime had infiltrated the New Jersey criminal justice system. A grand jury probed possible ties between Local 464a officialdom and the Passaic County prosecutor's office. They found quite a few. The first assistant prosecutor, John Niccollai Jr., was the son of John Niccollai Sr., Local 464a's secretary-treasurer. Steven Kaplan, an assistant prosecutor, was the son of Irving "Izzy" Kaplan, Local 464a's founder and president. Sam Kohen, a business agent for the local, had a brother working as a county investigator.[10]

Following the probe, John Niccollai Jr. made a career change. He resigned from the prosecutor's office and got a job with his dad's union. (The senior Niccollai had just been indicted for the fourth time.[11]) The junior Niccollai's ascendancy to the presidency came in 2002, when the incumbent president was charged with taking bribes and pleaded guilty to a lesser charge.[12]

Two years later, Mr. Niccollai was identified by the *Philadelphia Inquirer* as having received the highest yearly pay of any union official in New Jersey or Pennsylvania. He earned $407,656.[13] Niccollai also has a dauphin, John II, who serves as a $156,000-a-year "director of operations." And, finally, there is Gloria Niccollai, who receives a more modest salary as a clerical employee. When asked in a telephone interview if she was related to the president, Ms. Niccollai replied, "I have no comment at this time."[14]

Across the river, in the town of Hastings-on-Hudson in southern Westchester County, lay another troubled UFCW family fiefdom. It belonged to the Vetrano family, who ruled quietly until March 2005, when the family patriarch, eighty-three-year-old James Vetrano, was indicted on charges that he helped the Gambino crime family steal Local 305's benefit funds. Vetrano was alleged by the U.S. attorney's office to have cooperated with famed Westchester Gambino boss Greg DePalma in a plot to make wiseguys beneficiaries of the plan even though they weren't legitimate union members. Vetrano faces thirty years' imprisonment.[15] But even if he is imprisoned, there's another Vetrano in the pipeline—Secretary-Treasurer Ray Vetrano. When asked what relation Ray was to James, a spokesperson for Local 305 declared, "I'm not going to answer that, sir."[16] A spokesperson for the parent union was no more communicative. Asked if the UFCW would force the elder Vetrano to step down, she replied, "I can't comment on that."[17]

NEW GOSPEL, OLD CORRUPTION

Had Sweeney's talk of a "New Labor" been spin from the very beginning? Well, mostly, yes. A prime concern of delegates to the 1995 convention was the Federation's bad public image. Gallup polls regularly showed that labor leaders ranked near the bottom in ratings of professional ethics. Sweeney showed his determination to change those perceptions by outsourcing his job to Washington's top public relations firms, pollsters, and speechwriters—mostly from the Clinton White House. Sweeney's pollster was Stanley Greenberg, Clinton's pollster. Sweeney's autobiography was written with David Kusnet, Clinton's principal speechwriter from 1992 to 1994. The prominent firm of Greer, Margolis, Mitchell, and Burns came up with a report on "core positioning and message discipline." They provided what Jo-Ann Mort, then communications director for UNITE, called "the new gospel." Union media should always foreground "the economic concerns of all working families" and put the union "as an institution" in the background. The whole effort took a little more than a year to gear up. "The repositioning campaign launched by the AFL-CIO began in 1997," recalls Mort, "with ads and slogans airing in five test markets."[18]

The campaign flopped. By 2002, the public esteem in which labor leaders were held had fallen even further. In 1997, according to a Gallup poll, only 17 percent of Americans had thought the ethics of labor leaders were "high or very high." But five years later the figure had dropped to just 14 percent. Only some salespeople—telemarketers, used car dealers, and insurance salespersons—were ranked lower.[19]

The 1995 contest between the two presidential rivals, Sweeney and Thomas Donahue, had been portrayed as "the first contested election" in the Federation's history. The implication was that a real election was finally going to take place. But a genuine vote would have meant a direct election—one that respects the country's democratic norms. Ever since the passage of the Seventeenth Amendment in 1913, even the United States Senate has had direct elections. But in only a handful of the AFL-CIO's fifty-eight affiliates do the members get to vote for top officials. When direct elections do take place for the highest offices in American unions, it's usually because of a court-ordered consent decree: The leaders opted for elections only because they were faced with a decision—either allow genuine elections or stand trial on racketeering charges.

The last time union candidates with alternative programs faced each other in a real contest was at the AFL's 1895 convention. An alliance of Populists and labor radicals backed United Mine Workers of America president John McBride. He actually defeated the conservative AFL incumbent, Samuel Gompers.[20] But it was a last hurrah for radical politics—or for any politics in the Federation. The Gompers forces crushed the McBride insurgency after only a year. A weak confederacy of autonomous fiefdoms will never provide a theater for genuine politics. Instead of settling arguments by persuasion and mobilization of opinion, those who find themselves in the minority simply leave the organization.

A century later, the delegates could choose between two former officials from the same union who stood for almost identical goals and strategies. Thomas Donahue, the older of the two, who was serving as interim AFL-CIO president, had actually given Sweeney his first staff job in the SEIU's 32BJ—the largest of the union's janitorial locals and one of the most corrupt, going back to its founding in the 1930s.[21] Initially, Donahue had been Sweeney's choice for president. Both were bald-headed Irish Americans from the Bronx. In fact, three of the last four AFL-CIO presidents have been bald-headed Irish Americans from the Bronx.[22]

And what about New York's janitors Local 32BJ—now the mother of AFL-CIO presidents? Why wasn't serving as a top official in the New York janitors union an outright disqualification? James Bambrick, who founded the union in 1935, had struggled unsuccessfully to free himself from mob control. He wound up paying protection money to George Scalise, the former pimp who had become the union's international president with the approval of the Capone gang.[23] Bambrick was succeeded under dubious circumstances by David Sullivan, who'd been the union's secretary-treasurer. Sullivan had also been indicted for allegedly participating in the payments to Scalise as well as pocketing funds. The indictments were dropped and the prosecuting attorney was hired as Local 32BJ's general counsel. Like Sweeney, Sullivan would use 32BJ as a springboard to the presidency of the international union. But Malcolm Johnson, a Pulitzer Prize–winning journalist whose series of exposés turned into *On the Waterfront*, described the local's saga as a paradigm of labor racketeering.[24] If Sweeney's predecessors were tainted, so was his immediate successor, Gus Bevona. In 1999, Bevona, often reckoned the nation's highest-paid union official, decided to retire after settling a civil suit by dissidents charging him with using union funds to hire a gumshoe to harass a member who had complained about "Greedy Gus"'s $400,000-a-year salary.[25]

Sweeney's relationship with Bevona perfectly illustrated the patron-client relationships at the heart of the American labor movement. Bevona, who lived at members' expense in a 3,000-square-foot marble-clad penthouse atop the union's Sixth Avenue headquarters, was widely regarded as an embarrassment. He allegedly once told a crowd that he'd kill President Clinton if he was in the room.[26] Sweeney was the labor movement's rising star. Yet Sweeney and Bevona were joined at the hip—and cash was the glue. Basically, Bevona paid Sweeney protection money. After being elevated to the SEIU's presidency, Sweeney stayed on as Bevona's consultant, at a salary that reached nearly $80,000 a year. But the job was no sinecure, Sweeney insisted; he was involved. True enough. When Bevona used union funds to go after his principal critic, Sweeney approved the use of union funds plus legal expenses to defend Bevona. Sweeney also approved a sweetheart real estate deal Bevona made with two cleaning company contractors that allegedly cost the union $200 million in extra lease payments. It was part of a rental arrangement on the union's headquarters, which the members were made to believe they owned.[27]

Sweeney's rival Donahue connived at even grosser corruption. When six officials of 32E, the parent union's Bronx affiliate, were convicted of taking bribes from landlords in exchange for sweetheart contracts, Donahue was brought in. It was his job to supervise the long-overdue reform of the local. Ever since Scalise founded the local in 1938, installing Sam "Firpo" Abrams, a convicted bank robber, as president, every local president had gone to jail or been murdered.[28]

Donahue let a slate of convicted officials run again, and they were all re-elected. Donahue advanced to the assistant secretaryship of labor in the Johnson administration.[29]

Not that it made all that much difference whether Sweeney or Donahue served as AFL-CIO president. Both had established their qualifications for a job that demanded more discretion than dynamism. The AFL-CIO was not a centralized organization that put a lot of power in the hands of a single leader. The presidency was mostly an honorific position, and the occupant acted as a spokesperson for a collection of completely autonomous affiliates. The affiliates in turn were made up of 20,000 largely autonomous locals. The president couldn't call a single strike or organize a single worker—any rebuilding of the Federation's strength had to start at the local level, where the money and power were located. It was often not in the interest of these leaders to bring in new members or to do much more than perform routine maintenance on the political machines that kept them in power.

CORRUPTION'S SOURCE

A major journalistic conceit is the importance of character. By probing the lifestyle, background, convictions, ethnicity, and gender of the actor, you understand the person. If you understand the person, you understand the behavior of his institution.

If character is so decisive, how come union problems all seem so much the same, year after year, no matter who runs the institution? Whatever the gender, race, or intellectual background of the leaders, corruption has been a constant. District Council 37, the 120,000-member New York affiliate of the American Federation of State County and Municipal Employees, is run by a seventy-eight-year-old black woman, Lillian Roberts, a former nurse's aide. Her critics accuse her of responsibility for kickbacks, election irregularities, nepotism, benefit fund scams, and poor contracts. In 1998, her predecessor, Stanley Hill, a black man, resigned in the face of similar charges. But many of the rackets uncovered at the time by prosecutors originated in the era of his predecessor, Victor Gotbaum, a Jewish man who'd been an intelligence officer and served on the Council on Foreign Relations. Regardless of temperament or background, the job requires a certain combination of iron and rubber—an iron hand and rubber principles. The occupant either has them to begin with or acquires them soon.

Academics generally don't do character analysis. They have bigger theoretical fish to fry: globalization, the shift of manufacturing to the third world, the rise of the information economy, the feminization of the workforce. These universal trends are supposed to explain our unions' problems. How come, then, American unions are so different from unions elsewhere? Except in officer salaries and total union financial assets, where we're far ahead, the U.S. labor movement comes in last or nearly last in just about every other important respect: the lowest density, the longest decline in membership, the least success in social welfare legislation, the fewest strikes—America hasn't had a real general strike since 1877.

The American labor movement is not only weaker than others, it's also a lot more corrupt. Of course, some corruption is probably inevitable. But the scale and scope of corruption and self-enrichment in "old Europe" remain relatively underdeveloped. In other advanced industrialized countries, you don't find insignificant local leaders earning over half a million a year. Nor do you find whole unions run by crime families—not even in Sicily or Calabria.[30] To realize their dream of becoming union leaders, young thugs like James "Big Jim" Colosimo, the founder of the Chicago Laborers and the longest-serving crime boss in the city's history, had to migrate in 1895 from southern Italy.[31] Only in America!

The fundamental actors in American labor are institutions—the unions themselves. It's the union institutions that act and have identity, that manage or succumb to trends, and that shape the character of their leaders. The real question is not "Who is John Sweeney?" but "What is the institutional character of a labor movement that turns out John Sweeneys generation after generation?" What needs scrutiny is less the adverse macroeconomic trends than why the AFL-CIO has been so notably unable to handle them. American unions share the problems of unions every-where, but they also have deeper, characteristic problems.

Call it the fiefdom syndrome—a kind of protection system based on exclusive jurisdictions, exclusive bargaining, and job control. Those who control the jobs become the bosses; those who want the jobs become their clients. Loyalty to the boss becomes the highest virtue. It's an ethic of de-pendence rather than solidarity, one that promotes the most wide-rang-ing corruption. Corruption in turn produces atomization, weakness, demoralization, and apathy, which in turn promote further corruption. Solidarity—united action on behalf of the common good—turns into a slogan that produces only crooked smiles.

It's this special character that explains why the American labor move-ment fares so poorly in the vital tasks unions are designed to perform: im-proving the material living standards of the majority of working people, ending the dependence of workers on the will of the employer, and reduc-ing the blatant economic inequality that tends to develop between those who run corporations and those who work for them.

HOW CORRUPTION HAS UNDERMINED THE UNIONS

Defenders of the AFL-CIO status quo argue that friends of the labor movement should shut up about corruption. Exposés of labor bosses, they say, only aid corporate bosses. The unstated assumption is that cor-ruption has no damaging consequences of its own. It's just the *perception* of corruption that's harmful.

But corruption is not cost free, and in many ways its consequences are more serious than ever. This is true even though the gross symptoms are less obvious. It's not like in the late 1920s or the early 1930s; we don't have gunfights on street corners, with the Capone and the Moran gangs blast-ing away at each other for control of the Teamsters, laundry, janitors, and bartenders unions. Nowadays in Chicago, the Outfit has no rivals, and their bullets are delivered in envelopes, meant to scare dissidents, not kill them. Maintaining a territory requires a lot less firepower than seizing it in the first place. But the slow strangulation of genuine labor union impulses and energies has had its effect. The devastating results of the curse—five generations of corruption—can be measured in seven specific ways.

The continuing shrinkage in membership numbers. Most critics point to a decline in dues-paying membership as the Federation's biggest problem. It's not. If the AFL-CIO's 13 million members were active, participating members, if they were connected in action and in sympathy with non-dues-paying workers in a genuine labor movement, if current union leaders had any moral authority, American labor might still be a powerful force in the country.

Still, the numerical decline says something about the fortunes of the Federation. When the AFL-CIO was created fifty years ago, it had 16 million members, and private sector union density stood at nearly 40 percent. Now in the private sector, it's 8 percent. Public sector membership stands much higher, but it has stopped growing, and public sector workers constitute only about 15 percent of U.S. workers. Two Princeton labor economists predict that, given present trends, the entire U.S. labor movement—in the public and private sectors—will eventually bottom out at 2.1 percent.[32]

Theories abound to explain the decline—including outsourcing, deindustrialization, globalization, the Reagan Revolution, bad labor laws, employer resistance, and the decline in the species of male, blue collar workers. But lacking is any recognition that stagnation is the natural state of official labor in America. From the dawn of the twentieth century, the periods of decline (1919–1934 and 1955–2004) are greater than the periods of growth (1900–1919 and 1934–1955).

Historically, the American Federation of Labor has tended toward stagnation for a lot of the same reasons corporate monopolies do. They are able to raise prices by restricting entry. They have little incentive to expand. Inefficiency, underinvestment, corruption, and inequality flow naturally from their restrictive efforts.

Understood as a loosely connected web of urban job trusts, the recent history of U.S. labor is easily told. Early in the twentieth century, the AFL steadily filled up the available monopoly niches—mainly in the construction, longshore, and transportation trades. Having reached a saturation point after World War I, membership naturally began to stagnate, at least until the 1930s, when a mass revolt of industrial workers shook the Federation and caused a split. Goaded by the newly formed CIO to defend its jurisdictions and aided by the federal government, the AFL poured resources into organizing, and membership tripled. But organizing stopped in 1955, when the two rival federations merged and agreed to respect each other's jurisdictions. A burst of organizing in the public sector during the 1960s proved to be only a speed bump on the road to stagnation.

Why, then, if there is an inherent tendency to decline, didn't organized labor disappear long ago—or at least fall to its 2 percent natural equilibrium level? Historically, what has prevented the AFL from death by attrition is foreign wars and opposing organizations. World wars have been tremendous stimuli for growth: in exchange for unions giving up the right to strike, the government promotes unionization.

Having a domestic opposition helps too. The AFL grows when it can provide a more acceptable alternative to employers than more inclusive, less corruptible organizations. About once a generation, a new labor movement comes along to challenge the trade unions. The Progressive Era produced a "new unionism" in opposition to the prevailing "business unionism" of the AFL. Even when the new unionists failed to consolidate their victories in the aftermath of the great strike in Lawrence, Massachusetts, led by the Industrial Workers of the World, they triggered an increase in the demand for unions. Above all, they produced the aspirations and forms of struggle that eventually led to the challenge of the more inclusive CIO.

But after the CIO merged with the AFL in 1955, all direct incentives to organize disappeared. The following year, organizing budgets fell more than 50 percent, and organized labor began its slow fifty-year fade. The inherent tendency for the local monopolies to stagnate was abetted by their unwillingness to spend money on bringing in members who might tip the political balance within the union.

The failure to organize. The total may represent only a third of the civilian labor force, but the AFL-CIO cites polls indicating that 45 million workers would like to join a union.[33] Yet the AFL-CIO has only 13 million members. Neither Sweeney nor anyone in official labor was willing to admit that it simply wasn't in the interests of many unions to spend money on organizing. That's why they never did—and never will. But at least Sweeney didn't hide behind the old excuses that employers were mean and the government's election rules unfair. He squarely blamed his predecessor, Lane Kirkland, for failing to lead.

Under Kirkland, Sweeney noted, organizing efforts had hit rock bottom. In 1990, the worst year, there were only 3,628 elections for union representation covering 230,000 workers. Winning only about 50 percent of the elections meant bringing in less than half of the 300,000 new members a year the labor movement needed just to keep from shrinking. Sweeney's target was a million a year, which in ten years would bring the Federation back to where it was at the time of the merger. AFL-CIO headquarters hired 200 new organizers, and the affiliates hired thousands more. The goal was to get every affiliate to increase its organizing budget to at least 20 percent.

The upshot was even fewer new members: a steep and steady decline in the number of elections and in the number of workers brought into unions through elections. In sheer numerical terms, Kirkland, whose organizing specialty was alleged to be Georgetown soirées, actually produced better organizing numbers than Sweeney. In 2003, there were one-third fewer elections than ten years earlier, under Kirkland, and the number of workers brought in through union elections was only 47,000. When the number of members lost via employer-sponsored decertification elections—where the members vote to get rid of the union—was figured in, it left only 30,000 new members, or about 3 percent of the target of 1 million.

Why should this come as a surprise? The U.S. fiefdom model of unionism operates a lot like old-style cartel capitalism. Of course, it's in the interests of organized labor to have more members. But it's not necessarily in the interests of each local to spend the money to organize. It's also in the interest of business as a whole for each individual firm to invest. One firm's spending benefits another. But if the firm has a monopoly, extra investment may lower profits. There has to be a competitive threat.

In the 1930s, the threat of the CIO forced the AFL to organize. In fact, when challenged, the AFL was able to out-organize the CIO.[34] With the gradual taming of the CIO and its ultimate incorporation into the AFL, employers had less incentive to recognize the more employer-friendly, corrupt AFL affiliates. The main point of the merger was to save money by calling off the battle for members. The big falloff in membership started with the agreement between the two federations to stop competing for members. Jurisdictional boundaries between unions became more secure than ever before.

Certainly U.S. laws governing union recognition are a disgrace. They abridge a fundamental human right—the right to organize and bargain collectively with employers. But the most towering obstacle to organizing remains the AFL-CIO itself, a patchwork realm of 20,000 self-regarding local fiefdoms. That's where 75 percent of the money for organizing lies.[35] Many have little incentive to organize. Others aren't equipped to organize even if they wanted to.

In the classic trades—construction, longshore, and certain elite locals in the Teamsters, unions don't organize because bringing in more members wouldn't raise the income of those already organized. It would lower them. Many blacks, immigrants, and women would like to become plumbers and electricians, and many would like $100,000-a-year jobs on the docks. But from the union standpoint, bringing in these groups wouldn't increase the number of unionized jobs, just the number of workers sitting in the hiring hall waiting for jobs. There's also the danger that black members might dilute the political base of the white leadership.

Then there is the most unmentionable of internal organizing obstacles: corruption. Why didn't the Teamsters' Joint Council 25 boss, Bill Hogan, try to organize low-wage United Service Companies employees at the Las Vegas Convention Center? Why, in 1999, did he try to replace Las Vegas union workers making $20.00 an hour with employees from United making $7.90? Because his brother was a big executive in United, according to a Teamsters Internal Review Board, which expelled him for life.[36] Why didn't Hogan's boss, Hoffa Jr., set him straight? Most likely because gaining new members was less important to Hoffa than keeping the political support of his powerful regional baron.

Why don't union carpenters have a bigger share of the work in midtown Manhattan? Because the head of the New York City Council of Carpenters allegedly took an envelope with $10,000 inside. Prosecutors said it had been given to him by the son-in-law of the DeCavalcante crime family's godfather. The exchange took place after the two quaffed beers at Hooters, just a few steps from the Park Central Hotel. In exchange for the ten large—a down payment on a $50,000 bribe—Mike Forde, the Council's boss, agreed to allow lower-paid, non-union carpenters to replace his members on the Park Central remodeling job. Forde was convicted of the charges in 2004, but the conviction was later overturned by the presiding judge, Jeffrey Atlas, because of alleged anti-union sentiment on the part of some jurors. Atlas accused them of holding the view "that the case resembled a *Sopranos* episode."[37] Perhaps the problem of juror bias could have been solved by excluding those contaminated with knowledge of the union's history. A decade earlier, Martin Forde, Mike's dad, was brought down on similar charges. The same charges doomed an almost unbroken series of District Council officials going back to the late Teddy Maritas, who allowed Genovese crime families to control a non-union drywall empire in the Bronx until he disappeared just before his trial.

The decline in the number and effectiveness of strikes. Just consider the past fifty years. There was no great spike in strike activity in the 1950s— nothing like the strike wave following World War II, after price controls were lifted. But in 1952 there were 470 major strikes involving 2.75 million workers. The totals have dropped pretty steadily since. There was a flare-up in the 1970s—inflation again. But the numbers in the Nixon-Ford era never reached those of the Truman-Eisenhower period. And by 1992, there were only thirty-five strikes involving 364,000 workers. The percentage of work time lost by strikes fell to an oceanic depth of 0.02 percent— *two hundredths* of 1 percent.[38]

Although it hardly seems possible, strike activity has fallen substantially since then. The 1997 Teamsters strike against UPS—heralded as a "watershed" by the secretary of labor and "a major triumph and an omen of future success" by the *New York Times*—proved to be a false dawn.[39] The two-week strike didn't even change the ratio of full-time to part-time workers at UPS, much less reverse the decline of the U.S. labor movement. The downward trend continued unabated. In 2004, there were only seventeen strikes affecting only 0.01 percent of precious work time.[40] The strike rate in the United States is only a fraction of what it is in major western European countries.

Labor experts at the Heritage Foundation, a conservative think tank, predict that globalization will bring with it the triumph of the U.S. industrial relations model. This may be wishful thinking. Despite setbacks and scattered signs of convergence, it hasn't happened yet. On the contrary, in western Europe, South Korea, and Israel, general strikes, nationwide labor protests, thought to have gone out with cloth caps and lunch pails, have returned. Most seek to stop the dismantling of the welfare state. Perhaps the most successful general strike took place in France, where a three-week job action in 1995 brought down the conservative government and led to the passage of legislation guaranteeing a thirty-five-hour workweek.[41] General strikes in Italy brought down the first Berlusconi government; since then they have become almost routine. In the winter of 2004, the second of two massive actions saw over a million demonstrators in fifty Italian cities protesting changes in pension eligibility.[42] Likewise, in France during the winter of 2005, when the conservative government of Jacques Chirac tried to repeal the thirty-five-hour law, over a million workers went on strike in protest.[43]

Not all the general strikes were defensive. In the late 1990s, a largely successful Danish strike for a sixth vacation week had 10 percent of the Danish population in the streets. The Danes stayed out for two weeks, demanding parity with workers in other Scandinavian countries. Seventy percent of the Danish population supported the action. When the vacation legislation was enacted, employers complained that Denmark had become "a workers' dictatorship."[44]

At least that's one threat America doesn't face. It's not just that multinational employers have an easy time of crushing the isolated, uncoordinated protests of their employees, who are trapped in the ever-shrinking archipelago of organized labor, or that U.S. labor laws uniquely favor employers by allowing the use of "replacement workers." There's also the cynical indifference of the higher union officials to the struggles that take place at the lower levels of their own organization.

Consider the desperate but doomed efforts of 300 workers at Domino Sugar's Brooklyn refinery who tried to resist management's plan to lay off a third of the workforce. On June 15, 1999, the members of Local 1814 of the International Longshoremen's Association (ILA) challenged Lyle & Tate, the multinational owners of their 143-year-old plant, by going out on strike.

The union ranks held for twenty months—not one single member crossed the picket line. By the end of February 2001, the members were driven back to the factory by hunger, a member's suicide, and the glacial indifference of labor's leadership—including their own. Domino Sugar's other unionized U.S. plants worked overtime to turn out the sugar lost by the Brooklyn strike. Explained the head of Baltimore's United Food and Commercial Workers Local 1101, "If my contract were expired, I would have joined them 100 percent." The Domino Sugar workers also got no help from the head of the New York State Federation of Labor. "It bothered me from the beginning that the union wasn't strong enough to put this together," recalled the official.[45] But it was the silence of AFL-CIO president John Sweeney that resounded loudest in Brooklyn. After the members had surrendered, strike leader Joe Crimi commented, "God Bless our labor leaders who must have thought this strike was a waste of time," he said. "But what makes me mad is I stopped [the] members from putting up the RAT [a fifteen-foot inflatable rodent signifying "scabs at work"] against Sweeney. Two-year strike, one death, totally destroyed membership, a contract book that took more than sixty years to accomplish slashed to shit. God knows the money they lost, families disrupted. And I stopped them. Why? Because I didn't want to hurt the labor movement."[46]

Crimi's strikers didn't even get any help from their own international union, the International Longshoremen's Association—not even strike funds. John Bowers, the ILA's president, who kept office even after a 1990 racketeering suit charging he was a mob puppet, couldn't be bothered.[47] Nor could the top leaders of Local 1814. These weren't the same mob associates charged in the 1990 suit—they were new ones. But they were busy, too, running errands for the Gambino crime family, extorting payments from members for cushy waterfront jobs, collecting kickbacks from bosses for labor peace, and intimidating trustees of the local's health plan to award contracts to companies owned by the Gambino and Genovese families. These activities are the charges in the 2002 indictment brought against Local 1814's president, Frank "Red" Scollo, who was indicted along with fifteen other crime family members and associates. Scollo eventually pleaded guilty.[48]

The collapse of labor standards. "America Needs a Raise" was the title of John Sweeney's book. His premise was that by putting resources into organizing unions, Americans could get a raise. But increasingly, many American unions weren't capable of getting raises that exceeded the non-union rate or sometimes even the minimum wage. Union wages below or only slightly higher than the legal minimums were common in the grocery stores and chicken-plucking factories represented by the UFCW,[49] in factories and warehouses represented by the Teamsters, and, above all, in the restaurants and garment shops represented by UNITE–HERE.[50]

For the immigrant workers represented by UNITE, attaining even the minimum wage was their American Dream. In 1997, a Bureau of Labor Standards report revealed that New York City, where UNITE had its headquarters, had the worst sweatshop problem in the nation. About two-thirds of the garment shops in the city were sweatshops, in violation of wage and hour or safety standards. The stunning finding, though, was that three-quarters of the *union* shops were sweatshops. The results seemed to conflict with the common wisdom that "a bad union is better than no union."

In fairness to union-run sweatshops, the government study didn't take into account that UNITE members had health and pensions benefits and non-union workers didn't. Still, the level of union benefits was extraordinarily low: a typical pensioner was receiving only $60–$70 a month—and that after a lifetime of body-destroying work, breathing air filled with cotton particles, bent over machines that required repetitive motion, often seven days a week, twelve hours a day.

UNITE's leaders had long ago given up any effort to improve conditions in the shops or even defend their contracts, which called for thirty-five-hour weeks and nearly double the minimum wage. Since the 1960s, their overt strategy was to maintain membership—and their dues base—by tacitly matching non-union contractors with dollar-for-dollar concessions. While they succeeded in keeping wages low, membership fell by three-quarters anyway.

Much more successful was UNITE's innovative public relations campaign, which positioned the union as leader in the battle against sweatshops—not here in the United States, but overseas. The National Labor Committee, which began as the union label division of UNITE's predecessor organization, exposed the terrible conditions faced by Central Americans and Chinese in overseas garment shops. But if UNITE wanted to battle against sweatshops, why didn't it just enforce its own contracts here in the United States? Occasionally the hypocrisy was on display. One day during the Christmas season, the union-led activists in a lower Broadway demonstration protested sweatshops in Mexico while dozens of UNITE workers were demonstrating literally across the street against the union's failure to enforce their contract in a particularly revolting sweatshop at 446 Broadway.[51]

UNITE officials never took the slightest responsibility for conditions in the shops. Not without some plausibility, they invoked overseas competition, Wal-Mart, and the docile character of their members, who were often undocumented immigrants. But invoking those forces didn't explain why shop conditions in New York City were worse than elsewhere. How come totally non-union San Francisco, which had the same undocumented immigrants and produced the same type of garments, had only a fraction as many sweatshops?

A lot of the reason New York's rag trade was the worst was that it had the worst mob problem. Mobsters owned trucking and garment companies. The Lucchese crime family had deeply infiltrated the union and, according to a 1998 report by the Office of Labor Racketeering, an associate ran UNITE's largest local. Mob infiltration of the union was an old story. But whereas the mob's emphasis was once said to be on price stability—making sure no one undersold their clients—now it seems to be on helping them with cost control.[52] The racket *du jour* is pay not to play. Depending on the size of the bribe, contractors could get a friendly business agent, a break on benefits, or simply get rid of the union altogether.

The crisis of the $350 billion multiemployer pension system. America's labor leaders manage a huge sum: over $350 billion in pension funds. Unfortunately, though, this sum is not nearly enough. Obligations exceed assets by at least $150 billion. Officials explain that the market's been down, and they talk about actuarial problems. But simple corruption and the fragmented character of the unions perhaps explain a great deal too.

One reason why there's not enough money to pay future obligations is that there are too many plans. Why does the AFL-CIO need to have 2,100 separate pension plans for its 13 million members? That's a plan for every 6,200 members. Social Security has one plan for all 280 million Americans. Social Security's administrative costs run about $11 a year per person. Take a Teamsters pension plan at random—Long Island City's Local 814. Administrative costs run about $420 each per year for the 2,700 member-participants, who mostly work for moving companies. That's nearly forty times more per capita than what the Social Security Administration charges. The Bush administration insists that the sky is falling for Social Security because it will be able to meet only 70 percent of its obligations in 2040. *Today*, the Local 814 plan has only 55 percent of the funds it needs to meet its obligations.[53]

It might well be that decades of control over Local 814 by the Bonanno crime family has shrunk the assets it needs.[54] Still, a simple reduction in the number of union plans could save members billions in administrative costs—costs that consume a substantial portion of the plans' investment gain, and sometimes all of it. But consolidating the plans would mean less patronage and less power for the local union leaders who get to name trustees and hire outside vendors—and less opportunity for racketeering conspiracies.

Labor racketeers love pension funds. In 2002, a report by the Department of Labor's Office of the Inspector General showed that there were 357 pending racketeering investigations; 39 percent involved organized crime, and 44 percent involved pension or welfare plans.

It's often pension plan looting—not just adverse macroeconomic trends like low interest rates—that helps explain why union-run plans are so dangerously underfunded. The Teamsters' Central States Plan, "the Mob's piggy bank" during the 1970s and 1980s, can't pay its obligations today.[55] UPS, the largest employer of Teamsters, touts *its* pension plans as fully funded. One of the saddest facts about the American labor movement is that the putative beneficiaries of union-run plans have been historically less likely to get a pension than workers who are beneficiaries of company-run plans.[56]

But Sweeney's New Labor agenda never included reforms aimed at reducing pension fund pilferage, lowering administrative costs, or even ensuring that members actually got their pensions. Instead, Sweeney committed himself to a very different type of pension reform. He vowed that labor unions would use their prodigious pension fund assets to become corporate watchdogs. Union pension fund activists would compel the Fortune 500 companies to treat workers better, fight for the public interest, and force unwilling companies to recognize AFL-CIO affiliates. Sweeney started a public relations operation called "Paywatch" that targeted corporate malfeasance.

The summer of 2002 found him on Wall Street baying against corporate pension crooks from Enron, WorldCom, and Arthur Andersen. Strangely, though, Sweeney chose to focus on "the sorry spectacle of Gary Winnick, the CEO of Global Crossing, selling off $734 million in stock while urging his employees to buy more."[57]

What Winnick did was unconscionable, but he had help from a company on which Sweeney served as board chairman—Ullico—Union Labor Life Insurance Company, the AFL-CIO's insurance company, founded in 1925. Ullico was present at the creation of Winnick's non-union Global Crossing.[58] Winnick wanted labor leaders on board, and in 1997, he reportedly solicited more than two dozen of them to participate in the company's initial public offering. Ullico got shares worth $7 million, which turned into shares worth an incredible $2 billion before Global Crossing collapsed five years later, nearly taking Ullico with it.[59]

None of Ullico's directors wound up with a $92 million house in Bel Air, like Gary Winnick did. Their entire swag amounted to a comparatively trivial $5.2 million. But they were playing the same game: using their insider status to benefit themselves at company expense.

It was very easy to fleece the beneficial owners of Ullico stock—the union members who were participants in the various union plans that actually owned it. Ullico stock wasn't publicly traded. The directors themselves set its price—which was effectively based on the price of Global Crossing stock. As Global Crossing stock went up, up went Ullico stock. The directors and officers had the company sell them stock on favorable terms denied to everyone else. When Global Crossing went down, the insiders lowered the price of Ullico stock, but not before selling their stock back to the company at its peak price. Sweeney didn't participate in the transactions, but he approved them.

Many of the directors who did profit from the trades had also gotten in trouble for alleged misuse of their unions' pension funds. Among them was Plumbers Union President Marty Maddaloni, who'd lost at least $200 million in pension fund money on the reefs off Hollywood, Florida, in the effort to rebuild the mob-linked Hotel Diplomat. In addition to helping pay back $11 million to the Plumbers' fund, in August 2004 Maddaloni agreed to pay back $200,000 to Ullico.[60]

Also among them was Doug McCarron, the six-foot-five, white-haired boss of the United Brotherhood of Carpenters, who bears a striking resemblance to Charlton Heston's Moses. Whether or not McCarron actually broke the Sixth Commandment, he resigned from the Ullico board after returning about $200,000 of the $276,000 he earned from stock swapping with Ullico.[61]

McCarron is a veteran of pension fund controversy. He'd been the target of a civil suit charging that he'd paid excessive advisory fees to money manager Richard Blum, who is Senator Diane Feinstein's husband. In an eight-year period during the 1990s, Blum got $54 million in advisory fees from the Southern California Carpenters' Fund, although he handled only a small part of the fund.[62]

Blum's fees were awarded by McCarron and Ronald Tutor, co-chairs of the $2 billion fund. Tutor, southern California's largest contractor, had been a major supporter of McCarron during his rise to power. Tutor and Blum were also business partners. At one time, Blum was the largest investor in Perini Corporation, a construction company later taken over by Tutor. It was the allegedly imprudent investment by Southern California Carpenters in Perini that initially triggered the civil suit.[63] Blum sued the plaintiff, retired carpenter Horacio Grana, for libel. He then dropped the libel suit. Grana's death ended the litigation.

Besides McCarron and Maddaloni, Communication Workers of America (CWA) boss Morty Bahr was another Ullico director who got the message that money could be made from insider trading. A month before he got caught taking $27,000 in stock trading profits, Bahr lambasted Global Crossing for "corporate arrogance" and "secret dealings and employee abuses."[64]

Bahr hadn't always been so critical of Global Crossing. In 1999, when Global Crossing was battling Qwest in a takeover battle for Frontier Communications, he came out strongly for Global Crossing. Insisted Bahr: "Qwest stands for an old-style slash and burn merger strategy, while Global Crossing stands for growth."[65]

Actually, Global Crossing, although it appeared robust, was already in its death spiral. It didn't have the cash to buy Frontier's assets. It paid for the company with its own stock—which was achieving stratospheric heights on the engines of accounting fraud. A few months later, Bahr and the rest of the Ullico directors got opportunities to become minor partners in the Global Crossing Golconda.

Things turned out differently for CWA's members at Frontier Communications. Employees with 401(k) plans had balked at having their life savings in Global Crossing stock, but CWA officials had put their fears at rest. A local CWA official who represented Frontier employees exclaimed bitterly, "[They've] lost everything they've worked thirty, thirty-five years for, they're devastated."[66]

For official labor, though, the biggest casualty may have been the AFL-CIO's "No More Enrons" campaign. In March 2002, AFL-CIO secretary-treasurer Richard Trumka had planned a big public relations offensive attacking the appointment of a former Enron director to the board of Lockheed Martin. By April, as the Ullico revelations piled up, Trumka decided to pull the plug. A union official explained to *Business Week*, "He didn't want us to look like hypocrites."[67]

Failure of union reform. In the 1990s, beginning with the election of Teamsters president Ron Carey, labor activists—the AFL-CIO left—were convinced that they had unleashed a wave of reform that would have irreversible effects. More than a decade later, the impact is hard to detect. A lot of the same unions that were run by thieves, racketeers, and gunmen fifty, eighty, or a hundred years ago—the New Jersey Longshoremen, the Chicago Projectionists Union, the Boston Teamsters, the Ironworkers— remain corrupt today. Nine Ironworkers officials have been indicted for embezzlement; four have pleaded guilty, including the president, Jake West.[68] It was worse in 1913, when thirty-three officials were sent to prison for participation in dynamite bombings. But the Chicago projectionists are still setting off bombs in theaters; the Gambino and Genovese crime families continue to extort their respective longshore locals on both sides of the Hudson River; and the Irish gangs continue to provide the muscle for the Teamsters in Boston's Local 25.

There's a tendency in all large organizations for the reformers to get spit out or worse—to get digested without a trace by the system. The labor movement, though, has a particularly strong digestive tract. The reformers go in, and they may capture a few locals and win what are seen as major victories. But either they don't get far—like Ken Paff, head of Teamsters for a Democratic Union, who has fought the good fight for thirty years, with increasingly less impact—or they do as "Uncle Dan" Tobin did: he began in 1905 as a Teamsters reformer and eventually became general president of America's most corrupt union.

It's the fiefdom nature of the system—the localness, the complexity of the ties between leaders and members—that makes it almost impossible to build a broad base across the whole membership or keep from being co-opted by the demands of loyalty.

While the protection game between leaders and members explains a lot of corruption's persistence, so do the symbiotic relations between lower-level leaders and higher-level leaders. It goes right to the very top of the AFL-CIO.

Credit Sweeney with generous impulses and a desire to speak authentically with a New Voice. He wasn't a free citizen. He had to compete with longtime Kirkland aide Thomas Donahue for votes from the affiliates. Many of the affiliates had deeply rooted organized crime problems. In 1986, the President's Commission on Organized Crime had identified the four most mobbed-up unions: the Teamsters, the Laborers, the Hotel and Restaurant Workers, and the East Coast Longshoremen. Although Sweeney was widely portrayed as battling the Old Guard, three of the four supported Sweeney; the fourth, the Longshoremen, went for Donahue.

At the 1995 convention, the four historically most mobbed-up unions were far from holding a pariah status. They controlled over 2.5 million out of 13 million convention votes. Competition for their allegiance was fierce. Laborers president Arthur Coia Jr. made the most of his strategic position. "Right now you got one guy in a position to determine the whole presidency of the AFL-CIO," said Coia, who controlled 750,000 votes. Referring to himself as "the kingmaker," he added: "Not bad for a small-time, hometown guy from Providence, Rhode Island."[69]

If Coia could name the king, the realm was in big trouble. He would later admit in sworn testimony that he owed his first national office in the Laborers to a meeting he had with Chicago Outfit boss Vincent Solano, who at the time ranked no. 42 on the Fortune list of America's top fifty mobsters.[70] Arthur Coia Sr. was about to retire. To step up to his father's no. 2 position in the union, Coia Jr. had to have Solano's blessing. An Outfit associate summoned Coia Jr. from Providence to meet with the aging crime boss in a coffee shop at O'Hare Airport. The audience took only about fifteen minutes. "It was like out of a movie," Coia recalled.[71]

With campaign debts to supporters like Coia Jr., the battle for reform wasn't going to get much help from the AFL-CIO's president. It would have to come either from inside the individual AFL-CIO affiliates or from outside, through government prosecutorial efforts.

Government-led reform is clearly the least desirable course. It bends toward government control of unions and encourages efforts by union leaders to find politicians who will protect them from the prosecutors. But without the outside prosecutors, it's also clear that leaders like Arthur Coia, whom the Justice Department described in a 212-page complaint as a "mob puppet," would still be on-stage performing their herky-jerky routines.[72]

In the case of Arthur Coia, the Clinton administration devised a novel arrangement. In place of an independent board, Coia was allowed to hire Robert Luskin, his personal defense attorney, to clean up the union. The deal was worked out in a February 1995 White House meeting that included not just Luskin but also Harold Ickes, a former Laborers' attorney who served as a top Clinton aide.[73] Skeptics noted that Coia contributed nearly $5 million to the Democrats during the next two election cycles, and before that, he lent $100,000 to Clinton's inauguration. Skeptics also pointed out that Luskin did eventually force over 200 corrupt officials to leave the Laborers—mainly by providing them with financial incentives to leave.

Rather than wiping out the mob problem, though, the ultimate outcome of the Clinton Justice Department's most celebrated cleanup may have just shifted the locus of Mafia influence in the union from Chicago to New York. Coia was under pressure to deliver heads. He naturally chose to deliver those of his adversaries. Historically, the Outfit had run the Laborers from Chicago, and that changed under Coia. The Chicago mob sent two representatives to Coia Sr.'s 1993 funeral to register their displeasure with his son. Coia says they accused him of "stealing and taking the presidency from Chicago."[74] But the Chicago boys were mercilessly purged anyhow, even though no evidence was ever presented that the ousted Outfit associates who ran the Chicago locals were guilty of labor racketeering.

On the other hand, with few exceptions, Coia's mob supporters in the east got to run their fiefdoms pretty much as they liked.

The AFL-CIO's "barren marriage" to the Democratic Party. Unions give much more to political campaigns than media accounts suggest. Yes, corporations give more, but unions are surprisingly competitive. According to the Center for Responsive Politics, seven of the top ten campaign contributors in the last decade are not Fortune 500 corporations. They're AFL-CIO unions. And overwhelmingly they give to the Democrats; union giving is much more one-sided than corporate giving. The corporations divide their contributions into about 60 percent to the Republicans and 40 percent to the Democrats. In the 2002 election cycle, the AFL-CIO spent nearly $100 million on candidates, with over 90 percent going to the Democrats. That's just in federal elections, and it doesn't include most in-kind contributions, like "volunteer" phone banking. While it's hard to know precisely, it's unlikely that very much of the $100 million in cash was given to candidates to advance a common agenda for working people. Most goes to promote very specific purposes of individual union leaders.

In descending order of public benefit, these aims are, first, to improve contract terms for their respective unions; second, to increase their membership—sometimes at the expense of other unions;[75] and third, union leaders write checks to protect themselves. They're buying Get Out of Jail Free cards—or, more strictly, Stay Out of Jail cards.

Between 1996 and 2000, three of the top union givers—AFSCME, SEIU, and the Teamsters—were headed by presidents who were under federal investigation, although only Ron Carey was charged. The presidents of the Laborers, the Ironworkers, and the Hotel Employees and Restaurant Employees (HERE) also came under scrutiny. They all had to resign, but at least they didn't do time. The total membership of these unions whose presidents were under criminal investigation is equal to half the membership of the AFL-CIO.

The point here isn't that labor's money mainly goes to keep union leaders out of prison. It's that the portion that probably does illustrates a huge and widely underappreciated fact that is denied on both sides of the transaction—even by Republicans, who try to scare their base by suggesting that the money is going to advance John Sweeney's "radical agenda": "legalizing abortion, legalizing marijuana, forcing the Boy Scouts to admit homosexuals and atheists," and so on.[76] But it's not what's going on in the Boy Scouts that explains why union leaders and Democratic pols hook up. Nor do broad public policy reasons do much to illuminate the relationship. On trade, tax policy, labor law, minimum wage policy, welfare reform, and so on, labor gets so little. Why the fidelity?

Even the far left accepts the two sides' own account of why they're together. In the 1980s, Mike Davis, the brilliant and scholarly Trotskyist truck driver, in his *Prisoners of the American Dream*, described the relationship between the AFL-CIO and the Democratic Party as a "barren marriage." Quite convincingly, he portrayed how little the unions got, in public policy terms, from their courtship of the Democrats; how far short the unions were falling in the effort to make the Democrats into European-style social democrats.[77] Davis was assuming that social democracy is what the AFL-CIO is truly aiming at.

The natural conclusion of Davis's critique was the same as Leon Trotsky's: that the great task of organized labor in America was to break with the Democrats and create its own party. Davis, however, didn't fully embrace his own conclusions. He argued that the labor left had to break with some Democrats and ally with others, particularly with the Rev. Jesse Jackson, who had battled Walter Mondale for the party's 1984 presidential nomination. Davis's strategy was to form militant rank-and-file caucuses in AFL-CIO unions and steer them toward an alliance with Jackson's Rainbow Coalition forces.

Jackson, however, had already allied with Jackie Presser, the roly-poly, 300-pound former car thief who'd risen to the Teamsters general presidency with the help of the FBI and the Cleveland mob. Even less than most mob associates, Presser was no friend of rank-and-file caucuses. To combat Teamsters for a Democratic Union, Presser organized BLAST—Brotherhood of Loyal Americans and Strong Teamsters: goon squads designed specifically to intimidate and break up dissident rallies.[78]

At Presser's own rallies, after his indictment on labor racketeering charges, he deployed Jackson.[79] At one "Don't Send Jackie to Jail" rally at the Cincinnati Convention Center, Jackson enumerated, one after another, all the Reagan officials who had been indicted. "If you live in a glass house, you don't throw stones," said Jackson, bringing the crowd to its feet.[80]

After the speech, Jackson and his entourage boarded Presser's private jet, only to voice his disappointment with the surprisingly proletarian fare available on Air Jackie. "Where's all the grand food, the lobster, the shrimp, and the caviar?" complained Jackson loudly. "Don't tell me that fat son of a bitch hasn't laid out a supper for me."[81]

After a few drinks, Jackson got over his pique. According to Duke Zeller, a Presser aide, Jackson and Jackie had actually been together for some years. Public policy hadn't been the basis of their mutual attraction. Jackson always wanted money from Presser. And Presser, continually harassed by the Justice Department, needed the political cover that the Chicago-based civil rights leader brought to Teamsters events.[82] After Presser died, Jackson found an even bigger trade union teat: Hotel and Restaurant Union boss Ed Hanley. A close ally of Presser, Hanley was also a creature of Midwest mobsters.[83] Facing federal investigation, Hanley put nearly a dozen Rainbow/PUSH Coalition staffers on the union payroll, including Jesse Jr., although before he became a U.S. congressman. In 1999, Karin Stanford, the mother of Jackson's love child, also got a HERE salary while she worked for Rainbow/PUSH.[84]

The relationship between trade union bosses and Democratic Party politicians may be a "barren marriage," but only by the standards of modern Western-style marriage. It's true that the unions and the Democrats don't have a relationship of equals based on shared common ideals and goals. It's more of an old-style patriarchal marriage. Union leaders are like traditional brides who must bring a dowry. Democratic Party politicians are the grooms who assume the dominant role. When it comes to party affairs, the trade union role is in the kitchen, preparing "grand food." The unions accept their role because the Democratic Party politicians let them do what they please in the kitchen; how the union leaders manage to put the shrimp on the table is up to them. Still, both sides know that their relationship is being judged by more demanding standards, making for frequent furtiveness, pretension, and hypocrisy.

When major institutions in society become corrupt, the point is to identify what has gone wrong, mobilize indignation, and undertake necessary reforms. With unions, however, there is a danger that they've been weak and corrupt so long that it's no longer clear what it is they contribute to the health of the society. When major drug companies knowingly put lethal drugs on the market, the public doesn't say, "Let's get rid of drug companies," because people realize that America needs world-class companies to manufacture drugs. But most don't think they need world-class unions. Americans haven't seriously reckoned with the burden of bad unions.

CHAPTER TWO

The Hidden Cost of Corrupt Unions

What difference does it make that labor unions play such a small and sorry role in American life? Why should those of us whose pensions don't depend on a continuous inflow of union dues care if organized labor is in trouble? Maybe labor's problems are like the perpetual crisis that plagued the Austro-Hungarian Empire in its last fifty years: terminal but not truly serious. That is, perhaps the United States needs a labor movement no more than central Europe needed an empire. That's essentially the position of free market conservatives who argue that labor unions are a thing of the past. Unions were a creation of blue collar manufacturing workers in the nineteenth-century nation-state. Now nation-states have been undermined by globalization, and the digital revolution has rendered blue collar workers obsolete.

The left, too, for the most part, has lost interest in the labor movement. Its most fashionable thinkers no longer address workers at all; U.S. workers' interests aren't seen as having any special significance or legitimacy. As philosopher Richard Rorty has observed, today's left "thinks more about stigma than about money, more about deep and hidden psychosexual motivation than about shallow and evident greed." The shift in concerns took place, he notes, at the same time that "intellectuals began to lose interest in labor unions."[1]

It's not just the intellectual elite. On a list of issues that Americans feel are important, the sad state of American unions doesn't show up anywhere—not even on a list of economic concerns. Americans worry about job security and the rising cost of health care. They fear outsourcing.[2] They don't fear that some union leader is going to steal their pension or sign a sweetheart contract giving away their dues money.

Although Americans may know where it hurts, they may not know what's causing them their pain. That throbbing you feel in your throat may not come from your throat. It may be from acid reflux disease in your stomach.

For many Americans, the idea that their economic pain might be connected with the state of the unions would be a stretch. Many workers have no direct contact with unions, clean or dirty. The numbers are especially telling among young people. Of those under twenty-five, only about one in twenty are union members, compared with nearly one in four among workers over sixty.

The AFL-CIO is an archipelago of fiefdoms in a sea of unorganized workers. As the sea level rises, the state of the labor movement's shrinking domain hardly seems to matter any more. But if politics and material life still matter, the state of the labor movement makes a gigantic difference. *New York Times* columnist David Brooks inadvertently makes clear what's at stake when he writes that Americans are "the hardest working people on the face of the earth. The average American works 350 hours a year ... more than the average European."[3] But is this because of our "strong work ethic," as Brooks believes, or, far more plausibly, because of the weakness of American labor? And why is it so weak?

STRONG WORK ETHIC OR WEAK LABOR MOVEMENT?

It's the lack of a powerful collective voice, one that speaks with genuine moral authority, that has turned millions of Americans into semidependent creatures incapable of exercising a meaningful choice in the workplace. Non-union employees—92 percent of those working in the private sector—have no collective voice whatever. Their working lives are still largely shaped by the ancient Tudor doctrine of "employment at will," as interpreted in a seminal American legal treatise written in 1877 by Horace G. Wood entitled *Master and Servant*.[4] Unless they want to give up employment entirely, they can't refuse the boss's order to work overtime. They can't ask for a raise, so they take that extra part-time job even though it means less time with their families.[5] Workers in the private sector can't go on vacations like the globetrotting Germans because they don't have unions that are capable of winning the right to take long enough vacations. Millions in the Home of the Brave are afraid to risk being seen going to the toilet on company time.

Ours is the only country in the advanced capitalist world in which there is no national legislation mandating a minimum vacation time. In Europe the minimum is four weeks.[6] We are also unique in lacking a statute guaranteeing long-term paid sick leave. The average in Europe is fifty-four weeks at 62 percent pay.[7] Another sign of American exceptionalism is our lack of a federal law guaranteeing paid maternity leave. It's common in Europe, where the maximum is eighteen weeks at 89 percent pay.[8]

Maybe there is a uniquely American work ethic. We could find out if national legislation were passed giving employees the right to take vacations, get sick, and become pregnant without penalty. If workers chose nevertheless to keep on working the same number of hours, Mr. Brooks would be proved right.

In nations around the world, the stronger the unions, the less inequality and insecurity and the more "social democracy"—the more workers are free to choose whether to work more or go on vacation; the more rights they can claim against employers, like the right of French workers to walk off jobs they deem to be unsafe; and the more collective goods they enjoy, like universal health insurance, free child care, and job security.

There are two widely used measures of union strength: union density—the share of union members in the workforce—and union coverage—the share of workers who benefit from union contracts. These measures are far from complete, but countries with high rates of union density—like Sweden, Italy, and Germany—or union coverage—like France—have more workplace rights and a wider distribution of collective goods. They also have less inequality, violent crime, and social exclusion.

AMERICAN DREAMS, EUROPEAN REALITIES

It may be that the Europeans are making the wrong choices. Most U.S. conservatives think so. Writes David Brooks: "The European model is foundering under the fact that billions of people are willing to work harder than the Europeans are."[9] America's penchant for low taxes, high income inequality, reduced social benefits, workplace insecurity, and long hours, it's claimed, represents the most sensible strategy for growth in a global economy. Perhaps. But that's not the issue here. Nor is the statistical sleight of hand that allows Brooks to claim that the sloth of European workers has reduced them to a standard of living comparable to that enjoyed by the typical resident of an Arkansas trailer park.[10]

Nor is it material that European welfare states are under tremendous pressure, or even that European unions and labor-led parties aren't what they once were. Many continental unions find themselves with a shrinking, aging membership, bargaining at lower levels, fighting against concessions, and defending social benefits won years before. In Germany, the unions and the Social Democratic Party have divided over "flexibility," with the party insisting that the unions give up free weekends.[11] In the late 1980s, the Italian unions gave up *la scala mobile*: national legislation won by mass strikes in the 1970s that had pegged wages to the cost of living.

But it's one thing to be giving ground while defending a social democracy, and another never to have achieved one at all. The question is, what explains the *choice* of models—the direction of development? Why has most of Europe gone in the direction of social democracy, while the United States, after a brief and comparatively mild fling beginning in the 1930s, turned around in the 1970s and adopted the nineteenth-century model of capitalism that the rest of the Western world had abandoned— unrestricted free trade, poor laws, seventy-hour work weeks, the night watchman state, and the hangman—institutions that were already being satirized by Charles Dickens in the 1840s?

The most plausible reason is inequalities of power. If power is the capacity to make others act contrary to their will, American workers have little of it. Such leverage as they do have is unnaturally fragmented, monopolized by a comparative few, and used without benefiting most American wageworkers, who simply lack any influence over corporate management, either in the boardroom or in the streets. Unlike countries in the European Union, America lacks laws mandating works councils that allow workers to have a say in determining work rules. Nor can American workers mount nationwide strikes of the type that force governments to retreat or fall—as they have in France, Italy, and Denmark.

American workers, unlike European workers, can't compensate for their lack of private sector power with political power. In Sweden, the relations between the governing Swedish Workers Party and the union movement are very close. Labor governments have run the country most of the time since 1929, creating an unrivaled social democracy—albeit one that emphasizes the opportunity to work rather than the chance to get on welfare.[12] It was the British Labor Party, which came to power in 1945, that introduced national health insurance to the Anglo-Saxon world. In France, a union-backed government of the left came to power in 1997 and enacted the key demand of the unions: reduction of the workweek to thirty-five hours.[13]

The comparative futility of American labor's involvement in national politics is stunning. It's not just that American unions don't have a party. They probably spend more on elections than all the labor movements of the rest of the world combined—an estimated $250 million in the 2004 election cycle. Yet the dividends for ordinary workers are hard to identify. The last truly significant piece of pro-worker legislation—the creation of the Occupational Safety and Health Administration (OSHA)—passed in 1970, under Richard Nixon.

America's lack of a strong labor or social-democratic party is something that's been chewed over for a hundred years. But the reasons debaters once found compelling now seem terribly dated. Observers formerly pointed to the huge divergence between American and European living standards. The difference, some argued, was due to the American model of trade unionism, which had modeled itself on American business. Progressivism, famously observed the German sociologist Werner Sombart, "foundered on the reefs of roast beef and the shoals of apple pie."[14]

But that was in 1906, when, as Sombart also noted, "the American worker makes two or three times what his German counterpart makes."[15] A few years later, in 1909, AFL president Samuel Gompers, who took a five-month European grand tour, also noted the huge difference in living standards. Gompers claimed he had never seen such poverty as he saw in Amsterdam or Brussels. The Belgian pushcart drivers were so poor they didn't even have horses. They hitched up dogs to their carts.[16]

European workers were less well off because they were badly led, he concluded, with labor officials espousing an effeminate social welfare philosophy as well as a primitive egalitarianism. To French trade union critics who disparaged his penchant for staying at the Ritz with an entourage, Gompers vaunted the difference between European and American labor movements. The French unions had only $75,000 in their treasury, he pointed out, while the AFL "counts its deposits in banks by millions of dollars."[17]

American workers were rich, Gompers explained, because of the AFL's steady leadership. He ended the account of his 1909 grand tour with a pleonastic tribute to the organization that paid his salary: "In unity and capacity for organization, progressiveness of propaganda, thoroughness and clearness in scope and purpose, militancy of spirit, soundness of finances, adaptability in administration to the ends sought or continuity and rapidity of development, the national movement in no foreign country can compare with the AFL."[18]

Did American workers owe their comparative prosperity to the AFL, as Gompers claimed? It's hard to see how. At that time, membership in American unions stood at just 10 percent in the private sector. While that's higher than today's 8 percent, it wasn't high enough to materially affect the wages of the other 90 percent. AFL membership was concentrated in urban occupational niches like construction, trucking, and longshore. The far higher level of American wages can be explained by the far higher levels of productivity in American manufacturing and agriculture. American unions had scant presence in either sector.[19]

What Gompers utterly ignored on his grand tour was the huge upsurge in European labor in the first decade of the twentieth century. By 1907, the United States was already far behind every country but Belgium in union density. Sweden's main labor federation, the Swedish Trade Union Confederation (known as LO), had organized nearly half the country. Proportionately, Germany had about three times as many workers organized as the United States did.[20]

It would take a long time for Europe to match the United States in roast beef. But by the 1990s, the dogs in Brussels were no longer pulling carts but strolling on leashes or perched on laps. Belgium had reached 98 percent of U.S. labor productivity. And the Netherlands wasn't far behind.[21] As European and American productivity converged, it was possible for

Europeans, with their much more powerful labor movement, to reduce their hours and distribute the wealth they produced more equally. While in the United States the number of hours worked per year had increased since 1980, France had reduced hours worked by 244, Spain by 210, and Germany by 489.[22] If official statistics can be believed, the average wage of Italian workers in the 1990s nearly equaled the declared income of jewelers and hotel owners.[23]

Social democracy may not be the end of history, but social-democratic regimes accomplished what their adversaries had insisted was impossible. First, they've proved capable of incorporating capitalism's main strengths —openness to technology and the value of innovation. According to the World Economic Forum, four of the top six countries in the world in terms of competitiveness are Scandinavian social democracies.[24] Second, social-democratic regimes remedied the gross inequality and insecurity produced by early free market capitalism. By the nineteenth century, as anthropologist Marvin Harris reminds us, "Factory hands and miners were putting in twelve hours a day under conditions that no self-respecting Bushman, Trobriander, Cherokee or Iroquois would have tolerated. At the day's end, after contending with the continuous whine and chatter of wheels and shafts, dust, smoke and foul odors, the operators of the new labor-saving devices retired to their dingy hovels of lice and fleas."[25] What transformed these conditions was not improved technology and freer markets but organized movements of the miners and factory hands themselves.

Perhaps the reduction of inequality and insecurity is an ignoble societal objective. Friedrich Nietzsche denounced these concerns as the product of "slave morality." To stop fast-growing social-democratic movements, he advocated reducing workers to serflike status so they could better provide leisure and security for the artist class.[26] In parallel fashion, American social Darwinists like William Graham Sumner opposed unions, social programs, and even private charity because they restricted the freedom of the robber barons—the genuine benefactor of the Forgotten Man.[27]

In Europe, opponents of social democracy lost the argument and lost the war. Here in the United States, neo–social Darwinists have regained the upper hand. In no small measure, America's domestic social democracy deficit is due to the desertion of its practical advocates. The problem isn't simply that the bosses have the upper hand, or even that American union leaders have been poor advocates and practitioners, but, more seriously, that the genuine interests of the trade union establishment lie elsewhere. The AFL-CIO hasn't fought for social legislation that would reduce insecurity because it seeks to maintain union-controlled private health and pension plans—plans that serve as pillars of patronage, kickbacks, and self-enrichment for union leaders. Then, too, American unions can't fight inequality effectively because by their very structure they serve as amplifiers rather than ameliorators of wage differences.

Losing the Battle Against Inequality. "American Exceptionalism" used to suggest the question "How come America escaped European-style class differences?" Now it raises exactly the opposite question. For at least a generation, with the exception of the late 1990s, the United States has been moving proudly, confidently, and almost inexorably toward greater inequality. Among the advanced nations, what is striking about American income isn't the sheer extent of it so much as how unevenly it's distributed. According to a study of fourteen advanced countries, the median income among the rich—defined as the top 10 percent—is higher in the United States than in any of the other countries—and in relation to the bottom 10 percent, way higher. The rich in America earn 5.4 times what the bottom tenth earn; in the other thirteen countries, the rich average only 3.5 times what the bottom tenth earn.[28]

Since 1970, the U.S. national income has more than doubled. Who has benefited? Not the poor—the bottom 10 to 15 percent of the population. Compared with seventeen other advanced nations in the Organization for Economic Cooperation and Development, our leadership in poverty is substantial in the most widely measured categories: we have the highest—and the deepest—rate of child poverty, the highest percentage of elderly poor, and the highest percentage of people who are poor in their lives at least once. And notwithstanding the folkloric claims about the superior mobility of American society, we have the highest percentage of people who are poor for protracted periods in their lives.[29]

The broader middling strata in the United States have no reason to celebrate either. U.S. workers experienced the longest period of wage stagnation in modern American history: median nonsupervisory worker wages fell between 1971 and 1995. Then came the five years of the Clinton bubble, when wages shot up, especially for the bottom quartile. But since the stock market crash in 2000, wages have resumed their downward trajectory. By 2003, the median non-supervisory wage for male workers was less than it was in 1973. Overall, for this generation, what has kept incomes from cratering despite falling wages is greater work effort: an extra 172 hours a year per person since 1973, and for a family in the middle fifth, about 500 extra hours.[30]

In plutocratic America, much of the gain in national income has gone to the top 1 percent. Since 1979, this group's income in real terms has more than doubled.[31] A *Forbes* article entitled "In Praise of Inequality" boasts that the United States has more billionaires per capita than any other country. There are dozens of nations where the gross national product doesn't equal the personal fortunes of the wealthiest Americans, like Bill Gates ($46.6 billion) and Warren Buffett ($42.9 billion).[32] But the *Forbes* data also show that the most fertile countries for growing billionaires aren't necessarily the wealthiest. In poor countries like Mexico and Russia, where corrupt institutions make it easier to appropriate the wealth of others, wealth tends to concentrate in the hands of a few.[33]

Among the world's economies, the United States stands out like Martha Stewart at a Tupperware party: fabulous but faintly suspect. Our economic profile—as cast by what economists call the Gini index—resembles third world countries like Venezuela and Mexico more than first world countries like Sweden, France, and Italy.[34] By the peak of the 1990s New Economy, American CEOs earned 500 times what the median worker earned. By 2003, the ratio had fallen to a mere 300 times. But that's still an order of magnitude greater than in continental Europe, where it stands between 11 and 19 to one.[35]

What happened? Clinton administration economists explained that people don't cause inequality, computers do. The introduction of information technology provided higher returns to those who had acquired the new information-based skills.[36] Others have stressed increased trade and globalization. But Sweden and Japan have computers too, and they're also major trading nations, and neither comes close to our level of inequality. Plus, here in America, the era of the great technology boom (1995–2000) was the one period since the late 1970s when wage inequality was reversed.[37]

As the "irrational exuberance" of the late 1990s waned—or rather was channeled into real estate speculation—federal investigators discovered that many of the most successful CEOs had acquired their fabulous incomes through rather traditional skills, like stock swindling, accounting fraud, and pilfering from the company. Bernie Ebbers, the Mississippi mogul who created the $55 billion telecom giant WorldCom by making over seventy acquisitions, managed to conceal for years that the company was worthless. In 2002, WorldCom finally sank, taking down over $30 billion in debt and 17,000 jobs. Ebbers was eventually found guilty of perpetrating an $11 billion fraud. Global Crossing's Gary Winnick—bankrolled in part by the AFL-CIO—buried $34 billion worth of fiber optic cable in the ocean, where it remains 98 percent unused. After taking Global Crossing into bankruptcy, Winnick then bought a $60 million house in California. Then he fixed it up—for a total cost of $94 million. Winnick's castle sheltered his personal assets from workers who were trying to collect $34 million in lost pensions.[38] The unrivaled emperor of excess, though, was probably Tyco International's Dennis Kozlowski, another merger wizard. At the high point of Kozlowski's reign, Tyco had a market value of $120 billion. Kozlowski, who slept on $5,960 sheets and used a $17,000 toilet kit, celebrated by staging a $2 million birthday party in Sardinia that made Trimalchio's banquet seem like the South Beach diet. The *pièce de résistance* was an ice sculpture of Michelango's David that dispensed vodka from its penis for celebrity guests.[39]

Vulgarity may be the least of the problems presented by the Kozlowskis of the corporate world. The practical justification for inequality has always rested on the claim that investment—and therefore jobs—depends on the rich. Yet the investment of the late 1990s may ultimately have created fewer rather than more jobs. The number of jobs in 2004 stood lower than the total in 2000, at the stock market peak. Literally trillions in assets were destroyed. Like the unbridled Soviet-era communists, whose uneconomic heavy industry projects still litter a ravaged landscape, the renegade CEOs carried out a huge, arrogant misallocation of wealth, destroying more capital than they created. At least the robber barons of the nineteenth century built the railroads.

How has power shifted so strongly in favor of a self-aggrandizing corporate elite? And what could cut them down to size? The popularity of TV reality shows like *The Apprentice*, featuring Donald Trump, suggests that Americans simply love arrogant billionaires who shout "You're fired!" at them. The show has high ratings, and Trump has millions of fans. But he also has some of the most negative ratings of anyone in public life.[40] Other polls show that Americans aren't a lot more tolerant of inequality than Europeans.[41]

European and American unions treat their tycoons very differently. In the United States, the AFL-CIO played the role of pilot fish to Gary Winnick's shark, swimming in the wake of his company's initial public offering of stock, secretly benefiting through insider trading from what dropped from his jaws. It was a scenario often repeated by Ullico with other corporations and by other union funds.

In Europe, the rise of an overweaning plutocracy has been largely checked, at least until recently, by labor-driven political action.[42] Through tax policy, labor and social-democratic governments redistribute income. Although tax rates on upper brackets have come down almost everywhere, the top marginal rates in Europe are still substantially higher than in the U.S.—50 percent or higher in every major continental country.[43] Through wage policies, European countries have established a higher basic minimum wage than the United States has—as high as 70 percent of the median wage, as opposed to less than 40 percent here. In other European countries, union collective bargaining contracts are extended to non-union workers. France has about the same share of union members as the United States, but over 90 percent of French workers are covered by union contracts.[44]

In the private sector, too, European unions flatten out wage differences. They push for a "solidarity" wage whose ideal is the strong helping the weak. In European unions, the spread between union leaders' salaries and members' wages is generally negligible. In America, the highest-paid union leaders make as much as the lowest-paid Swedish CEOs.[45] Egalitarian sentiments ring out from the nation's founding document. Decades later, Alexis de Tocqueville, a distinguished French visitor, observed in his travels across America that equality was "the fundamental fact from which all others seem to be derived."[46]

But today the United States lacks effective institutions capable of translating egalitarian values into action. The problem with labor's legislative efforts isn't only the unions' lack of leverage, it's also how the leadership chooses to exercise what leverage it has. But the real sources of income in-equality are in the private sector, where employees face off for shares of corporate revenue against corporate managers and stockholders. If labor were more successful in the market, the need for legislative redistributive action would be a lot less.

In the private sector, unions can reduce inequality in two ways. They can use their bargaining power to raise the share of corporate revenue that goes to wages, and they can use their persuasive power on their own mem-bers to sell them on compressing the spread of wages—convincing the strong to help the weak.

In the past half century, American unions haven't ventured very far down either road. Capital's share of national income has been rising[47] and wage inequality has been increasing.[48] It's a twin failure that can't be ex-plained just by pointing to falling union membership, lack of market power, low union density, and so forth.[49] Low union density itself has to be understood as a principal outcome of American-style unionism.

A few economists, particularly those close to the AFL-CIO, blame ris-ing U.S. inequality on falling rates of union membership.[50] Their solution is to allow existing unions to add dues-paying members; eliminate the need for cumbersome National Labor Relations Board elections, which are heavily stacked against labor; and repeal the Taft-Hartley Act, which took away big portions of labor's bargaining clout. It's unlikely, though, that legislative changes—however desirable from the standpoint of assur-ing workers' rights—would reduce income inequality. If today's unions had more members, they'd be bigger but not better attuned to broader so-cial welfare issues; they'd be richer, but not more egalitarian. The problem is not just that American unions don't have enough members; it's that they organize in ways that tend to leave most workers out, creating substantial wage differences among workers who do the same work and amplifying economic inequality.

Besides creating inequality within unions themselves, unions have lost their power to reduce inequality between union and non-union workers. They aren't able to raise the wages of less skilled workers. In the garment, retail, grocery, hotel and restaurant, and meat processing industries, the problem isn't that unions have no presence, it's that their presence doesn't make a difference.

Unlike continental European unions, which have no geographical jurisdictions, territorially based American unions naturally seek exclusive territorial monopolies. The successful monopolist restricts supply. That's what keeps wages high for those shielded by the monopoly's protective wall, and the high wages attract workers who want to join. But if a territorial union were to let all applicants in, the number of union jobs in the territory wouldn't increase, just the number of members seeking those jobs. Adding more members would dilute the market power of those already in the union. "Organizing the unorganized" sounds like an obvious idea until one realizes how it threatens the wages of the already organized and the political base of the incumbent union leadership.

Under the U.S. fiefdom model, the point is to find a rich territory and occupy it. Little incentive exists for the occupiers to extend the benefits of the union to low-paid outsiders. Nor is there much inclination for the union and the employer to fight each other for shares of revenue. For one thing, the union monopoly depends on the employers' monopoly. And a lot of the employers' strength comes from having an agreement with a union that monopolizes the labor—whether skilled, like plumbers, or strategically located, like longshore workers. Occasionally there will be a falling-out, but usually it's in the interest of both sides to work together quietly to gouge the public.

The still-powerful New York City construction unions, totally intertwined with the contractors, perfectly illustrate the monopoly model. The New York construction unions have the nation's highest wage and benefit scale. The New York contractors have achieved the nation's highest construction costs. And the city has the lowest rate of housing construction among all American cities experiencing population growth.[51] It goes without saying that the construction unions, many historically run by crime family associates and some even by made guys, have had little to contribute to the civic debate about low-cost housing or alternatives to a market where the median apartment in 2004 sold for $1.2 million.

Even so, the union scale might promote equality if it were more widely shared. But how many of the city's 125,000 construction workers—union or non-union—actually get the $75-an-hour wage and benefit packages called for by the contract? It's hard to know for sure. But union density appears to have slipped over the past couple of decades; one estimate puts the level at 18 percent.[52] And in all but the best of times, there are thousands of members who "put their union card in their shoe" while working for non-union contractors so they can work at all.

Most notoriously, the "Theme from *The Godfather*" regularly serves as background music whenever six-figure construction jobs are in play in New York City. It's hard to avoid the strong arm of the wiseguys when there's so much money to be made from the huge spread between the union rate and the market rate. The contractors can hire non-union labor for as little as $10 an hour with no benefits. Then they charge the owner, the developer, or the government the union rate. The difference will be pocketed by the contractor, minus the cost of bribes to union officials to look the other way. Mob guys—if they're not the contractors themselves—will wind up with at least a couple of points. It's the fee they charge for protection—a vital commodity in the construction field. The more the spread between wages, the more union members getting the premium wages need protection against those seeking their jobs and the more officials who are betraying their members will need protection against those who covet their territories.

In other words, job control unionism requires protection, and protection bends toward the mob. Thus the mob becomes the ultimate guarantor of wage inequality.

The tilt toward inequality isn't restricted to the skilled construction trades in the conservative-minded former AFL unions. Take the International Longshoremen's and Warehousemen's Union (ILWU). Organized by communists, born out of the San Francisco general strike of 1934, and adopting the Wobbly motto "An injury to one is an injury to all," the ILWU has been identified as the reddest of all American unions. Its founder, Harry Bridges, whom the government tried to deport for alleged communist leanings, was the West Coast director of the CIO. On May Day, 1999, his avatars shut down ports all along the West Coast in sympathy with radical journalist Mumia Abu Jamal, who was convicted of murdering a Philadelphia policeman. At the front of 20,000 demonstrators, an ILWU contingent marched chanting, "An injury to one is an injury to all! Free Mumia Abu Jamal." It's hard to imagine a comparable job action on the East Coast, where the International Longshoremen's Association (ILA) holds sway. Since the 1930s, the ILA has been run by the

Gambino and Genovese crime families—rarely noted for their progressive sympathies.

Long ago, communists and mafiosi effectively divided the nation's ports. The reds got the West Coast and the mob got the East—and never, you would think, the twain shall meet, which is why it's jolting to see how much alike the ILA and the ILWU have become in key respects.

Both unions practiced successful job control unionism. Each controlled the hiring hall and thus became the gatekeepers doling out steady work and high-wage jobs. The ILWU avoided the most corrupting effects of job control. At least on the West Coast, you didn't have to be a wiseguy's nephew to get the best job. But, insensibly, the Los Angeles docks became fiefdoms, too. By 2004, when West Coast port officials announced a lottery for 3,000 new casual jobs and over 500,000 applications were received, it turned out the lottery had been blatantly rigged in favor of ILWU officials' relatives.[53]

More broadly, officials of both organizations have used the union's power over jobs not to create more equality—equal pay for equal work—but rather to create *status* groups—legally defined categories of workers who have sharply distinct rights to work and opportunities for earning income. Some workers get to work more hours than other workers. They get called first when jobs are available. The work they perform is less demanding. The mob-run and the progressive-run unions display a similar pattern of multitier union membership, nepotism, radical income inequality, and racial and gender discrimination, and the majority of port industry workers never get into the union at all. In Boston, Port Authority investigators charged ILA officials from three area locals with issuing union cards to their children—some as young as two years old. Casual dockworkers would then be assigned to work in place of the children for a few hours every year, building up valuable seniority for the union bosses' kids. When the children grew up, investigators explained, instead of starting at $16 an hour, they would earn $28. About thirty children were involved in the alleged scheme, which was uncovered in 2005 and dated back about two decades. Suspicions were first aroused when a dockworker was discovered using the same name as the ten-year-old granddaughter of an ILA boss.[54]

In L.A. they call longshore work a "million-dollar job." It's dangerous and requires substantial upper body strength, but it doesn't demand a lengthy apprenticeship or a college education. Yet ILWU members in the port of Los Angeles–Long Beach average nearly $90,000 a year plus $30,000 in benefits. Then there are the clerks, who work with clipboards, inspecting the cargo and reporting damage; they average $125,000 a year plus benefits. Union-chosen foremen ("walking bosses") get more.

The problem is getting to be a full-fledged member. Until 1980, when a federal court intervened, blacks and women were almost totally excluded from membership at any level. To reach the six-figure brackets today, you not only have to be in the union, you have to be an A-list man in the union. It's an exclusive club. The ranks of the A men come from the ranks of the B men. It takes 8,000 hours of work for a B man to become an A man. The B men in turn come from the ranks of casuals, who earn $18–$21 an hour when they work—and weeks can go by when they don't. Casuals wait, shelterless, in a parking lot, near an auto-dismantling yard where dead bodies sometimes turn up. Meanwhile, it takes an average of seven years to get from casual status to the B-list.[55]

Altogether, the 5,000 union jobs are only a fraction of the 40,000 long-shore jobs in the Los Angeles port. Many of the non-union port jobs don't pay a lot more than the California minimum wage.

The evolution of the left-led ILWU shouldn't be seen as some kind of unique betrayal by self-seeking sellouts. It only duplicates the history of the even more radical Industrial Workers of the World (the Wobblies), which before World War I captured the docks in Philadelphia. The Wobblies began by insisting on equal wages for all port workers. The more they raised wages, though, the more desirable longshore jobs became. They opted finally for a two-tier system that protected the well-connected Wobblies and excluded "floaters." Expelled by the national organization, the Wobbly-founded Local 8 disappeared into the ILA. Progressive ideals will always founder on the reefs of job control unionism.

Still, if growing inequality is a concern, it's hard to see which is worse—job control unionism or the loss of job control. That's what has happened to old AFL unions like UNITE-HERE, the warehouse workers in the Teamsters, and, despite strong membership gains, the UFCW. These unions have found it harder than organizations in the skilled construction trades to monopolize work; they also lacked control over choke points in the economy, which the longshore unions had. It was in the 1960s and

1970s that these weaker craft began to lose market power. Long accustomed to relying on mob muscle, they found there was little the Mafia could do to help with problems of deregulation, import competition, and runaway plants. But wiseguys could help employers get the lowest wages possible. In UNITE's New York garment locals, the mob regularly collected bribes from employers who were allowed to pay sub-minimum wages. In the Teamsters Joint Council 16, the most mobbed up in the country, officials signed off on a liquidation of a local whose warehouse contract called for $18 an hour and transferred the membership to a corrupt New Jersey local whose contract paid $5 an hour less. In the UFCW, officials grew rich while wages and conditions reverted back to the days of *The Jungle*.

Call it "Wal-Mart unionism"—low wages every day. The union leaders' strategy—most successful in the case of the SEIU and the UFCW, and least successful in the case of UNITE-HERE—has been to gain members and increase income by adjusting to employers' demand for low wages.[56]

Today, UNITE workers include the lowest-paid union workers in the advanced industrialized world. Some in UNITE's flagship Local 23-25, the trimmers in Chinatown garment factories, earn as little as $1 an hour. Seven-day workweeks are common. Many earn below the federal minimum wage. Contracts go unenforced by tacit agreement. The mob still flourishes here too. The downtown racket is a variation of what goes on in midtown construction. In construction, the contractors pay the mob for using non-union workers; in garment, the contractors give up bribes for the right to pay union workers at the non-union market rate.

It's in these neo-craft, immigrant-based unions, where wages are typically 50 percent below the national median, that the highest salaries among officials in the U.S. labor movement can be found. In the UFCW, for example, where nepotism, mob control, and failed strikes have been a tradition, presidents of obscure locals can earn more than the president of the United States. There's Jack Loveall, president of Local 588 in Rosemont, California, whose salary comes from dues paid by low-wage baggers and checkers. Loveall earns $547,000 in annual compensation. His sons Jacques and Adam Loveall, both vice presidents, get $143,000 and $174,000, respectively.[57] UFCW Local 770 president Ricky Icaza, who headed the 59,000-member coalition of grocery store workers who were badly defeated in the 2004 southern California grocery strike, earned $274,000. His no. 2 actually earned more: $308,000. Another local president, who was part of the wrangling coalition whose members fought over TV face time, topped out at $345,000.[58] The overpaid UFCW bosses wasted the courage and sacrifice of their members, who returned to work after a four-month strike under terms worse than those they initially rejected.

By contrast, the three-week French general strike in 1995 that led to the fall of a conservative government headed by premier Alain Juppé bent on increasing drug copayments and social security taxes was run by union officials who typically made far less than the chauffeur of the Washington, D.C., Teachers Union.[59]

Unlike AFL-CIO leaders, whose pay is routed to them directly by the employer without ever passing through the hands of the members, the French leaders get their pay through voluntary contributions. "We have these little books," explained Jean-Pierre Page, a former Air France worker who serves as head of the International Department of the Confédération Générale du Travail (CGT). "Every month we go around to the workers in the factories or the office and ask them to buy a stamp and paste it in their book."[60]

This stamp gathering, or *philatelism*, as it is sometimes self-deprecatingly called, costs workers anywhere from half a percent to 1 percent of their pay. (Low-paid southern California grocery store workers pay their leaders $61 a month after a $400 initiation fee—that is, more than four times as much in percentage terms.) It's not easy to create a fortune on French union dues. "We make the equivalent of $2,400 a month," said Page, "about what a skilled worker in the Paris region makes." Even Page's boss at the time, Louis Vainnet, the head of the CGT France's largest union, made no more. Declared Page, "We are poor, but militant."[61]

OFFICIAL LABOR: ALLIES OR ADVERSARIES OF THE WELFARE STATE?

President Ronald Reagan raised the retirement age. President Bill Clinton abolished welfare "as we know it." Hillary Clinton's health care plan imploded. President George W. Bush seeks to privatize Social Security.

While it's too early to write obituaries for the American welfare state, it may not be premature to ask what has gone wrong. What explains America's unique status among advanced economies in the welfare world? It's not just that we're alone in failing to provide universal health coverage; it's also that the programs we do provide are generally the least generous and the least universalistic, relying the most on stigma and means testing.[62]

Just like America's penchant for overwork, our welfare state—which finds its model in the Victorian Poor Law—is usually explained by invoking American values:[63] the work ethic, of course, but also individual initiative, risk taking, and hostility to big government. Internationally, sociologists observe, American values are off the charts on the "individualism vs. group solidarity" scale. We're five times more likely than Japanese to think that corporations should be concerned with just making profits. (Still, revealingly, 60 percent of Americans reject this idea.)[64]

As long as the discussion remains in the cloudland of "values," America's mean-spirited welfare state seems like a populist preference. Sturdy, independent Americans disdain big government handouts. The results change drastically, though, when pollsters' questions are sharpened. If you ask, "Do you want universal health care coverage?" by two to one, Americans reply yes.[65] If you ask, "Do you want the government to invest Social Security funds on Wall Street?" they say no in nearly the same proportions, 61 percent to 38 percent. How about increasing the retirement age? Over two-thirds oppose it (although only a minority is aware that Reagan already raised it).[66] An NBC/*Wall Street Journal* poll found that 77 percent of the American public supported universal coverage, regardless of health or employment status. Support was back to where it was before the failed effort to pass health care legislation during the Clinton administration.[67]

Why aren't American preferences translated better into welfare legislation? The short answer is that organized labor—which in other countries provides the chief impetus—lines up on the wrong side in the United States. If both organized capital and organized labor oppose a piece of legislation that affects them, it's not going to pass.

In every country the battle over the welfare state divides into two opposing interest groups with opposite strategies. On one side are the wealthy minority, who are doubly opposed to the programs because they don't benefit from them and would have to pay a disproportionate share of their cost. On the other are the less wealthy potential majority, who would receive a disproportionate share of the benefits without fully paying for them. Those who support a welfare state seek to create universal benefits that would give everyone—not just the needy—a stake in the program. Their strategy is to upgrade the benefits to meet, as one Swedish social democrat puts it, "even the most discriminating tastes of the new middle class."[68]

Those opposed to the welfare state try to limit benefits to the most desperately indigent. Their strategy rests on the "less eligibility" principle, well illustrated in *Oliver Twist*, where conditions for the poor are kept less preferable than those experienced by the lowest-paid laborer.

But the order of battle isn't defined only by the opposing interests of rich and poor. Just as important are special interest groups. Auto manufacturers' interests may be served by having taxpayers subsidize their health care costs. (General Motors says its health care costs run $1,400 per vehicle produced; its European competitors, who shift the cost to taxpayers, pay nothing.)[69] GM would benefit from state-provided care. If doctors' salaries are low, as they were in the Progressive Era, it may be in physicians' interest to have the government increase demand for their services. On the other hand, the life and health insurance companies are dependably on the side of the wealthy minority. They don't want to lose market share for their services to the government. By restricting government benefits to those who can't afford their product, they stay profitable.

Where do organized labor's interests lie? In Europe, they fall unambiguously on the side of the welfare state. Occasionally, welfare legislation was enacted by the European right to blunt labor's appeal. To steal the thunder of the Social Democrats, conservative German chancellor Otto von Bismarck put the country on the road to national health insurance. Proclaimed Bismarck in 1881: "The cure of social ills must be sought not exclusively in the repression of (socialist) excesses but simultaneously in the positive advance of the welfare of the working class."[70] Legislation soon followed mandating employer-funded health, accident, and old-age insurance. Mostly, though, welfare state legislation was a direct product of union agitation, labor efforts, or popular front governments.[71] In post–World War II Britain, the Labor government created the National Health Service, improving on the 1911 National Insurance Act, which covered only workers earning less than 1 pound a day, by providing free health care for all.[72] The health minister was the leader of the Welsh miners, Aneurin Bevan, whose father, David, also a miner, had died of black lung.

Why does Canada have national health insurance and we don't? Seymour Martin Lipset, one of America's leading political sociologists, says that it's because of a difference in national values. We Americans, of course, value individual initiative and a weak state. Up north, they hold to strong Tory values, among which Lipset identifies communitarianism, group solidarity, and a strong state.[73]

But whatever role Tory values may have played in priming the pump, the Tories themselves didn't do much to initiate or enact Canada's universal health care legislation. The credit belongs to Tommy Douglas and the Canadian labor movement. In 2004, Douglas was voted "the Greatest Canadian" in a CBC-sponsored poll, beating out several figures better known to Americans, like Wayne Gretzky, Pierre Trudeau, and Alexander Graham Bell.[74] Douglas's achievement was to get the union-backed Cooperative Commonwealth Federation to support something he called "universal health care."

What would grow into a nationwide system of universal care was first tried out in the small town of Swift Current, in Saskatchewan, after World War II. But as a programmatic idea, universal health care began in the 1930s when the four labor parties of the western provinces merged to form the Cooperative Commonwealth Federation and pledged to support universal care. The Federation came to power in Saskatchewan in the 1940s, with Tommy Douglas as the premier. Along with a pension plan that provided medical and dental services, Douglas was able to enact a public insurance plan for hospitalization in Swift Current. People in Swift Current liked universal coverage. From there it spread to other towns in Saskatchewan, and from Saskatchewan to the other nine Canadian provinces. In 1962, the health care movement advanced another step, again radiating out from Saskatchewan, only this time providing universal coverage for doctors' services outside the hospital.

Of course the coverage stopped at the U.S. border. But in the United States there had been a similar party with a similar objective formed in Minnesota. The Minnesota Farmer-Labor Party actually served as a model for the Canadians. It was founded earlier, and its candidate for governor, Floyd Olsen, won office earlier. But the Minnesota organization never managed to achieve universal coverage, even in a small town.

In the United States, the problem hasn't been chiefly that there were no figures like Tommy Douglas, who advocated universal health care. It's that they could never persuade official labor to support the cause. Instead, official labor often found common cause with the wealthy, the financial institutions, the HMOs, and the insurance companies. The upshot is that Americans simply do without programs Europeans and Canadians take for granted—principally universal health insurance, but also programs like universal free child care. Although child care is the third-biggest expense for young American families, a national plan for child care is nowhere on the agenda of the AFL-CIO. The official approach is to secure child care benefits through collective bargaining, but only about 1.6 million union members are covered for child care benefits through their union contracts.[75] (Even the jewel in the crown of our welfare state—Social Security—fails to shine with anything like the sparkle of continental Europe's benefits. In fact, when measured by criteria such as how much a retiree receives as a percentage of the median wage, how many years it takes to qualify, and how many retirees actually receive a pension, the United States ranks below every European country except Ireland.)[76]

You don't get as chintzy and as mean-spirited a welfare state as ours overnight. It takes generations to fall so far behind. A huge opportunity was lost early in the twentieth century. On the eve of America's entry into World War I, it looked as if the United States would follow Germany and Great Britain in enacting a national health insurance law. It was the high tide of the Progressive Era. In 1912, the Progressive Party had come out for national health insurance, and even the American Medical Association and the National Association of Manufacturers were cautious early supporters. Largely because of opposition from the insurance companies, backed up by organized labor, health insurance never happened.

Naturally, the better-endowed insurance industry led the struggle. Metropolitan and Prudential both jumped into a fateful 1917 referendum in California with the message that the advocates of health benefits were trying to turn America into the Kaiser's Germany. Health insurance lost by more than two to one. Observed Frederick L. Hoffman, vice president of Prudential, "Unhappily, most of the kindly thought of the world is wasted upon those who least deserve it."[77] Later, Hartford-based insurance giants would announce a program touting golf as means of reducing sickness and promoting longevity among company workers.[78]

The interests of the insurance companies were obvious: they had policies to sell and markets to protect. But at the time, so did organized labor. It is said that organized labor acquired interest in the pension and health benefits industry only after the passage of Taft-Hartley in 1947. But as early as 1907, notes historian David Brian Robertson, eighty-four of the approximately 125 AFL affiliates had benefit funds. Nineteen of them, including the main craft unions in construction, such as the carpenters and the painters, offered disability benefits.[79] The wealthy railroad brotherhoods were also deeply involved in the insurance business.

Were union leaders just protecting their markets, or did they really believe that a British-style health care system based on employer mandates would undermine the American character? It's impossible to tell for sure, but what we do know is that support for or against national health insurance broke down pretty much along the lines of institutional interest. Official labor's support for national insurance was limited to industrial unions that didn't offer pension or health benefits, such as the Mineworkers and the Amalgamated Clothing and Textile Workers. "In so far as the attitude of organized labor is concerned," observed a lawyers committee investigating the issue, "it is opposed or indifferent to any compulsory health insurance laws."[80]

Throughout the Progressive Era, AFL boss Sam Gompers was the public face of labor's battle against health insurance. Most of his arguments came from the insurance industry, which provided him with data showing that health insurance hadn't worked in Germany or Britain. Some arguments, though, could only have come from Gompers. American workers didn't need a government-run health plan, he insisted; all they needed was a union contract. It was collective bargaining that led to the reduction of hours and the monitoring of safety conditions that were the workers' best guarantee of physical and mental health. Gompers didn't address how the 90 percent of American workers who were not in AFL unions would maintain their physical and mental health.

Worse than no coverage for Gompers was the specter of an iron heel crushing strong men, reducing them to effeminacy. If a national health insurance program were passed, the employers' sway would no longer stop at the factory gates, predicted Gompers, but would extend that jurisdiction to the workers' homes.[81] Gompers insisted that the health insurance schemes passed in 1911 by a Liberal-Labor parliament had "taken much of the virility out of the British unions."[82]

Not only were the English now less virile, but they were also less healthy than Americans. "Are the health conditions better in any other country than ours?" Gompers asked at a meeting of the plutocratic National Civic Federation. "Is the length of life of the people of other countries greater than the length of life of the people of the U.S.? Statistics can demonstrate that easily." What was the world's healthiest nation? he asked rhetorically. The United States of America, he answered, where there was no health insurance at all.[83]

But might not health insurance make Americans even healthier? Perhaps, but that wasn't the point, Gompers argued. The issue was freedom. "Shall the toilers surrender their freedom for a few crumbs?" he asked in the subtitle of an article replying to the arguments of Meyer London, the socialist congressman from New York City's Lower East Side. "Sore and saddened as I am by the illness, the killing and the maiming of so many of my fellow workers," Gompers insisted, "I would rather see that go on for years and years, minimized and mitigated by the organized labor movement, than give up one jot of the freedom of the workers to strive and struggle for their own emancipation through their own efforts."[84] Perhaps, too, Gompers feared the effect of government legislation on the demand for unions. That's why he opposed federal restrictions on the length of the working day. "If we can get an eight-hour law for the working people," he warned in 1914, "then you will find that the working people themselves will fail to have any interest in your economic organization."[85]

On the other hand, if you were a member of Gompers's United Cigar Makers and you wanted to stay healthy and free, Gompers had an insurance plan he would sell you. Unfortunately, like many other union plans of the period, the Cigar Makers' plans kept having financial difficulties, and frequently benefits had to be suspended. The union plans of the period suffered from a lack of regulation. No effort was made to apply real insurance principles, like funding or community rating, and union leaders freely took money out of the plans for non-insurance purposes. A lot of money went into the union kitties, and comparatively little came out in the form of benefits. In 1916, the amount of money the entire American labor movement paid out in all forms of benefits—pension, health, and unemployment—came to about a dollar and a half per member.[86]

But Gompers was just a spokesman for the affiliates. More closely identified with union financial institution building and the movement to defend unions against the threat of compulsory health insurance was Warren Stone, the distinguished-looking president of the Brotherhood of Locomotive Engineers. In 1917, he'd led the fight against health insurance as labor's ranking member of the National Civic Federation's Committee on Health Insurance. "Instead of trying to bail a leaky boat," Stone argued, "we would stop the leaks, that is begin at the other end and pay a living wage. The whole idea of the workingman is to avoid paternalism."[87]

After the war, the issue of national health insurance began to fade. Warren Stone was asked to join Warren Harding's cabinet, but he declined, turning his attention to financial empire building. Stone founded a fast-growing Cleveland-based chain of labor banks, which he touted as a remedy for labor-management conflict—especially after the collapse of the great strike wave in 1919.

With Grand Chief Engineer Stone at the throttle, organized labor had entered into its own era of Frenzied Finance. Labor-owned banks, insurance companies, and real estate and investment companies were springing up all across the country. Stone's coast-to-coast empire alone was valued at $150 million—well over $1.5 billion in today's dollars. In 1920, he issued his own $5 bills as legal tender, displaying President Benjamin Harrison's picture and, underneath, Stone's signature.[88]

It was about the same time that Charles Ponzi began his investment enterprise in Boston. Stone's operation, though, was far more elaborate, long-lasting, and, ultimately, more damaging. His banks lent money to individuals and businesses that couldn't pay them back. The bad loans were then fobbed off on union pension and health insurance funds. The funds became insolvent too. Meanwhile, Stone lived in a luxurious parkside apartment and hired his son to serve as his second in command.[89] By 1927, Stone's entire enterprise came crashing down. By dying in 1925, however, he escaped opprobrium. On news of his death, flags flew at half-staff throughout Cleveland, the headquarters of the Brotherhood Bank.[90]

With Gompers's demise just the year before, Stone had departed as America's most prominent labor union leader. He's been almost completely forgotten by contemporary labor historians, but it's an unfortunate erasure, one that obscures the origins and continuity of official labor's long struggle for union financial enterprise and against government meddling in health care.

At various times in the history of organized labor, various avatars of Warren Stone have manifested themselves at key times to save American workers from losing their freedom for "a few crumbs."

In the 1970s, the danger of national health insurance being passed was the greatest since the crisis of 1917. Franklin D. Roosevelt had decided not to include health insurance as part of the 1935 Social Security Act. Harry Truman had been forced to back off his national health insurance plan. But in 1971, conservative Republican Richard Nixon actually proposed a national health insurance plan—at a time when the Democrats controlled Congress.

Nixon's plan was far more generous and comprehensive than any plan being discussed by either political party a generation later. It required employers to pay three-quarters of the costs of health insurance for their employees; for those not covered by employers, the government would pick up the bill. The coverage was truly comprehensive, including not only doctor and hospital bills but also lab work, nursing homes, and mental health care—the works. Nixon's bill also cut red tape: no forms to fill out—just show your "health card."[91]

"Comprehensive health insurance is an idea whose time has come in America," Nixon announced in sending his bill to Congress. He was, of course, dead wrong. The plan was immediately attacked by the U.S. Chamber of Commerce as "revolutionary," "radical," and an "outright handout." The Chamber was joined by the AFL-CIO, which attacked the plan just as vehemently from the left. Requiring employers to offer health insurance (so-called employer mandates) was a thinly disguised measure to allow bosses to replace full-time workers with part-timers.[92]

So instead of supporting the bill as a beginning, something to build on, organized labor opposed it from the left. The plan just wasn't good enough. Labor's two wings—AFL-CIO president George Meany for the conservative trades and President Leonard Woodcock for the more progressive UAW—joined to promote an alternative scheme based on the single-payer model in which the government would pay all health bills, not myriad insurance companies. The union-backed plan was more in line with the most advanced legislation in Europe. But at the time, it had zero chance of passage. Labor urged congressional allies not to vote for the Nixon plan. This was like breaking down an open door, since few Democrats wanted to give Nixon a historic social policy victory, especially before an election. On the same grounds, liberals and labor helped defeat Nixon's guaranteed annual income plan.[93]

For the next two decades, the threat of national health insurance receded sharply. But in the early 1990s it surfaced again, with the Democrats in control of both houses of Congress and George H.W. Bush's reelection prospects threatened by a severe recession. The momentum for putting health insurance back on the national agenda, though, came less from organized labor than from embattled U.S. manufacturers.

Overseas carmakers were gaining market share at the expense of the Big Three—Ford, GM, and Chrysler. While health care costs for foreign automakers were socialized, for U.S. automakers they came out of Detroit's bottom line. Chrysler chief Lee Iacocca even became the head of something called the National Leadership Coalition on Health Care, which included some Fortune 500 companies supporting a Canadian-style plan. Iacocca supported a single-payer approach because it was cheaper. Administrative costs eat up over 30 percent of U.S. health costs, compared with about 17 percent in Canada's single-payer system.[94]

For the companies selling insurance—which earn nearly a quarter of all the corporate profits in America—a single-payer plan would have been devastating. But they didn't have to face that threat alone. Just as in 1917, the insurance companies found a major ally in organized labor. In the 1990s, the avatar of Warren Stone was Bobby Georgine, head of the AFL-CIO's Building and Construction Trades Department. He also headed Ullico, which has a subsidiary, Zenith, that administers health and pension plans for many AFL-CIO affiliates, mainly in the buildings trades.

Georgine became notorious in 2003, when his role in engineering the Ullico insider trading scheme was exposed (see chapter 1). It was in the early 1990s, though, that he played his most significant public policy role. He cast what was said to be the deciding vote in the AFL-CIO on whether to support a single-payer plan or to back a proposal preserving the private health insurance plans.[95]

About a year before Clinton won the presidency, Georgine had been on one side of a noisy and uncharacteristically heated controversy at the Executive Council in Bal Harbour. "Most years," one veteran observer wrote, "the hot topics during the AFL-CIO's annual meeting are less heated than a debate over whether the clams should be cold or steamed."[96] This time the two sides argued over whether to continue fighting for a single-payer plan or to back a revived version of the previously despised Nixon plan.

Narrow, purely institutional interests divided the two camps. On one side were the industrial unions—just as in 1917. The UAW and the steel workers did have health and pension benefits, but unlike their Bal Harbour peers in the construction unions, they had less control over them. And they were under constant pressure from employers to shift health costs to the public sector. Allied with the industrial unions was AFSCME. A union that represents government workers obviously had little to lose from the expansion of government-administered health plans. But there was also little to gain. When the Clinton administration announced its employer mandate plan, AFSCME dropped its support for the single-payer plan. According to Charles Lewis of the Center for Public Integrity, President McEntee even paid for the Clintons' bus tour to sell the insurance company–backed plan to the heartland.[97]

On the other side were the traditional enemies of universal health insurance—the building trades and the union representing HMOs and the health care industry—the Service Employees International Union. The SEIU boss at the time was John Sweeney, soon to become head of the AFL-CIO. He also headed the AFL-CIO's committee on health care issues. The leader of the building trades on health care issues was Ullico's Bobby Georgine.

Construction trades officials looked to Ullico for directorship fees, for financing of local union contractors, and, as it turned out, for insider trading opportunities. Even more important, the leaders of the old-line trades had their own health care plans and their own administrative apparatus, which paid out benefits. As for Georgine himself, ending the single-payer system would have been a personal setback. Without Ullico, who would pay his million-dollar-a-year salary and keep him aloft in private jets? Georgine and his allies approved the Clinton plan because, as Georgine explained to a House Committee, it preserved the status quo in the industry.[98] In Bal Harbour, though, Georgine explained his positions strictly in public policy terms. "I wouldn't want to be tilting at windmills, I want to do what's doable," he claimed.[99] When the AFL-CIO health policy committee later took a vote on whether to endorse a single-payer plan or to maintain the status quo, Georgine cast his deciding vote.

Georgine's biggest ally outside the building trades was John Sweeney, who in 1995 would become the AFL-CIO president but whose voice had grown in authority since the 1980s as SEIU added numbers in the burgeoning health care field. As chair of the AFL-CIO health plan committee, Sweeney could be expected to defend his dues base: the private health care industry. In the mid-1990s, about a third of Sweeney's 1.2 million members worked for HMOs, for-profit hospitals, or private nursing home facilities. A single-payer plan was not in the interest of his for-profit employers. Sweeney's fingerprints, writes Professor Marie Gottschalk, "were all over the AFL-CIO's doomed health care strategy."[100]

In America's century-long failure to produce a national health care system, organized labor looms as a major culprit. Labor leaders' actions can be explained, first, in terms of what benefits them as individuals, second, what benefits their respective organizations, third, what their employers want, and lastly, if at all, what's good for American working people as a whole. Samuel Gompers actually accused national health insurance advocates of letting concerns for the $1.50-a-day worker drag down the $5-a-day man.

In the final presidential debate in 2004, President Bush attacked Democratic candidate John Kerry's health plan as a "government" plan—although in fact it left the role of private insurers entirely intact and merely reduced the number of uninsured to 25 million. Warming to the attack, the president channeled arguments made in 1917 by Gompers and health insurance executives: Americans don't need reform because we already have the best health care in the world. "Just look at other countries that have tried to have federally controlled health care," said Bush, "they have poor quality health care. Our health care system is the envy of the world because we believe in making sure that the decisions are made by doctors and patients, not by officials in the nation's capital."[101]

America's system may be the envy of insurance companies around the world, but the World Health Organization's rankings suggests little reason for envy elsewhere. The United States ranks no. 1 in per capita health expenditure and no. 1 in the amount spent as a percentage of gross domestic product. But it does far less well in terms of life expectancy, infant mortality rate, and the universality of coverage. The upshot is that our system stands only thirty-seventh in overall performance, just barely ahead of Cuba but behind countries like Morocco, Dominica, and Costa Rica. (France and Italy, with far stronger labor organizations, rank no. 1 and no. 2.)[102]

It would be stretching things quite a bit to say that the U.S. labor movement is the architect of the American poorhouse state. To be an architect of anything, you would have to have a plan. The AFL-CIO is too divided, too distracted by parochial interests, too bogged down in institutional corruption to come up with any credible alternative to the main drift. The 20,000 fiefdoms that constitute labor in America lack sufficient coherence to mount even a noisy national protest. In 1996, when President Clinton signed the Personal Responsibility and Welfare Reconciliation Act, he eliminated the right to welfare that was established in 1935 when FDR signed the Social Security Act. Down went food stamps and out went Medicaid for legal immigrants. It moved the country back toward the spirit of the Poor Law. In any of a dozen European countries, its passage would have set off a general strike. Sweeney sent off a telegram.

Ross Clark, writing in the weekly *Spectator*, reminds us how bitterly the British came to resent the legacy of their own welfare system, based on the Poor Law and "less eligibility." He recalled the humiliations George Orwell described in *The Road to Wigan Pier*, including unemployed miners being forced to evict elderly bedridden parents to qualify for means-tested relief. Miners president Aneurin Bevan described the regime as "a principle that eats like an acid into the bones of the poor. In the small rooms and around the meager tables of the poor, hells of personal acrimony and wounded vanity arise." More than any other factor, Clark says, means testing explains the British people's flight to democratic socialism in 1945.[103]

The same deprivations and miseries exist today in America. For a similar turn to take place successfully here, though, labor would have to completely reinvent itself. It got off to a bad start.

PART 2
Origins

CHAPTER THREE

The Revolt Against Solidarity

Who speaks now of New York's notorious Sam Parks? Or Cornelius "Con" Shea, the first president of the Teamsters, who began his career as a professional bomber for hire at age sixteen?[1] Or P. II. "Pinhead" McCarthy, the carpenter boss who became mayor of San Francisco as the head of the Union Labor Party? In power for most of the first decade of the twentieth century, the ULP produced the once-famous "paint-eating" city supervisors—so rapacious for bribes, their mentor complained, they would eat the paint off a wall. In one ULP administration, sixteen of eighteen city supervisors—mainly union officials—pleaded guilty to bribery.[2]

Nearly a century ago, these men—known as America's labor czars—were far more than just colorful thieves. Protecting their members from the bosses and the bosses from their members, they created a whole "made in America" industry: the labor peace racket. It provided them with leverage over critical areas of the American urban economy, such as construction, longshore, and trucking. Sam Parks was mentioned authoritatively in the same breath with J. D. Rockefeller and J. P. Morgan as a shaper of American destinies. Ordinary New Yorkers knew that this almost illiterate Irish immigrant held the entire $250 million construction industry in his work-callused, graft-grabbing hands.[3]

For the most part, labor history has pushed mainstream rascals like Parks, Shea, and McCarthy into the background and pushed the martyrs and the rebels into the foreground. Along with the elimination of the labor czars, some of labor history's most violent and seemingly indelible seminal events have been rendered delible by the improving pen. In Chicago in 1905, nearly three times more people were killed in a Teamsters strike than were later machine-gunned by Al Capone's goons in the St.

Valentine's Day massacre. If it seems that the violence takes place on completely different moral planes, it has to be realized that the man who led the job action, Con Shea, took bribes from employers to stage fake "sympathy" strikes against their competitors, and that Shea would later become a prominent member of the gang that Capone tried to wipe out on St. Valentine's Day. In fact, Shea and Capone were in the same business: labor racketeering.

Of course, the historians who were inspired by the new social movements of the 1960s did not start out with the aim of lopping rogue ancestors from labor's family tree. But as new leftists and ex–Communist Party members, they had a dilemma. While they were drawn to labor's cause, they found it hard to feel good about America's corrupt, complaisant, and racially exclusionary unions.

In the 1960s, the chasm between the idealism of the civil rights movement and the corruption of the unions couldn't be ignored. Early in the decade, Robert Kennedy published *The Enemy Within* (1960), a bestseller illustrating "how unions were bought and sold, and the members taken." For those Rip Van Winkle Marxists whose idea of labor leaders was formed in 1937 at the Battle of the Overpass, where the indomitable Reuther brothers endured savage beatings by Henry Ford's goons for their efforts to bring industrial unionism to Ford's River Rouge plants, Kennedy told some amazing stories, with settings from central Florida, where the Teamsters' Jimmy Hoffa managed to dupe his members into buying underwater lots in a phony retirement community to Apalachin, New York, where America's top crime organized figures scheduled a 1957 meeting at which twenty-two of the fifty-six in attendance were union officials.[4]

Then there was the embarrassment of race. Nineteen sixty-four was the year of Mississippi Summer. Hundreds of Northern college students risked their lives to campaign for black voting rights in the Deep South. Two students, Andrew Goodman and Michael Schwerner, along with black civil rights worker Andrew Cheney, never returned from Philadelphia, Mississippi. Meanwhile, up North, the resistance to civil rights was coming not from the Ku Klux Klan but from the head of the AFL-CIO. In the Bronx, at Hunts Point, a new produce market was being built. As on most city projects, the unionized construction workers were nearly all white. When the city's Human Rights Commission insisted that qualified blacks be allowed to work alongside whites, the members of George Meany's old Plumbers Local 2 walked off the job, backed by Meany himself, who was now running the AFL-CIO. The other trades joined in, combining to bring off one of the most effective general strikes in New York City history. Government hearings showed that some construction unions had few or no blacks in their membership. New York's Sheet Metal Local 28 hadn't admitted a black person since the 1930s.[5]

These events put young leftist academics in a bind. As historian Alice Kessler Harris rather delicately puts it, "Labor historians of the 1960s struggled to reconcile the promise of trade unionism in the abstract with the reality of unions far removed from their members' lives."[6] Rather than try to find out why the promise hadn't been realized, though, the young historians found creative ways to sidestep the issue.

Labor's founding fathers, all white and male, were hustled off the historical stage. You could almost hear the horns of Aaron Copeland's "Fanfare for the Common Man" as ordinary working people of all races and genders entered the textbooks stage left. And instead of the AFL, the direct institutional ancestor of most of today's unions, the new leftist historians would celebrate the AFL's more progressive but mostly defunct adversaries: the IWW, which wanted to organize "one big industrial union"; the socialist Eugene V. Debs, who argued that the AFL was too corrupt to be reformed; and the early CIO, which arose in a revolt against the AFL's exclusionary craft system.

Under the guise of writing labor history "from the bottom up," however, the bottom-up historians simply turned it upside down. So much has been written about the origins of the CIO, you would think that the crusading Walter Reuther became the head of the AFL-CIO, instead of his hidebound AFL antagonist George Meany, who was first installed as secretary-treasurer of the Federation by labor racketeer Joey Fay. Yet of the AFL's origins, there has been almost total silence for the past thirty years.[7]

Even more broadly, historians would simply change the subject, talking about "work" in place of unions; workers' "culture" rather than their politics; workers' "consciousness" instead of their institutions. As Professor Harris puts it, "In searching for the clues to workers' consciousness, new labor historians expanded their search to the streets, the saloons, and the concert halls."[8] But the new labor historians largely ignored the political dimension of workers' lives. They ignored the governance of union hiring halls, the admission to apprenticeship, union meetings, and the business agent system. You could find out a lot about workers' "consciousness" by examining the world they face in the hiring hall, its rules and customs— who got sent out, who sat on the bench, what you had to do to get on your business agent's good side.

In providing labor with nobler ancestors and a more reputable past, the new labor history seems to have borrowed from the psychology of "self-esteem." To be successful in their daily battles, workers must feel good about themselves and their history. So labor historians teach that the American working people created a common culture of mutual support and solidarity; they provide a detailed, painstaking picture of "the daily self-assertion of craftsmen on the job."[9] The daily self-abasement of craft unionists to their business agent went unnoticed. You would never know that jurisdictional strikes—strikes of workers against each other—vastly outnumbered strikes against employers, or that some of the largest race riots in American history began as AFL job actions. Doggedly, labor historians continue to insist what is plainly untrue: that American workers and their organizations yield to none in their militancy and effectiveness.[10]

But what is to be gained by poking around organized labor's forgotten past? Is the revisionist goal merely to replace sentimentalism with cynicism? Or is it just a matter of restoring "balance" to the history of American labor? Actually, it's the choice of explanatory history over exemplary history.

Present-day labor historians want to provide "a usable past"—one that is useful as an inspiration for present-day activism. The aim is to provide collective and individual role models. It's an academic expression of a late-1960s movement chant, one that still echoes, however faintly: "Debs, Debs, be like him! Dare to struggle, dare to win."

In this respect, the new labor history was about as new as Titus Livy's Roman histories, which provided glorious accounts of Horatius at the Bridge, defending the young republic against invading Etruscans; Publius, the great lawgiver; brave and stalwart generals like Scipio; tyrant slayers like Brutus; the unshakable courage of the Roman plebeians united behind their tribunes against patrician power.

No doubt exemplary history has its place. But it has to be handled carefully. One big difference between Horatius and Publius on the one hand and "Big Bill" Haywood and Gene Debs on the other is that the former duo really did found a republic, whereas the true founders of the American labor republic were men like Con Shea and Sam Parks. It was Con Shea's corrupt practices that turned into the mores of the Teamsters, America's largest union for much of the twentieth century.

Explanatory history tries to answer the question of how things happened and thus to be useful in a different way. Its principal subject is institutions, which set the rules that establish how people will be treated. Ideals are embedded in the rules, which explains how institutions are able to create their own culture. If you don't understand how institutions work, how practices turn into rules and rules into values, if you merely feel their effects, how can you change them?

CORRUPTION AS HISTORY?

Preoccupation with corrupt acts of individuals often seems to be the product of a small and censorious mind. So it seemed to many Church officials who couldn't understand why the young monk Martin Luther got so enraged at Johann Tetzel, a Dominican friar who had developed a brisk sixteenth-century business selling indulgences to German peasants. Obviously, they conceded, Tetzel was a rascal. He promised he could get your soul out of purgatory even if you'd deflowered the Virgin Mary. His sales pitch, "When the coin in the coffer rings, a soul from purgatory springs," was coarse beyond question. But ninety-five theses? Nailed to the door of the Wittenberg Church? Surely Luther was overdoing it. If pressed, Church apologists conceded that it was often possible to bribe ecclesiastical judges, but they asked pointedly, Why pick on the Church, when the corruption of secular authority was so much worse? Besides, a lot of the money for indulgences went for a good purpose—Pope Leo's additions to St. Peter's. Ultimately, they reasoned, by attacking the Tetzels, Luther only aided the Turks.

But Luther's approach can serve as a model for all serious reformers.

While steeped in specifics, his attack on Church corruption actually pointed well beyond the myriad shakedown artists who flourished under the protection of Pope Leo X, the Medici aristocrat to whom all the Tetzels tithed. Neither the sale of indulgences nor the commerce in Church offices served as Luther's ultimate target. These were not "abuses"; they were inevitable expressions of an institution that he charged was corrupt in its essence.

Corruption flowed from the aims and structure of the institution, above all, from the excessive and absolute authority of the hierarchy—from which flowed the low spiritual involvement of the laity—and the shallow concepts of sin, salvation, and obligation. What else could be expected from an institution whose goal of defending the faith had long since been replaced by the defense of its dues? Corruption was not a matter of bad prelates who had somehow wormed their way into office; rather, the forms of corruption were identical with the relationships the Church leadership formed with the membership.

The corruption of American trade unionism isn't the result of a few Tetzels either. It, too, must be understood in terms of its own peculiar aims and structure. Although the Church became corrupt, the AFL was corrupt at its inception—and, arguably, before.

The AFL was founded in 1886 as a weak association of local craft unions that themselves had only recently developed national organizations. Even then, they were carrying the racketeering virus. By the 1890s, with the rapid growth of AFL big-city locals, the labor czars had already established their fiefdoms.

The careers of the labor czars express the corrupt possibilities of a certain primitive form of labor organization—the trade union. Trade unionism—dividing workers by particular skills or "trades" and then further dividing them by sovereign territorial districts or "jurisdictions"—is just one variant of unionism. But it's the form that uniquely triumphed in the United States. As industrial capitalism swept across Europe and America in the mid-nineteenth century, drawing workers into cities, the local trade union was always the first form of labor organization to appear because it was simplest to organize.

Trade unions seek the narrowest possible objective—a trade agreement with a boss. They pursue it by forming the most elementary, amoeboid form of organization. Like neighborhood youth gangs, the early trade unions are small, local, territorial, and frequently engaged in turf battles with each other. The membership is exclusive, made up of the workers from the same trade who tend for one reason or another to have more economic leverage than their fellows and who frequently share blood and ethnic ties. The organization tends to be run by an authoritarian leader who often physically dominates the men. He provides jobs and job protection to the members. In return, the members offer him their loyalty. Broadly speaking, it's a patron-client system. The strongest ties are vertical between the members and the leaders, not horizontal between the members.

Europe started out with trade unions too. But by the dawn of the twentieth century, continental workers were on their way to developing more powerful, more inclusive organizations with wider objectives. Instead of a loose confederation of local unions, they formed national unions that bargained with employers on a national basis. From there, national unions naturally formed national political parties. By contrast, American local unions naturally tended to hook up with local urban machines. Moreover, because European unions didn't maintain jurisdictional boundaries, they didn't waste their time constantly fighting each other in turf battles. Except during the fascist period, European unionism ceased being compulsory; the closed shop disappeared as an issue; and members didn't have union dues automatically deducted from their paychecks. Since union leaders didn't control the members' jobs, they couldn't reduce them to clients. The classic criticism of European social-democratic unionists was that they were bureaucratic and reformist.[11] But at least in continental western Europe, union corruption never became a serious issue—not even in Italy, the land of the Mafia.

In America, by the mid-1880s, it looked as if a wider, more advanced, more inclusive form of labor organization than the trade union would develop too. Friedrich Engels, coauthor with Karl Marx of the *Communist Manifesto*, was sure of it. The future, he explained patiently, belonged not to the "narrow trade unions" but to the Knights of Labor, a truly national organization and one that had voluntary dues, admitted blacks and women, included skilled and unskilled workers, and had reached a total membership of nearly a million. The Knights minted slogans like "The strong must help the weak," "One Big Union," and "An injury to one is an injury to all." Just as the more advanced species ousts the less advanced, explained Engels, the more advanced form of labor organization will push out the more backward. It was a dead certainty, "as surely as historical evolution has, like natural evolution, its own immanent laws."[12]

But in America, unlike in Europe, the hairy, big-jawed, low-browed Neanderthals displaced the smoother, flat-faced *Homo sapiens.* Terence Powderly, "Grand Master Workman" of the defeated Knights, didn't like it a bit. He saw the AFL victors as "a lot of . . . leather assed, empty headed, two-faced, itchy palmed scavengers in the field of labor reform."[13] What explains the victory of the lowbrows and itchy palms?

The very creation of the AFL represented a revolt against union solidarity in favor of separation over unity and local autonomy over concerted national action. Critics called it the "American Separation of Labor." "The AFL couldn't have a general strike if they wanted to," observed the IWW's Big Bill Haywood. "They are not organized for a general strike. They have 27,000 different agreements that expire 27,000 different minutes of the year. It is not a labor organization. It is simply a combination of job trusts."[14]

And mostly it has stayed that way. The possibility of joint action seems as remote as ever. While the Federation's budget has swollen from $1,500 a year in Samuel Gompers's time to $172 million in John Sweeney's,[15] the AFL-CIO is still just an umbrella organization that can't so much as shut down a lemonade stand, much less call a national strike. Autonomy remains the overriding issue in the Federation. The latest proposals for reforming the AFL-CO, advanced in 2005 by SEIU leader Andy Stern and his coalition, would weaken the Federation even further, drastically cutting the national staff and returning half the dues revenue back to the affiliates.

Why did the ever-warring warlords ever decide to get together? It was because of the Knights of Labor. Without the Knights threatening Samuel Gompers's rule over the Cigar Makers in the early 1890s, he never would have sought to pull his organization and the other national trade unions together in a protective alliance. For him the Knights "deserved no legitimate place in the field occupied by trade unions."[16]

The issue was jobs. The stout, hard-drinking Gompers, who was born in England, didn't think the eastern European immigrant cigar makers who worked in New York tenement houses and used molds to shape cigars deserved the right to compete with the members he represented: skilled, native cigar makers who hand-rolled their product in factories. Gompers got the state legislature to put the "tenement trash" out of business.[17] But a New York state court ruled Gompers's law banning cigar making in tenements unconstitutional. The immigrants wound up taking over his union and electing his rival. When the Knights sided with the rebellious immigrant workers, Gompers began to organize the AFL.[18]

Perhaps the best brief summary of the stakes in the battle between the Knights and the trade unions—the clear turning point in American labor history—comes from an older, pro-AFL historian. "The struggle," writes Selig Perlman, a prominent early-twentieth-century progressive historian, "was one between groups within the working class. The skilled men stood for the right to use their advantage of skills and efficient organization in order to wrest the maximum amount or concessions for themselves. The Knights of Labor endeavored to annex their skilled men in order that the advantage from their exceptional fighting strength might lift up the unskilled and semi-skilled. From the viewpoint of a struggle between principles this was indeed a clash between the principle of labor solidarity and that of trade separation."[19]

Why did solidarity lose in America and win in many western European countries? Maybe it was because the Europeans had less immigration pressure, more homogeneity, weaker bosses, and smaller national territories. But whatever the reasons, Europe's skilled workers were more willing to throw in their lot with the less skilled and form common organizations for common goals.

MAINTAINING A MONOPOLY

In America in the 1880s, self-interest beat solidarity. Still, did that mean the AFL had to be corrupt forever afterward or that it had to remain organized labor's chief alternative?

In the twentieth century, there would be two other major challenges to AFL's institutional monopoly, but neither had the potential of the

Knights. In many ways, the IWW modeled itself on the Knights. It adopted the slogan "One Big Union" and attacked AFL exclusivity. "There are 35 million workers in the U.S. who can't get into the AFL," pointed out Big Bill Haywood. "By improving the labor power of a few individuals, keeping others out with initiation fees and closing the books . . . . [t]hey form a little job trust."[20]

But with a flair for direct action and a weakness for sabotage, Haywood's factionalized Wobblies could never agree among themselves whom they ought to be organizing: all the industrial workers of the world or just "the militant minority"? Mostly they concentrated on the poorest, most exploited workers. It was a strategy that produced some of the peak moments in American labor history—like the famous Bread and Roses strike in Lawrence, Massachusetts. But there were some terrible valleys. After four American Legionnaires were killed by IWW sharpshooters while parading on Armistice Day, November 11, 1919, in Centralia, Washington, anti-Wobbly hysteria broke out. A lynch mob castrated and hung one of the Wobblies, Wesley Everest, in his army uniform. More than a thousand IWW members were arrested. By the early 1920s, the IWW had just about ceased to exist.[21]

The early CIO would prove to be a more formidable rival than the IWW: it required less risk and had a broader appeal. Against employers, it used IWW sit-down tactics, but no guns, explosives, or sabotage. By including all the craft and unskilled workers of an enterprise in a single industrial union, the CIO was more inclusive than the pure craft unions of the AFL (or, for that matter, the IWW, which in practice tried to organize the poorest and most oppressed).

In contrast to the AFL, which would have half a dozen separate, feuding craft unions in a single industry—as it still does in the airline industry—the CIO managed to organize millions of workers into single, more centralized unions—the autoworkers, steelworkers, rubber workers, communications workers, and so on. But the CIO still relied on compulsory membership; it signed only exclusive, closed-shop contracts; and it was territorial, just like the AFL. As a national federation, the CIO structure of loosely affiliated national unions was almost identical to the AFL's. Overall, within the labor movement in the Western world, the CIO stood closer to the AFL than to European labor unions.

Still, the differences were substantial enough for the AFL and the CIO to have fought each other with a passion they rarely displayed when battling employers. The two rivals did more than boycott each other's products. Exchanging not just blows but bullets, they fought a nationwide war for control of America's workplaces. By 1939, the AFL had clearly won. AFL carpenters beat CIO woodworkers; the AFL's AFSCME largely eliminated the CIO public employees union. In Minneapolis, a few months before Pearl Harbor, out-of-town muscle men—one bunch led by Detroit's Jimmy Hoffa, the other by Denny Lewis, the brother of CIO boss John L. Lewis. The two clashed violently for control of the local Teamsters. Hoffa won. They fought a rematch in Detroit in a battle that began with clubs and ended with pistols. Hoffa and the AFL won that engagement too.[22]

The AFL victories were not achieved without outside help, however, which came first from employers. Under American labor law, it's really the employer who decides which union will represent the workers. An agreement with one union legally bars the efforts of a would-be competitor. Bosses much preferred the more decentralized, corruptible AFL.

A second set of helpers in the anti-CIO struggle came from the Capone gang—perhaps the most powerful warlords in the Federation. For several decades, the Chicago-based criminal enterprise managed to dominate as many as seven international AFL affiliates—the Laborers, the Building Service Workers, the hotel and restaurant workers, the brewery workers, the motion pictures workers, the Teamsters, and probably the meat cutters. The Outfit didn't just muscle in, it knew how to organize: under mob dominance, Capone-controlled unions turned into the fastest growing affiliates in the AFL.

Led by Murray "the Camel" Humphreys, the Chicago mob's chief labor strategist, the Outfit went on the offensive in the early 1930s, taking over one local after another, often murdering CIO progressives in the process. From Hollywood studios to Detroit construction sites to Brooklyn butcher shops, the Capone gang and its Midwest allies beat, kidnapped, and assassinated their rivals in the bloodiest labor battles in American history. At the 1936 Rochester Convention of the hotel and restaurant workers union (HERE), mobsters opened fire, shooting three delegates and killing the president of Manhattan-based Local 16.[23]

More consequential, if much less well publicized than the Rochester shootings (which were handled by special prosecutor Thomas E. Dewey), was the 1939 murder of a crusading head of the Chicago Waste Handlers Union. He was shot by a small-time associate of Humphreys, who immediately replaced the murdered progressive with Paul Dorfman, setting up a Teamsters dynasty that would last until the early 1980s, with terrible consequences for the integrity of the Teamsters' pension funds.[24]

Besides help from what amounted to the "Capone International," the AFL also received tacit support from FBI director J. Edgar Hoover. His one-sided law enforcement priorities—insisting that the mob didn't exist while wiretapping the major CIO unions for subversives—helped check the CIO's drive. Battling the mob, the FBI, and the AFL as well as the employers and crippled by infighting between communist and anticommunist factions, the CIO soon stopped being a going concern, and by 1955 it was merged into the AFL.

Whatever animal vitality existed in the American labor movement largely disappeared after the AFL-CIO merger. Neither the AFL nor the CIO unions had to defend their jurisdictions. The merged Federation settled into its "sleepy monopoly" mode.[25] A wave of strikes in the 1970s stimulated some radical hopes, but organizing efforts had dropped precipitously. The percentage of American workers who were union members began declining the year after the merger.

Still, the AFL declined less rapidly than the CIO. Before the merger, the autoworkers ranked as America's largest union.[26] Today the four largest unions in the Federation are all AFL unions: the American Federation of State, County, and Municipal Employees, the Teamsters, the Service Employees International Union, and the United Food and Commercial Workers. Eight of the top ten are AFL unions. The most prominent of the AFL's former antagonists—the UAW, the Steelworkers, and the Mineworkers—would all together fit in any one of the top four.[27] Another clear sign that the AFL retained its dominance is that every AFL-CIO president, and in fact every candidate for the AFL-CIO presidency, has come from the AFL.[28]

Still, labor experts have routinely treated the CIO as the wave of the future. America's most influential sociologists—most notably C. Wright Mills and Daniel Bell—wrote as if the AFL's corrupt Old Guard was doomed. The sun was setting on the mobsters who had dominated the

AFL unions. Bell, in his classic *End of Ideology*, described them as mostly old geezers tottering on their last legs. The next generation of Italians, he prophesied, would opt for more mainstream professional careers. Mills explained that mob control was obsolete because of increased government regulation of industry.

Bell and Mills both believed that the CIO's better-educated, more progressive "new men of power" were taking over. George Meany wouldn't last much longer, predicted Bell in 1958; he'd "already written his page in history."[29] As for America's best-known union crook, Bell said, "what ultimately will curb Hoffa is a craving for respectability."[30] Labor's future belonged to the CIO's Walter Reuther, who would lead the labor movement into a more vigorous battle for social democracy: "better housing, more schools, adequate medical care, and the creation of a more 'humanistic' work environment." (Actually, much to the consternation of his social-democratic allies, Reuther wound up taking the autoworkers out of the AFL-CIO and into an alliance with Frank Fitzsimmons and the Teamsters.)

The "New York intellectuals" like Bell and Mills believed that larger "modernizing" forces would drive history and carry the progressive cause along with it. Big minds tend to study big trends: globalization, bureaucratization, alienation, suburbanization, concentration of capital. The corrupt workings of small, retrograde, local institutions tend to escape their notice.

In principle, though, it's not hard to understand the anomaly of the AFL that's at the heart of labor history—and perhaps even of modern American history—namely, that the most backward union movement in the advanced industrialized world has been able to monopolize power in the most advanced industrialized country, burying all its rivals. Winning early meant winning big. Once the AFL succeeded in locking in the workers who had the most leverage, its monopoly was hard to challenge. But what explains the AFL's formidable propensity for corruption? What makes corruption not merely an abuse but the substance of union governance?

FOUNDATIONS OF MONOPOLY

After an initial court rebuff, American unions got their coercive powers comparatively early. America's first permanent union, the Philadelphia Shoemakers—known then as "cordwainers"—had been active for a dozen years when the court's decision in the 1806 cordwainers conspiracy case put them and all other unions out of business for more than a generation. Unions, it was ruled, could not coerce employers and could not injure nonmembers by excluding them.[31] Then in 1842, *Cordwainers* was reversed.[32] Ever since, union leaders have been uniquely allowed to impose their services on client and adversary alike.

The most important coercive powers of American trade unions are perfectly legal. They come from the trade agreement or contract, which is far more than a "deal"—it's a regime, a form of government, and, like the U.S. Constitution, it gives rise to an all-embracing political system, one that tends to develop into a kleptocracy. Monopolies do tend toward corruption, especially political monopolies, and every trade agreement contains an exclusive bargaining provision.

That most eminent of American labor historians, John R. Commons, noticed this potential a century ago. He observed that the trade agreement contained features whereby "unions may become cat's paw of the employers, and may subject its officers to corruption."[33] Commons didn't say how, but if you read his essays on the New York construction industry and the Chicago Teamsters, it was easy to see how. The progression ran from coercion to collusion, from collusion to protection, and from a protection system to a protection racket.

Why should the union leader and the contractor fight when they could make a deal and shift the cost to the owner—who hired the contractor— or to the consumer? Collusion would be possible insofar as the union and the contractor could monopolize the market. The union could help secure the monopoly by restricting entry into the trade and by picketing competitors.

The colluding partners transform the trade agreement into a defensive wall behind which both parties can prosper. The employer is shielded from the bids of other contractors, and the workers are protected from the competition of their fellow tradesmen. The more exclusive the union, the higher the wages. And depending on how well they get along with their business agent, the members are also protected from the competition of other, less well situated workers in the union—the A-list workers from those on the B-list, top-tier workers from the bottom tier, full-timers from adjuncts.

The contract's protective features require a filtering system to determine who gets into the union and who fills the most desirable slots. It's in the interest of the leaders to select members who will be loyal not to other union members or to broad union principles but to themselves. Personal loyalty is best promoted by personal rewards—jobs and perks in exchange for votes and favors. But blood ties—family, ethnicity, and race—tend to encourage a narrower loyalty too.

The system turns into a protection racket almost from the beginning. It's always in the interest of the contractor to find a union leader who is most willing to let him cut the corners from the contract. In exchange for concessions, the contractor rewards the union leader with discretionary jobs for his members. The union leader is allowed to choose who works and who sits on a bench in the hiring hall waiting to be called. Soon the union leader has gathered around himself a retinue of clients that further protects him from the broader membership.

The trade agreement, initially designed to protect the members from the boss, winds up protecting the boss from the members. It transforms the local walking delegate (today's business agent) into a full-blown labor czar—the holder of a great fiefdom, which he acquires by virtue of the power ceded to him by the employer to hire and select workers.

Meanwhile, the union, which was intended to bring workers together in concert, to reduce their dependence on the arbitrary will of the employer, actually winds up atomizing them and turning them into individual clients of a union boss. As clients, however, the union members are by no means simple victims of the system. They're also its beneficiaries.

The result is a regime that's corrupt in more than just the thin, conventional, modern-day sense of the term. In ordinary discourse, it's chiefly corporate leaders or public officials who can be corrupt. In our political vocabulary, corruption means strictly the use of office for private benefit or stealing from the public. In classical antiquity, corruption had a deeper meaning and a wider scope of reference. Early modern republican writers like Machiavelli, Rousseau, and Jefferson revived this older usage when they insisted that not only kings could be corrupt, but commoners too. Both could have a disintegrating effect on the republic. The ordinary citizen was deemed corrupt when he became dependent on the will of a despot or dictator. In fact, the main danger to the survival of the republic came not from official chicanery but from citizens giving up their autonomy, trading their rights and duties for the dole or for special status as members of Caesar's entourage. Totally preoccupied with maintaining individual privileges and benefits, the ordinary citizen becomes a client, the intellectual a courtier; both give up any genuine concern for the common good on which the survival of the republic depends.[34]

The triumph of the trade agreement—the precursor of the modern collective bargaining contract—doomed working-class republicanism in America. The mushrooming growth of the AFL at the turn of the century, nearly quadrupling between 1897 and 1903, would have a perverse effect.[35] Instead of reducing American inequality, the AFL regimes—"job trusts," as Big Bill Haywood tabbed them—tended to aggravate the differences.[36] Inequality, in turn, as Machiavelli argued, historically served as the seedbed of republican corruption.[37] It would prove to be a classic feedback mechanism.

CHAPTER FOUR

The Fall of Sam Parks

Only in America would Sam Parks have been honored as the Grand Marshal of the Labor Day parade. Here was Parks, the nation's most infamous labor racketeer, veteran of half a dozen indictments for bribery, embezzlement, and assault, only six days out of Sing Sing. But on September 6, 1903, mounted on a white horse, sporting a white cowboy hat and a golden sash emblazoned with the letters "S.P." across his red silk shirt, the boss of the local Ironworkers was given the honor of leading thousands of workers down New York's Fifth Avenue in the nation's oldest labor parade.[1]

Why Parks? How was a forty-year-old Irish immigrant from County Down able to dominate not just the city's labor movement but also its $100-million-dollar-a-year building industry at the time of its most spectacular growth? Parks's reign (1896–1903) certainly wasn't due to his eloquence in labor's cause. Parks rarely gave public speeches, and when he spoke it was in short, barking sentences, mostly profanities. Nor was it because of the pamphlets he wrote defending workers' rights. Parks was practically illiterate. And he wasn't at the head of the parade because of election to some lofty official position. Parks wasn't even president of his local union. He was the "walking delegate" from Local 2 of the city's 4,500-member Ironworkers union.

The actual president of Parks's Housesmiths' and Bridgemen's Union, a Dutchman named Robert Nedig, stayed home on Labor Day. "I won't march behind that jailbird," Nedig said. "I am prepared to take the consequences."[2]

Almost from the AFL's inception, the trouble wasn't that it had crooks in its ranks, it was that they were at the front of the parade, determining the route. Honest workers either had to march behind them or stay home.

At the turn of the century, if the walking delegate said "March" it was a brave member—whether the president or not—who would refuse. Nedig got a license to carry a revolver. He even wore it under the tail of his black coat when he sang in the choir on Sunday. Parks's notorious "entertainment committee" of thugs might come after him, but they'd pay a price, he warned. "If an attack is made on me, a man may die before it is settled."[3]

Some of Parks's power rested on violence and intimidation. More of it was based on law and economics. Parks recruited his entertainment committee from the ironworkers who depended on him for jobs. Building trades jobs were all "closed shop."[4] To get a job, you had to be a union member first. And the union, through its apprenticeship system and hiring hall, decided who became a member and which member got the job. Proponents insisted that the alternative, "open shop," meant no unions at all. "A device of the employers to maintain a workplace," explains one authority, "where there is a union but nobody is required to join it."[5] In the open shop, AFL supporters insisted, workers could have no rights against management. In the closed shop, opponents claimed, they could have none against union leaders. Whether or not a third way actually existed, none emerged. Only in America did there develop a system of exclusive representation and winner-take-all elections that turned jobs into fiefdoms controlled by warlords like Sam Parks.[6]

If you were a union member out of work, the walking delegate was the indispensable man to see. If you wanted a better union job—say, foreman, and the foreman's job meant less work, less danger, and nearly twice the hourly pay—you had to be on the right side of the walking delegate.

Even if you got the job, if you wanted to receive the full union scale, you had to be approved by the union bosses. Longtime New York painters union leader Philip Zaussner recalls: "The official scale was $4.00 per day, but the majority of contractors paid less than $3.00 and some as little as $2.00 or $2.25. The actual wages paid to the member depended on the amount of protection (from the union politicians) the contractor was able to get. Protection was in any event cheaper than paying the scale."[7] But if you were a member under the protection of the walking delegate, you could get $4.00 even while all the other painters were getting $3.00 or less.

Although walking delegates weren't even citywide officials, they were seen as national figures. In *Shame of the Cities*, Lincoln Steffens identified Parks as one of the dominating figures in American society, along with Rockefeller and Morgan.[8] At a time when the last absolute ruler in the Western World spoke Russian, walking delegates were called "labor czars" both by the membership and by the national muckraking press.[9] Novels were written about them. Parks and Nedig were the fictionalized protagonists of Leroy Scott's *Walking Delegate*, published in 1905. In an age that took workers' attempts at organization more seriously, there was even an opera with the same title.[10]

THE WALKING DELEGATE AS WARLORD

In truth, however colorful and expressive, the term "labor czar" was a bit misleading. At any one time, there was only one czar in Russia, one Peter or Catherine the Great. In the AFL, there was no absolute ruler at all. Certainly AFL president Samuel Gompers was no Sam the Great, exercising autocratic powers over a vast empire through a swollen bureaucracy. Instead there was a realm ruled by a numerous petty boyars—purely local potentates whose absolute power stopped at jurisdictional boundaries. At the turn of the century, each big-city construction industry was likely to have one. Besides Sam Parks in New York, the most notorious ones were "Skinny" Madden in Chicago and P. H. "Pinhead" McCarthy in San Francisco. They operated less like Romanoffs in the Kremlin than Somalian warlords in *Black Hawk Down*. Petty, brutal tyrants, ruling their local territory by force and guile, utilizing clan alliances, but with no motive higher than greed and no purpose larger than self-aggrandizement, these early labor bosses were just as likely to switch sides overnight and join the enemy as to attack him without warning—all depending on how much the enemy had to offer.

Like the Somalian or Afghan warlord, the turn-of-the-century walking delegate could demand tribute because he controlled a local territory. In his hands was concentrated all the power of today's business agents and the union's executive officers. His job was to enforce the contract. If there was a violation, Parks could order the ironworkers off the job; when he said it was OK to go back, they picked up their rivet guns. There were no votes.[11]

Understandably, the contractors didn't want to get on the wrong side of Sam Parks either. Not only would they lose time and money if he called a strike, they also had to pay the union for the hours lost by the members— "waiting time." Whether or not the "waiting time" money paid to Parks ever went to his men, contractors had to pay it. So, then as now, contractors cultivated good relations with the union delegate by hiring the men he preferred to have hired. The most powerful walking delegates were those who had the most jobs to give out. The delegates with the most jobs had the most leverage with the contractors. It wasn't the methods that walking delegates used that counted, it was the results. A delegate who kept his men supplied with steady work could expect to remain a delegate indefinitely.

Essentially, the walking delegate was running a local protection racket. He protected the contractor from the members and the members from the bosses. The turbulent conditions of late-nineteenth-century American laissez-faire capitalism had given rise to a system more than faintly redolent of the chaos of the European Dark Ages. The seventh-century Merovingian state couldn't protect its subjects. As Gothic invaders burned fields and fought for booty, the small cultivator found himself in desperate need of protection. Peasants turned to powerful local men, offering their services and a portion of their produce in return for protection. The local strongman who offered protection might in turn offer a portion of his rents to an even stronger regional boss, a count or a duke, in order to receive his protection. In the early twentieth century, the AFL was formally committed to local democratic rule. But with its weak national president and its strong local fiefdom holders, who received obligatory tithes and services from the members in return for protection, AFL governance was more Merovingian than Jeffersonian.

Jeffersonian democracy depends on a community of more or less equal, independent, smallholding yeomen. "Dependence begets subservience and venality, suffocates the germ of virtue, and prepares fit tools for the designs of ambition," wrote Jefferson. The ratio of independent people to the dependent members of society, he thought, "is a good enough barometer whereby to measure its degree of corruption."[12]

American journeymen in the building trades started out on an equal

footing. What turned some into union bosses and others into their dependent clients? Chiefly it was the way they responded to the modern urban speculative building industry and its system of contractors and
subcontractors. The new mass production of flats in cities like New York
dissolved the structure and stability of the ancient trades. Urban building
booms attracted huge waves of itinerant craftsmen from cheaper cities
who poured in to the boom cities. What made the unskilled competitive
with the trained local journeymen was the spread of piecework, payment
by the quantity produced instead of by the hour. Piecework required only
unskilled "lumpers." Skills were subdivided and subcontracted. Working
days lengthened. Wages fell.

In 1881, the United Brotherhood of Carpenters was founded to stop the
flow of itinerant greenhands and check the spread of piecework. Each local of the Brotherhood issued its own cards. Someone had to check the
cards. In the mid-1880s, the "tramping committees" of urban construction workers who made their way from building project to building project to check cards and enforce contracts against lumping gave way to the
single walking delegate. Essentially a middleman between the contractor
and the union, the walking delegate was a full-time paid officer. He could
shut down jobs. He could provide jobs. It was a powerful position.[13]

Parks got to be a labor czar because he was a powerful man—as tough as
any man in the West Side's Hell's Kitchen. Even off his horse, Parks was an
imposing physical specimen. He had the stature and build of someone
who'd survived the hardest physical work the country had to offer: he'd
been a lumber man in the North Woods, a coalheaver on the Great Lakes
docks, a roustabout sailor, a railroad brakeman, a bridge builder. "Time
was," wrote Ray Stannard Baker, the original muckraking journalist, "when
unerringly balanced on a steel beam, two hundred feet in blue space, he
could drive more rivets to the hour than any other man in the trade."[14]

Even his most formidable and ultimately fatal antagonist, William
Travis Jerome, the district attorney allied with the city's landowning aris-
tocrats, respected Parks's abilities. "Only a fool would underestimate his
power," said Jerome. "He has personal magnetism and power to convince
others his word is law. He has physical bravery, daring and a dashing style
of leadership . . . his shrewdness is beyond question."[15]

With his big muscular shoulders and ham-sized fists, Parks bragged that he'd rather fight than eat. He claimed that he once had "twenty separate fights in a single day." That's how he organized stubborn West Side ironworkers—perhaps the toughest and most fearless workers in a hard-hitting industry. Often there would be someone on the number 1 line subway, the IRT, who didn't want to join the union. "I gave him a belt on the jaw," recalled Parks, "and that cleared his mind."[16]

By Labor Day in 1903, however, Parks's organizing and fighting days were well behind him. Now he was riding about in a cab, wearing diamonds, walking around with his blooded bulldog, breeding race horses, picking up the tab in bars for the house. "Sam Parks is good hearted all right," testified one Local 2 member, "if he takes graft he spends it with the boys."

Just where Parks's money came from—if he had any at all—was hotly contested. The *New York Times* ran a sympathetic feature story on Parks in 1903, a year before his death, while he was gravely ill. Parks and his wife lived in middle-class but not particularly luxurious circumstances. At $40 a week, his salary was three and a half times what the members made,[17] but not much more than what a foremen earned. And even if he did take bribes from bosses, said one Local 2 official, in an argument that would resonate down through the century to the days of Jimmy Hoffa and beyond, "He pulled up the wages from $2.25 to $4.50 a day, and that is enough for us."[18]

Still, Parks had a personal account of $11,000 in the Garfield National Bank—about $234,000 in 2005 dollars. Many suspected that some of the cash came not from shaking down the bosses but stealing from the members. There was $150,000 in union funds that Parks had spent in 1901 and 1902 that he couldn't account for.[19]

Some did come from contractors, District Attorney Jerome showed. And members were kidding themselves if they thought Parks's cash flow didn't ultimately come out of their pockets. Why would a contractor give money to a union leader? Basically, there could be two reasons. One is that the employer wants to prevent a potential harm the union leader threatens—like a strike. That's extortion. The other is to gain a benefit, such as not having to use union workers or pay union scale to union workers. That's bribery. Obviously, it's the members who are the victims of bribery—they don't get the benefits of the contract. But they may also be the ultimate bankrollers of the premiums contractors paid Parks for strike insurance. Union leaders have to call needless strikes, otherwise contractors won't pay to avoid them. Union members suffer when leaders call needless strikes—they lose work. What seems like a tax on contractors can actually be shifted to the members.

If contractors gained and members lost, why did business attack the labor czars? Why was Parks a notorious national figure, resplendent on his white steed in the illustrated pages of *McClure's*? Why was there such opposition to the legal foundation of his power, the closed shop? First of all, the contractors didn't oppose the closed shop, not even after the most violent strikes, like those in Chicago and San Francisco, where many were killed.[20] Why would they? The closed shop served as the legal foundation for their highly lucrative construction cartels: the building trades unions agreed to work only for specific contractors; the contractors in turn agreed to hire only members of the signatory unions. Unions could force their members not to work for the competition. It was the *consumers* of construction who paid the higher cartel price—they were the principal objectors—the building owners, the landowners, and their financial backers—the banks and insurance companies. These interests formed the substantial core of the opposition to the political machine boss and the labor czar in every city.[21]

There's a difference between wanting to change an institution—the closed shop—and wanting to do away with an abuse of the institution—Sam Parks. No contractor, however much he might benefit from the closed shop, wants to be the object of a shakedown. And many of Parks's strikes, the D.A. showed, were shakedown strikes against a single employer. In the Hecla Iron dispute, it all started when Parks had the company's superintendent meet him in a Manhattan bar. "You've never done anything for the walking delegates," Parks observed. "Ain't it about time?" He also accused the company of violating the contract. But he said he would "leave them alone for $1,000." Hecla's superintendent refused indignantly. "I'll give you two minutes to get out of here," he said. Parks did leave, but then he called strikes that cost the company $50,000 and threw 1,200 men out of work for weeks. Humbled, Hecla's president, Robert Poulsen, on the advice of the general contractor, Fuller Construction, asked Parks for an appointment.[22]

The meeting took place at the Flatiron Building, Fuller headquarters. What did he have to do to get the men back to work? "I'm it; you pay me," said Parks. "You can go to work when you pay Sam Parks." Poulsen testified that he inquired, "What about the men who are striking?" to which Parks was supposed to have answered, "To hell with those ___." He went on, "I don't care a damn for the law or for any damn man on the face of the earth. I'm going to get square with the Hecla Iron workers if it takes me to the end of my days, and I'll settle this strike when I get good and ready."[23]

Actually, $2,000 sufficed. It's possible that under oath the witnesses distorted or made up what Parks said. But the D.A. displayed the check proving that Hecla gave Parks the $2,000. His office leaked to the press that the check was cashed by Parks's employer, Fuller Construction.

Parks's cynicism seems breathtaking. But in sheer contempt for his union vocation, he was outdone by Lawrence Murphy, his colleague on the union-run Board of Trades. Murphy, the Stone Cutters Union treasurer, wasn't parading with Parks on Labor Day as usual, because he had been caught taking bribes—a common occupational hazard under the regime of the crusading New York D.A.

Murphy was charged with receiving a hefty $200,000 in bribes—over $4 million in today's dollars. He was also charged with stealing $12,000 from the union. What made Murphy's bribery case unusual was his cynical use of "the highwayman's defense." The prosecution charged that Murphy was part of a ring of corrupt officials who met in a bar to plan hold-up strikes. They would earn between $10,000 and $50,000 for threatening and then calling off strikes. The swag was always divided fairly among the six principal officers in the stonecutters union.

Murphy conceded the facts, but through his attorney, he argued a novel legal theory. Think of the union, he suggested, not as an association of workers but as what it really was: a gang of highwaymen. Can highway robbers demand that one of their gang members return his share of the loot? Who were the stonecutters union to demand their money back? The stonecutters had no case against Murphy because the money he was accused of stealing from the union had been extorted from employers and consequently did not belong to the union. After all, a highwayman has no title to the property he has obtained by force or duress and therefore has no cause of action against another highwayman who takes the stolen property from him. The jury took twenty minutes to convict Murphy of grand larceny. On hearing the verdict, he blurted out, "This is a put up job. The others got as much as I did. They are trying to do me in."[24]

Murphy bossed only the small stonecutters union. Parks had better lawyers and better political connections. Above all, he had William "Big Bug" Devery. In the Hecla Iron case, Devery, the former New York City police commissioner and a 1903 mayoral candidate, bailed him out.

Devery was a natural political ally of the old school. Parks ran a union machine. Devery ran a political machine. But Devery was really a nineteenth-century figure out of a Thomas Nash cartoon. He could never find a place in the "New Tammany" machine, the reformed organization that avoided blatant extortion and concentrated on George Washington Plunkett–style "honest graft"—pay-to-play contributions, no extortion. Devery had mastered the shakedown routines. In 1894, he'd been a principal target of the city's Lexow Commission inquiry into police graft. In other words, Devery and Parks plied the same trade, one as a police officer, and the other as a union officer. Neither attacks by the muckraking greats, like Lincoln Steffens, nor exposure by the Lexow Commission stopped Devery from rising from police captain to police chief.[25] Or from accumulating a great fortune. To the awe of the assembled crowd of Parks's supporters standing outside Sing Sing in the summer of 1903 protesting his imprisonment, Devery—whose campaign tactics included throwing coins into a crowd—peeled off $5,000 from a huge wad of bills. "This whole roll," said Devery, "is for my friend Parks. It is all money earned by honest labor, and will go to get an honest man, who is under arrest, out. There is nothing crooked about Parks. He is the workingman's friend, and so am I."[26]

The whole crowd, with Devery and Parks in the lead and Tammany politicians in tow, then moved en masse to Alderman Foley's saloon on Center Street. But before stepping inside and setting up drinks for everyone, Devery mounted a bootblack stand to give another speech. "I am heartily in sympathy with the laboring man," Devery said. "I am glad to help this man," he went on, pointing to Parks, "because he is the friend of labor too. He has gotten higher wages for the ironworkers, who have to risk their lives twenty or thirty stories up in the air without any law to protect him." Asked whether he would include Parks on a Devery ticket for Manhattan borough president, the former police chief replied, "I guess that is right, Sport, I'd like to have Parks run if the workingmen want him, and I guess they do."[27]

But District Attorney Jerome wanted Parks too. Just weeks before the parade, he indicted Parks again. It was another shakedown case. Once again, Jerome had not only testimony from the contractor but also his canceled checks to prove the bribery claims. Once again, Parks made the journey from the Tombs, the newly built men's prison, to Sing Sing. To show solidarity with their imprisoned comrade, Parks's fellow union leaders on the Board of Delegates—the governing body of the building trades—decided to have the Labor Day march led by a single riderless white horse. Just days before the march, though, after only a few weeks in custody, Parks was released on a certificate of reasonable doubt from his two-and-a-half-year sentence to hard labor.

Now both Parks and the horse were ready for a triumphal moment. In a procession more redolent of victory marches in Imperial Rome than those characteristically organized by American workers, Parks rode the white steed down Fifth Avenue, sporting his golden "S.P." sash. Marching on foot directly behind Parks were his centurions, Richard Carvel and Tim McCarthy, who had been indicted for extortion too. And there was mayoral candidate Big Bill Devery, riding in a carriage. Seated besides him, resplendent in her diamonds, was Mrs. Sam Parks.

Imperial Roman triumphs concluded satisfyingly with the ceremonial execution of the captured enemy general. New York's triumphal Labor Day parade ended ignominiously with Parks nearly captured by his union adversaries. An estimated $3 million in wages had been lost by members because of Parks's penchant for shakedown strikes. Members' wives ran up to the carriage carrying the bejeweled Mrs. Parks and shouted that they needed shoes for their children. Workers along the line of march offered revisionist interpretations of the initials "S.P." emblazoned on Parks's Grand Marshal's sash. "Stolen Property," shouted one. "State's Prison," another. Parks was cursed and hissed. He escaped serious injury at the hands of the members. It didn't escape the notice of the *New York Times* that the march had been poorly attended. The year before, 25,000 had marched, but fewer than 9,000 showed up this time.[28] Parks was vulnerable.

His next fall came quickly, and it was no mere stumble. In October he was found guilty again of extortion. Another ex–police chief—not

Devery, who had abandoned him—offered to bail him out. But this time the presiding judge denied bail. On the day of his sentencing, he resigned from the union. Parks gave up. According to *Harper's Weekly*, it was because he knew detectives had collected evidence that he'd conspired to murder the international president of the Ironworkers union.[29] Parks wound up in Sing Sing for the final time. He died there in 1904 of cardiac arrest.

How exceptional was Parks and his Ironworkers local? Labor's academic friends insist that the vast majority of unions—well over 99 percent—are honest.[30] But Parks wasn't just any AFL leader in New York. He was the topmost figure.

Nor was Parks's style of leadership foreign to New York's governing body of the building trades unions, the United Board of Delegates—or, for that matter to Chicago's Board of Business Agents, run by the Steamfitters president for life, Martin B. "Skinny" Madden, "the personification of graft, violence, and intimidation."[31] Both associations were organized on the "highwaymen model"—a few leaders cutting up bribes in exchange for selling out their members—a model that applied pretty well to the supreme soviets of the building trades.

Contractors paid up because the locals were monopolies. In New York City, the United Board of Delegates was the mother of monopolies. In 1902, it represented about 60,000 New York City construction workers in thirty-four unions. To get premium wages as a craft member in New York City, it wasn't enough to be in a craft union, or even to be in favor with the walking delegate of your union. Your walking delegate had to have a seat on the Board of Delegates. Only that way could he have real leverage against general contractors. The delegate took his grievance to the board, and the board would decide whether a sympathetic strike—shutting down the job—should be called.[32]

Whether or not the delegates decided to call a sympathy strike often had nothing to do with the justice of the workers' demands, let alone with "sympathy." If the contractors could put up enough cash, the board would side with the employers. In 1902, when the painters union (the Amalgamated) made a demand for $4 a day, it antagonized the painting contractors. They decided to ignore the Amalgamated's demands and find a new union to negotiate with. Instead of calling a sympathy strike, the board weighed its offers. The rival International Brotherhood of Painters was in the bidding. The Brotherhood had long coveted the Amalgamated's lucrative New York jurisdiction. The obstacle was getting the Board of Delegates to replace the Amalgamated with the Brotherhood.

With enough cash, any obstacle could be overcome. But the Brotherhood bosses, it turned out, couldn't come up with enough money to tempt the city's parliament of walking delegates. The president of the Brotherhood offered the delegates $2,500, which they indignantly refused. The Brotherhood then turned to the painting contractors, who took up a collection; fifteen of seventeen members of the association donated a total of $17,000, which was then distributed among the Board of Delegates.

After the cash was divided, Parks's second in command, Richard Carvel of the Derrickmen, was designated umpire between the two painters unions. The Amalgamated, he ruled, had to dissolve itself and join its rival. In another stipulation, the Brotherhood publicly agreed not to let its members work for less than $4 a day. Secretly, however, the Brotherhood agreed to the contractors' demand that the rate fall to $3.25 and $3.50 a day. Thus the Amalgamated disappeared from the New York City labor scene. Labor historian John R. Commons called it "probably the most amazing act of the board during its career." Commented one prominent New York labor leader, "I knew that the end was coming when the unions began to graft on each other."[33]

Actually, Parks's career as New York's labor boss served as both an end and a beginning. It marked the end of easy illusions that the AFL could ever be transformed into a real union—one that would fight for the common good of American working people. The point of American-style unionism was not to obtain labor's rightful share of the nation's wealth; rather, it was to extract whatever the local traffic would bear for workers who, for whatever reason, happened to have strong local bargaining leverage.

But Sam Parks also represented a beginning. Compared with what would come in the 1920s, Parks's era was almost a golden age. Corruption, while pervasive, hadn't yet permeated the rank and file; union leaders hadn't yet given up control of their organizations to organized crime; machine-gun methods of enforcing union rules were unknown. Baser periods would soon follow.

Robert Brindell, who succeeded Parks as New York's labor boss, created nostalgia for Parks. He was far more powerful, with a broader reach, and he stole immensely more. Under the Brindell regime, every building tradesman in the city had to pay him a dollar a month. Non-union workers bought $10-a-week "privilege to work" cards from Brindell. Even union business agents had to pay tribute to the boss. It added up: A state investigating committee estimated that in 1919 alone, Brindell took in $1 million. Parks had been treated by city officials as a public enemy; Brindell was a city official—a housing commissioner, appointed by Mayor John Hylan.[34]

In 1920, Brindell exited the labor movement just as Parks had—via a prison term in Sing Sing for extortion. He would be New York's last labor czar. By the early 1920s, there were no more labor czars anywhere. "Skinny" Madden, Chicago's labor czar, died in 1912. After a violent interregnum, state authorities in 1922 indicted fifty-three union leaders for extortion, conspiracy, and murder. The same year, in San Francisco, the nation's last surviving labor czar, Pinhead McCarthy, a former two-term mayor and boss of the Building Trades Council for over a quarter century, was finally driven from office after revelations of bribe taking. The local labor potentates were simply unable to maintain a two-front war against big capital and the criminal justice system.

In the 1920s, no new union strongmen emerged. Labor became a conquered province as much more violent, better armed, more specialized racketeers blasted their way into control of local union movements. The early crime syndicate bosses—Arnold Rothstein, Louis "Lepke" Buchalter, and Jacob "Gurrah" Shapiro in the garment unions and Dutch Schultz in the restaurant and hotel trades—dominated the muscling-in era of the 1920s. They imposed a street tax on labor's shakedown artists just as they did the other illicit operators. Crooked labor leaders joined the bookies, bootleggers, pimps, and numbers runners, who all paid protection money too.

The shift occurred most violently and spectacularly in Al Capone's Chicago and with almost industrial efficiency under New York's Murder Inc., but in cities all across the country—with the Purple Gang in Detroit, Johnny Lazia in Kansas City, Moe Dalitz in Cleveland, Buster Wortman in St. Louis, Nig Rosen in Philadelphia, and Longy Zwillman in New Jersey—

the formerly independent labor boss came under the domination of the organized crime boss.

But the labor boss would sink lower. By the 1950s, the old Jewish bosses had either been assassinated, like Zwillman, or come under the protection of Italian crime families, like Moe Dalitz, who had moved to Las Vegas. There, Dalitz supervised crime family operations, including the tapping of the Teamsters' Central States Pension fund. While the labor leader could still dominate his own members, in many affiliates he was now just a tertiary figure in the power structure of organized crime. The labor boss answered to a mob associate who answered to a mob boss. The mobsters themselves grasped the meaning of the power shift. Explained Vincent "the Fish" Cafaro, a Genovese boss, "We got our money from gambling, but our real strength came from the unions. With the unions behind us, we could shut down the city, the country for that matter, if we needed to get our way."[35]

Besides representing the elementary stage in the evolution of union corruption, Sam Parks also stands at the beginning of a unique American labor tradition: the rogue hero.

For at least a century, labor's defenders have insisted that big business is just as corrupt, or even more corrupt, than unions. Unquestionably, major Wall Street and corporate malefactors like Daniel Drew (watered railroad stocks), Sam Insull (utility stock fraud), Michael Milken (junk bonds), and Bernie Ebbers (WorldCom) have made off with sums that make Parks and his successors seem like subway turnstile jumpers. But it's a dubious argument. U.S. corporations are uniquely organized around greed and the promise of individual self-enrichment. They don't pretend to a higher vocation. Unions do.

And Wall Street doesn't honor its convicted crooks by having them ring the opening bell at the New York Stock Exchange. Corruption, if proven, is treated as a badge of shame. Crooked Wall Street operators are rarely allowed to run their enterprises from jail. The imprisoned union leader giving orders from prison, as Sam Parks did, would be a common feature of the labor movement. In the AFL and later the AFL-CIO, indictment for bribery or financial misconduct became an automatic pass to the front of the Labor Day parade—or, if the indictment came down early enough in the year, the St. Patrick's Day parade. President Paschal McGuinness of the

District Council of Carpenters, an alleged crime family associate, was the St. Paddy's Grand Marshal in New York City in 1992 after his indictment for bribery. His predecessor was indicted and then disappeared, presumed to have been murdered. Each of McGuinness's successors wound up indicted too.

Finally, Parks's place in labor history is justified by his indirect but important role in labor's crime of the century. At the Ironworkers' convention in Kansas City, just after the 1903 Labor Day parade, Parks lost the international presidency by only a handful of votes—43–40. But he had enough strength among the delegates to elect the vice president and treasurer, John J. McNamara. In 1911, AFL would proclaim Labor Day "McNamara Day." Three months later, McNamara and his brother James would plead guilty to carrying out the bloody bombing of the Los Angeles Times Building—setting back the organizing hopes of the American labor movement for a generation.[36]

CHAPTER FIVE

Dynamite Organizing

At first, no one thought it was a bomb. At 1:07 a.m. on October 1, 1910, 200,000 Los Angeles residents were awakened by a mighty roar. Many feared it was an earthquake. Just four years earlier, a huge eruption had leveled and burned downtown San Francisco. In fact, the sound was dynamite echoing through "Ink Alley" at the rear of the Los Angeles Times Building. Two minutes after the initial explosion, the entire building was filled with gas and flames. Those trapped on the upper floors leaped out windows to their death. Of the nearly 100 workers in the building, a score escaped uninjured. Twenty-one were killed.

The next day, Harrison Gray Otis, the owner of the *Los Angeles Times*, which then had a circulation of about 11,000, ran an editorial blaming organized labor for the blast. "Oh ye anarchic scum," wrote Otis, "you cowardly murderers, you leeches upon honest labor, you midnight assassins, you whose hands are dripping with the innocent blood of your victims . . . go mingle with the crowd on the street corners, look upon the crumbled and blackened walls, look at the ruins, wherein are buried the calcined remains of those whom you murdered."[1]

Otis was widely recognized as organized labor's most inveterate enemy. Most readers thought he had gone way beyond the evidence. Where was the proof? About a year later, though, beginning with the confessions of the McNamara brothers, two officials of the Ironworkers union, evidence began to pile up that Otis had actually underestimated the extent of the labor plot. The bombing of the Los Angeles Times Building turned out to be only one in a series of no fewer than a hundred and perhaps as many as a thousand explosions set off to destroy public buildings, bridges, and railroad yards.

The campaign—rolled out in December 1905 by the Ironworkers, who had links to the West Coast construction unions—may have been the most wide-ranging terror operation in twentieth-century American history. But the perpetrators had little in common with Hamas or al Qaeda. The men who set off the bombs were mostly highly paid professionals, and the motives of the officials who served as their paymasters were purely commercial. The point was to extort closed shop agreements from construction companies.

It's hard to justify the murder of innocent workers for commercial purposes, but the McNamaras' defenders insisted that the closed shop transcended ordinary business: It was the soul of American trade unionism. The explosions were a desperate means to a desirable end: the dignity and prosperity of American workers.

But was the Ironworkers' closed shop campaign a necessary means for a necessary end, or just a means to extract bribes from employers? Perhaps both. American-style unionism is no more possible without the closed shop than are American-style drug companies without exclusive patent laws. On the other hand, monopoly power not only invites abuse, it provides a vocation for those likely to abuse it. The political pedigree and postincarceration resume of the bombmaster, J. J. McNamara, were dubious. He was an ally of Sam Parks, and after McNamara got out of prison for the *Los Angeles Times* bombing, he was soon back in, first for extortion and then for embezzlement of union funds.

The Ironworkers' leadership continues to be united in pursuit of criminal vocations right down to the present. Between 1999 and 2002, nine top officials of the union, including its president and general vice president, were charged with multiple counts of stealing. All pleaded guilty except President Jake West, who was also implicated in the Ullico insider trading scandal. A federal judge ruled that West was "medically incompetent" (he was ill) and postponed his trial indefinitely.[2]

The latest batch of convicted Ironworkers officials went down quietly. In contrast, nearly a century ago, the strongest voices of organized labor, from Samuel Gompers to Eugene Debs, supported both McNamaras until the day of their shocking confessions. Gompers's support might have been more than moral. He came close to being indicted himself.

After the McNamaras lost innocence as their defense, they cited the pressures of the class struggle. But this position became far-fetched, given who these men were and the spirit in which they acted. A lot of the bombing was carried out in a lighthearted spirit. There were jokes about the campaigns at Ironworkers conventions. Explosives were very much part of the union's ordinary activities: Bombing materials were stored in the union's Indianapolis headquarters.

The canonization of the brothers as working-class martyrs had to wait until memories had dimmed. But then none of the McNamaras' defenders ever put the *Los Angeles Times* bombings in the context of the five-year Ironworkers terror campaign that preceded it. Disconnecting the L.A. bombing from the antecedent campaign makes it easier to emphasize the improbability of the McNamaras' guilt.[3] It doesn't figure, the argument runs among sympathetic historians. Why would they have blown up the *Times*? Open-shop, low-wage L.A. was in the middle of the most promising union organizing campaign in its history. Hard as it may be to believe now, more than ninety years later, a Socialist, attorney Job Harriman, was the favorite candidate in the race for mayor. The Socialists won eight of nine L.A. council races. Harriman won the mayoral primary. "Confident and growing," writes labor historian Michael Kazin, "the labor movement certainly had no reason to destroy its own peaceful reputation."[4]

Eugene Debs, the editor of a much bigger paper than the *Los Angeles Times*—the weekly *Appeal to Reason*, with nearly half a million subscribers—agreed completely.[5] What's more, Debs, the Socialist Party's candidate for president, thought he knew who was responsible for the explosion in Ink Alley—Harrison Gray Otis himself. It was all too suspicious. Otis just happened to be in Mexico on a business trip, instead of in the building. Otis's son-in-law Harry Chandler, the paper's general manager, had gone home early. It stood to reason, argued Debs, that the *Times* managers were "themselves the instigators, if not the actual perpetrators" of the crime.[6] Urged Debs: "Deliver the carcasses of the plutocrats to the furies."[7]

While Debs had no real evidence, Otis fit perfectly the labor left's profile of the ideal perpetrator: an imperialist butcher turned open shop crusader. As a commander of U.S. troops in the Philippines, Brigadier General Otis had fought guerrillas by destroying their villages. "The slaughter of women and children was frightful," wrote one eyewitness.[8]

When he returned from the war, it was as if he'd brought the war back with him, only the L.A. union men were now the enemy. Otis became the commander in chief of a campaign to defeat the most promising labor movement in L.A.'s history—the drive to organize the city's metalworkers.

In 1910, an organizer for the metalworkers described L.A. as "the great stronghold and citadel of the organized enemies of organized labor." While San Francisco ironworkers earned $4.00 an hour for eight hours, ironworkers in L.A. were paid anywhere from $1.75 to $2.25 for ten hours. Anyone caught at a union meeting would be promptly fired. L.A. was known as the "Otistown of the Openshop."[9]

The *Times* publisher aimed to keep it that way. He attacked organized labor with all the ferocity he'd displayed against the Filipino independence fighters. The *Times* headquarters was transformed into a military fortress. Otis drove around town in an armor-plated car with a machine gun on a turret.[10] For his adversaries, Otis was a man of such malignancy that it was easy for them to conclude either that he had set the blast himself or, more charitably, that the cause was management's negligence: a gas leak in the ink room.

A little more than a week after the event, however, on October 11, the case for an accidental explosion clouded considerably. "Infernal machines"—nitroglycerin bombs connected to timing devices—were discovered in the homes of Harrison Gray Otis and Felix J. Zeehandelaar, who headed the Merchants and Manufacturers Association, an open shop organization founded by Otis. Many pro-labor supporters argued that Otis had planted these devices, too, and then conveniently had them found before they exploded in order to discredit the labor movement.[11]

Within fourteen months, though, Otis—"the most notorious, most persistent and unfair enemy of trade unionism on the North American continent"—wound up completely vindicated and his AFL accusers utterly discredited. The bombers confessed. They were the McNamara brothers, John and James. Both worked for the AFL-affiliated ironworkers union, the International Association of Bridge, Structural, and Ornamental Ironworkers.

The *Los Angeles Times* bomb was placed in Ink Alley by James, a twenty-nine-year-old former printer. His older brother John, an attorney, who provided him with lucrative bombing contracts—$200 per job (about

$4,000 in 2005 dollars) and an expense account—served as secretary-treasurer of the Ironworkers. John in turn owed his career to Sam Parks.

At the 1903 Kansas City convention, just before he went off to Sing Sing, Parks brought his local electioneering tactics to the international. Parks had Frank Buchanan, the president, beaten by a half dozen members of Parks's "entertainment committee"; they also beat and intimidated other rival delegates. Parks lost his own bid, but his supporters wound up in control of the executive board, and they succeeded in putting John J. McNamara in office as secretary-treasurer.[12]

McNamara's bombs were a Sam Parks legacy in two other major respects. Parks was a dynamite pioneer. Others in labor had used dynamite earlier—the Haymarket anarchists, to choose just one example, used explosives in 1886 as a method of revolutionary labor protest[13]—but Parks may have been the first conventional AFL leader to deploy explosives in an urban setting as part of a strategy aimed at getting an ordinary trade agreement.[14]

THE IRONWORKERS VS. THE STEELMEN

The Ironworkers would probably never have been convicted if they hadn't taken on U.S. Steel. Eugene Debs, in his *Appeal to Reason*, which had a circulation of 40,000 in L.A., plausibly portrayed U.S. Steel as the aggressor. "The conspiracy," he wrote, "was hatched in Wall Street soon after the steel octopus was spawned. Morgan brought down his fist and hissed 'GOD DAMN THEIR SOULS, THE UNIONS HAVE GOT TO BE WIPED OUT.'" Debs warned that "if Morgan, Guggenheim and Otis and the Merchants and Manufacturers Association want red hell they can have it, but let them take notice that when it comes, the working class alone will not furnish all the victims."[15]

In fact, one of the first acts of the steel octopus was to offer the Ironworkers a closed shop contract. Parks's nemesis, the Ironworkers' international president, Frank Buchanan, wanted to sign the agreement in January 1902. But approval of the deal wasn't just up to him: The agreement had to be ratified by the big locals. Parks led the successful campaign to reject it. It was union politics: Parks wanted to replace Buchanan as president.[16]

It's said that small dogs sometimes challenge much larger dogs because they don't realize they're small dogs. The Ironworkers' leadership may have suffered from this kind of misperception. The ironworkers founded their organization—the International Association of Bridge, Structural, and Ornamental Ironworkers—the same year as the steelmen founded U.S. Steel—1901. U.S. Steel was a merger of moguls—Henry Frick, Andrew Carnegie, J. P. Morgan, and John "Bet-a-Million" Gates. The union was a tough but scraggly amalgamation of twenty-seven locals with about 6,000 workers. By 1905, it had grown to 16,000. Compared with the billion-dollar corporation, the union had only about $1,000 in the bank, with its outstanding liabilities "about $2,000 less than nothing."[17]

Still, the Ironworkers knew how to use the weapons of the weak. They would need them, since U.S. Steel decided to change its tactics after its offer to recognize the union in a closed shop agreement was rejected. U.S. Steel lined up the biggest steelmakers and steel erectors in the country to form the National Erectors Association. If they couldn't bend the Ironworkers union, they decided, they'd break it. In 1905, America's most powerful corporate leaders launched a nationwide campaign for the open shop in construction.

In response, the Ironworkers launched a clandestine nationwide bombing campaign against the open shop alliance. A new pro-dynamite president, Frank Ryan, sent cash to local presidents with thinly veiled instructions about how to use the money. The local presidents would send back news clips of their bombing jobs.

Most of the union's dynamiting wasn't carried out by the local presidents. The bulk of the bombing was managed in Indianapolis by the International itself. There were two men directly in charge. One was the union's secretary-treasurer, John J. McNamara, who mainly supervised his brother James, who actually placed the bombs. The other was Herbert S. Hockin, whose job was to handle Ortie McManigal, who in turn carried out many of the biggest jobs. Most of the Ironworkers' targets were bridges and viaducts in obscure places. But there were some well-known civic institutions too. Before the *Los Angeles Times* explosion, the Ironworkers blew up a Cleveland hotel (1906), the Detroit City Gas Company (1907),

Blackwells Island Bridge in New York (1908), and the Boston Opera (1909).[18]

The campaign didn't stop after the terrible loss of life at the *Los Angeles Times*. It only deepened the resolve of the Ironworkers' national office. In 1911, John McNamara wanted to expand the campaign by hiring an additional "eight or ten good men." In the meantime, his strategy was to keep both coasts "lit up" as best he could with his limited resources—about $1,000 a month. "When there would be an explosion in the west," he explained, "there would be an echo in the east; and when an explosion happened in the east, there would be an echo in the west; so as to keep them guessing as to who it was."

On the East Coast, McNamara's biggest post-*Times* job was the destruction of the Springfield, Massachusetts, municipal building on April 11, 1911. On the West Coast, in L.A., about three months after the *Times* explosion, he had the Llewellyn Iron Works destroyed. Llewellyn was actually one of five targets that had been marked for destruction, including the Alexandria Hotel and the L.A. Hall of Records. There was allegedly even a plan to blow up the Panama Canal because one of the contractors on the job wouldn't sign a trade agreement with the union.[19]

Altogether, what was the damage? Officially, the government charged the Ironworkers with ninety-four blasts. However, William J. Burns, the private detective who'd been hired by the National Erectors Association to investigate the earlier bombings, claimed in his bestselling book *The Masked War* that the union was responsible for a total of nearly a thousand attacks over the six years from 1905 to 1911. Burns's estimates were taken seriously because it was he—not the government—who actually cracked the case.[20]

It was James McNamara's post-*Times* follow-up jobs—particularly the failed effort in L.A. to blow up Otis and Zeehandelaar's homes—that put Burns in a position to identify the nation's biggest homegrown terror plot. The same type of dynamite used in the attempt to dynamite Zeehandelaar's house had been used to destroy a girder in the Ironworkers' earlier bombing campaign in Peoria, Illinois.[21]

The Peoria bombing had been carried out by Ortie McManigal. He'd been under surveillance since 1907, when he blew up the Detroit Gas Company headquarters. After his arrest, prosecutors turned him easily. Yes, explained McManigal, James McNamara had planted the *Los Angeles*

Times bomb, and he'd been given the assignment by his brother John. But the Ironworkers were just subcontractors on the *Times* job. The project had been paid for by top San Francisco building trades officials, who were behind the L.A. metal trades organizing campaign.

McManigal's statement gave detective Burns most of the leads he would need to identify the complex structure of the secret bombing apparatus. He would prove that the dynamite for both the *Times* and the Llewellyn Iron Works jobs had been paid for by Olaf Tveitmoe, the editor of the San Francisco building trades weekly, *Organized Labor,* and the no. 2 official in the San Francisco building trades. Tveitmoe would be indicted with two other Bay Area building trades officials.

A forty-year-old Norwegian immigrant who led the Bay Area crusade against nonwhite immigration, Tveitmoe was not your typical bombing suspect. He was Sam Gompers's chief West Coast ally and the principal spokesman and theoretician for the San Francisco building trades—widely recognized as the most powerful municipal building trades organization in the country. A few years after the building trades–controlled Union Labor Party came to power in 1901, Tveitmoe was appointed a city supervisor. (He was not, however, one of the notorious "paint eaters" mentioned in chapter 3). Tveitmoe's immediate boss in the building trades, P. H. "Pinhead" McCarthy, was the mayor of San Francisco.[22]

The "barons," as San Francisco building trades bosses were known, besides creating labor's most effective urban political machine had fashioned what may have been the narrowest, most parochial labor organization in America. Pinhead McCarthy forced the San Francisco craft unions to disaffiliate from the state federation of labor. He tried, with some success, to get the local unions to cut off their affiliations with their own internationals. Overall, McCarthy's commitment to labor solidarity could be accurately gauged from his behavior one Labor Day when he had the building trades march not just separately from the rest of the San Francisco movement but in the opposite direction. Why would the barons get involved in organizing exploited workers in L.A.?

They had no choice. The barons had been given an ultimatum by the local metal trades employers. Work was shifting to L.A. Either the San Francisco building trades brought L.A. wages up to the San Francisco level or there'd be no more contracts.[23]

To put some fear into the local L.A. bosses, Tveitmoe had reached out to the L.A. Ironworkers. The Ironworkers had a formidable reputation, and of all the L.A. unions, they stood to gain the most from a successful organizing campaign. A local official in the L.A. Ironworkers contacted Ironworkers president Frank Ryan. "If you have a good live one back there (not a kid glove man) that you could send us here," he said, "I believe he could accomplish a great deal of good." After a lot of back and forth, the International decided to send James McNamara. It was McNamara who allegedly told his bombing colleague McManigal that the San Francisco people "wanted the *Times* put out of business."[24] It was a Christmas present for "the old man"—Tveitmoe.[25]

McManigal claimed that there were documents that would corroborate everything he said. But the documents were in the Ironworkers' safe in the American Central Life Building headquarters in Indianapolis. Armed with a warrant to look for explosives, the prosecutors' investigative team entered the building, then followed a tip from a janitor to look in the basement, where they found a vault. Inside the vault were letters and files, and beneath the documents were eighty-six sticks of dynamite, alarms, fulminating caps, dry-cell batteries, a fuse, and a case for carrying nitroglycerin.[26]

The Ironworkers' leadership apparently wrote everything down. They even dutifully recorded how much they were paying in blackmail and to whom. John McNamara wrote about plans to kill his blackmailing ex-girlfriend. Naturally, he had no desire to see these facts come out.

Nor did AFL president Samuel Gompers want the details of the Ironworkers' five-year bombing campaign aired out. When word came down that the McNamaras had pleaded guilty, Gompers had just returned from an AFL convention in Atlanta. Bursting into tears, he cried, "I have been grossly imposed upon." A *New York Times* reporter interviewing him at the Hotel Victoria asked, "Can you explain how it happens that you were kept in ignorance?" Gompers, who was accompanied in his suite by Olaf Tveitmoe and Tveitmoe's aide, Anton Johannsen, replied, "Explain! Kept in ignorance? Why, we want to know that ourselves. We who were willing to give our encouragement, our pennies, our faith, why were we not told the truth from the beginning? We had a right to know." Tveitmoe and Johannsen, who were both later indicted in the bombing conspiracy, nodded in agreement.[27]

Weepily, Gompers explained that he'd been set up. He had no idea that the McNamaras had been guilty. "If they were guilty, if they did this thing, and if they had told me so, I would have said to them to plead guilty. I believe in truth. I believe in candor. I do not believe in violence. Labor does not need violence."[28]

Gompers's plea of ignorance risks claiming credulity. Although there's no evidence that he was in any way involved in the bombings, he had to know at some point before it was announced that the McNamaras were guilty. He was paying the bills for famed attorney Clarence Darrow to defend them. Before the McNamaras' decision to change their plea, Darrow called Gompers to advise him of the new developments in the case—the arrival of the documents.

The murkier question is not whether Gompers knew about the guilty plea before it was announced but whether he knew about the bombings before they took place. Ortie McManigal, the government's chief informer, said he did, but he had no documents to back up the charge. Detective Burns, whose every public accusation was proved correct, charged that Gompers was part of the bombing conspiracy. Some members of the L.A. prosecution team hoped that by charging Darrow with jury tampering, he would provide evidence on Gompers. According to historian Sidney Fine, the prosecution finally turned down what was said to be Darrow's offer to give up Gompers in exchange for immunity and a $10,000 fine.[29] While Darrow was more credible than McManigal, the prosecutors doubted that it was possible to bring down Gompers on Darrow's word alone.

If Gompers knew and said nothing, it would have been illegal, but it didn't mean he sanctioned the bombings or personally approved of them. Acting as president of the AFL wasn't like serving as president of the United States. Gompers wasn't at the top of the Ironworkers' chain of command. McNamara didn't have to clear bombing targets with Gompers.

It was the prosecutors who needed to go to the top to get permission to try the rest of the Ironworkers leadership. What they called the "real crime of the century" was not the L.A. bombings but the entire six-year Ironworkers bombing conspiracy. To stage the trial, however, they needed a go-ahead from U.S. president William Taft himself.

When Taft said yes, the Justice Department mobilized all its resources. The government called 499 witnesses; trial testimony consumed 21,000 pages; the prosecution's documentary exhibits ran to over 5,000 pages. On January 1, 1913, a federal judge sentenced thirty-three defendants, including president Frank Ryan, to prison terms in Leavenworth.

Olaf Tveitmoe was also convicted, in Indianapolis. Just after the *Los Angeles Times* bombing, Tveitmoe had offered a $7,000 reward for information leading to the conviction of the bombers. He himself was convicted specifically of financing the dynamite purchase.

Right after the McNamaras' devastating admission, Olaf Tveitmoe had written, "Tell all union men, women and friends to keep heads cool and their feet firmly on the ground. Labor's fight does not rest with a few individuals. It is rooted in the eternal struggle for freedom and justice."[30] In fact, the reckless action of "a few individuals" set the ground afire under the feet of the entire American labor movement.

First to topple was Tveitmoe's own organization. In San Francisco, after winning four of the previous five mayoral elections, the Union Labor Party disappeared completely. San Francisco was widely considered the strongest union town in America. Yet in the 1920s even the building trades in San Francisco went open shop.[31]

The McNamara verdict sent L.A.'s labor movement into a vegetative state for a generation. Socialist mayoral candidate Job Harriman, who had finished first in the primary, got less than 40 percent of the vote in the general election. The campaign to organize the metal trades collapsed. The backlash may even have been permanent. Despite the CIO's organizing efforts in the 1930s and 1940s, L.A.–Long Beach, the largest metropolitan labor market in the United States with 4.8 million workers, remains—except for public sector and janitorial workers—almost entirely non-union.

Surprisingly, given that they sustained the heaviest legal blows, the least permanent effect of the prosecutions was felt by the Ironworkers' union. Gompers quickly made amends for his public criticism of Ironworkers violence. He addressed the 1913 Ironworkers convention, saying, "I am not your accuser." President Frank Ryan, convicted of terror bombing, had his sentence commuted by Woodrow Wilson and wound up working for the AFL. By 1919, eleven of the Ironworkers officials convicted in Indianapolis for conspiracy were back in office.[32] Mass indictment of the leadership became a kind of folkway, part of the leadership tradition: in 2002, the seven top Ironworkers officers, from former president Jake West on down, were all under federal indictment for one crime or another.

It was the AFL, though, that suffered the steepest loss of public confidence. Gompers had financed a huge public relations effort to convince America of the McNamaras' innocence. He had a special stamp made, bearing a portrait of John J. McNamara. AFL members were to put it alongside the regular two-cent stamp bearing George Washington's likeness on all outgoing AFL mail. Hundreds of thousands of buttons were made that read "McNamara Brothers Not Guilty," "Justice for the McNamara's," and "Kidnapped." Labor Day 1911 was officially designated as "McNamara Day." The AFL even produced a film entitled "A Martyr to His Cause" tracing McNamara's life from the age of seventeen to his abduction and confinement by the government; 50,000 people saw the Cincinnati premiere.[33]

Labor historian Philip S. Foner has rescued the script of the final two scenes of "Martyr to His Cause" from AFL files:

HIS MESSAGE TO ORGANIZED LABOR
Scene 19: Cell. Mac, seated in his cell, is writing. As he finishes, flash on sheet, the following:
TO THE BROTHERHOOD OF ORGANIZED LABOR:
In this second attempt to crash and discredit the cause we represent I realize fully the desperation of the enemies of labor arrayed against us, but I am of good heart, for it will fail. That I am innocent of any infraction of the law in word or act needs no emphasis from me, for the truth is mighty and will prevail right speedily; and for it I shall contentedly wait.

I send to all brothers and friends of union labor the world over my earnest and affectionate greetings, with the assurance there is no villainy of which we are afraid. I am also confident that it is not asking too much of the public to suspend judgment in these matters until opportunity for a full and fair defense has been afforded. J.J. Mc.

(Back to picture) Mac with head bent low, reads the paper, then dissolve into Scene 20: The home fireside. Close-up of mother, alone, weeping over a letter from her son.[34]

The dual confessions shocked and disillusioned the hundreds of thousands of workers who had marched in cities across the country protesting the McNamara brothers' innocence. Wearers tore off their "Kidnapped" buttons and threw them in disgust into the street. At an L.A. labor temple, workers discussed a necktie party for Darrow and AFL officials who had proclaimed McNamara's innocence.[35] AFL spinners tried to mitigate the damage by pointing out that until the L.A. campaign, the bombings hadn't killed anyone. (Although not for lacking of trying, considering the explosive devices that didn't go off at Zeehandlaar's and Otis's houses.)

But the campaign against the open shop steel erectors wasn't restricted to bombs. There were also many beatings, or "sluggings" as they were then known.

In cities like Cleveland and New York, the slugging campaigns were especially successful. They persisted because the sluggers were rarely prosecuted by city officials. Thomas Slattery, a former aide to Sam Parks who was the boss of the Ironworkers Brooklyn local, was arrested again and again for assault charges. Except for a single $10 fine, he always escaped conviction. "Slattery," remarked an official of the National Employers Association, "must be one of the best citizens of Brooklyn and evidently has no trouble in obtaining friends to testify to this fact in court." Tim Murphy, president of a Cleveland Ironworkers local, got a $1 fine and eleven days in the workhouse for beating an American Bridge timekeeper. At the end of the year, the city appointed him the city bridge inspector.[36]

Some of the sluggings were brutal. Tom Dorsey, of the Manhattan local, hit a non-union worker in the face with an eight-pound hammer, knocking out his teeth and breaking his jaw. During the five-year slugging campaign, four workers went not to the hospital but to the morgue.[37]

The McNamara affair did much to unmake the AFL as a bearer of progressive hopes. But labor intellectuals never made it all the way through the five stages of grief described by Elisabeth Kübler-Ross. Denial, yes; anger, yes. But they never reached the final stage of acceptance. They refused to acknowledge that there was something deeply wrong—actually inhuman—about multiple killings of innocent workers simply to gain a closed shop trade agreement. They insisted on playing down the consequences. Except in L.A., no one got killed. Most common was the "social explanation." In pro-AFL accounts of the *Los Angeles Times* bombing, Eugene Debs was brought in as the closer.

For Debs, just because General Otis turned out to be formally innocent of bombing his own paper didn't mean that the McNamaras were truly guilty. "The McNamara's," Debs wrote, "are the product of capitalism. . . . If you want to judge McNamara you must first serve a month as a structural ironworker on a skyscraper, risking your life every minute to feed your wife and babies, then be discharged and blacklisted for joining a union. Every floor in every skyscraper represents a workingman killed in its erection. It is easy enough for a gentlemen of education and refinement to sit at his typewriter and point out the crimes of the workers. Put him in the ironworker's shoes," argued Debs, "and he will hesitate to condemn them as criminals who fight against the crimes of which they are the victims of such savage methods as have been forced upon them by their masters."[38]

Louis D. Brandeis, a future U.S. Supreme Court justice, was no socialist, but he reasoned just like Debs. He too pointed to the "underlying causes" of the bombing. It was the great trusts and corporations who were at fault. "What was it," asked Brandeis, "that led men like the McNamara's really to believe that the only recourse they had for improving the condition of the wage-earner was to use dynamite against property and life?"[39]

The progressives' defense would have been more effective if either of the McNamaras had actually been wage earners.[40] John didn't work on an office building, he worked in one: the Ironworkers' Indianapolis headquarters, in the American Central Life Building. He provided his brother with a $1,000-a-month expense account—nearly $19,000 in today's dollars. Most of it was spent on the union's dynamite projects, but a lot went to his several mistresses.[41]

Progressives recognize, of course, that not all union violence is carried out by victimized workers desperate for revenge. Sometimes, they point out, it's executed by class-conscious revolutionaries anxious to accelerate the progress of the progressive movement. Marx himself acknowledged the need for force "to sweep away" the "old conditions of production."[42] Of all the bombers, James McNamara seems to fit closest to the progressive profile of the class-conscious revolutionary. By 1941, when he died of cancer in San Quentin, McNamara had become a member of the Communist

Party. He issued a last statement, which read, "I will find my freedom only in the liberation of the working class. Whether that occurs while I am at San Quentin or out is of minor importance to me."[43]

But McNamara's embrace of Marxism was a jailhouse conversion. He was one of the early members of the Militia for Christ. The whole point of this organization, founded by the German Roman Catholic Church, was to promote conservative trade unionism by routing the advocates of class struggle from the labor movement.[44] No more than his brother, who was also a member of the Militia, had James McNamara ever worked at the trade.[45]

Besides confusing union staff with working stiffs and revolutionaries with conservatives, progressives also got the dynamiters' mood all wrong. First of all, the bombings weren't something done spontaneously by workers out of anger at the exceedingly dangerous, oppressive conditions they faced. They were executed by highly paid professionals and planned by union leaders as part of a methodical and rational, if occasionally light-hearted, campaign.[46]

Those involved in the day-to-day Ironworkers campaign were businesslike independent contractors. The executive board agreed on a standard fee of $200 per bombing. For a really big job, like the Blackwells Island Bridge in New York City, the bomber could earn $950—nearly a year's earnings for a skilled worker. For jobs that might involve loss of life, union bombers could expect $1,500 to $2,500.[47]

Far from being frantic gestures of desperation, the bombings were premised on cost-benefit analyses. Bombers justified their high fees on business grounds too: "Well, you know," explained one bomber, "it costs something to get the wind to blow the right way."[48]

Union leaders were a model of rational choice behavior. Their goal was to increase the costs to contractors in terms of damages and security so that a closed shop union contract was cheaper. This was the argument McNamara advised a leader of one of his Missouri locals to use in selling the bombing campaign. Tell the open shop contractor building a bridge across the Missouri River, he advised, that unionization was the safer policy—that open shop firms experienced difficulties completing their work.[49]

It wasn't all business, though. The bombings were also designed to lift spirits. In a letter to his "missionary workers," John McNamara explained that he wanted to have a bombing completed before a quarterly Ironworkers meeting. Speed was important because McNamara wanted "to make the boys feel good."[50]

In the union's national magazine, the *Bridgeman*, they liked to joke that it was meteors that actually caused bridges to collapse. After the dynamiting of the Pan American Bridge Company's New Castle plant—which had led to a closed shop contract—the local's business agent wrote, "Halley's comet passed through here on time and found about thirty of our members working for the Pan American Bridge Company. . . . This was a scab job to start with, but this company had to be shown that Union men were the cheaper."[51]

Another moment of levity was supplied by the Brooklyn slugger and business agent Thomas Slattery. He introduced a resolution that didn't appear in the union's official convention proceedings but was probably made from the floor. He moved, just months before the L.A. explosion, "that no more bombs or explosives of any kind be exploded while this convention is in session."[52]

The problem with the "social explanation" is that it explains the crimes of institutions by examining the motivations of individuals. Capitalism drives the individual workers to desperation. The dynamite campaign, however, was not carried out by isolated individuals, much by less poor, exploited individuals. The target of the campaign wasn't necessarily non-union workers. In the case of the Halley's Comet blast, officials targeted the union's own members who were working non-union.

John McNamara and Olaf Tveitmoe were top-rank AFL officials. On his release from prison, McNamara was given a job as a business agent with an Indianapolis local and resumed his efforts to unionize by extortion. He was arrested again and received a five-year prison term.[53] What put an end to his union career, though, was getting caught embezzling union funds.[54]

Unlike the McNamara brothers, Tveitmoe and the members of his circle were radicals. But notwithstanding the articles published in their journal, *Organized Labor*, supporting municipal power and Henry George, they weren't economic radicals. Certainly they weren't egalitarians.

Tveitmoe surrounded himself with men like Anton Johannsen—

"thick-fisted, bull-necked dynamic men." Johannsen and Tveitmoe were indicted together in the *Los Angeles Times* bombing. Their participation should have come as no shock. Louis Adamic, who interviewed the *Organized Labor* crowd, says that they laughed at naïve socialists who were conducting classes in economics. "'What we need,' they said with great emphasis, 'is not classes in economics, but classes in chemistry.'" They also laughed and winked a lot about Teddy Roosevelt's insistence on the need to talk softly and carry "a big stick."[55]

Neither had much concern for the "laboring stiffs" outside the building trades unions, notes Adamic. They did what they could to exclude them. One of the few campaign pledges honored by Pinhead McCarthy, the Union Labor Party's candidate who won the San Francisco mayoralty, was to dismiss all immigrant workers from city jobs.[56] After the influx of construction workers, to repair the damage following the 1906 earthquake, the union men made sure the "earthquake mechanics" left town.[57]

Organized Labor, edited by Tveitmoe, frequently invoked the notion of class struggle—it was in vogue a century ago—but Tveitmoe's real editorial passions were stirred by racial struggle. "The almond-eyed Mongolian is watching for his opportunity," he warned, "waiting to assassinate you and your children with one of his many maladies." The Chinese deserved no compassion. They were doomed, Tveitmoe explained, having "long since outlived their usefulness in the world's history." Thus, San Francisco must cease to be "an asylum for these Silurian ghosts."[58]

There was no common justice possible for the yellow man and the white man. Life was a pitiless racial struggle. "I would rather see California without a solitary man within it," observed Pinhead McCarthy, "than to see California Japanized or Chinaized."[59]

McCarthy's scorched-earth racial radicalism was pretty common at the time in the AFL. (In 1901, Gompers wrote *Meat vs. Rice: American Manhood Against Asiatic Coolieism*.)[60] The use of dynamite became common. So did the garden varieties of corruption. Each was a joint by-product of the AFL protection system. The union existed to protect its mostly homogeneous members against the labor of nonmembers.

"Organizing" therefore didn't involve a drive to open up the union to outsiders. It meant coercing employers to sign trade agreements for the benefit of your people. Once the union got the contractor to sign the trade agreement, relations tended to go from coercion to collusion. The way the leader could provide jobs for his people was by cooperating with the employer. In return for allowing him to protect his people, the leader gave back contract concessions to the employer.

That's the way the labor game was played in the Progressive Era. The marvel is that it has changed so little. In the Progressive years, many of America's most powerful institutions—the Southern Pacific (known as "The Octopus"), the corporate meatpacking and public utility trusts, the urban machines, even John D. Rockefeller's Standard Oil—were pushed to carry out some semblance of reform. But the AFL would remain unreformed and unscathed.

Since the 1960s, historians have tended to emphasize the limits of Progressivism. As Howard Zinn pointed out in his bestselling *People's History of the United States*, Progressives didn't make "fundamental" reforms; they were just a middle-class movement; businessmen acted "reluctantly" to forestall greater threats to their property.[61]

It's true that Progressivism did stop at regulation of the meatpackers, not their expropriation. Teddy Roosevelt merely broke up Standard Oil, rather than nationalizing it; Woodrow Wilson's income tax only nibbled at income inequality. And little progress was made in the direction of improved labor laws, health benefits, and pension benefits along the lines achieved in Germany and Great Britain.

A big reason why progressivism didn't push the United States farther along the road to social democracy is that the trade unions were missing in action. Progressive goals ran counter to the interests of AFL leaders like Pinhead McCarthy, John McNamara, and Olaf Tveitmoe. What they cared about was getting as many collective bargaining agreements as possible. In that endeavor, bombs and urban terrorism were a lot more effective than ballots and federal legislation.

Dynamite worked. Federal legislation worked the wrong way—it told workers they could get their rights and benefits from the government and not from AFL barons. These antireform sentiments were the creed not just of AFL rogues like McNamara but of its saints, like P. J. McGuire, the ex-Marxist who founded the Carpenters and then cofounded the AFL itself. "We have come to the conclusion," he intoned five years before the actual creation of the Federation, "that wherever we can help ourselves we will do it, without asking the aid of the government, and if we want to make a law, we will make it in our own trade unions and try to enforce it through them by contracts with our employers."[62]

McGuire's contractualism would define the position of organized labor in America from Gompers—who opposed a federally imposed eight-hour day—through the health care debate of 1994, when the AFL-CIO fought the replacement of HMOs by a Canadian-style single-payer system—but perhaps with this crucial exception: the trades would be the adversary of progressive government at the federal level but the ally of corrupt, Tammany-style government in cities all across the country.

CHAPTER SIX

Solidarity for Sale, Chicago, 1905

Potentially, there's a colossal frontier, a moral divide that separates a genuine labor movement from any conceivable countermovement of employers. What splits them is not that one group owns the means of production and the other doesn't or that the employers are rich and the workers are not. That's sociology, not morality. The real difference is a moral sentiment: solidarity. Insofar as workers feel that other workers' concerns are as important as their own, if they show real willingness to make sacrifices for other workers—sharing jobs, risking their jobs for the well-being of other workers—they can never be written off as just another special interest. Big corporations may cooperate in strikes and lockouts, but what group of investors would ever voluntarily give up their earnings to another?

What could make solidarity more than a pious moral sentiment is a certain kind of strike. In all strikes, workers temporarily stop working and thus stop getting paid. The strikers' end is to achieve some demand by hurting the boss more than they hurt themselves. It's a pain-gain calculus. But sympathy strikes—supporting the strikes of others by going on strike—involves pain with no immediate opportunity for personal gain. At the turn of the century, even the strongest unions with the most skilled workers were lucky to win half their strikes, and workers who lost strikes lost jobs. Lost strikes sometimes even meant that the union disappeared.

From its inception, the problem with the American labor movement has always been that it's so divided by separate jurisdictions that true solidarity has been comparatively rare. It's not simply that Americans are selfish. Under our system, certain kinds of work in specific places—for example, unloading materials on a construction site in lower Manhattan—

belongs to a certain union. Unfortunately, multiple unions—operating engineers, carpenters, laborers—claim the same work and battle each other for the right to perform it.[1] Until the 1930s, most of our strikes were jurisdictional: workers on strike against each other. Then, too, there were so many thousands of jurisdictions with contracts expiring at different times that a general strike of the European type was simply inconceivable.

That's why the legacy of the 1905 Chicago Teamsters strike has been so important to American labor historians down through the years. Maybe we didn't have any nationwide general strikes like the Europeans, but we did have local sympathy strikes in which workers of one or more trades would walk off the job in support of the demands of another. In Chicago in 1905, for one shining moment, it seems, the strongest union in Chicago, the mainly Irish American Teamsters, who had humbled the city's powerful merchant princes, stood shoulder to shoulder with some of the weakest—the city's tailors, who had been out of work for more than six months.

Boston-based Cornelius "Con" Shea, the newly elected president of the International Brotherhood of Teamsters (IBT), took command of the Chicago situation, giving the order himself to his Montgomery Ward drivers. Over forty drivers walked off the job in support of a comparative handful of garment workers who were on strike against Ward's.

What turned the strike into one of the biggest and bloodiest in American history was not Shea's rather measured action but the reaction of Chicago's elite employers, who saw an opportunity to break the union. They locked out about 4,000 teamsters and brought in strikebreakers, and the city's downtown area was in deadly turmoil for the next three months.

Eventually, the employers won. They broke the strike. Nearly half the locked-out teamsters lost their jobs permanently. The rest went back to work on whatever terms they could arrange.

But historians like to see in the fighting spirit of the Teamsters—and their willingness to take risks for the less favorably situated workers—the germs of American solidarity. Yale Professor David Montgomery has perhaps gone the furthest. He compares the Chicago Teamsters strike of 1905 with the St. Petersburg revolution of 1905, which overthrew the czar of Russia.[2]

But in the glorifying accounts, nothing really adds up, certainly not the motive for the job action. The Teamsters didn't act in solidarity. The first batch of strikers—the Ward's drivers—were ordered off the job by Con Shea. If they had disobeyed, they'd have been kicked out of the union, and without union membership they would have lost their jobs. The remaining 4,000 teamsters didn't decide to go on strike on behalf of the garment workers either. They were locked out.

The sentiment for solidarity had to come from the Teamsters' official leadership. In Chicago, then as now, the locals were famous for corruption, racketeering, and collusion with management. Con Shea was by no means a credible exponent of solidarity. He was a lifetime labor racketeer who started out as a professional bomber at age sixteen. Two years after the Chicago strike, Shea was expelled from the Teamsters by a rival faction. He found his way back to Chicago, where he continued his vocation as a professional bomber, eventually working his way back up to the leadership of a local under the protection of the Capone gang's principal Irish rival.

No wonder there were skeptics one spring morning in early April, when Shea went down to the main truck barn serving Chicago's Montgomery Ward & Co. to announce that he was pulling his members off the job. It was a small action for the biggest Teamsters boss in the country. Forty-seven Ward's drivers, Shea explained, would on his orders act in sympathy with seventeen members of the United Garment Workers Union. The garment workers had been locked out by Ward's six months earlier. But they were only a handful of the 10,000 tailors who'd gone out on strike in November 1904 against employers all over the city. At the time, the garment workers had appealed to Shea to stage a sympathy strike. He'd refused. But now, in the spring, with the strike seemingly over, he'd changed his mind.[3] Why? A $1,500 bribe from Sears, a Ward's competitor, his accusers would charge. Sympathy for the oppressed, insisted his supporters.

Few that spring could have imagined that Shea's order was about to produce one of the most violent strikes in twentieth-century American labor history. But by the time the strike ended 105 days later, in a brutally hot Chicago summer, twenty-one deaths would be recorded and over 400 injuries and nearly 900 arrests. In terms of fatalities—mainly involving African American strikebreakers—the Chicago strike was exceeded in twentieth-century U.S. labor history by the horrendous East St. Louis massacre of 1917, which also had its origins in an AFL-sponsored job action and degenerated into a killing spree where whites actually scalped black women.[4] It was an era when job actions could turn into race riots and race riots into racially divisive strikes, like the 1919 Chicago riot that cost thirty-eight lives.[5]

The blood-soaked 1905 strike nearly destroyed the newly founded IBT. From the very beginning of the Ward's sympathy strike, employers seemed to be straining for a chance to break the 35,000-member union—at the time, Chicago's largest and most powerful labor organization. The city's State Street merchant princes, the La Salle Street banks, the railroads, and the express companies swiftly bulked up a newly created entity called the Chicago Employers Association. They invested millions in wagons, purchased 1,000 horses, and brought up 2,000 blacks from the South to replace the strikers. Teamsters all across the city who refused to handle Montgomery Ward merchandise were locked out. Shea retaliated by spreading the strike, leading to more lockouts.

Lockouts can be counted on to produce strong feelings. And turn-of-the-century Teamsters strike tactics—wagons blocking the streets and wild horses running out of control in the intersections—carried with them a high probability of violence. But the 1905 strike was unprecedented. Strikebreaking blacks were lynched in the Little Hell and Back of the Yards neighborhoods, torn apart and beaten to death by the mainly Irish crowds who supported the predominantly Irish Teamsters union. Terrified blacks, deputized as city marshals and armed by the Employers Association, brandished weapons and fired into the mobs, further inflaming the neighborhoods. After a few weeks, the United Garment Workers asked the Teamsters to spread the strike to the big garment employers. Shea refused, and the UGW withdrew support for the Teamsters' action.

Shea tried to cut his losses. But what had begun as a sympathy strike became a survival strike when the employers refused to hire back the teamsters. Shea couldn't settle without getting his 4,000 members' jobs back. By July, though, with strike pay exhausted, a spontaneous back-to-work movement began. Having won none of their objectives and been berated by President Theodore Roosevelt, who came to town to uphold law and order, the teamsters returned to their jobs—at least those who still had jobs; 1,700 teamsters, nearly half of those on strike, were let go by management.

The Teamsters survived, but only in pieces. What hurt the Teamsters' image as much as the strike violence and the loss of jobs were accusations that Con Shea's action against Ward's had been bought with a $1,500 bribe. However, grand jury testimony couldn't prove that Shea had taken the money, and he beat two trials—one in a hung jury, the other in an acquittal. But witnesses pulled the curtains back on a union that regularly served as a clearinghouse for employers who wanted to damage their competitors. A few thousand dollars in the right hands could start a sympathy strike that would abruptly halt all deliveries to a business rival. The employers' competitive greed was being greased by corrupt labor bosses who piously packaged it as union solidarity.

Shea beat back a movement by reform opponents to unseat him at a wild IBT convention in August 1905 marked by gun waving, fistfights in the aisles, and open bribery of the delegates. In 1907, Shea was finally toppled, but reform Chicago Teamsters had already pulled out of the IBT and didn't come back for a generation.

The Chicago Teamsters strike of 1905, a shining moment for American labor? So it would seem from reading labor history. The classic four-volume history of American labor edited by John Commons, America's foremost labor historian, explains: "The picture of self-centered craft unions, callous to the plight of the helpless groups, is greatly overdrawn and based on extreme instances. It is enough to recall the unselfish aid given by the Chicago Teamsters to the struggling garment workers which embroiled them in the disastrous struggle of 1905."[6]

Commons was no AFL apologist. He had identified the problem of phony sympathy strikes as early as 1902: they crowded out genuine strikes in New York. "The friendly employer who hired only union men and also the unfriendly employer," he observed, "were used as clubs to hit the opposing union." Simple graft was now the main motive behind building trades "sympathy strikes."[7]

But it didn't have to be that way, Commons argued.[8] The problem with the AFL model of unionism was exclusivity—the failure to extend the benefits of craft unionism to the unskilled crafts. Commons described how, in Chicago, Teamsters leaders had taken a despised occupation, in which workers labored 80 to 100 hours a week, cut their hours by a third and raised their pay. Unionized Chicago teamsters now made as much as skilled craftsmen. The Chicago example showed how closed shop craft unionism didn't have to remain a monopoly of skilled workers. It could spread to the nonskilled trades. The Chicago Teamsters were now the biggest union in the nation's most unionized city. True, he conceded, the creative process had been messy. For a while, there'd been a corruption problem, he acknowledged. But the reformers were now in charge. Wrote Commons of the Shea-led Teamsters: "Men of integrity and self-respect secure the offices, and the worldly wisdom of the Teamster makes him amenable to reason and fair dealing."[9] "Sympathy strikes," he wrote hopefully, "seem to have been eliminated."[10]

Who was Shea? *Harper's Weekly* described him as "a little rotund person, with a round, heavy face, a keen gray eye, and a rumpled mass of brown hair prematurely shot with white." Shea, thirty-three years old and from Cambridge, Massachusetts, had been arrested a few times for assault—once for beating up his cousin, Margaret Shea.[11]

He was a formidable adversary: quick-witted, imperturbable, eloquent. Shea knew how to turn the funeral of a member killed by a strikebreaker into a great strike rally. In the hot summer of 1905, he led the mourners to Chicago's City Hall, where, standing on a window ledge above the crowd, he delivered a moving oration. Afterward, as Shea drove away in a carriage, members of the crowd pursued his vehicle trying to shake his hand.[12]

Shea was no pushover. He could take a big punch and hang on. Once he discovered that his venture had brought down the organized might of Chicago's most powerful employers, he refused to swing back wildly. He resisted all demands to extend the strike—the clothing workers' demand to widen it to more garment employers and his striking members' demand that he call out the rest of the city's 35,000 Teamsters.

He could counterpunch too. When accused of taking a bribe to start the strike against Montgomery Ward, he didn't just deny the charge. He offered to testify that Montgomery Ward tried to bribe him to stage a walkout against Sears. And when grand jury testimony revealed that he'd been the guest of John Driscoll, head of the truck owners association, at Sparrow Park, an upscale Chicago whorehouse, he threatened to get unionized cab drivers to give him the names of all the Employers Association big shots who patronized the same place.

The most damaging revelation of the June grand jury testimony was not that Shea was associating with Driscoll's prostitutes but that he was associating with John Driscoll. After Shea admitted to the association, the IBT executive board met in emergency session to consider having him removed. What saved him was that he was leading a strike that threatened the union's survival. To take him down in the middle of the strike was to cede its outcome.

By June 1905, Driscoll had become a pariah in both the labor and business communities. But only a few years earlier, he was the business half of one of the most remarkable teams in the history of industrial relations: Driscoll, head of the Coal Team Owners Association, and Al Young, boss of the Coal Teamsters Union. They were Chicago's coal dust twins. It was by staking out a spot next to the main bridge across the Chicago River that Al Young had founded his local. Coal wagons had to cross this spot. When they did, Young had non-union drivers knocked off their wagons.[13] Of Young it was said, "When he pulls up, the city stops short. No coal moves from railroad to boiler room. Nothing moves."[14]

The industrial relations script called for Driscoll and Young to act out their parts as eternal enemies. But instead, by practicing the subtle arts of cooperation in lieu of the militant tactics of class struggle, they became, briefly, the industrial arbiters of the city. They met daily in a dingy Dearborn Street office and planned how to crush competitors and wipe out scabs. They even dared to target the city's greatest merchant prince, Marshall Field. Field had been humbled by the duo, who forced him to rip gas pipes out of his stores and replace gas heating with coal.

Field was outraged. If Driscoll and Young weren't stopped, he thundered, it would spell doom for Chicago's prosperity. But working Teamsters had to love the odd couple. Before Young and Driscoll, Chicago teamsters typically worked seven days a week, 80 to 100 hours. In the first year that Driscoll and Young teamed up, they were able to raise wages 20 percent. In the second, they doubled wages. Some members of the Chicago Teamsters, the beer truck drivers, would soon be making as much as $35 a week, when the average income for American workers was less than $10 a week. At the same time, the union was able to cut hours so that members were working a six-day week. Then Young and Driscoll did the same thing for teamster helpers.[15]

Swollen with success, Driscoll grew bolder and less imaginative. He used Young to play the timeworn good cop–bad cop act once too often. Driscoll would ask Young to threaten a sympathy strike, and then he'd step in with an offer to mediate the strike. The levelheaded Driscoll would persuade the hotheaded Young to call it off. What took the team owners so long to get wise to this simple and transparent routine? They weren't stupid. It's just that they had no real interest in bringing Driscoll, their representative, to heel. Who, after all, was really being hurt by this routine? Not the team owners. They simply passed on their increased labor costs to their big customers—the Marshall Fields and the Wards. For the coal team owners, who hired drivers for their horse-drawn teams, Driscoll was a bonanza. Without his tactics, they wouldn't have contracts with the biggest corporate customers in the city.

At first, the team owners' customers were grateful for the chance to get the job actions canceled. After a while, though, they realized they were being set up. Marshall Field and Montgomery Ward, who had initially encouraged Driscoll to create the Associated Teaming Interests, turned hostile. It was probably because of pressure from their big customers that the team owners fired Driscoll.

Meanwhile, Young was having more success in national union politics. He was trying to leverage his control over his Chicago Teamsters—the largest teamsters organization in the country—into control of the Teamsters nationwide. Before they joined forces in 1903, there were two competing Teamsters internationals. Young controlled the smaller one, the Teamsters' International Union. When he quietly hooked up with Shea, who had a strong base in the Boston local of the larger rival, the IBT was born, with Young as the kingmaker and Shea as the general president.[16]

Once in national office, Shea presided over the early mushrooming growth of the Teamsters: 821 locals in over 300 cities by the time of the great Chicago strike. Having more to lose and sensing a new mood of confrontation among employers, Shea asked the delegates at the first IBT convention in 1904 to draw back from promiscuous use of the sympathy strike.[17] The impetuous members, he noted, naturally tended to sympathize with their trade union brothers. But sympathy strikes had given the union a bad reputation. He called for and received from the delegates constitutional restrictions on sympathy strikes.[18]

Shea also seemed to be acting cautiously in December 1904, when he was asked by the United Garment Workers to support their strike. They were in a losing battle over the closed shop with the thirty-eight-member National Wholesale Tailors Association. The employers had replaced their 10,000 tailors with strikebreakers in November. That's when a sympathy strike would have been decisive, but Shea turned the UGW down. While the garment union continued to list the strike as ongoing, it wasn't having any effect on the employers.[19]

What caused Shea's reversal in April 1905? On the merits, it's hard to tell. A Teamsters strike could have hurt Ward's—they had a large mail-order business that relied on delivery trucks. But the big department store employed only seventeen garment workers. How would a Teamsters strike pressure the employers of the nearly 10,000 remaining garment workers unless the Teamsters spread the strike to the big employers—which Shea absolutely refused to do? "It is true," said the UGW's Robert Noren just before resigning from the Montgomery Ward strike committee, "that we are gaining nothing from a fight which ostensibly is in support of our cause."[20]

It was Noren, testified Young, who had convened a crucial April 6 meeting at the Chicago Stock Exchange Saloon. A day before the start of the Teamsters' job action against Ward's, Noren had invited Shea, Young, and two other Teamsters local presidents. Noren called them together for two reasons: first, to plan the Ward's sympathy strike, and second, to divide up $1,500 in bribe money he'd brought with him. Young described how Shea "chuckled" when his share of the money was placed in his hands. According to Young, Shea said "it felt so good" that he gave Noren back $20 of his share.

"What happened the next morning?" asked the prosecutor.

"We called out the Teamsters on Montgomery Ward Co."

"Did you say anything to Shea regarding the advisability of calling out the drivers?"

"Yes, I told him I believed he had made a mistake in calling the strike because it had not been called in accordance with the laws of the IBT. It takes a two-thirds vote of the local union to inaugurate a strike and it must be also referred to a joint council and sustained by a two-thirds vote there."

"What did Shea say then?"

"He said, 'To hell with the laws.'"

Young's evidence failed to convict Shea on conspiracy charges. His hostility toward the defendant was too obvious. But his testimony brought out some uncontested facts that can help make sense of Shea's otherwise contradictory behavior.

It was a fact that Shea had pushed successfully to make sympathy strikes unconstitutional.

Why first make sympathy strikes illegal and then carry one out? One plausible reason was to make sure that genuine, freely given solidarity was legally impossible. That way he could sell his ersatz brand. Employers want to know who can turn strikes on and off. To the extent that workers made their own decisions, Shea would have been superfluous.

Actually, two Teamsters strikes took place in Chicago in 1905, and neither was a genuine sympathy strike. First there was the April action against Ward's. That was the shakedown strike.

The second strike was an exercise in racial solidarity. But the Teamsters didn't choose that action either. It was more a spontaneous reaction than a deliberated decision. After a few weeks, the Employers Association replaced about 4,000 white, mainly Irish Chicagoans with blacks from St. Louis. The strike quickly turned into a slow-motion race riot, one that revealed two of the principal dimensions of the AFL protection system. It wasn't just that union leaders protected the bosses from the members. The corrupt mandate of the leaders rested in large part on the protection they provided members from the competition of non-union workers—at first chiefly eastern and southern European immigrants, and then, increasingly, blacks.

The introduction of black team drivers enraged the whole South Side Irish community, where the main truck barns were located. Thousands would get up early to watch the police escort several hundred blacks to work. "Scab-herding" was the *Tribune*'s caption. It wasn't unusual for mobs of 1,000 to 1,500 to chase a scab truck as it rolled down urban canyons. The scenario resembled episodes in Western movies where the stagecoach traveling through the gulch would try to run a gauntlet of bushwhackers. Strike sympathizers led by union teamsters would surround and attack a single truck. The point was to free the horses, destroy the load, and punish the scabs. But the black strikebreakers, armed with rifles and deputized as city marshals, were no easy mark for the mobs.

Violence peaked on May Day, when gunshots, brickbats, knives, and paving stones killed one and injured over 100 people.

By mid-May, the battle had been redefined. First the strike had lost its sympathetic character when the garment workers pulled out. Then it lost its class character as the fear of blacks taking their jobs swamped all the strikers' other concerns. The widely anticipated arrival of Samuel Gompers on May 17 to arbitrate the strike was pushed into the background by the shooting the same day of an eight-year-old white boy.

A black strikebreaker wearing a deputy sheriff's star killed the boy in front of his home in the Back of the Yards neighborhood. At 6:15 p.m., about twenty children had gathered to harass two blacks who had just gotten off work at Peabody Coal Yards. According to eyewitnesses, the men at first ignored the children's taunts, but suddenly they wheeled and drew revolvers. The children scattered as the men opened fire. Eight-year-old Enoch Carlson was hit in the side and fell, mortally wounded. A white neighbor saw the shooting and called for help. Almost immediately, a crowd of armed whites was pursuing the blacks. "The Negroes turned about several times," a witness reported, "but evidently were in a panic and resumed their flight." Aided by a white shopkeeper who thought they were riot victims, the two escaped through a yard after the shopkeeper locked the gate behind them. The frustrated white mob gathered with ropes, ready to lynch any blacks in the vicinity. Chicago police soon arrived to protect "unoffending negroes." Authorities later apprehended the black strikebreakers from Peabody Coal.

Ultimately, the settlement of the strike turned on what to do about the black strikebreakers. A courtroom colloquy between Shea and Mayer Levy, the attorney for the Employers at the peak of the strike violence, illustrates how the terms of engagement had been transformed:

"You have been importing Negroes by the hundred—do you mean to say you refuse to discharge Negroes and reinstate the old men, white men?" Shea shouted.

"So long as a teamster in present employ behaves himself and does his work he will not be discharged, be he black or white," replied Levy.

"That is an outrageous stand," said Shea. "You have brought these Negroes in here to fight us, and we answer that we have the right to attack them wherever found."

"Then do so at your peril," answered Levy. "These black men breathe the same air and spring from the same divinity as you."[21]

Neither Shea nor his turn-of-the-century Chicago Teamsters had a monopoly on racial hatred. The pro-employer *Chicago Tribune* ran vicious anti-union cartoons on its front page but couldn't resist attempts at racial humor. Under a half-page headline, "How to Break up the Strike Breakers," the *Tribune* cartoonist depicted a wagonload of apelike blacks wearing derby hats. They were shown leaping off a wagon simultaneously in order to grab slices of watermelon brought to them by "union pickets." In another issue, a photo portrait of an African American strikebreaker ran under a caption, "A Typical 'Black Beauty' from St. Louis." Under the subhead, "Head Harder than Brick," the paper claimed that a black strikebreaker was struck on the head by a rock thrown off a building that chipped a piece off the sidewalk. The Negro scratched his head a second, cast a glance upward and remarked, "Something 'pars to be flying round heah."

Racial hostility was palpable at every level of Chicago society. Was Shea wrong to insist that employers had inflamed racial sensibilities by bringing in black strikebreakers? Attorney Levy talked piously about each man being a child of God. But surely he must have realized that violence would break out, just as it always did, and would discredit the strikers.

Employers brutally exploited the opportunity that the AFL system created. The closed shop wasn't just closed against non-union workers. Depending on the union, it was closed against particular ethnic and racial groups—and, of course, women. And naturally so. How could a system based on personal loyalty not be discriminatory? Racial ties reinforced family and ethnic loyalties. Not only were Jews, women, and eastern and southern Europeans generally excluded from the construction trades, they couldn't get into the UGW either. Blacks, of course, couldn't get into the Teamsters.

No wonder the African American strikebreakers weren't exactly crippled with ambivalence at having to fire at the Irish American trade unionists. As former Wobbly and Communist Party founder William Z. Foster observed of blacks in the great steel strike right after World War I, "Most of them seemed to take keen delight in stealing the white man's jobs and crushing their strike."[22] Like the fierce Gurkhas assisting the British in colonial India, black workers made highly motivated, militant scabs in multiethnic Chicago. Had the Teamsters opened up their unions to blacks, they would have deprived the employers of this divisive weapon.

By 1905 the Teamsters were well on their way to becoming the most corrupt force in American trade unionism. They just needed to bulk up their membership—which they began to do in the 1930s. What ever happened, though, to Con Shea? After he was finally ousted from the IBT in 1907, Shea stayed in Chicago and returned to his earlier vocation as a bomber. After a long absence, he turned up on the front pages in 1921, indicted this time for killing a policeman and setting off bombs in Chicago's construction wars.

By the 1920s, bombing had become more than just a sideline for Shea. He was an active, if very senior, figure in Chicago's booming contract bombing field. According to the 1929 Report of the Illinois Crime Survey, Shea was a member of James Sweeney's gang. Sweeney's people hung out at Harrison and Halstead Streets, not far from the scene of the great 1905 riots. Union business agents were their primary clients. But Sweeney & Co. were, as the report puts it, "in the bombing business." Along with bombing went slugging: "Shea and another man bombed the Schreiber Laundry and had also received a list of twenty-five persons in all parts of the city to be slugged."[23]

In one of Shea's last public appearances, in 1924, he was identified as a labor leader at a testimonial dinner for the top Chicago mobster, Dion O'Bannion. The remnants of the O'Bannion gang, merged into Tommy Moran's crew, would be almost entirely wiped out by Al Capone in the St. Valentine's Day massacre. But that night, almost the entire North Side gang was there to present O'Bannion with a platinum watch encrusted with diamonds. Shea, who was serving as secretary of the Chicago Theater and Janitors Union, sat beside Louis "Two Gun" Alterie, the president.[24] Alterie's entry in the *World Encyclopedia of Organized Crime* credits him with inventing the machine gun ambush. Unfortunately for Alterie, he would get the same treatment himself from the Capone gang, dying in a volley of bullets in front of his Chicago apartment.[25] But Shea, his trade union colleague, died peacefully in his bed after an operation for gallstones.[26]

It was 1929: the dawn of the Capone era and twilight for union leaders who could act without Scarface's approval. It would not begin peacefully. But it would end in a kind of order.

PART 3

Corrupt Unions—A Contemporary Survey

CHAPTER SEVEN

Totally Mobbed Up

DAILY LIFE IN THE LABORERS UNION

THE DEATH OF AN UNKNOWN SOLDIER

When sixty-eight-year-old Gaspar Lupo died in the late spring of 1989, it marked the end of two meticulously intertwined careers: one open, the other secret. In his public calling, Lupo had served for more than two decades as the president of the New York Mason Tenders District Council, the umbrella organization for a dozen locals and 10,000 laborers in the five boroughs and Long Island. He'd operated at the highest circles of the New York labor movement, earning nearly $400,000 a year; the state AFL-CIO elected him a vice president, and he served on the executive board of the New York City Central Labor Council.

It was Lupo's hidden calling, though, that explained his eminence in organized labor: Gaspar Lupo was a made member of the Genovese crime family, the largest, most powerful criminal organization in the United States.[1] As president of the Mason Tenders District Council, Lupo was elected by delegates from the locals. With one exception, the locals were all run by New York City crime families. The Gambinos ran one local and the Luccheses three, but the Genoveses controlled all the rest, so the majority mob ruled.

The Mason Tenders perform the hardest, most dangerous jobs in the building industry: removing asbestos, demolition, and doing grunt work for plasterers and masons. They make anywhere from $30 to $43 an hour plus substantial benefits.[2] But because laborers are comparatively unskilled, they're highly vulnerable to being replaced by non-union laborers, who may earn as little as $8.50 an hour for the same work.

This is where Lupo and his *goombata* came in. Officially, it was their job to enforce the contract, protecting the members from employers who would otherwise hire $8.50-an-hour workers. Unofficially, though, Lupo & Co. made sure the employers could hire all the low-wage, non-union workers they wanted, in exchange for bribes. It was a service officials claimed to be proud of. "Have we screwed the worker?" an attorney for one of the Mason Tenders locals asked rhetorically when confronted by an accusatory reporter. "Some schnook who can't read or write gets a job at $10 an hour? Hey, we made him a person."[3]

In criminological circles, the Genovese crime family is known for the discipline and discretion it imposes on its members. All his life, Lupo lived on the down-low as an obedient Genovese soldier. He avoided publicity. His typical attire—rep tie, pastel jacket, and dark slacks—made him look more like a typical senior citizen than a wiseguy; there were no pinkie rings on his thick, stubby fingers. He followed the rules and took orders—even from much younger men. His obedience caused more thuggish mobsters to laugh at him behind his back. "Gaspar's a good, good man. He'll do anything I tell him," boasted James Messera, the Genovese capo to whom Lupo reported. "Anything, I mean anything. I don't give a fuck if I tell him to jump off the roof, he'll jump from the fucking building."[4]

In public, of course, Lupo gave the orders. Every five years, someone on the Mason Tenders' Genovese-controlled executive board would move to nominate, second, and reelect Lupo. It was the same ritual that had been practiced in the 1920s when Lupo's father-in-law, Charles Graziano, presided over the Mason Tenders.

The locals were just miniature versions of the district council—each, it seemed, had its reigning family. In Local 66 on Long Island, there was the famous Vario family—Paulie Vario was "Paulie Cicero" in Martin Scorsese's *Goodfellas* (played by Paul Sorvino). In Manhattan, there was the Giardina family, who ran Local 23 for the Gambinos. There were two branches of the Pagano family, both affiliated with the Genoveses; one ran Local 59, the other Local 104.[5] Mostly they'd been around for generations.

But within five years of Lupo's death, largely because of his successors' flamboyant lack of Genovese discipline, the extraordinary enterprise that the family had built up over three quarters of a century would be shaken to its foundations. Federal authorities charged more than twenty officials with labor racketeering. Lupo's oldest son would go to jail. The government would take over the union, wipe out the Genovese locals, and create fewer, larger locals, which would in theory be less vulnerable to Mafia control. Dozens of made guys and associates who'd battened on the payroll were banned for life. For the city's crime families, it would take years to recoup even a portion of their former influence—and income.

Meanwhile, ongoing court proceedings exhumed family secrets about the district council and the individual locals—how mob-connected officials enriched their non-union construction companies; how they carried out their pension fund scams; and how their awards of health care contracts to obvious quacks destroyed the health funds. It added up, investigators claimed, to perhaps the biggest fund rip-off in labor history.

But the total sums—estimated at over $65 million—were soon dwarfed by scandals in several other construction unions. Plumbers officials, for example, would be charged with misappropriating four times that amount.[6] There was certainly nothing new in running a labor peace racket, however comprehensive. The novelty lay not so much in what was done, or even in who was doing it—mob influence prevails in most New York City construction trades—but in the matter of degree.[7] The Mason Tenders were totally mobbed up. Union governance was simply a matter of mob protocols. All decisions of consequence were made not by union leaders in the Mason Tenders headquarters on Eighteenth Street but by a Genovese capo in the family clubhouse on Mott Street. Ultimately, though, what the revelations added up to was that the Laborers in New York City faithfully mirrored the history and operation of the parent union, the 800,000-member Laborers International Union of North America (LIUNA).

In the Laborers, a century-long tradition of corruption had transformed the casual nepotism of the labor movement into a rigid, almost pharaonic dynastic system. Mob guys didn't have to marry their sisters or undergo ritual mummification, but they maintained a similar ancestor cult for similar reasons—the promotion of loyalty, stability, and trust. And even if they've still got a long way to go to rival the 2,500-year span of the Old, Middle, and New Kingdoms, they've also managed to parlay inherited office into life-and-death control over their subjects.

LIUNA was probably the first U.S. union to come under the control of organized crime, and for more than a century, precedent and practice, custom and mores have maintained the most direct and most complete

Mafia rule over a union anywhere in America and probably anywhere in the advanced industrialized world. The Laborers thus serve as an archetype of what's wrong with the domestic labor movement, and the New York Mason Tenders are a faithful embodiment of the type whose dimensions have been made unusually clear by the marvels of electronic surveillance.

How can it really be said, though, that the Laborers are even more mob-dominated than the Teamsters or the Longshoremen or the Hotel and Restaurant Workers Union? All four AFL-CIO unions were identified in the president's 1986 Crime Commission Report as the most mobbed up in America.[8] What's so special about the Laborers?

Fewer degrees of separation. Compare, for example, the government's 1988 RICO (Racketeer Influenced and Corrupt Organization Act) case against the Teamsters with its 1993 draft complaint against LIUNA.[9] In the Teamsters, only a dozen out of about 2,500 locals were charged with being run by actual members of organized crime.[10] Most were crime family associates—union officials who weren't formally inducted into the mob but who owed their positions to mob backing and who reciprocated by taking mob orders and sharing bribes, kickbacks, extortion fees, and benefit fund loot.

In the Laborers, though, it was far more common for the head of the local or a district council to be a made guy—like Gaspar Lupo, who actually went through the traditional Mafia ceremony, where you swear allegiance for life and they burn the saint's picture in your hand. In several cities the head of the local Laborers union was actually the *head* of the local crime family. Like the pharaoh, who wore two crowns—red and white, symbolizing two kingdoms—John Riggi, the New Jersey boss of the DeCavalcante family, was also the business manager of LIUNA Local 394 in Elizabeth.[11] In 2003, Riggi—already in prison on extortion charges—pleaded guilty to the murder of Fred Weiss, a Staten Island contractor. The murder was a favor, Riggi testified, to John Gotti of the Gambino crime family. Gotti feared the contractor might cooperate with law enforcement. "I and the others met and we agreed Fred Weiss should be murdered," Riggi explained. "Pursuant to that agreement, Fred Weiss was murdered. That's it."[12]

Riggi had paid the price of wearing the dual crown. Serving as the head of a major labor organization had raised his public profile. But in taking more risks, he had reaped more rewards: the fewer people between you and the swag, the more there is to earn. Besides, why waste all those six-figure union official salaries on people who aren't even in the family?

THE OLD KINGDOM

Francis Ford Coppola, director of *The Godfather*, says he modeled Vito Corleone in large part on Vito Genovese, founder of the Genovese crime family. To understand Vito Corleone and his enterprise in New York, Coppola takes us back to Corleone, Sicily. But to grasp the malignant dimensions of the present-day Genovese influence in the New York Laborers and the union as a whole requires a double flashback, first to Italy and then to Chicago.

The Laborers are the most mobbed-up union in America mostly because they've been mobbed up the longest. Not only the tradition of force but the force of tradition combine to repel countervailing influences. It wasn't until the 1920s, the muscling-in era, that unions all across America came under the control of organized crime. But in the Laborers, the mob had almost a generation's head start. In fact, organized crime control over the Chicago locals preceded the foundation of the international union itself.

But Chicago has to be seen against the background of southern Italian immigrant tradition and Sicilian labor racketeering. The Old World racketeering system wasn't transplanted directly or all at once to America.[13] It proceeded in stages, starting with immigrant laborers trapped in the padrone system. In the late nineteenth century, Italian immigrants from southern Italy paid exorbitant commissions to better-established Italian American immigrant labor bosses in exchange for work. The contractors paid the padrone, and the padrone, after taking a hefty cut—the *pizzu*—paid the worker. Essentially it was a kind of peonage,[14] but with a typically American twist in which successful peons sometimes wound up as padrones. And the most successful padrones sometimes ended up as pioneer crime syndicate bosses.

It was a former padrone who became the patron saint of organized crime in Chicago and the founder of the Chicago Laborers union.[15] Al Capone gets too much credit. He simply added, by violent means, to a trade union empire that had been built from scratch in the Laborers by James "Big Jim" Colosimo. A generation before Capone, even before the 1903 creation of the Laborers as an international union, Colosimo had become the principal force in the Laborers. As a young pimp, he'd married a middle-aged madam and gone on to control a chain of South Side whorehouses. Colosimo later established Chicago's first Italian American crime syndicate—but it was his founding of the Laborers union in Chicago that made him a different kind of crook.

Colosimo created the Chicago Street Sweepers and Street Repairs Union: the "White Wings," so called because of their white uniforms. Controlling the White Wing votes gave Colosimo leverage over the Chicago South Side Democratic Party machine, which in turn favored his members—and his hookers. It was the first fiefdom in what would be Colosimo's steadily expanding trade union domain, consisting mostly of pick-and-shovel laborers' locals, employing mainly Italian American workers.[16]

What made Colosimo such a pioneer in the organized crime field was that he was the first to take over otherwise legal institutions—labor unions—and bring them together with illegal operations in whorehouses, liquor, and gambling to create an integrated, citywide crime conglomerate. Wider territories gave Big Jim the power to hire more shooters, bribe more politicians, and out-intimidate his rivals.

Colosimo did so well he was able to turn over the day-to-day affairs of the local unions to younger subordinates. The White Wings, he awarded to his bodyguard, "Dago Mike" Carozzo. Although Dago Mike had once been indicted for murder, it scarcely slowed his ascent in the American labor movement. He wound up running over two dozen mob Laborers locals in Chicago. By the 1920s, Carozzo was a fixture on the executive board of the AFL. He joined another Italian American Laborers official from Chicago, "Diamond Joe" Esposito, head of Sewer and Tunnel Workers Local 2. Like Carozzo, Esposito had also been indicted for murder without any damaging vocational effects. Like Colosimo, he'd also been a padrone. But Diamond Joe's reign lasted only a few years. It was cut short, allegedly on orders from Al Capone. Fifty-eight garlic-tipped bullets were found in Esposito's body.

In the 1920s, Chicago led the nation in elaborate and closely watched gangster funerals. The meticulously organized last rites became the simplest way to grasp the politics of union succession: just observe who buried whom. In 1921, when a young local Laborers leader, Joe Moreschi, appeared as one of the six pallbearers at the funeral of the Sicilian Mafia boss of Chicago, it was a reliable sign of future eminence.[17] Sure enough, in 1926, Moreschi became the first mob-controlled president of the International Laborers and Hod Carriers Union.[18]

Moreschi would last as long as any of the most tenacious pharaohs in the Old Kingdom. He held on to the ruling position until 1968—forty-two years. During most of his reign, no conventions or elections were held. When he died, at eighty-four, he was replaced by another Chicago dynasty: the Foscos—Peter Fosco (1968–1975) and, after Fosco's death, his son Angelo (1975–1993). The Foscos' continuous rule simply expressed the continuation of mob control in the Chicago Laborers locals. The old White Wings became Local 1001, representing 2,700 sanitation workers. But they're still controlled by Colosimo's descendants—the Outfit—according to a 2004 complaint by a government-sanctioned internal prosecuting attorney.[19] And in 1999, Diamond Joe Esposito's Local 2 was put under trusteeship for alleged mob control.[20]

At last, though, with Angelo Fosco's death in 1993, a real rupture took place—the wresting of the international union from the Chicago mob's control. Practically on his dying day, Fosco was pulled out of bed and ordered by the Chicago Outfit to jet off to a meeting of the LIUNA executive board in Miami. There he was supposed to support the transfer of power to an Outfit-backed successor. He got as far as the lobby of the Bal Harbour Sheraton. Then, as he was being wheeled in on a gurney in a tangled array of tubes and needles, attended by nurses and aides, "he croaked."[21]

Fosco's death allowed the incumbent general secretary-treasurer, the no. 2 official, Arthur Coia Jr., to round up the votes he needed to steal the general presidency away from the Outfit. Coia could afford to risk Chicago's anger because he had the apparent backing—and presumably the protection—of the eastern crime families, principally the Genoveses, who now controlled the international executive board. They had supported his father, Arthur E. Coia, for the no. 2 job, and now they supported the son for the no. 1 position.[22]

Coia Jr. was almost immediately identified by the Justice Department, in a 212-page complaint, as a "mob puppet."[23] Still, he managed to last seven years before the government took him down on felony tax charges.[24] He survived until 2000 by skillfully cultivating Bill Clinton on the one hand and the Genovese-led eastern block of families on the other. Nevertheless, Coia acquired a reputation as a Mafia-busting reformer. Under an unprecedented agreement that allowed him to run the cleanup of his own administration, the Justice Department insisted on getting many scalps, so it was scalps that Coia provided. Mostly, though, they belonged to his Chicago adversaries, not his own eastern supporters.

Coia was particularly careful not to bruise the foreheads of the leadership of the Genoveses' flagship union—the New York Mason Tenders. In 1994, when the feds issued their 214-count racketeering complaint against Lupo et al., it was inevitable that some wiseguys would have to go. But for Coia Jr. to keep control of the Laborers, it was also crucial that many bad guys would have to stay.

It was a testament to his survival skills that Coia Jr. managed, for longer than anyone would have supposed, to maintain two faces. To the government, he appeared as the great scourge of union corruption. To the mob associates and dynastic families who had run the Mason Tenders for generations, he was their indulgent uncle, recommending them for top positions in the new, "reformed" Mason Tenders, and then, when the court monitor dug in his heels, sending the wiseguys off to top administrative jobs with the Laborers' Albany, New York, welfare funds. Displaying both guile and grace under pressure, Coia surmounted a deadly threat to his political base. Never before in more than three-quarters of a century of operation had the mob-controlled New York Mason Tenders faced federal prosecution: how had they finally got caught?

POWER IN THE NEW YORK KINGDOM

Gaspar Lupo's aggressive displays of loyalty may have concealed a streak of independence or just simple common sense. Perhaps it was just nice luck and good timing, but as long as Lupo occupied the top office, the Mason Tenders managed to stay out of major trouble with the criminal justice system. Under Lupo, the number of people allowed to steal from the funds was kept within reasonable bounds. The amounts stolen were never so great as to impair the funds' ability to pay out benefits, and pension thieves didn't advertise their thefts by conspicuous consumption.

Within a year of Lupo's death, capo James Messera was organizing huge rip-offs of the funds that were so blatant that even the Mason Tenders' lawyer, who participated in Lupo's routine rip-off schemes, was afraid to OK them. Eventually, $50 million to $60 million disappeared from pension, health, and annuity funds. Members with AIDS lost their health coverage. Most of the money disappeared in crooked real estate deals. The purchase of the West Eighteenth Street Mason Tenders headquarters building, according to prosecutors at the time, produced one of the biggest thefts in pension fund history.

No sooner had the Eighteenth Street deal gone down than Messera's principal scam partner, a Long Island strip club operator, went out and bought four Mercedes Benzes and a yacht. In 1990, the U.S. attorney for the Southern District indicted Messera and half a dozen members of his crew on unrelated charges. Most of the made guys did time. Messera himself got thirty-nine months. Finally, in 1994, Messera was indicted for his role in the pension fund scam.

Both of Lupo's sons, Frankie and Jimmy, the boys he'd groomed to take over the Mason Tenders after he died, were indicted too. Lupo would get his wish—his sons would follow him as president. But their terms as top union officers would turn out to be little more than brief apprenticeships for prison life.

For a couple of generations at least, criminologists have debated whether or not organized crime might perform some essential social function. Primarily because the FBI was able to bug the Genoveses' clubhouse at 262 Mott Street and because James Messera, the Genovese capo who ran the Mason Tenders, was such a blowhard, we have a clearer idea of what mob guys really do in unions.

Diego Gambetta, an Italian sociologist whose book *The Sicilian Mafia* has become an academic classic, suggests that mafiosi are chiefly in the business of providing protective services. The "men of honor" help stabilize transactions in a world lacking in trust.[25] Less academically trained observers have suggested that the mob is made up primarily of thieves, not genuine businessmen. Probably both are right as far as they go: a principal occupation for the mob is providing protective services for thieves, but stealing on their own account can't be ignored either.

Yet neither the emphasis on protective services nor the focus on thievery captures the key *political* dimension of mob unionism. The mob leaders of the Laborers are some of the most murderous people on the continent. But notwithstanding the muscling-in era of the 1920s and 1930s, the Mafia has been able to capture and maintain control of trade unions less through overt violence than through their mastery of the politics of job trust unionism.

Mob leaders will kill without hesitation whoever seems to constitute a threat, particularly snitches and those who might grab their territory. But ordinary union members don't constitute a threat, so there's no point in worrying about them. Would-be union opponents can't muster much of a following in an institution dominated by the politics of patronage. Members aren't involved in any decisions, so they don't have any information that would be useful to prosecutors.

John Riggi, a DeCavalcante boss who served as head of the Elizabeth, New Jersey, Laborers local, has made this point clear. He's a confessed cold-blooded murderer. But he drew the line at rough stuff against his members. It was unnecessary. When a dissident faction of African Americans began protesting discriminatory hiring practices at a Local 394 meeting, Riggi's dad, the union's former business manager, wanted to go after them. "Don't argue with these guys, Pop," Riggi told his father, according to testimony before the National Labor Relations Board. "I'll hit him in the pocket book where it hurts." The ringleader of the protest wound up working twenty-six hours in two years.[26]

An ordinary non-mob union boss might have applied the same sanction. In fact, there's a lot of overlap: hiring hall favoritism, no-show jobs, spreading around contractor kickbacks to subordinates—how different is the mob union leader's game from the ordinary corrupt trade union leader's? Not very. The aims and the rules aren't all that different. It's just that the mob's game is played at a much higher level. Ultimately, the union political game is not based on issues or programs or on principles of solidarity but on personal loyalties. And the mob knows how to play that game above the rim. For one thing, fear inspires loyalty. Mob guys know how to create closer, more reliable, more proactive social networks. They uphold and revere tradition; they use ritual and kinship organization. They use family institutions to substitute for normal political institutions like open conventions or meetings. A hereditary officialdom requires a closed selection mechanism. The mob funeral has evolved for this purpose.

LUPO'S FUNERAL: A WISEGUY JOB FAIR

In bygone days, mob funerals were decorous extravaganzas. In 1924, at the wake for Dion O'Bannion, a top Chicago gangster, the Chicago Symphony Orchestra played Handel. *Chicago Tribune* reporters described how the body "lay in state" as mourners silently filed by. Then the pallbearers, led by labor racketeer Maxie Eisen, president of the Kosher Meat Peddlers Association, bore the casket to the hearse.[27]

Nowadays mob funerals are more utilitarian and less liturgical, and more like rowdy job fairs than ceremonies of last respect. Retainers jostle each other for better positions and more lucrative contracts; loud arguments break out over rights of succession and threaten to drown out the organ music.

At the funeral of Arthur Coia Sr., in Providence, Rhode Island, in 1993, Coia Jr., the Laborers' newly selected general president, complained about two thick-necked mourners who arrived from Chicago. At full volume, they threatened trouble if Coia didn't return LIUNA to the hands of those who owned it. A generation before, it had been the Chicago mob that enforced funeral discipline. At Peter Fosco Sr.'s 1975 funeral, Terence J. O'Sullivan, the father of the reigning LIUNA president, was forced into early retirement as punishment for disrupting the proceedings with his importunate demands for higher office. Similar threats and barely suppressed violence marked Gaspar Lupo's final hours above ground.

Frankie Lupo, Gaspar's oldest son at forty-five, stood next in the Lupo line of succession for the $391,000-a-year president's job. He complained about the buzzing crowd of favor-seeking retainers at Vernon C. Wagner's two-room funeral parlor in Hicksville, Long Island. In one room lay the body and the principal mourners. In the other, recalled Frankie Lupo, "there were all these officials having loud conversations. You go to your father's funeral and you've got some person that doesn't even have the respect to wait till the funeral's over to talk about jobs."[28]

But Frankie Lupo himself turned out to be the biggest favor seeker at his father's funeral. Not only did he want the top job for himself, he wanted his brother Jimmy to get the no. 2 job.

At least that's how Genovese boss James Messera remembered it. "Now at the funeral the first day I was there," Messera recounted a few weeks later, "Frankie [Lupo] was there. And I told Frankie, 'You got the number one position there.' He says, 'Can I put my brother there?'" Frankie was asking for the two top Mason Tenders positions—president for himself and business manager for his brother. His father had held them both. Besides the salaries, whoever got the positions could serve as a pension and benefit fund trustee.

Messera claimed he wanted to divide the patronage plums more evenly. "'You know,' I says, 'Frankie, I want to put Baldo [Mule], give him a shot. He'll retire in six and a half years. . . . Let him retire with a little dignity out of this fucking joint. Your brother ain't ready for it yet.'" Frankie's brother Jimmy was eight years younger. Baldo Mule was the fifty-seven-year-old son-in-law of Joe "Lefty" Loiacono, Messera's predecessor as Genovese captain in charge of the District Council.

Mule was almost family. He was an adult. And Frankie Lupo, no roof-jumper like his father, needed supervision. Putting Mule in one of the top two Mason Tenders positions, as Messera explained to a family member, would mean a pair of ears at the top reporting back directly to the family. At the same time, Mule's ascension would mean less independence for Frankie Lupo, who was an associate, not a trusted member of the family like his father.[29]

It was obvious that what was at stake in the arguments at the funeral was power—above all power to award jobs and take bribes as well as to control $200 million in pension funds. But Lupo and Messera talked around the main issue, speaking in terms of legitimacy and respect.

"You know, my family always had the number one [and] number two position," Messera recalled Frankie Lupo saying, "My father held the positions until later on in years he brought me in."

"Well you ain't going to hold two positions," shot back Messera.

"Please Jimmy," said Frankie, "I won't get no respect in that joint. Fifty years, a member of this family held the one and two spots. Besides, I know my father would want it this way."

Messera disputed the old man's intention. "Gaspar," he recalled, "had no fucking use for that kid [Jimmy Lupo]." He "treated him like a jerk-off." Lupo never brought Jimmy along when they would eat together. Still, Messera decided to be generous and grant Frankie's wish. "All right Frankie, if it means that fucking much, all right."

The real lines of authority in the Mason Tenders weren't on paper. The actual headquarters of the union at the time wasn't on Thirty-seventh and Park Avenue South. It was at 262 Mott Street in Jimmy Messera's social club. Messera didn't appreciate the comments of Nino Lanza, who had taken sides at the funeral with the Lupos and even told Messera he should restrain his generosity toward his associates. "Do me a favor," Messera said. "Tell this fucking Nino we'll make the decisions here, not him. Lou [Casciano] and Al's [Soussi] getting a raise. Give them the fucking cars I think they should get. Get a nice Oldsmobile or get a nice Buick. Whatever the fuck he's looking for. You know, one of these sporty-looking motherfuckers. I just said to Frankie, 'He's getting a fucking raise and he'll get any fucking car he wants. And give that fucking message to Nino.'"

The night after Lupo's funeral, the recollection of Lanza's insubordination ate away at Messera. "I didn't sleep a wink," he complained. "I was walking the fucking floor." Messera decided to give Frankie Lupo something to think about too. He ordered a subordinate to call Lupo. "Tell him his fucking brother ain't got the number two spot. Baldo got number two. And tell your brother because of that loudmouth motherfucker [Sal Lanza, Nino's brother] he ain't got number two spot."[30]

Later Messera would explain his concerns about Gaspar Lupo's son Frankie to a member of his crew. "If I gotta worry about . . . his son fuckin' me, then he ain't gonna last. He won't be there five minutes. I don't give a fuck if it's Lupo's son. I'll take this motherfucker down in one second and he won't be there anymore."

WHICH SIDE ARE THEY ON?

The Mason Tenders tapes show that while Messera didn't have the total control he boasted of, it was only because other factions in the Genovese crime family had to be taken into account. Evidently, the Genoveses had the power. What did they do with it?

Despite America's longtime obsession with the Mafia, it's still not at all clear what the members actually do—besides practice colorful rituals, talk dirty, and whack people—especially in unions, which have been among their most important businesses. "It's our job to run the unions," Gambino boss Big Paul Castellano once observed in an FBI-recorded lecture. Mobsters are frequently charged with "labor racketeering"—but what's the racket? Evidently, the mob doesn't work *pro bono*. But *cui bono*? There are only two sides in a market transaction. The buyer—the boss—and the seller—the worker. Where does the mob put its leverage?

On questions of this sort, scholars connected with academic labor studies programs have practiced an *omertà* rivaling the Mafia's own.[31] Lawyers and prosecutors have been less reticent. But their concern is chiefly with law enforcement, not with the union as an institution in civil society. Hollywood has provided only a bit more illumination. The classic modern mob movies—Coppola's *Godfather* series and Scorsese's *Goodfellas* and *Casino*—ignore mob unionism. Elia Kazan's *On the Waterfront*, made over half a century ago, gives us a sidelong glance via longshore leader Johnny Friendly—smooth, brutal, and inhuman. Obviously he's with management; he wears an overcoat, like the ship owners, not a bomber jacket, like the members. He has thugs to beat and kill informers who threaten his rackets with the ship owners. But it's not really clear what the rackets are. A Hollywood close-up of labor racketeering, like full-frontal male nudity, remains beyond the pale.

But the Mason Tenders case brings the mob's presence in unions into clearer focus. In the New York Mason Tenders, mobsters were charged with a huge number of racketeering acts—the 1994 RICO complaint itemizes over two hundred, and for each act, there might be as many as forty or fifty counts. The overwhelming majority are for bribery: taking money from contractors to avoid payment of union wages or benefits, or both, or maybe just ignoring overtime.

The bribes at the shop steward level from subcontractors for allowing non-union labor on a particular site ranged from $250 to $1,000.[32] Local officers who controlled larger jurisdictions could nick subcontractors for a lot more: $1,000 to $4,000 for the same thing—the use of cheap non-union labor. Higher up the hierarchy, though, the Mason Tenders "field representatives"—all "connected"—who were supposed to patrol construction sites to make sure contractors paid their contributions to the funds, actually earned more substantial sums by letting them ignore or discount the payments.

The complaint didn't include a single count for extortion. The absence of extortion charges against what may have been the most mobbed-up union in America is notable, especially given what mob-involved contractors have customarily claimed when they are indicted—that they were extorted. Going back to Thomas Dewey's 1937 prosecution of the Dutch Schultz restaurant racket, the classic employers' defense has been that they paid money to mobsters only because they were afraid. It's true that it's often hard to distinguish between a bribe and extortion. Ultimately, though, the distinction turns on whether you get a real service for your money. Are they avoiding an additional cost or acquiring a significant benefit? In the restaurant racket case, the jury thought there was a benefit. The ten defendants, union leaders and restaurant owners alike, were pronounced guilty on all counts.

Calling strikes and then demanding bribes to call them off is the classic shakedown threat. Bosses pay just to avoid the greater cost of a strike. That didn't happen in the Mason Tenders. And on the basis of available evidence, such naked extortion may be on the way out. The mob seems to be more solicitous nowadays of its contractor clients. In the case of one contractor who paid the Gambinos to have a job action called off, it turned out that Mason Tenders Local 23's Louie Giardina couldn't deliver. The contractor who paid $50,000 and got no relief felt cheated and threatened to go to the district attorney, but instead of getting whacked, he got a full refund and an apology.[33]

For the Mafia, pension fund pilfering may represent the canoli of labor racketeering, but bribery is the everyday pasta. If most of what ordinary unionism is about is getting and enforcing contracts, most of what mob unionism is about is undermining contracts. Instead of making sure that the contractors live up to the contract, mobsters make sure that the contractors are all paid up for the right not to have to live up to them.[34]

One dialogue that took place in 1989 in Little Italy is a virtual one-act play illustrating how the natural impulses of the legitimate trade unionist to uphold the contract are thwarted by mob control. The two characters are real: Al is Al Soussi, one of the Genoveses' "field reps" at the Mason Tenders District Council. The job of the field rep is to enforce the contract—to make sure that the wages and benefits called for in the contract are being paid to the members. Carl is an ordinary laborer in the Mason Tenders. He wants to help the union by calling in the name of a non-union company. Al is furious because the non-union company belongs to him.

> Carl: I give him the name of the company. He goes, 'No, it's not union,
>   but we're gonna get it unionized in a couple of days' . . .
> Al: What was the name of the company?
> Carl: D-E-P, something like that.
> Al : D-E-P's my company, you cocksucker, what're you crazy?
> Carl: No.
> Al: Yeah, that's my company. Yeah, yeah, yeah, D-E-P, yeah, yeah, I got
>   the shake on 'em. What're you interferin' it?
> Carl: No, I called—
> Al : (Yelling) Yeah, yeah, you called the delegate on me! Now what?
> Carl: It's on Seventy-sixth . . .
> Al: Yeah, now what? Now what d'ya do, now that you ratted on me?
> Carl: How do I know?
> Al: (Shouting) Why didn't you keep your fuckin' mouth shut?[35]

Whatever the Mafia's origins as "primitive rebels," today's mobsters in the labor movement are no populists.[36] Clearly, a big reason why mafiosi tend to side with the bosses instead of the members is that they *are* the bosses. A mob-dominated union is no more than a particularly virulent form of employer-dominated union.

PENSION FUND LOOTING FOR DUMMIES

As the union's trustees, the Genoveses could be trusted to skim the benefit funds and steal the pension money. Welfare annuity and benefit fund money turns over much more quickly than the money in pension funds. With benefit funds, the main focus is on kickbacks. Benefit fund vendors pay for the right to overcharge for real or bogus services. The truly grand larceny goes on in the pension funds, which are required to have large reserves. In the New York Mason Tenders, the pension fund's total stood at over $250 million worth of assets. Gaspar Lupo once confided to an undercover informant that he had about $150 million he could move into phony real estate deals.[37]

Given those sums, it was understandable that along with the succession question, the most avid discussions in the bereavement room at the Hicksville funeral parlor involved plans for stealing from the pension fund. Messera tells Frankie Lupo about some real estate properties that he was getting ready to sell to the union. In a deposition, Lupo recalled, "He [Messera] asked me if I could . . . go ahead with the purchases. I told him I'd give it to the lawyers. If everything was okay, there'd be no problem."[38]

Under Messera's direction, the share of funds invested in real estate would more than quadruple to 25 percent of all fund assets. Since nearly all the value was bogus, the pension fund was impaired. The members never really found out what happened to the money. The subsequent leadership of the Mason Tenders—including the business manager and secretary-treasurer who later would resign after being charged in 2004 with misappropriating union funds—told the members that the problem in the fund had been caused by bad investment advice on the purchase of derivative contracts and that the money had been recovered—both totally false.

Stealing from pension funds is a quiet, undramatic crime that is hard to discover and attracts relatively little notice. In 1978, when the Luccheses robbed German airline Lufthansa of $6 million, the theft provided tabloid headlines for weeks. At the time, the heist was the largest successful cash robbery in American history. It would serve as the dramatic armature of Scorsese's *Goodfellas*. But in the 1990s, when the Genoveses were discovered taking out ten times that sum from the Mason Tenders pension fund in real estate swindles, the story created barely a ripple.

It's easy to see why Hollywood chose to portray the robbers rather than the real estate operators. The amount of long-term planning, the split-second timing, and the genuine risk involved in the Lufthansa heist far outstripped what was required to steal the Mason Tenders' money. In the Lufthansa robbery, there was a guard who had to be struck senseless; half a dozen employees who had to be taken unawares and handcuffed; a supervisor who had to be plied with a hooker while his keys were stolen; alarm systems to deactivate; and two technologically challenging vaults to unlock with the duplicated key.

In the case of the Mason Tenders, the custodians of the fund didn't need to be overpowered or deceived by the thieves. They were the thieves.

No one tried to stop Messera from stealing the money—not the lawyers; not the accountants; not the trustees—either from management or the union side; not Nino Lanza, the trust fund administrator; nor his assistant Carlo Melacci. (Although later Melacci, who would eventually provide a deposition for the prosecution, would find bullets whizzing through the windows of his house.)

Messera knew how easy it would be. At the funeral he predicted that on the sale of Brooklyn real estate to the Mason Tenders' pension fund, he would make "close to a million or more, cash."

Gaspar Lupo's death on June 13, 1989, interrupted the scheme. But at the June 19 funeral service, Messera gave Frankie Lupo the instructions needed to keep the plan in operation. Lupo was directed to go to the Wall Street law office of the Mason Tenders' trust fund lawyer, Bill Davis. There he was to meet Genovese associate Ron Micelli. It was from Micelli that the pension fund was expected to buy the overvalued Brooklyn properties.

The point, of course, was to make it seem as if the properties weren't overvalued. For this, it was necessary to reach out to "connected" real estate appraisers. Alfio Di Franco, an Ozone Park realtor and a Genovese associate, explained how the abandoned, decrepit buildings in central

Brooklyn near the Holy Cross Cemetery would soon be worth even more millions than he was estimating: "Real estate in this general area is now coming into its own," he explained in his report to the pension fund trustees, "with values excalaterating [sic] due to the unique structure of the subject."

Satisfied by this analysis, the trustees asked no questions and bought the Brooklyn properties for over $3 million. The plan was to rehabilitate the buildings. But only four months after the purchase, one of the Brooklyn tenements, which was being used as a crack house, collapsed before its anticipated "excalateration" in value.[39]

Four years later, when interviewed by assistant U.S. attorney Alan Taffet, Frankie Lupo seemed at a loss to recall exactly how much he took in bribes from the contractors who were carrying out the rehab job on the Brooklyn properties. "I think it was around—between $100,000 and $130,000, I'm pretty sure."[40] Of course, the passage of four years can erode memory, but an ordinary person would probably remember whether he'd gotten $130,000 or $30,000 less than that. For the median New Yorker, $30,000 is close to a year's income. But for Lupo, who was earning ten times that in salary, perhaps it's understandable how it might all begin to blur—there were so many kickbacks, so many bribes.

Generally, the Mason Tenders real estate swindles were carried out in two phases. First, the trustees would buy a property at inflated value from mob-connected sellers. Then they would renovate the property in order to get kickbacks from the contractors doing the work.

In the Miami real estate scam, where the trustees pretended to be building a home for retired laborers, the real money was made not in phase one but in the bribes collected from the contractors carrying out the renovations. The year before Gaspar Lupo died, the welfare fund had already purchased property for $1.45 million at 6060 Indian Creek Road from Marie Buscemi. "Marie Buscemi" was an alias of Messera's mom.

After some sham negotiations designed to make the eventual purchase price of the Indian Creek Road property seem more legitimate—allegedly attorney Bill Davis's idea—the trustees paid a little over twice the true value.[41] "We knew that the price was inflated high, my father and myself, and we went along with it," admitted Frankie Lupo in his deposition. "Bill Davis knows too, because he's the one who suggested we make it look like we lowered the price, to make it look a little better. In turn, . . . he wanted to be on retainer so he can get his monthly fee, because [he] was the only one [who] had a Florida license, and . . . he subsequently did go on that retainer for years to come."

One reason Davis stayed on retainer for so long was that it turned out Messera's mom didn't actually own the Miami property that the union had bought from her. She lacked a clear title. And Davis forgot to check. "That was another ongoing problem for years," recalled Lupo, "trying to clear up the title." But by spending a few hundred thousand more of the members' money, the fund finally owned the dilapidated hotel on Indian Creek Road.[42]

Now it was time to wreck it and begin the renovation phase of the swindle. The members were told at first that the fund had purchased a hotel in Florida so it could be turned into a retirement home for laborers. Employer trustee Joe Fater began to engage contractors to demolish the structure and a general contractor to build the new Laborers' retirement home. In the renovation phase, the fund spent a total of $18 million. The building was transformed successively from a hotel to a retirement home to a commercial hotel to a hospice, but throughout all these transformations, the appraised value of the property never exceeded $4 million.

In all these transactions, Frankie Lupo and Joe Fater were a model of labor-management cooperation. Sometimes Fater picked up bribes for Lupo. Sometimes Lupo for Fater. "Basically, I would pick up the money and go to Joe's office on Park Avenue," Lupo told the assistant U.S. attorney. "When he collected the money, I'd go up to [his] office and he would give me the money and I would give him what I wanted to give him out of that check."[43]

FLIPPING THE UNION HEADQUARTERS

Frankie Lupo recalls Messera directing him at the funeral to "get together with Ron." Ron Micelli was a forty-two-year-old owner of a Long Island topless nightclub, the Mirage Bar, where the "Girls of Goldfinger" danced. Together Messera and Micelli cooked up a deal on the remodeling of the union's Chelsea headquarters that would make the Brooklyn and Miami scams seem like sound investments.

Union leaders commonly get kickbacks from contractors when they build or remodel their headquarters. The contractors pay the kickbacks because it means they're free to overcharge the union for their work. But the Genovese team managed to wring about $28 million worth of graft out of the project.

Their treasure was an eighty-four-year-old twelve-story vacant loft at 32 West Eighteenth Street. Although the property was not that far from what is now the red-hot Flatiron District, in 1990 the Manhattan real estate market was headed downward, and 32 West Eighteenth Street hadn't had a tenant in four years. Still, Micelli told his lawyer to contact Davis, the Mason Tenders fund lawyer, to prepare documents for the deal. Davis rounded up the usual phony appraisals from the mob-connected real estate guys, who established the building's value at $15.85 million. Twelve months later, a non-connected appraiser found the property to be worth about $8 million. Indeed, the building's owner had just bought it for $7.5 million.

The initial idea was a classic "flip": a purchase at the market price and then a sale for an excessive amount to a party that knowingly allows itself to be bilked—in this case the union. And what a flip it was! Double the purchase price of $8 million. But Messera got greedy.

Instead of having Micelli, who'd been the "developer" of the Brooklyn properties, simply buy the properties and turn around and sell them to the union for double what he paid, Messera insisted that there should be a double flip—or back flip. First Micelli would buy the Chelsea property for $16 million, with the union lending him the money so he could make the purchase. Then, ten months later, Micelli would turn around and sell the building back to the union for $24 million.

According to Frankie Lupo, the size of the fraud scared off Davis. He refused to go ahead, putting Lupo in a tight spot.[44] Lupo wasn't about to tell Messera that the deal had gone bust. "I mean there was . . . no way after I committed myself to these people, Jimmy and Ron," said Lupo, "that I was going to turn around at that point and back out of the deal then."[45]

Frankie Lupo chose to get mad at Davis rather than at Messera, the mob capo who got him into the deal in the first place. "At this point, after telling me everything was fine, now you're telling me we can't do it," he complained to Davis. "I'm not going to tell Jimmy at this point in time that we're not going to go ahead with this."

Understandably, Lupo didn't want to be responsible for taking millions out of the mobster's pocket. Labor-management cooperation to the rescue. Management trustee Joe Fater brought into the deal his own lawyer, who agreed to take over from Davis and prepare the necessary documents. "All I basically did was sign the checks at the very end," explained Frank Lupo. "He [Fater's lawyer] put this whole thing together."

Now that the fund owned the property, phase two of the rip-off—renovations—could begin. Messera's partner, Micelli, chose the renovating contractors. Complained Lupo, "They had no concept of construction 'cause the building was as bad as when we started. Everything was wrong, the codes, everything."

Still, the incompetent contractors did reward Lupo with $150,000 in kickbacks.[46] Along with his $300,000-plus salary, the extra income enabled to Lupo drive a Mercedes and a Lincoln. The members earned an average of $30,000–$35,000, although about 25 percent of them were unemployed at the time.[47]

Altogether, with the renovations and the flips, the trustees had poured $32 million into the Eighteenth Street headquarters. By the mid-1990s, the twelve-story building was appraised at $4 million and had produced no income. In 1998, the trustees sold it for $8 million. The combination of the Miami, Brooklyn, and Eighteenth Street frauds broke the pension fund and as well as the welfare funds, which had also been mobilized by the trustees for the real estate investment program.

TOWARD A NEW MOB KINGDOM?

"As we know, the LCN [La Cosa Nostra] has mutated
and has been restructured. The children of the made
are well educated. They know that to pull a Gotti is to
find a cold jail."

■

—Ron Fino[48]

Ancient Egypt's New Kingdom emerged in defiant reaction to the invasion and occupation of the territory. By driving out the invaders, Egypt's rulers were able to unify Upper and Lower Egypt, the two feuding realms, enabling their successors to hang on to power for a few hundred more years. In the Laborers, for the Upper and Lower Kingdoms, substitute the Midwest and the East and their capitals, Chicago and New York.

In 1994, when the feds began to prosecute the New York Mason Tenders, the Justice Department seemed poised to take over the entire union, now run by the younger Coia. The action threatened to disrupt the continuity of a freshly established eastern dynasty, which had just emerged after a struggle with the midwestern bosses.

In November, the Justice Department released the 212-page draft complaint detailing the pattern of mob activity in the Laborers going back to the 1920s. It seemed as if the Clinton administration was heading down the same track as the Bush administration, which in 1988 filed its RICO case against the Teamsters and then ousted the leaders and put the union under the control of an independent court-approved board.

But Coia was able to avoid the Teamsters treatment. He didn't have to resign, like the Teamsters leaders. He didn't have to put up with an independent board that could purge him or his people at will. Instead, in February 1995, a deal finally emerged after months of negotiations in which Coia was represented by his defense attorney, Harvard-trained Robert D. Luskin. Under the terms, Luskin would serve as Coia's in-house prosecutor. The in-house clean-up presumed that Coia—a man whom Justice had designated just a few months earlier as a "mob puppet"—would cut his own strings and resolutely battle his puppeteers. How was such a one-sided pact possible?

The simple answer, provided by Republican congressmen who held hearings just before the 1996 election, was that Coia had kissed up to Bill and Hillary Clinton. He sent them thoughtful gifts and provided millions in cash for Democratic campaign funds. LIUNA's political action committee, the Laborers Political League, paid out $2.3 million during the 1995–1996 election cycle, with the bulk of the money going to Clinton allies. Coia hosted a Democratic National Committee dinner that raised $3.5 million. DNC chief Terry McAuliffe wrote a memo in January 1995, a month before the deal with Justice, that identified Coia as "one of our top ten supporters." The cash drew Coia and the Clintons closer. Bill and Arthur exchanged gifts of golf clubs. Coia gave Clinton a club with the presidential seal on it. In appreciation, Clinton wrote, "Dear Arthur, I just heard you've become a grandfather. . . . Thanks for the gorgeous driver—it's a work of art." Clinton then gave Coia a Calloway "Divine Nine" club. In all, according to Republican Party accounting, Coia had over 120 personal contacts with the Clintons, including private breakfasts with the first lady. About the time the draft agreement was being finalized, Hillary Clinton addressed a Florida LIUNA convention despite Justice Department warnings that "we plan to portray him as a mob puppet."[49]

None of this damning material was false. But, to hear Robert Luskin argue the case, it seemed almost irrelevant. The LIUNA-Justice agreement was neither one sided nor unproductive, he insisted. Look at all the bad guys he'd ousted—over 200. The Justice Department got their scalps without having to go to court, saving the taxpayers millions. Coia got to keep his job and even escaped direct supervision. "But Coia knew that if he didn't let me do my work," Luskin explained in an interview in his Washington, D.C., law office at Patton & Boggs, "Justice would bring down the hammer and take over the union just as they had done in the Teamster case."[50] Besides, the Justice Department eventually did remove Coia on the basis of charges Luskin had originally filed.

None of Luskin's exculpatory material was false either. But in substance, it was quite misleading. How great a blow against the eastern dynasty was Coia's ouster? In 2000, the LIUNA president had been charged with failing to pay sales tax on several heavily discounted Ferraris he'd bought from a mob-linked auto dealer who had an exclusive contract with the union. Coia paid a fine and became LIUNA's emeritus president, at just about his former salary. His top assistant, Terence O'Sullivan Jr., took over as general president.[51]

Had Coia been removed in more than name? That was the question raised by Ron Fino, a former Buffalo mob associate. Fino's opinion carries special weight. He was the son of a mob assassin, but he rejected the role assigned him by birth and became a voluntary undercover operative for the FBI. Beginning in 1969, Fino was a model asset, gaining the confidence of LIUNA's top bosses. He was also a model labor leader. As business manager of Buffalo LIUNA's Local 210, Fino was even voted AFL-CIO's "man of the year." Perhaps most important, he'd worked as an investigator for LIUNA's independent hearing officer after the 1995 agreement. But Fino said he became disillusioned when he was told that his investigations of Coia and his allies were off limits. In a bitter 2004 letter to the U.S. attorney in Chicago, Fino reminded him of his prediction that Terence O'Sullivan Jr. would eventually get either the no. 1 or no. 2 position.

The prediction was easy to make, because mob-dominated organizations are reliably nepotistic. O'Sullivan would move up because his father, the former LIUNA secretary-treasurer, had been so close to the Coias— they'd all been indicted together in the 1980 Hauser welfare fund scam case. O'Sullivan Sr. had been booted out of the union, not for being indicted but for violating mob etiquette. "I was at the funeral of Peter Fosco Sr. and present at the discussion to remove O'Sullivan Sr.," Fino recalled. Just like Frankie Lupo at Gaspar Lupo's funeral, O'Sullivan Sr. had pushed the succession issue too hard. He'd insisted on replacing Fosco, antagonizing the Chicago bosses, who weren't about to give up the no. 1 position to a candidate linked to the eastern families.[52]

Fino was also deeply skeptical about Luskin's nine-year prosecutorial efforts. "The bare truth is: this whole consent decree program has been a sham," he wrote, "a vehicle to remove Coia opponents and replace them with Coia loyalists, a vehicle where certain Genovese family controlled officials have been allowed to escape prosecution and allowed to strengthen their position."[53]

Fino's prime example of a sham cleanup was the Mason Tenders District Council in New York. He knew the players intimately: it was his body recordings that had furnished the evidence leading to the RICO suit against the Mason Tenders.[54]

Arthur Coia himself had portrayed the overnight reform of the Mafia's most deeply rooted enclave in New York as a triumph of his Clean Team. "The Mason Tenders have made tremendous strides in transforming a once corrupt organization into a democratic organization," Coia announced on the occasion of the first elections.[55] A full-time public relations official on staff made sure the public was aware of the transformation.

It wasn't a hard sell. The media loves to tell transformational stories. How often have we heard the saga of the failed oilman, a middle-aged alcoholic who finds Jesus and in ten years becomes a national political figure? With the Mason Tenders, the total makeover took months rather than years. Both the *New York Times* and the *Daily News* ran feature stories about the union's rebirth. The Mason Tenders' principal unit, Local 79, became famous for a fifteen-foot inflatable rat, which officials placed in front of organizing targets. The president of the New York City Central Labor Council was quoted: "I use Local 79 as a model of the new labor movement everywhere I go."[56]

Louise Furio, for one, was highly skeptical. She'd been fired from her clerical supervisor's job in the Mason Tenders benefits division—let go by Frankie Lupo—in retaliation for helping the FBI in its investigation, she said. "If the union was really clean, they'd have called me back to work," she said. According to Furio, the new administration was less a Clean Team than a Second Team made up of mob relatives and associates.

After working nine years in the headquarters, Furio knew who was who in the Mason Tenders' ruling families. She demonstrated how little had changed in a leaflet she passed out under the noses of the Clean Team bosses as they filed past her to attend a general meeting.

Richard Ello, the central figure in the cleanup and now the Mason Tenders' new funds trustee, she pointed out, was Gaspar Lupo's nephew.[57] And when James Lupo, Gaspar's son, suddenly disappeared—just before his arrest—Ello moved into his house.[58]

The fund's management trustee, Furio's leaflet noted, hadn't even been replaced.[59] And the fund's clerical office was still being used to provide top officials with no-show jobs for their wives.[60]

Daniel Kearney, the new Mason Tenders secretary-treasurer, rushed up to Furio, grabbed her leaflets, and tore them up, shouting, "It's all garbage!"

Actually, it wasn't. In 2004, Kearney and the entire top New York Laborers leadership—including the president of the Mason Tenders District Council—would be forced to resign under the weight of hundreds of embezzlement charges.[61] Since then, the union has again been placed under trusteeship.

The huge inflatable rat turned out to be an authentic icon for the Laborers reform movement. Had Arthur Coia been sincere about ridding the New York Mason Tenders of the Genoveses, he would never have had his personal representative recommend Mike Pagano Jr. to head Local 79, the new flagship local.[62] From the Genovese standpoint, of course, Pagano would have been the logical choice. Their top guy, Messera—whom Pagano had appointed to be his field representative—was then in jail. As former head of Local 104, the Genoveses' old flagship local in the Mason Tenders, Pagano was the highest-ranking Genovese associate from the Mason Tenders still on the street. But how did the choice of Pagano aid the reform cause? He'd been charged in the original complaint with three racketeering counts. And his family had been running the local for four generations. Mike Jr. had taken over from his uncle Anthony Pagano Jr., and Anthony had been preceded by his uncle Sam Pagano. Sam in turn had been preceded by Anthony's father, Anthony Sr., who had founded the local in the 1920s.[63]

Unaccountably, though, the FBI agent in charge of vetting the Clean Team approved Pagano. Only the intervention of the court-appointed investigations officer, Mike Chertoff, now the Bush administration's Homeland Security chief, kept Pagano from the no. 1 position in New York City. Eventually, Pagano was banned for life from the Mason Tenders in New York City, but not from the Laborers in Albany, where he served, until his 2004 retirement, as the assistant director of the New York State Laborers' Tri-Funds, based in Albany.[64] Once established in the state capital, Pagano might have encountered Harold Ickes, who after his ouster from the White House began representing the New York State Laborers political action committee in Albany. His law firm also served as the Laborers' lobbyist.[65]

Instead of Pagano for the head of Local 79, the union chose his subordinate out of Local 104, Joe Speziale. The family principle was upheld again when Joe's brother Sal got to run the other big New York Mason Tenders Local. Since the 2004 embezzlement scandal, both Speziale brothers have dropped out of sight.

But the Clean Team wasn't just a pack of ordinary thieves, gnawing away at the treasury. There was more going on. In the fall of 2004, federal indictments implicated Local 79 in a multimillion-dollar mob scam of the Metropolitan Transportation Authority. Eddie Garofalo, the brother-in-law of Sammy "the Bull" Gravano, got contracts for demolition and asbestos removal at the MTA's headquarters at 2 Broadway. He used non-union labor but charged the MTA for union labor. To keep the giant rat from showing up on the site, Garofalo paid $1,000 a week to an official of Local 79.[66] The renovation was supposed to cost $150 million. But with the help of two crime families and three mobbed-up construction unions—including the Mason Tenders—it cost $375 million. Shades of the Eighteenth Street Mason Tenders headquarters remodeling job.

The 2004 federal indictments also throw a sad and eerie light on the great MTA demonstration that shook midtown New York in the summer of 1998. As many as 40,000 construction workers surrounded an MTA construction site on Fifty-fourth and Ninth Avenue. They were protesting Roy Kay Co., which had gotten a $35 million non-union contract. "No scabs! No scabs!" they shouted. "Whose streets? Our streets! Whose city? Our city!" Leading the demonstrators was Joe Speziale of Local 79. "Do what ya gotta do"—he told the men. As the work-hardened trade unionists rushed the site, the handful of cops protecting it went flying; terrified young officers panicked and wound up macing themselves.

For the first time in more than a generation, New York City had a sense of the raw, concentrated, muscular power of the labor movement. Roy Kay tried to continue the work. But the daily demonstrations, featuring Local 79 and the rat, proved too disruptive. The company couldn't take the daily doses of harassment, the threats, and the constant anxiety. Finally, Kay signed an exclusive agreement.

It was a famous victory. But in retrospect, you have to wonder why the rat never found its way to MTA's downtown headquarters. What was the difference between Roy Kay Co. and Eddie Garofalo, the crime family boss? Both had MTA contracts. Both used non-union labor. Kay at least paid the prevailing wage. Garofalo was alleged to have paid as little as $8.50 an hour. One got the rat treatment, the other the silent treatment. How come? Five generations of Laborers history, stretching back to Big Jim Colosimo, should be enough to explain why.

CHAPTER EIGHT

DC 37

A PROGRESSIVE KLEPTOCRACY

"Everybody takes a little from the kitty."

■

—Al Diop, president, Local 1549, 1983[1]

A PERFECT DAY FOR BALLOT STUFFING

The great blizzard of '96 that began on Sunday afternoon, January 7, shut down all of New York City for two days. Fourteen inches of snow fell on Monday, seven more on Tuesday. Even the post office had to close. City businesses lost billions. Six New Yorkers lost their lives. But the howling winds that blew snow into drifts nearly six feet deep along Broadway must have seemed heaven sent to four top officials of District Council 37 of the American Federation of State, County, and Municipal Employees (AF-SCME), America's largest municipal union, with fifty-six separate locals and 120,000 members.

The officials had spent the weekend in the union's headquarters at 125 Barclay Street rushing back and forth from the basement mailroom, where filled-out election ballots had been stored in boxes. They hauled the boxes of ballots on a hand truck into the elevator and up to their fifth-floor executive offices. There they steamed opened the envelopes and discarded the ballots the members had marked "no." Changing hands frequently and using multicolored pens, the union officials checked the "yes" box on blank ballots run off especially for the occasion. Then they stuffed the freshly marked "yes" votes into the original outer envelopes mailed in by the members.

Altogether, the ill winds of January blew the DC 37 ballot stuffers a lot of good. The storm's approach cleared out the building, leaving them to work undisturbed and providing time to carry out what may have been the costliest vote fraud in American trade union history. The leadership got to approve an unpopular five-year $14 billion citywide contract that the members had voted down by a substantial margin. The disruptive impact of the storm gave them a made-in-heaven excuse for a decision they'd reached in December: to extend the four-week voting period another week so they could manufacture more "yes" votes.

Both parties to the contract talks—Mayor Rudolph Giuliani for the city, the leaders of DC 37 for the members—had strongly endorsed the unpopular agreement. It called for no raises in the first two years for all city workers and a modest 11 percent increase over the three years after that. Although promoted as guaranteeing job security, the agreement made 10,000 employees in the city hospital system particularly vulnerable to layoffs.

Still, potentially, the pact was win-win for negotiators on both sides. Mayor Giuliani was under heavy pressure from the financial and real estate communities to keep salaries down.[2] The mayor could claim he'd saved the citizens roughly $4.8 billion over the life of the agreement.[3] The members would complain, and the opposition might make angry charges. But the DC 37 leadership figured to stay on the good side of Mayor Giuliani, who could reward them with cushy perks and small favors; he was also a legendary prosecutor of labor malefactors whom they had ample reason to not to antagonize.

Vote fraud in the DC 37 tradition was both normal and seminal. The union owes its virtual monopoly in representing the city's non-uniformed workers to a 1965 election against the Teamsters. In the last real chance city employees ever had to choose their union, DC 37 won by 800 votes. "We stole the election," acknowledged an aide in the campaign who claimed to have stuffed 300 ballots.[4] Stanley Hill, the union's executive director from 1986 to 1998, pointed out that he'd been a vote fraud victim himself nearly thirty years earlier. In 1970, the ballots that might have ensured his reelection as president of the social workers union were thrown down a stairwell.[5]

Generally speaking, those who stole votes also stole money. If a kleptocracy is an institution run by thieves, DC 37 fits the definition literally. Just take its executive board—over half of its members were charged with felonies and either resigned in disgrace, died before they could be tried, or wound up convicted.

According to the union constitution, the heads of the biggest locals got to send the most representatives to the delegates council, which elected the top District Council officers. Union protocol determined that they got the highest salaries and got to steal the most money. Al "the Fox" Diop, head of the second-largest local, the clerical local, whose members often made only poverty-level wages, was convicted of stealing $1 million. Diop lived in his own secret penthouse atop the union's Barclay Street headquarters that could be reached only by a private elevator. The union paid for his maid service, his limousines, even his prostitutes. But Diop was outpilfered by Charlie Hughes, head of the largest unit, the Local 372 school lunchroom workers, whose members made even less than Diop's. Hughes wound up pleading guilty to stealing $2.25 million. Much of the proceeds found their way to Millen, Georgia, where Hughes built a mansion and provided no-show jobs for his relatives.

But thanks to DC 37's executive director, Stanley Hill, it wasn't just the big barons who got to live large. Hundreds of lesser gentry got at least a taste of expense account life. In September 1998, when AFSCME held its convention in Hawaii, Hill brought along 600 of his retainers at members' expense. They stayed at the Sheraton Waikiki. Hill himself slept in the $935-a-night Executive Suite. Acknowledged a grateful hotel spokesperson, "It was the largest single booking in Honolulu's history."[6]

By 1999, the saga of DC 37's gilded leadership and gelded membership had gotten the *60 Minutes* treatment, complete with Mike Wallace. The tabloids were pounding the case relentlessly; even the *New York Times* had piled on. The combined media pressure plus a couple of dozen indictments had forced AFSCME's boss, Gerald McEntee—never indicted, but under federal investigation for his role in a Teamsters election money-laundering scandal—to oust Hill and impose a trusteeship. When Lee Saunders, the able and articulate trustee, arrived from Washington, he promised a thorough cleanup. But there were limits to how far and how deep any probe launched by a McEntee satrap could go. DC 37's benefit fund rackets hadn't gone on without McEntee's complicity—he'd gotten a piece of the action himself for his daughter and his ex-wife.

Besides, DC 37 wasn't really ready for reform. The remaining DC 37 leadership was deeply divided into reform and Old Guard factions, but both wanted Saunders to go. And he did, back to Washington. Then the two factions settled down to a steady campaign of mutual vituperation. Yet no one on either side was about to cut up his American Express card. Indeed, it was the rare crusader in DC 37 who was willing to saddle up for much less than $200,000 a year plus perquisites.

All the while, the looting continued. In 2004, the biggest single rip-off yet was uncovered—$4.5 million missing from the treasury of the Local 375 Civil Service Technical Guild and its legal services funds. The looted money had capitalized a small real estate empire in the Bronx. Perhaps not coincidentally, Roy Commer, the former president of Local 375, who had called for an audit of the legal services fund, had been summarily expelled from the union on a silly, trumped-up charge.[7] At the 2000 AFSCME convention in Philadelphia, President Gerald McEntee himself had led thousands of green-shirted delegates in booing and hooting as they voted the meddlesome Commer out of the union for life.[8]

THE MEANING OF THE MIASMA

Chances are, if you were introduced to a leader of DC 37 in the 1990s, especially a leader of one of the big locals, you met a crook, someone who was stealing money and rigging elections. That this became well known was highly embarrassing for the labor movement in New York City—even more, perhaps, than the damaging revelations about the Laborers, Carpenters, Teamsters, Operating Engineers, Plumbers, and a dozen others.

Unlike them, DC 37 had a notable history of involvement in civic life. The union had displayed a devotion to progressive causes that went back to the days of the civil rights movement. The union burnished its image in the 1970s during the city's "fiscal crisis" when the leadership accepted a 22 percent cut in membership through firings. When bankers closed their coffers to the city, DC 37's leaders opened theirs: they organized a $2.5 billion bailout from workers' pension funds.[9] More recently, in the fall of

1996, a couple of years before the mass indictments came down, DC 37 had helped finance the Columbia University "Teach-In with Labor." The big meeting, attended by over 1,000 people, signaled a revival of the long-dormant relationship between organized labor and the left intelligentsia. Theologian Cornel West, feminist Betty Friedan, and historian Eric Foner all threw AFL-CIO president John Sweeney bouquets. So did Richard Rorty, America's most famous philosopher, who insisted that corruption and mob rule in the labor movement were no more serious than in "American academic departments."[10]

The wave of indictments should have embarrassed Giuliani. He had treated DC 37 kleptocrats like labor statesmen, attending their funerals, taking their campaign contributions, and performing special favors for them that few besides fiscal watchdogs would notice. But "The World's Mayor" was hard to shame. When his special DC 37 favorite, Charlie Hughes—who hugged him effusively in mayoral campaign commercials—was indicted, Giuliani was dismissive. "What did it amount to?" he asked rhetorically.

What indeed? In Hughes's case, the thefts reached only a couple of million dollars. Giuliani had prosecuted labor leaders who were a lot worse. DC 37's executive director, Stanley Hill, may have been guilty of conflicts of interest—secretly taking money from Health Insurance Plan of New York (HIP), the union's main health care provider—but he wasn't a made guy in the Mafia, like Gaspar Lupo, the boss of the Mason Tenders District Council.[11] Actually no one was able to demonstrate that Mafia involvement in DC 37 was more than marginal, if it existed at all.

Why, then, bother to air out DC 37's extensive, flagrant, continual, but still not truly world-class corruption? Principally because of what DC 37's corrupt governance says about the dismal state of public sector unionism in America, which has followed the same numerical and moral trajectory as private sector unionism.

Like the Depression-era efforts to organize industrial workers, and the earlier struggle to organize the construction trades in the 1880s, the battle to bring unionism to city clerks, park workers, teachers, cops, and firefighters began as a high-minded crusade. In 1968, the struggle for union recognition brought Martin Luther King "to the mountain top" in Memphis. He had come to help AFSCME's all-black Local 1733, representing sanitation workers, get their first contract. King thought he could help link the civil rights and labor movements.

So did the legendary James Farmer, a founder of the Congress on Racial Equality, who worked for a time as an organizer for DC 37. He had some success in kindling a revolt among Italian Americans against New York City parks czar Robert Moses. But then Farmer was transferred uptown to work on the fateful 1965 contest between the Teamsters and DC 37 to represent Harlem Hospital workers. The brutality of the internecine battle soured him on union organizing. "I'm gon' cut yo' fuckin' throat," he was warned by a rival organizer. "If I had to die violently," recalled Farmer, "I wanted it to be on the front lines of the fight for racial equality, not in the dark alleys of a union jurisdictional scuffle."[12]

Once the jurisdictional scuffles were settled, though, the winners sat down to enjoy the spoils. Although many of the levers and a lot of the most lucrative opportunities for graft were lacking, public sector unionism hasn't been a lot less corrupt than private sector unionism. Nor is there much reason to believe that standards of integrity in DC 37 were significantly below those of other large public sector unions in the city or around the country.

Some recent stories of public sector unionism on the march:

- The president of the Washington, D.C., local of the American Federation of Teachers, Barbara Bullock, along with some of her aides, stole over $5 million from members. With the loot, the sixty-eight-year-old former teacher filled her closet with designer clothes and $35,000 worth of purses. Bullock's $90,000-a-year union chauffeur laundered the money.[13]

- A Broward County jury convicted Walter J. "Buster" Browne and his sister, Patricia, of running their 7,000-member municipal employees union as a racketeering enterprise. Besides embezzling funds, shaking down vendors who bid on union contracts, and handing out no-show jobs, the pair also plied the labor peace trade, receiving $500,000 from eight companies in exchange for not organizing their workers—or organizing them if a more honest union was threatening to come in.

- In 2003, an AFSCME father-daughter team was convicted on 195 counts of embezzlement and kickbacks. Gary Rodrigues, head of Hawaii's second-largest public employees union, was sentenced to five years for arranging consulting fees for his daughter to be paid by health and dental insurance companies. The daughter, Robin Rodrigues, did no work. The health insurance company charged inflated rates and eventually went bankrupt, leaving many of the union's 15,000 members with unpaid bills.

- Stephen Gardell, a much-decorated NYPD detective who served as a trustee for the Detective Endowment Association, was charged with conspiring to turn a $175 million annuity fund over to Mafia families.[14] In 2002, Gardell pleaded guilty to a lesser charge.

- United Teachers of Dade boss Pat Tornillo got a two-year federal sentence in 2003 after admitting to stealing $3.5 million from his members. The seventy-eight-year-old Tornillo took a deal that gave him immunity from charges that he accepted a $900,000 bribe for swinging a $195 million contract for HIP-Florida—a troubled health plan that eventually had to be taken over by its New York parent. Tornillo chose HIP after taking a 1995 safari to Zimbabwe with AFT president Sandy Feldman and her husband, Arthur Barnes, an HIP senior vice president for external affairs. "Purely social," was how a Feldman aide described the member-financed safari.[15]

Sometime in the near future, public employees unions will represent most of the U.S. labor movement. They're almost there now. But while nearly 47 percent of American union members in 2004 were public employees, the *share* of public sector unions keeps growing, not because they're adding members but because private sector unions are shrinking faster.[16]

After a promising start, public sector unionism quickly settled down to becoming a racket like the rest of the American labor movement—and for the same institutional reasons that were fully on display at DC 37. Except for the one election in 1965 at Harlem Hospital, the members never got to choose which union they wanted to join. They were simply assigned to one or another of DC 37's local fiefdoms. The local officials were given freedom to graft by the District Council officials, who were dependent on the local votes. And the District Council officials got the same deal from international AFSCME leaders like McEntee, who depended on them for votes. Heavy patronage, weighting of the governance system, and vote fraud as a last resort meant that reform attempts were largely futile and politics became, at best, a game of the ins versus the outs.

THE FIXERS

What made DC 37 officials different from other public sector union leaders wasn't that they stole dues money, siphoned benefit funds, or conducted crooked elections. It was the scale of their enterprise—and the fact that so many of them got caught all at once.

The key to turning DC 37 into a giant kleptocracy was control over the union's political system. In construction unions, the leadership controls who works, so politics mostly takes care of itself. Workers vote for whoever gets them work. Public sector union leaders lack the sticks and carrots of job control, but they get to count the votes.

While Hill's DC 37 regime didn't invent vote fraud, it may have perfected it. By the early 1990s, local presidents were routinely paying a dollar a vote to mailroom employees for blank ballots—which functioned like blank checks in the corrupt electoral system. The art of steaming open envelopes and stuffing them with premarked ballots was widely practiced. Once, in 1997, when customary techniques failed and a presidential candidate disfavored by the fifth-floor Barclay Street bosses actually won, the victory proved only temporary. Over the weekend, all the ballots disappeared from DC 37's locked security office—requiring a rerun and giving the incumbents another shot. There was even a U.S. Post Office, at 2727 Mermaid Avenue on Coney Island, that regularly served as a kind of vote fraud central for the blue collar division. Members would mail in their ballots, and incumbent officials would discard those cast for nonincumbents.[17]

So ingrained was the habit of electoral fraud that there seems to have been no serious deliberation about whether to fix the 1995–1996 city-wide vote. No one even appears to have asked, "What if we get caught?" True, some precautions were taken. Diop, the head of the second-largest local in DC 37 and the boss of the January 1996 ballot fraud crew, made sure that in his local the members' original ballots as well as the envelopes they came in were all destroyed. He also bought $4,300 worth of antibugging equipment and used it to sweep certain offices in union headquarters.

Still, a sense of invulnerability prevailed among the top officials—and it seems unjustified only in retrospect. After all, even if they were accused, who in the union would investigate the charges? And if the accusations were found to have substance, what then? No one could recall anyone ever having gone to jail for fixing a union election, much less a contract ratification vote.

There were immediate accusations and demands for investigations. Charles Ensley, president of the social workers union, spoke of a "stench" given off by incongruous totals when the results were announced in February 1996. "Nobody believes these results," he said.[18] Balloting had begun on December 4. It went on for six weeks. In locals that voted in open meetings, by raised hands, participants were astonished to learn that a meeting of thirty to forty people had produced over 400 votes recorded for the contract. Barclay Street meeting rooms that could have held no more than 100 people produced three or four times that many votes, nearly unanimously for the contract. In Al Diop's Local 1549, a union known mostly for the steady somnolence of its internal political life, apathy took a holiday. Turnout rose vertiginously from 28 percent at the time of the 1991 ratification vote to 54 percent.[19]

But in early 1996, the orchestrators of DC 37's vote fraud could still feel safe. Even if the latest performance of the Big Fix had gotten universally bad reviews, it didn't mean the long-running show would have to close or the directors would get fired. The worst that might conceivably happen would be that the Department of Labor or AFSCME, the parent union, would order a rerun. But the prospects were remote: AFSCME had never ordered a rerun in a ratification vote before.

Jail sentences must have seemed like an even more remote prospect. Ballot tampering was tacitly accepted by AFSCME's judicial panels, which treated incumbency as tantamount to innocence. It was widely ignored by the press, which didn't regard election thievery in unions as news, and abetted by federal judges, who considered it a shame, but not a crime.[20]

But history was about to change. Nearly four years after the great snow-storm, largely because of the investigations of an unlikely sleuth, the fifth-floor ballot stuffers all wound up either as witnesses for the prosecution or in jail. Mark Rosenthal, a forty-six-year-old former park worker turned local union president, not only figured out who stuffed the ballots, he managed to bluff one of the top conspirators into confessing, first to the Manhattan district attorney, Robert Morgenthau, then to Mike Wallace on *60 Minutes*. And in the forest of pointed fingers that quickly sprang up, it has been estimated that nearly 100 DC 37 officials cooperated with law enforcement officials, producing forty-one indictments covering thirty-one union officials and six union vendors.

As the indictments were announced in bunches by Morgenthau's office, the whole façade of political rectitude carefully built up over a generation at DC 37 began to crumble. Previously portrayed by mainstream journal-ists and prestigious academics as ceaselessly dedicated to progressive causes around the country and promoting maximum participation of its members in union affairs, DC 37, it turned out, wasn't even remotely what it seemed to be.

MR. DIOP AND MRS. DIGGINS

DC 37 officials knew that as long as they kept labor costs down and cam-paign contributions up, the mayor would never make trouble.[21] Every-thing, then, depended on keeping the members out of the life of the union. It was essential that all the crooked actions stayed within the kleptocratic apparatus. The ballot thieves weren't careful enough, however. Everyone who participated in the vote fraud shared common interests. They all worked for the enterprise—all, that is, except one volunteer—Marie Al-ston Diggins, who slipped through the carefully woven filter. Because in the end she had no reason to lie, Diggins provided the most important sin-gle piece of evidence that brought down the whole enterprise.

Before November 1998, the district attorney had indicted a couple of dozen DC 37 local officers for stealing. But there wasn't much media interest in the story. Nothing had leaked out yet about the big 1996 vote fraud conspiracy.

That changed when Mark Rosenthal got elected to the local 983 presidency and moved into an office next to "Turkey Joe" DeCanio, president of Local 376, the Laborers local. Turkey Joe liked to come to work early, when no one else was in the building—4 a.m. Rosenthal made it a point to be there early too. In one of their regular early morning talks, Rosenthal convinced DeCanio that the DC 37 leadership was about to rat him out. Rosenthal was just making it up, but the gullible DeCanio not only believed Rosenthal's story about the DC 37 leadership making him the scapegoat, he also took at face value Rosenthal's promise to use his influence with the prosecutors if DeCanio went to the D.A. with his side of the story. The terrified DeCanio, who let the whole conversation with Rosenthal be taped, ran to the closet to produce a handful of blank ballots he'd saved, left over from the ballot box stuffing operation. "Would this evidence help?" DeCanio wanted to know.

Assured that it would, DeCanio took his ballots and his damning stories to the D.A. It was dramatic evidence that vote stuffing had taken place; but proving that it was Al Diop & Co. who had done the stuffing was something else. Where was the proof?

In the end, it wasn't DeCanio's ballots that brought down Diop and his vote fraud team. It was a bogus memo falsifying the totals, dictated by Diop and typed by Marie Diggins, Diop's secretary. Diggins typed the phony memo as she was ordered. But Diop couldn't get her to lie to the D.A. about what she'd done. Diggins even saved a duplicate copy of the memo despite Diop's express orders to destroy it. Ultimately that's why Diop went to jail. It's a story that not only explains how the D.A. was able to bag the conspirators, it also illuminates the difference between genuine personal loyalty and its perversion, union sycophancy.

Al Diop thought he had limited participation in the vote fix to the right people. He'd ordered that word of the operation be kept secret from Stanley Hill, DC 37's executive director, who he believed had a discretion problem. And he made sure another official he didn't trust, DeCanio, who'd always been the go-to guy for DC 37 ballot fraud, was nowhere around during Local 1549's January 1996 ballot-stuffing operation. But Diop mis-judged Diggins, the long-serving secretary to his Local 1549 election com-mittee. Unlike nearly everyone else around Diop, she was a true volunteer. When the D.A. called her down to One Hogan Place in 1999, Diop did everything he could to keep her allegiance. He promised her a free DC 37 lawyer. He promised her cash. He repeatedly assured her that if she stuck to the cover story—denial—there was nothing to fear from the D.A.

As the secretary, Diggins was responsible for creating the "overrun" bal-lots, the extras printed for the members who had moved and reported not receiving a ballot. Usually 500 overruns sufficed. Diggins testified that she ordered 500 overruns as usual. "No, more," said Diop, according to Dig-gins's testimony. Later Diggins witnessed an argument between Diop and one of his subordinates, James Eady. The D.A. got Eady to give up his boss. Testified Eady, "I said, 'Okay 1,000.' Diop said, 'No, 5,000.' I said, 'Why so many? We never order more than 500. What the hell you need that many ballots for?' He said he wanted that amount, so order it."

But just because Diop had ordered lots of blank ballots didn't prove that he was guilty of vote fraud. What did was Diggins's eyewitness testi-mony plus the documents she secretly saved.

"Mr. Diop called me to his office," Diggins recalled, "and told me he wanted to be very discrete about this election. He said he didn't want no one to know the outcome of this election before he turned in the results. [He] had never before made such a request. He kept saying, 'Just be discrete.'"

Ms. Diggins's discretion was essential. She served as secretary of the election committee, the official responsible not just for ordering ballots but for typing up the official tally that would go to the Research and Ne-gotiations Department. She typed the election results at home: 9,202 "yes" votes, 3,067 "no" votes. She made three copies and gave one to Diop.

"Diop told me he would like to make a change in the report," recalled Diggins, "and I said to him, 'Why would you want to make a change in it?'" Diop's concern was that the conspirators hadn't stuffed enough "yes" bal-lots into the envelopes. He wanted to add another 800 yes's and subtract 800 no's.

Testified Diggins: "He was writing something and he handed the pa-per back to me and he subtracted 800 from the 'no' vote and then he made up the total along with it. He then said to me to check and see if this is correct. I looked at it and I said, 'Yes, this is correct.' So he asked me to retype it over in the office."

Diggins had gone along after Diop explained why falsifying the totals was necessary. "'The members won't be able to take care of their family if they lost their jobs,'" she recollected him saying. Diop asked her to shred the memo with the actual results. But Diggins shredded only two copies. Then, she said, "Diop asked me to retype the new memo in his presence."

The problem for Diop's machine was that Mrs. Diggins had no reason to lie. She couldn't be intimidated. In a political system saturated with patronage, Diop was brought down because the patronage dried up just at the point where it was most needed. Marie Diggins had been a member of the local's election committee for six years and had supervised fifteen to twenty elections.[22] Booting her off the committee for this election would have drawn suspicion and controversy. In other words, the system failed because it wasn't corrupt enough.

For want of one more patronage employee, the scheme failed. But why were a few hundred corrupt officials able to prevail over the common interests of 120,000 members? And where was the city?[23]

THE ENTERPRISE

In DC 37, they didn't just steal votes. If ballot tampering had been a DC 37 routine for decades, so had just plain stealing. In 1999, the union announced that upwards of $10 million in member money was missing from one local alone—the lunchroom attendants union. A $4 million audit conducted by KPMG was supposed to discover how much was missing in the various locals. But the AFSCME trustee who ordered the audit, Lee Saunders, kept the results secret. Information was power. His union allies got a pass. His adversaries wound up with the incriminating information on them gathered in the audit turned over to the D.A.[24]

Public exposure of the fraud was left to the Manhattan D.A. With few exceptions, prosecutors showed, the same officials who stole votes stole money. From DC 37's basement mail room, where phony ballots were produced in the print shop, to the secret tenth-floor penthouse apartment of the top vote fraud orchestrator, Al Diop, the entire building at 125 Barclay was filled with officials engaged in a bewildering variety of rackets, shakedowns, kickbacks, embezzlements, and thievery. Many of these were scams that assistant district attorney Jane Tully charged had been running in DC 37 for nearly a generation.

In DC 37, larceny had lost any taint of deviance. It was honesty that was illicit. You didn't want your boss to think you were an honest guy. Neal Desiderio, DC 37's mail room boss, who aided the 1996 vote fraud bosses by printing up fake ballots, didn't start out as a crook. What got him started in the early 1990s was a request for 500 ballots from Joe DeCanio, who was facing a tough opponent in his election for president of the Laborers' local. A couple of days later, DeCanio gave him $500. Desiderio begged off. "Just take it," DeCanio said. Why did Desiderio take the money? "Well," Desiderio testified, "because he was connected with, you know, organized crime figures, or so he said. I didn't want to not take it and have them think I wasn't going along with them."[25]

The boilerplate epithet for union officials involved, like DeCanio, in wrongdoings is "bureaucrat." But the union didn't operate like a bureaucracy. Bureaucrats operate according to universal rules. They treat people like cases. They advance in the hierarchy by taking tests.

That's not how top DC 37 officials got their jobs. In the blue collar division, the ultimate test for office was loyalty, and the preparation for it was often serving as the driver for your predecessor. In Laborers' Local 376, for example, three of the last four elected presidents had been chauffeurs first. In the other big blue collar local, park workers, after president Frankie Morelli either died of a heart attack or got whacked—the competing explanations—he was succeeded by his driver, the now imprisoned Robert Taylor. You don't get the top job that way in a real bureaucracy, like the IRS. But the chauffeur model of career advancement does operate in crime families and other organization in which secrecy and loyalty are the primary prerequisites. Before he became "Big Al," Capone served as driver for his boss, Johnny Torio.[26]

DC 37's officials behave less like bureaucrats than like figures in a premodern society, where rules depend on roles, and roles on rank. According to DC 37's mores, the higher and more powerful the officials, the more they were entitled to steal.

So it was predictable that the two biggest thieves in dollar terms would turn out to be the two officials who presided over the two largest fiefdoms in the DC 37 realm—Diop's Local 1549, with 23,000 clerical workers, and Hughes's 25,000-member Board of Education Local 372, representing school lunchroom attendants, school crossing guards, and school para-professionals. Although DC 37 had fifty-six locals, these two organizations had nearly 40 percent of the membership. Hughes and Diop had enough delegates to control the delegates council, DC 37's highest governing body. If they cooperated, they could determine who sat on the executive board and make or unmake the executive director.

Certainly no top official with an eye to longevity was going to confront either of the union's two reigning fief holders. In official circles, Hughes's lavish tastes, multiple mistresses, and financial problems were widely known.[27] He'd run up a $375,000 bill on his union credit card for purchases at stores like Victoria's Secret. When he asked DC 37's executive board for a onetime $1.1 million payment for "overtime," no one on board thought to portray the request as unreasonable. (Later, Hughes's attorney would explain the request as the product of a bipolar disorder.) The union's treasurer, Bob Myers, a confessed thief himself, simply wrote a check, handing over the million-plus to Hughes.

Myers understood DC 37 mores. Hughes, who earned $240,000 a year, was entitled to the check not because of what he had done—he certainly hadn't worked $1.1 million worth of overtime—but because of who he was.

Hughes was elected in 1968 and was never seriously challenged afterwards. Through his understanding of how city unions grow—by sucking up to the mayor—his local had edged past Diop's to become the District Council's largest fiefdom. Hughes's lunchroom realm was made up of the "little ladies in sneakers," the cafeteria workers. Their income averaged only $12,000 a year—one twentieth of what their leader earned—but they paid $900 a year in union dues, creating a huge budget and campaign war chest for Hughes. Hughes was the only African American and the only labor leader to appear in Mayor Giuliani's 1997 campaign commercials. No municipal union leader can add members if the mayor strongly disapproves of his leadership; the mayor can have the members reclassified so that they belong to another union.

DC 37's mores also help explain how Diop, head of DC 37's second-largest local, would be guilty of stealing the second-largest amount—$1.2 million, including charges on his union credit card for prostitutes. There was always gossip about Diop behind his back, but no one ever dreamed of confronting him on his expenses—certainly not Myers, DC 37's treasurer, who had been put in place by Diop.

In the pursuit of his dual life—in the union and in his secret penthouse apartment—Diop was sharp and discrete, like a knife in the water. Whereas Hughes was a legendary orator, an effusive man given to throwing his arms around Mayor Giuliani, Diop, a few years younger, was tall, thin, bespectacled, and undemonstrative, with an enigmatic smile. Known as "the Fox," Diop spoke quietly, never even raising his voice to hail a cab. Actually, Diop had no need for cabs. For union business, he could choose between his personal vehicle, for which he got a monthly union allowance of $665, or his Lincoln Town Car, which cost the members $135,000 over three years to rent.[28] For basic living expenses, Diop was entitled to $6,000 a month for rent plus $1,300 in maid service for his 125 Barclay Street union penthouse. But Diop must have found these accommodations cramping, because he ran up $161,432 in New York City hotel charges for 446 nights, including 128 on weekends. Diop's subordinates, including those who testified against him, were allowed lesser larcenies.

None of these revelations from Diop's fiefdom came exactly as a shock. Although only the inner circle of DC 37 officials ever got to see Diop's penthouse, its existence was common knowledge.[29] And, as Diop had explained back in a 1983 interview, defending a fellow DC 37 president accused of theft, the members didn't mind, and besides, "everyone takes a little from the kitty."[30]

Taking from the kitty wasn't just an individual enterprise, it was also a cooperative venture. In theory, local officials could have abused their credit cards on their own. But frequently, lower-level crooks depended on tacit approval from higher officials. More than 100 rank-and-file members of the City University of New York secretarial union, Local 384, sent a petition to Hill and McEntee in their campaign to get the union's president, Fran Autovino, to stop stealing.

They were trying to stop a woman who was obviously unhinged and out of control. In less than a couple of years, Autovino embezzled nearly

$200,000. The amount was no conjecture: in their petition to the AF-SCME bosses, the members included copies of American Express receipts and canceled checks to show that she was charging limos and cut flowers to her union credit card and taking solo trips to the Bahamas, Atlantic City, and, most obsessively, Las Vegas. In one month, Autovino hit the Mirage, the Desert Inn, Caesar's Palace, and Bally's, running up huge bills. The evidence was enough for the D.A. to send Autovino to jail, but neither Hill nor McEntee deigned to respond to their members' petition.[31]

THE TURKEY TRAIL

In the case of Autovino, top officials merely ignored the crimes of lower officials. In the case of the traditional DC 37 Thanksgiving turkey scam, cooperation was wider and deeper. The tradition's origins went back a long time too, if not to the pilgrims, at least back to the days of DC 37's long-serving executive director Victor Gotbaum. A civic hero to the New York City establishment for bailing out the city during the 1970s fiscal crisis with the members' pension funds, Gotbaum acknowledged in an interview that he knew about these "pockets" of corruption. He just didn't think it was a big deal. Gotbaum even knew about the role played by his own driver, Vinnie Parisi (now deceased). In the late 1960s, under the direction of Parisi, who became the boss of the Laborers local, dozens of DC 37 officials participated in a ring to cheat their respective locals on the giveaway of holiday turkeys.

How do you make money giving away free turkeys? First Vinnie Parisi would buy the birds at inflated prices from meat wholesalers who were in on the scam. He got kickbacks from the meat wholesalers, who pumped water into the turkeys to increase their weight.[32] Then Parisi and his turkey team would sell the fowls to union presidents at even more inflated prices. In return, the presidents would get a kickback. Finally, the grateful members would line up at Thanksgiving to collect their free, albeit waterlogged birds. Turkeys that might ordinarily cost $4–$5 wholesale wound up costing the union $25–$44 apiece.

When Parisi died, the scam was passed on to his driver and successor,

Joe DeCanio. It was DeCanio's enthusiasm for the operation that earned him the nickname "Turkey Joe." Every Thanksgiving, turkeys would be stacked to the ceiling at 125 Barclay—well over a thousand of the frozen gobblers would be passed out to the members, who would be lined up around the block. Half a dozen union presidents participated. But the biggest customer was Charlie Hughes's local. Hughes bought 8,000 turkeys yearly—at a cost of $275,000. Even though many of his members lived below the poverty line, most of the turkeys never reached the membership at all—they were given away to charity. A lot of turkeys wound up in Millen, Georgia, at Hughes's mansion.[33]

But turkey wasn't all that was on DeCanio's plate. There was the March on Washington scam and the annual Labor Day sandwich rip-off—DeCanio would inflate the prices of sandwiches that were supposed to be passed out to the members. The participating presidents would pay DeCanio for the sandwiches and get a kickback. DeCanio and the presidents then shared the proceeds with Mark Shaplo, a top Barclay Street official. The cash they gave to Shaplo was essentially protection money. He earned as much as $16,000 a year in tribute from a single local.[34]

Bigger sources of illicit revenue filtered down from the scheduling of union meetings, conventions, and parties. At Friar Tuck's in the Catskills, where a single "retreat" for officials could cost the members upwards of a million dollars, a 10 percent kickback went to whoever scheduled the event. All these ventures involved extensive cooperation among DC 37 officials.

Because the DC 37 scandal was a collective enterprise, once it sprang a leak, the DC 37 pirate ship went down quickly. All it took was DeCanio telling what he knew to the D.A. That produced an inexorable wave of confessions that sunk the enterprise. Within a year, fifteen members of the union's twenty-five-person executive board had either stepped down or been convicted of corruption charges.

It was quite a list: Hill, the executive director, resigned after his top aides confessed that they knew about the vote fix. President Victor Guadalupe said he was resigning for personal reasons. Myers, the treasurer, pleaded guilty to embezzlement charges. Martin Lubin, the associate director, was convicted of vote fraud. Nine vice presidents—Autovino, Cobb, Crilly, DeCanio, Diop, Hughes, McBryde, Taylor, and Tenenbaum—were either

convicted or pleaded guilty to major felonies. Eighty-four-year-old exec-
utive board member Shiekie Snyder, a mob associate and the boss of the
Off Track Betting (OTB) local, predicted he'd die before he'd be indicted.
He called his shot on what was probably an even bet.

WHO IS WILD BILL CUTOLO,
AND WHY DID GERALD MCENTEE GIVE HIM MONEY?

The mob dimension of the DC 37 scandal was never acknowledged by its
parent union, AFSCME, or its international president, Gerald McEntee. The trustee McEntee sent in to clean up the union never admitted to
the mob presence either. And except for the tabloids and some luminous
pieces in the civil service paper *The Chief Leader*, by editor Richard Steier,
the major national media, like *60 Minutes*, picked up the story but ignored
the involvement of organized crime in America's largest municipal
union.[35]

Many DC 37 presidents simply embezzled money from union treasuries on their own initiative. Others, especially in the blue collar division,
seemed to be controlled and coerced by the Colombo crime family. On
more than one occasion, thugs were sent to 125 Barclay Street to beat up
officers and intimidate officials. In 1995, one alleged mob associate demanded huge legal fees, to be paid out in advance by DC 37 officials to a
lawyer of his choice. When the money wasn't immediately forthcoming,
goons invaded the fifth floor, overturning chairs and tables and shutting
off the elevators, forcing officials to scurry into hiding. Top officials in AF-
SCME, all the way up to president McEntee himself, had allowed themselves to be the honorees of a charity run by Columbo crime family
captain William "Wild Bill" Cutolo. (Cutolo disappeared in 2000 and is
presumed to have been murdered.)[36] They put $40,000 into his coffers.
One former DC 37 official who spoke on condition of anonymity recalled
that in the early 1990s he saw Cutolo in the halls of 125 Barclay Street
about twice a week.

The mob–DC 37 relationship was no smooth-running conspiracy. In
1993, Frankie Morelli, then the president of DC 37 and a mob associate,

was roughed up in his fifth-floor office. He died a few months later. The funeral, attended by Mayor Giuliani, was a closed-casket affair.[37]

Officially, Morelli, a vice president of the New York State AFL-CIO, died of a heart attack. He was only fifty-nine. There were quite a few people who were relieved at the news of his death. Morelli was constantly making death threats himself—particularly against political opponents and union dissidents.

One of the city's assistant commissioners of transportation under Giuliani, Louis Hernandez, owed his job in part to Morelli. When Hernandez challenged Morelli's base by running against him for president of the park workers union, Local 983, Morelli threatened to kill him. "I feared for my family," Hernandez said. After multiple threats from Morelli, he said, "I actually started carrying a weapon for self-defense." One day, Morelli confronted him: "'Hey Louis,' he says, 'I hear you're packing a gun.' I said, 'You show me yours, I'll show you mine.'" On further reflection, Hernandez decided to give up his campaign against Morelli and switched to a career in management.[38]

Morelli's office was right next to the executive director's office on the fifth floor. The sounds of his beating could be heard by staffers in the executive offices. Sources say the ruckus caused two top DC 37 officials to run out of the building and hide in Beekman Downtown Hospital five blocks away.

That beating is literally hearsay—it was heard but not seen. But there was a witness to the beating of Vinnie Parisi, the chief of the Laborers' local. It seemed like a particularly gratuitous attack. When Parisi was assaulted in 1990, he was old and sick—a seventy-two-year-old chemotherapy patient. But the grand old man of the turkey trade had remained active in the union. He was head of the all-important—for graft—hospitality committee. The head of DC 37's hospitality committee decides where to hold conventions, retreats, conferences—decisions worth millions to those who can steer them properly. At a meeting with Cutolo, a Columbo crime family captain and an accused shooter in the Columbo family wars, Parisi rejected Cutolo's choice for a conference venue.

Parisi did more than that. According to an eyewitness, he told the feared mobster—who later beat charges that he'd murdered a dozen people— "go fuck yourself." According to the same eyewitness, Parisi went even further: he threw a wadded up piece of paper in Wild Bill's face. A few days later, Parisi and Ed Bennett, his son-in-law, who was then his driver and is now the Local 376 president, were coming to work in the morning. They had just crossed the parking lot and entered the rear of the building when they were met by five men. Parisi was beaten bloody with his own cane. He was being taught a lesson. Even an old man dying of cancer couldn't get away with showing disrespect to a Columbo crime family captain.[39]

When Bennett came home that night to tell his wife, Carol, what had happened to him and her father, she exploded. Figuring that it was Cutolo, she called Morelli, who was DC 37's contact person for Wild Bill. (If you wanted to leave a message for this accused killer, you left it with DC 37's president.)[40] "I called Cutolo every name I could think of," she recalled. Morelli not only relayed the message, he taped it and gave it to Cutolo.

Wild Bill himself then presented the tape of Carol Bennett's obscene tirade to Ed Bennett. "Sometimes the husband can get into trouble for what the wife does," said Cutolo. Bennett reported the threat to the FBI. He still has his complimentary tape from Cutolo.

Around DC 37, Wild Bill Cutolo wasn't just some shadowy figure who sent goons to beat people up. He was family. Cutolo's nephew, John Cardinale, was on the payroll in a no-show job as a grievance representative. An ex-girlfriend, the mother of one of his children, worked as a secretary in the blue collar division. Wild Bill himself was hard to miss in his cowboy boots and big brown ten-gallon hat.

At the Cutolo-controlled National Leukemia Research Association dinners, tables were $5,000 a pop. Cutolo himself was honored as the Man of the Year in 1988. McEntee and Diop were honorees in later years.[41]

When the *Daily News* broke the story in December 1998 about the mobbed-up charity, a spokesperson for McEntee explained that she'd had no idea of the connection between the charity and Cutolo. But it's hard to believe that at the time, 1991, no one was aware of Cutolo's connection with the mob. In 1990, he'd been thrown out of office as president of Local 861 of the Teamsters by a federally appointed judicial review board and expelled for life for being a member of a crime family.[42]

You didn't have to be an insider to know that top DC 37 officials were mob associates—or at least wannabe's. You just had to walk inside

Morelli's office. On the wall was a mural depicting him as "Frankie the Gent" along with "Big Vinnie" Parisi and a lower-ranking official of Local 983 who served as a trustee of the DC 37 benefit fund. The trio were dressed up in zoot suits, holding machine guns, leaning against a car whose bumper sticker read "Join the union or else."[43]

The mural had become a political issue in 1984, when Morelli challenged the incumbent president of DC 37, Joe Zurlo, for office. Zurlo's supporters distributed leaflet with a picture of the mob mural and the caption "Fear is the keynote of the opposition's campaign."[44] The leaflet asked if this was the kind of change the delegates wanted.

The answer delivered by DC 37's executive director at the time, Victor Gotbaum, was "yes." Asked recently why he backed someone he knew was a mob associate, Gotbaum explained, "Everyone knows the presidency of DC 37 is a meaningless office."[45]

True, the DC 37 presidency isn't a high-powered policy position, but that's why officials fight over it. The office provides a nice salary with minimal duties. The only plausible reason for supporting Morelli would be that he and his people could do more for Gotbaum than Zurlo and his people could.

Gotbaum reached out to Cutolo himself in 1986 when he ran for the presidency of the New York Central Labor Council as a progressive alternative to the Old Guard. Gotbaum admits that he met with Wild Bill, then an influential Teamsters leader, and he recalls the meeting. It was originally scheduled to take place at the Greenwich Village "candy store" owed by Cutolo but then was moved to a restaurant on the lower East Side. DC 37's top leaders were pushing Gotbaum to retire, and he needed a new perch. At the time, Cutolo controlled some other locals outside the Teamsters in addition to his own local. "Nothing came of it," Gotbaum said. "Flashy rings. He just wasn't my kind of guy."[46]

INVASION OF THE BOILER ROOM GUYS

The man who Gotbaum acknowledges set up the candy store summit is another alleged crime family associate from DC 37's blue collar division. Although he's gone now, Tommy DiNardo is a name still uttered in whispers. It was DiNardo's people who mounted the biggest and most disruptive assault on 125 Barclay Street—the 1995 attack to enforce a demand for a $450,000 retainer that DiNardo wanted turned over to an associate, an attorney named Adam Ira Klein.[47]

Officially, DiNardo's Local 1795 was known as the High-Pressure Plant Tenders local. More popularly, DiNardo's men were known as "the boiler room guys." They were well organized and intimidating. If the boiler room guys acted as if they owned their jobs, their proprietary attitude might have been understandable: it was alleged that many had bought them from union leaders.[48]

DiNardo demanded that DC 37 hire Adam Klein to get the boiler guys a raise. When there was no response, nearly 100 men from the local appeared one day at DC 37 headquarters with baseball bats. "It wasn't a decision that was made prior," recalled one participant. "We just got disgusted. We had ball bats in the trunks of our cars. People decided to go over to Barclay Street. 'Where's Stanley [Hill, DC 37's executive director]?' we're asking. We busted in the door, overturned chairs. 'We're looking for Stanley,' we told everyone. He was probably in there somewhere hiding in his office. We were told, though, that he wouldn't meet with us. So we shut down the elevators in the building. Security ran away. Then the cops showed up. They said, 'We don't want no problems. Make sure you're out of here in five minutes.' We hung around for a while. But we didn't turn the elevators back on. Finally we left."[49]

The bats broke the ice of negotiations. Immediately afterwards, Hill hired attorney Klein on a $450,000 retainer—that is, paid up front. Generally, payment follows work. But the advance payment proved to be no incentive for Klein, who was accused of doing little more to earn his money than DiNardo. Klein insisted otherwise, arguing that he'd devoted hundreds of hours to the case and that the boiler guys' raise would come soon.[50]

Ever after that, however, Stanley Hill became Klein's enthusiastic backer, defending him against charges that he did no work and kicked back part of the fee to DiNardo. "Adam is doing the best he could under the circumstances," Hill would explain. As for the sortie of 100 men swinging baseball bats, a DC 37 spokesperson denied that it ever happened.

"The elevators turn off automatically at 6 p.m.," she noted in a telephone interview. "That's probably how the story got started."[51]

IMPERIAL MAYORS, COLONIAL UNIONS

In his best-selling memoir, *Leadership*, Rudolph Giuliani recalls how in the 1980s, as U.S. attorney, he withstood pressure from within the Republican Party not to indict the Teamsters general president, Jackie Presser—"one of the few union leaders to back President Reagan." It was a vital case, Giuliani explains, both for moral and practical reasons. Union members were "stuck with people whose sole qualification was a willingness to get in bed with the mob"; corruption sullied the integrity of unions in general; and the substantial costs of corruption were passed on to consumers. But with help of Vice President Bush, Giuliani prevailed, and dozens of Teamsters crooks went to prison. The man *Time* called "The World's Mayor" concludes, "Standing up to bullies is not easy."

Given Giuliani's distaste for bullies, his deep convictions about union corruption, and his record as a prosecutor, you would have thought that as New York City's mayor he would have been all over DC 37's union crooks. Certainly, he would have kept his distance from them as a candidate, and he would have denounced their crimes from his bully pulpit—if not when the indictments first began to rain down, then at least when the officials confessed or were found guilty.

On the contrary, despite Giuliani's years of prosecutorial experience, he seemed to mistake Charlie Hughes and Turkey Joe DeCanio for labor statesmen. He took their money and endorsements and gave back praise for them and special treatment for their members.

Considering that thieves ran DC 37 and the Giuliani administration was headed by former prosecutors, the relationship was amazingly smooth. Their key project was the joint effort to deliver the substandard 1995 contract. In any collective bargaining negotiation, when the two sides finally agree, the negotiators are transformed from adversaries to allies who then "sell" the contract to their respective sides. But in the 1995–2000 contracts, the pressures were all on the union side. Giuliani had no sell job to perform—the business elites who had demanded a contract with wages substantially below the rate of inflation were quietly pleased. The mayor just had to make sure he didn't let his obvious satisfaction become too transparent. All the weight of persuasion fell on the DC 37 leaders, who had to bring their members along or end up on Rudy's wrong side.

But DC 37 leaders had to worry about crossing *any* mayor. The largely one-sided nature of the relationship between City Hall and city unions is obscured by myth, ancient history, and self-serving political clichés. Representing 80 percent of local government's 400,000 workers, New York City's municipal unions rank first in the country in cash flow and membership. But except for a brief period during the tumultuous 1960s, when unions still competed with each other for recognition and a green Mayor John Lindsay was being tested, municipal unions have always been thoroughly dominated by City Hall.[52]

It was in the 1950s, before getting official recognition, that employee organizations won their biggest pay gains. In the schools, several poorly financed, understaffed organizations competed for teachers' allegiance. Since the city hadn't awarded any of them exclusive bargaining rights, they competed in militancy. The pre-UFT teachers won raises of 47 percent in 1959 and 24 percent the following year.[53] Even in the 1960s, the springtime for municipal unions, wage gains were less than in the previous decade, before the labor movement had congealed into a cluster of jurisdictional monopolies.[54]

Nowadays the exaggeration of New York City union power to push up wages is considerable. Incomes that don't reach a "living wage"—$8.10 an hour—are more common in the private than in the public sector. But in 2002, there were over 50,000 public sector workers in this category.[55] Many middle- and upper-level city workers earn more than their private sector counterparts. In clerical titles, though, public sector workers earn 20 percent less.[56] And in some Board of Education aide titles, the starting wage is $18,000 a year.[57] Police, firefighter, and teacher titles lag substantially below the suburbs. On Long Island, where six-figure teacher salaries are common, the top compensation rung is nearly 50 percent higher than Gotham's.[58]

Giuliani treated union leaders the way criminology texts suggest the law should handle potential deviants—ensuring modest benefits for compliant behavior but making the penalties for deviance so severe that few are tempted. As mayor, Giuliani purged leaders who publicly criticized him. Alternatively, he made their unions disappear, as in the case of the transit cops. He took away all the "released time"—that is, city salaries—from the staff of his loudest critic, Jim Butler of Local 420. He even evicted his local from its union headquarters in the city's Goldwater Hospital. When the mayor imposed layoffs on the Health and Hospitals Corporation, only Butler's people got pink slips. Diop's members stayed on the job.

Giuliani also provided ample incentives for going along. Notwithstanding his reputation for civic virtue, he backed his principal trade union supporters no matter what. When Charlie Hughes went down, the mayor said he couldn't believe that Hughes, a major campaign contributor, would do anything dishonest. Despite the indictment, Giuliani kept Hughes on the Equal Employment Practices Commission. He even praised Hughes as "a terrific union leader" who "established a very, very strong union." As for Hughes's alleged wrongdoings, Giuliani remarked, "I don't know the details of this, and I have to leave it to Mr. Morgenthau's investigation and the union trustee who has come in to determine what happened. Was there any wrongdoing? What does it amount to?"[59]

It amounted to the $2.6 million in admitted thefts. For three years before the indictment, exposés had been published of Hughes's mansion in Georgia, his South Carolina relatives on the Local 372 payroll, and his million-dollar "retreats" at Friar Tuck's. Is it possible that Giuliani, with all his investigative resources and inquisitorial zeal, didn't know that Hughes was stealing from the members?

DeCanio was the first union leader to back Giuliani in the run-up to his 1997 reelection campaign. He eventually contributed $7,500—just a couple of hundred dollars less than Donald Trump. DeCanio wound up getting special treatment from the administration, which engineered $11,000 in raises for 200 of Turkey Joe's members.[60]

When DeCanio fell, Deputy Mayor Rudy Mastro, Giuliani's top aide in the Teamster case, mourned "a dear friend and a great union leader."[61]

EDITING AFSCME'S RAP SHEET

AFSCME's main line of rebuttal against critics was, "With us, corruption is an anomaly. DC 37 is just an unfortunate exception. We're putting it behind us."

The *de minimis* defense was shaken in January 2000, when an internal report itemizing official larceny found its way from Washington, D.C., to 125 Barclay Street and then onto the front page of the *New York Times*. It turned out DC 37 wasn't a renegade operation within AFSCME. The bonding company that insured the union against official theft listed $4.6 million in claims in one year alone from thirty-five locals around the country.

Larry Weinberg, AFSCME's chief counsel, minimized the report's significance. AFSCME had 7,000 locals. If only thirty-five had problems, "what you're looking at is a pretty small number out of that universe."[62]

In fact, the report was just a peek into criminal activity in AFSCME, not a survey. First of all, it covered only 1999, and not even all the embezzlement cases that year. An appendix listed twenty-three more pending cases of theft. Second, some of the biggest recent thefts were for some reason ignored altogether, like that of Washington, D.C.'s Thomas W. Waters, who pleaded guilty to stealing $761,000, and Boston's Joseph Bonavita, who ripped off $82,000. Third, the report really only dealt with embezzlement, leaving out various other crimes. Election theft wasn't tallied because its a cashless crime. Nor was shaking down union vendors and beating up members. As a result, some of AFSCME's most prominent criminal malefactors were left out, like Connecticut's Dominic Badolato, who was expelled from AFSCME for using illegal strong-arm tactics against his political opponents, and Philadelphia's Earl Stout, who was convicted of racketeering and mail fraud.[63]

Of course, it's true that AFSCME can't compare with the giants of corruption. What's impressive, though, is how corrupt AFSCME has become, in the seemingly unpromising field of municipal unionism. Commending AFSCME for abstaining from the crimes of the Teamsters and the Longshoremen is like praising someone who's afraid to fly for not hijacking airplanes.

CHAPTER NINE

UNITE's Garment Gulag

If the Teamsters union is the most demonized union in America, the garment union, UNITE!—now UNITE-HERE! after its merger 2004 merger with the hotel and restaurant workers union—may be the country's most idealized.[1] Dozens of historians and investigative journalists, following in the wake of prosecutors, have pursued Jimmy Hoffa and his successors with titles like *Mobbed Up*, *Vicious Circles*, and *Desperate Bargain*.[2] Garment union bosses have received a very different treatment. David Dubinsky, the revered head of the International Ladies Garment Workers Union—a UNITE predecessor—was the subject of numerous adulatory biographies, not the least of which was a short pictorial bio whose text was written by philosopher John Dewey.[3] Sidney Hillman, head of the rival Amalgamated Clothing Textile Workers Union, another UNITE predecessor, was the lionized subject of a biography by Matthew Josephson—one of America's outstanding popular historians.[4] Dubinsky and Hillman were both heroic figures in the best-selling *World of Our Fathers*, written by leading New York intellectual Irving Howe.[5]

And yet in many respects—union governance, collaboration with employers, the degree of corruption, and even the extent of mob domination—the garment unions and the Teamsters weren't all that different. In 1957, when John "Johnny Dio" Dioguardi, the feared Lucchese crime family boss, came under suspicion for having ordered acid thrown in the eyes of labor journalist Victor Riesel, two lines of investigation opened up: one from the articles he'd written about Dioguardi's involvement in the Teamsters, the other Riesel's investigations into garment racketeering.[6] In fact, Dioguardi served as the favored fixer for bosses in both industries who wanted sweetheart contracts or immunity from organizers.[7] As far back as the 1920s, a mob-controlled truck drivers local affiliated with the garment union has given the mob its leverage over the garment industry—a fact acknowledged by more than one garment union president.[8]

Yet the virtue of UNITE was never simply a myth. It was attained chiefly by transferring moral credit for the sacrifices and martyrdom of ordinary members—above all the victims of the 1911 Triangle Shirtwaist Fire—to the leadership. The garment unions were America's first urban industrial unions—the first to produce rank-and file immigrant heroes and heroines. The constant willingness of humble tailors, cutters, and sewers to give up their immediate interests—to go hungry and risk jail, injury, and death for the benefit of future workers—had produced by the early 1950s a combined garment union membership of about a million members.[9] Some garment workers actually earned autoworker wages. It was to evoke this great tradition that Democratic Party presidential campaigns regularly used to conclude with a rally in New York's garment center.

Perhaps, at least back then, it could be argued that the myth of the garment union—like the encompassing myth of the larger labor movement—had served some good. Theologian Reinhold Niebuhr insisted that mythical narratives are necessary. They inspire believers to fight more effectively for social justice. No doubt the often-repeated stories of the early Christian martyrs and the Biblical words of the ancient Jewish prophets have loosened more chains than all the revisionist histories and all the exposés of investigative journalists combined.[10]

Still, there can come a point when hope and history stop rhyming. That point was reached in the South during the 1960s. The resistance to civil rights in Mississippi jolted many into a reexamination of the accepted narrative of the South as the home of the Robert E. Lee and Rhett Butler virtues of honor, loyalty, kindness, and gentility. Something had gone deeply wrong in the South—and idealizing the world of their fathers wasn't helping southerners figure out what it was.

A similar point might have been reached during the late 1990s in New York City wherever garments were made—Sunset Park, Bushwick, Washington Heights, the old garment district, and particularly Chinatown—except that conditions were almost entirely hidden from public view, and official denial reigned. But the shops had largely reverted to nineteenth-century labor standards, with twelve-hour days and seven-day weeks and wages that rarely reached the federal minimum. In Chinatown, where most shops had union contracts, 90 percent of the factories were in violation of federal wage and hour laws.[11] The union no longer appeared to be even trying to enforce its contracts. Investigators from the Department of Labor's Office of Labor Racketeering thought they knew why.

In the spring of 1997, a dozen FBI agents swept past security guards stationed on the main floor of the giant twenty-five-story headquarters of UNITE's fabled Local 23-25.[12] Armed with a search warrant, the G-men took elevators to the tenth and eleventh floors. They carted away computers, software, and boxes of records belonging to top union officials. According to the April 3, 1997, affidavit that persuaded a judge to allow the seizure, the union was "facilitating organized crime control of Garment Center companies."[13]

For nearly ninety years, Local 23-25, originally of the ILGWU, had been known as the mother of trade union martyrs and feminist giants. Historians celebrate Pauline Newman, Fania Cohen, and Clara Lemlich, who had worked in garment factories and battled management on behalf of the union.[14] In 1909, from the shop floor they helped launch "The Uprising of 20,000" against New York City's brutal sweatshops. Historians have described it as "women's most significant struggle for unionism in the nation's history."[15] In the wake of the general strike, Local 25 won union recognition at Triangle Shirtwaist Co. But two years later, 146 members of the Local died in the Triangle Fire. Triangle wasn't just America's worst industrial accident. Behind the disaster lay a generation of union organizing, immigrant striving, and employer resistance. But the affidavit prepared by the Department of Labor's Office of Labor Racketeering portrayed Local 23-25, still the union's largest, as just another mobbed-up union.

According to the twenty-four-page document, the Lucchese crime family used Local 23-25 to exert its choke hold over New York's garment industry—a regime of extortion, murder, torture, and arson. Agent James Vanderberg described how Local 23-25 made possible a classic labor peace racket. Mobsters, after identifying non-union shops, would contact manager Edgar Romney, who would then "direct organizers to put pressure on companies with the threat of unionization, withdrawing the threat when an agreement with an organized crime family is made."[16] Eventually, the cash from the shakedowns wound up in the hands of Joseph Gambino, whose brother Tommy had married the daughter of the Lucchese crime family's founder.

Romney refused, despite repeated attempts to contact him, to comment on charges that he had taken orders from mobsters. The evidence in the affidavit came from the former acting boss of the Luccheses, a Local 23-25 business agent, garment shop owners, stakeouts, and electronic listening devices. Agents watched several transactions take place, including the pickup of the cash by Gambino. In one bugged conversation, a mob associate told a Local 23-25 organizer that he was going to sit down with "Edgar" to "discuss a couple of firms."[17]

The following year, the U.S. attorney, Mary Jo White, indicted seven Lucchese family members and associates on garment center extortion charges. Eventually they pleaded out—including acting boss "Little Joe" DeFede. A low-ranking Local 23-25 official, business agent Eddie Ko, had previously been convicted. Still, by 1998, he was the lone UNITE official charged. *Women's Wear Daily* speculated that indictments of some UNITE officials might actually come down.[18] But Irwin Rochman, a criminal defense lawyer hired by Romney, said, "I see not a shred of evidence" that union officials were involved in "anything of a criminal nature." If there were any evidence, he said, "they would have indicted [Romney]."[19]

As it turned out, neither Edgar Romney nor any high-level UNITE official was ever indicted, let alone convicted.[20] On the contrary, a few years later, Romney got a big raise and a promotion. As of 2005, he's UNITE's $223,000-a-year secretary-treasurer, supervising benefit funds.

Still, at the time, although only mobsters were indicted, UNITE's top leaders didn't emerge with their reputations completely unscathed. The same year that Local 23-25 offices were raided, results of an unpublished Department of Labor report surfaced in the *Wall Street Journal*. The survey of conditions carried out by the department's Wage and Hour Division showed that UNITE shops in the city were predominantly sweatshops—three-quarters of union shops were in violation of overtime, minimum wage, or safety regulations. It's often said, "A bad union is better than no union." But in Local 23-25's jurisdiction, union sweatshops were more common than non-union shops.[21]

The publicizing of the report coincided with a genuine uprising at 446

Broadway in 1997 by nearly 100 Local 23-25 members. Their protest against the union's alleged complicity in sweatshop conditions was played out on TV and in the press. Workers organized an unauthorized demonstration in front of their own factory complaining that they hadn't been paid in ten weeks. Before the paychecks had stopped, most hadn't been even making minimum wage. Seven-day weeks and twelve-hour days were common. The members complained that Freddy Menau, their business agent, did nothing. When Menau arrived at the protest, he explained that he didn't know about the ten-week pay lag.[22]

New York City's mostly unionized garment industry, with about 35,000 workers, had become a mob-dominated racket that made a mockery of collective bargaining while pushing wages down and hours up to the limits of human endurance.

The revelations sparked a 1998 congressional probe into Local 23-25's Chinatown sweatshops. Local 23-25 members testified behind a screen to prevent retaliation.[23] They had quite a story to tell, especially since UNITE had recently launched a high-minded crusade against overseas sweatshops and celebrity exploiters like Kathie Lee Gifford.

Local 23-25 had about 24,000 members—sorters, sewers, pressers, baggers, buttoners, and trimmers. They all had different piece rates, but the rates were fixed, so that few ever reached even the federal minimum wage of $5.15, much less the amount called for in the union contract. The wage rates in the contract were as imaginary as the vacations and the mandatory thirty-five-hour workweek. To maintain the fiction and keep their jobs, the Local 23-25 members even dutifully went along with the common industry practice of buying their checks. Essentially, they were paid a bogus sum by check, and they kicked back part of their wages in cash to the employer. It was a dodge designed to make federal inspectors think that the wage and hour laws were being observed. In many shops workers couldn't take breaks. They could be fired on the spot if they failed to meet piece rate norms. Repetitive motion injuries and asthma from breathing fabric fibers were endemic. Workers were even required to bring their own toilet paper to work.

As usual, garment union officials blew off the charges. Since the 1950s, when revelations of sweatshop conditions and mob control began to resurface after a decade's respite, union officials regularly dodged blame.

When *Women's Wear Daily* charged that the trucking unit, Local 102, was "an active tool of labor racketeers," Sol Chaiken, at that time president of the ILGWU—UNITE's predecessor—explained, "We have never been able to control 102."[24] Sometimes union leaders like Local 23-25's assistant manager, May Chen, blamed the members. "The bosses and the workers share the same ethnicity," she explained. "They're very close-knit. The odds are stacked against us."[25] Other times, they would claim that the terrible conditions persisted because no one ever spoke up. When Donna Karan employees, members of UNITE's Local 89-22-1, complained in a civil suit of working 100 straight days with eighty-hour weeks and no overtime at subminimum wages, factory manager Richard Rumelt said he simply had no idea. "If what's in the lawsuit is true," he said, "it's absolutely outrageous."[26]

Once upon a time, Local 23-25 had been known for leaders who fought sweatshop conditions rather than choosing to hide behind a smoke screen of feigned ignorance. Of the remarkable trio of garment activists—Cohen, Newman, and Lemlich—it was Lemlich whose career was tied most closely to Local 25—the predecessor of 23-25. Her most celebrated moment came a few months after she'd been severely beaten by gangsters for trying to organize a West Seventeenth Street blouse factory. She was in the audience at a Cooper Union meeting convened by Local 25 to discuss a proposed citywide strike. After a parade of officials, including AFL boss Samuel Gompers, finished speaking, it seemed as if there would be no strike. Lemlich pushed her way to podium. "I have listened to all the speakers." she said. "I have no further patience for talk, as I am one of those who feels and suffers from the things pictured. I move that we go on a general strike." Pandemonium broke out. After five minutes of cheering, the chairman of the meeting asked the audience, "Will you take the old Jewish oath?" Thousands of hands in Cooper Union shot up. They recited, "If I turn traitor to the cause I now pledge, may this hand wither from the arm I now raise."[27]

The next day, Local 25's offices on Clinton Street were inundated with women wanting to participate in the strike and join the union. In the long months that followed, the members suffered hundreds of arrests and beatings. But eventually the local gained 20,000 members, and many of its key demands were met, including a fifty-two-hour week.

The revolt of Local 25 women set off an even larger strike movement of workers in the men's clothing industry. By 1911, New York City garment workers had won a landmark agreement: the Protocol of Peace. Brokered by Louis Brandeis, it provided for a fifty-hour workweek, bonus pay for overtime, ten legal holidays, free electric power, limitations on overtime, and much more. Historians point out that in 1911, New York garment workers earned only $15–$18 a week on average.[28] But in real terms the wage levels of nearly a century ago compare favorably with what union members earn today; $15–$18 in 1911 is worth about $300 to $350 in current dollars, or about what garment workers earn today—only nowadays it would be hard to earn that amount working only fifty hours a week in Chinatown or the garment center.

The usual explanations for falling manufacturing wages in the United States include foreign outsourcing, competition with third world countries, immigration, and deunionization. They seem pretty convincing. Cheap imports and the flood of illegal immigrants certainly haven't raised wages. But garment wages in New York City started falling in the 1950s— before imports, undocumented immigrants, and outsourcing became common, and when the union represented most garment shops—as it has until very recently.

What has gone largely unexamined is the union's own labor market strategy going back to the 1950s—highly controversial at the time—which helped turn the city's biggest manufacturing industry from a medium-wage to a low-wage enterprise, rendering it much more vulnerable to over-seas competition.

Buried even more deeply from consideration has been the mob's role in destroying labor standards. Four of New York's five Mafia families divided up the garment industry. In the 1990s, before they were taken down, top bosses like Thomas and Joseph Gambino operated a $100 million garment empire that included sewing and trucking companies. Nor were the wiseguys just on the management side. It was the mob that controlled union "organizing." Union organizers were placed at the service of mobsters who used the union's leverage to extort millions in bribes. The payoffs allowed contractors to pay subminimum wages and cheat the union's pension, welfare, and health funds.

So while global forces were certainly at work, globalization alone can't explain why unionized New York City had the worst urban sweatshop scene in America. New York and San Francisco were in the same country. They had the same Chinese immigrants producing the same kind of sports clothes. Why, in 1999, according to Labor Department reports, were most of the shops in heavily unionized New York City not in compliance while in non-unionized San Francisco they were? How can shop owners today in San Francisco afford to pay the city minimum of $8.50 but in New York they can't pay the $5.15 federal minimum?[29] Nor can globalization explain why workers, after a lifetime of work in the shops, are retiring on pensions that average less than $85 dollars a month while top UNITE officials can receive over $15,000 a month.

The extreme reluctance to examine UNITE's bona fides was perhaps understandable. First impressions are everything. Brilliant beginnings enabled the union to build up a prodigious moral and financial capital. The Protocol of Peace seemed to point the way toward U.S. industrial democracy. But neither peace nor democracy were truly at hand. Infighting between communists and socialists, the influence of organized crime, and lost strikes all combined by the early 1930s to bring garment unionism to the brink of extinction.

The ILGWU was rescued by Russian immigrant David Dubinsky, who had served time in a czarist prison. He learned the cutters' trade in America, became adept at Amerikanski politics, and even founded a co-op restaurant on Tenth Street near Second Avenue that was frequented by Leon Trotsky. Shrewd and fiercely pragmatic, Dubinsky, the manager of the elite cutters' Local 10, brought the union back from near death. The CIO movement helped too, and so did wartime, with federal cost-plus contracts. Still, under Dubinsky, wages improved so prodigiously that by the 1940s, garment workers were making as much as autoworkers. And by the 1950s, ILGWU's national membership had grown to well over 400,000. First under Dubinsky and later under his successors, the ILGWU became a bulwark of the U.S. foreign policy and even the intelligence establishment.[30] And although by the 1990s UNITE had only about a quarter of its peak strength in membership, its financial assets had grown vastly: UNITE ran a financial conglomerate that included a bank, an insurance company, and a $28 billion mutual fund. One study rated it the nation's richest union in terms of per capita financial assets.[31] Local 23-

25's Seventh Avenue art deco headquarters—a block-long twenty-five-story building across from the Fashion Institute of Technology—was probably worth more than the total assets held by all but a handful of AFL-CIO unions. For UNITE's leaders—like President Jay Mazur, who earned over half a million dollars in his last year in office—representing impoverished garment workers now served as a kind of loss leader for their multifarious financial enterprises.[32]

WHILE WATCHDOGS SNOOZED

One of the best ways to dodge criticism is to attack the particular evil that the public suspects you're guilty of. John D. Rockefeller, thought to be a greedy oil monopolist, started giving away dimes to children. (At the time, a dime was worth nearly $2 in today's currency.) Similarly, UNITE, which supervised the Northern Hemisphere's biggest concentration of sweatshops, started a wildly successful media campaign in the mid-1990s that targeted sweatshops—principally those in Central America.

Charles Kernaghan, director of the UNITE-backed National Labor Committee, would become a celebrity himself by attacking celebrities who lent their names to sweated apparel products. In 1998, Kernaghan was asked to be the commencement speaker at twenty-three different universities. The invitations poured in after the 1996 Senate hearings in which Kernaghan nailed Kathie Lee Gifford—a daytime talk show host who was married to 1950s football star and *Monday Night Football* commentator Frank Gifford. Kathie Lee lent celebrity to a name brand of clothing, which was produced by subcontractors and sold in stores like Wal-Mart, JC Penney, Nordstrom, and K-Mart. Kernaghan portrayed the relentlessly chipper Gifford as the queen of Central American sweatshops. To dramatize his claims, Kernaghan sponsored a U.S. tour by Wendy Diaz, a fifteen-year-old Honduran who testified that she sewed Kathie Lee clothes for "43 cents an hour, sixty hours a week."[33]

The Local 23-25 workers at 446 Broadway, it turned out, were also making Kathie Lee clothes. But the National Labor Committee proved hostile to the idea of exposing Gifford's involvement in a sweatshop with a

UNITE contract. A spokesperson insisted that the NLC was fighting for human rights in areas like Central America. "It's incredibly arrogant to ask us to change our mission."[34]

Besides, how could you compare factory conditions in Manhattan to those in Honduras? It was a good question.[35] In Diaz's factory, the workers' wages were a much higher percentage of the median wage in Honduras than the 446 Broadway workers' wages as a percentage of the median U.S. factory wage.

On dozens of college campuses, where UNITE-run chapters of United Students Against Sweatshops were established, the term "sweatshop" completely lost its original, genuine meaning. A sweatshop was no longer a factory where wages and conditions were substantially below local standards. The term also lost any reference to the intensely competitive contracting system that first surfaced in the nineteenth century and that still reliably produced sweated conditions in big-city America. Instead, sweatshop meant just about all the garment factories in the third world—whether or not they measured up to local standards. Since no one was making as little as 43 cents an hour even in Chinatown, by this absolute standard, UNITE's sweatshops in New York City were, by comparison, run like Swedish auto factories. Under the new operational definition, what Gifford had done wrong was not making clothes in sweatshops, but making them in sweatshops that didn't have a UNITE contract.

There are a lot fewer union sweatshops in New York today. But it's not because the union finally started enforcing its contracts or because the government finally clamped down. Under President Clinton, the Labor Department stopped its investigators from asking in their wage and hour surveys whether sweatshops were union or non-union. Under President Bush, the department's survey made not only union sweatshops disappear, but most sweatshops throughout the city. In only three years, the Labor Department's Wage and Hour Division claimed that New York City went from about two-thirds noncompliance to majority compliance.[36] Private monitoring groups were skeptical, noting that the department had changed its methodology. Workers were now interviewed in front of their employers.[37]

Actually, most observers agree that factory conditions in Chinatown have grown worse, especially since September 11, 2001. If the population of illegal factories has dwindled, it's not because either the union or the government had done its job. The absolute number of sweatshops fell simply because the New York City garment industry—technologically backward, mob dominated, and totally dependent on undocumented workers—continues to shrink like a cheap suit that's been sent too often to the cleaners.

The union likes to present itself as the well-meaning little guy victimized by global and corporate forces. When UNITE president Jay Mazur appeared before a House investigating committee in the immediate aftermath of the 446 Broadway scandal, he acknowledged—after a ritual invocation of the Triangle Shirtwaist Fire—that most of the garment factories in the United States are sweatshops. Insisted Mazur: "Our union understands all too well the root causes of sweatshops."

But when UNITE identifies the "root causes," they invariably turn out to be people or forces outside the union's control—Wal-Mart, nonsignatory manufacturers, import competition, and the flood of highly vulnerable illegal immigrants.[38]

THE FIGHT FOR LOW WAGES

Most of the "root causes" of New York City's sweatshop problem are actually the effects of an industrial retention strategy heavily influenced by the union and aggravated by mob racketeering.[39] If New York's garment jungle had a chief strategist fifty years ago, it was Dubinsky. While he denied that the employer organizations like Greater Blouse Skirt and the Undergarment Association—made up of about 700 contractors—were "puppets" of the union, as some claimed, he acknowledged that the rag trade was different from other industries in the degree of union influence. In the 1950s, the union had the power to tell the manufacturers where they could manufacture and what contractors they could use. It was in the New York–based leadership's interest to keep the industry in New York.

New York ran the ILGWU because it had the votes, and it had the votes because it had the members. The leadership could keep the industry in New York only by steadily lowering wages to keep pace with the venues to which the contractors were moving. Since the new locations invariably had a lower cost of living, the strategy condemned New York workers to immiseration. "We adopted a plan," Dubinsky recalled in an autobiography written with *New York Times* labor editor A. H. Raskin, "that the lowest minimum of our contracts had to be ten or fifteen cents above the federal floor."[40]

To maintain bottom-feeding wage levels, the social-democratic Dubinsky embraced the most Dickensian version of capitalism—piece-rate wages, no-strike pledges, five-year contracts, opposition to the minimum wage, and opposition to government aid—complete with up-to-date Fagins in the form of the city's major Mafia families. This low-road strategy led naturally to a reliance on illegal immigrants and made the New York City industry more and more vulnerable to cheap foreign imports. Wal-Mart, which sold Kathie Lee clothes, didn't create the industrial conditions in which low garment prices were all that mattered. It merely proved best at exploiting them. The mob had done well when wages were rising, and it proved its flexibility when it adjusted to an era of falling wages. When Thomas Gambino was finally imprisoned in the 1990s on charges unrelated to garment industry racketeering, his net worth from the rag trade was estimated at $100 million.[41]

Of the cheap labor strategy, at least it could be said that it kept enough of the industry in place so that New York City officials could retain their power and retire on fat pensions. But the costs were great. The measures required to keep wages low destroyed the moral substance of the union. Ever poorer waves of unskilled immigrant workers had to be imported who would find life at the bottom acceptable. The once-vibrant political life of the union had to be extinguished. With constitutional changes, opposition to the leadership became difficult. Then, with undocumented workers constituting an increasingly large share of the membership, political opposition became unthinkable. Gradually, too, the sense of a special calling—and the insistence on low officer and staff salaries—became a hallowed memory, like Clara Lemlich's speech and the Triangle Fire. By the early 1950s, internal politics in the union were dead. Not because, as Irving Howe suggests in *World of Our Fathers*, nothing substantial remained to be accomplished, but because new immigrant members were effectively prevented from participating in the life of the organization.[42]

First came the domestic immigration of blacks from the American South; then Puerto Ricans from the island; and most recently, the poorest arrivals yet: Fujianese and Mexicans. But the entry of low-skilled, low-wage immigrants into the shops wasn't something that happened automatically because of market forces.

In 1959, the New York Central Labor Council proposed creating a New York City minimum wage that would be 50 cents above the federal minimum. The ILGWU representative didn't just oppose the plan. He threatened to withdraw the union's per capitas if the wage hike proposal passed. Four years later, the proposal resurfaced as a City Council bill. It was again opposed by the ILGWU. A letter from Teamsters Joint Council 16 to the Council Speaker was made public: "Surely you must or should know," it read, "that the ILGWU has a vested interest in the perpetuation of exploitation, low wage packets and poverty in New York City."[43]

Along with the struggle for lower wages, the union fought the lonely fight for lower skills.[44] When the government proposed federal manpower funds to raise skill levels in the garment industry, the research directors of the ILGWU and the Amalgamated collaborated in a fourteen-page memo in which they insisted that the government keep its money: "It is our considered judgment that the subsidized training of apparel workers is unnecessary . . . on the basis of our man-years of experience in the apparel industry, we are convinced that such training of apparel workers is not only a waste of federal funds but sets in motion forces detrimental to the health and stability of our industry." Advised the two union research directors: "The hiring of inexperienced workers by the industry is central to its functioning."[45]

In 1950, the city's apparel workers ranked second among manufacturing industries. By 1962, according to the Bureau of Labor Statistics, the industry had fallen to eleventh out of sixteen. By the late 1990s, New York City hit bottom. By any measure, it had the nation's worst sweatshop problem: the lowest percentage of shops in compliance, the most dollars fined, and the highest number of shops charged with violations, even though New York had fewer than half as many garment workers as Los Angeles.

Increasingly, the officials and the members came from separate ethnic groups and spoke different languages, so the native-born groups had no effective way of communicating with the immigrant members. The mutual incomprehension was compounded by a huge and growing divergence in educational levels. Top officials no longer came out of the shops. At the highest levels, they came from the Ivy League; one top UNITE vice president who had a Ph.D. had actually studied Mandarin. (Unfortunately, most of the Chinese members spoke not Mandarin but Cantonese or Fujianese.) It was no wonder that salaries began to diverge too. Dubinsky made only five times more than his average member; Mazur got about fifty times more.

Still, the union's member retention strategy failed even in its own terms. The New York City industry shrank anyhow, and so did the union. In 2004, the entire New York City industry counted only about 35,000 manufacturing workers, a poor second to Los Angeles, which long ago surpassed New York as the nation's garment center, and which now has 90,000 manufacturing workers—all non-union.[46] In Local 23-25's most recent filing, it has shrunk from about 25,000 to about 9,000 members.[47]

The massive shrinkage was inevitable. Even with immigrants from the world's most impoverished countries, the United States can't compete if its factories use the same technologies. But the New York industry, which still relies on the sewing machines your grandmother used, is not even on a par with third world garment factories. As MIT economist Michael Piore observes, "Most of the export-oriented garment factories [in China and Mexico] do not look like the ones uncovered in Los Angeles or New York City; in fact they seem like models of modernity by comparison: orderly, spacious, well-lighted, well ventilated and equipped with ample machinery."[48] The contrast is even greater with northern Italy, which exports billions of dollars of clothes to the United States made by workers who make two to three times what their New York counterparts make. The Big Apple may be becoming a backwater even compared with Los Angeles— where sweatshop factory conditions flourish too.

But at least in L.A. there are signs of change. In 1998, Dov Charney founded clothing manufacturer American Apparel Co. Charney eliminated subcontracting—once a demand of the early ILGWU—and created an up-to-date, completely integrated manufacturing system. Initially dismissed as a niche player, Charney employs over 1,000 workers and is now the nation's largest garment manufacturer. His non-union employees are mostly Mexican immigrants. They're paid an average of $13.00 an hour plus benefits.[49]

Focused and informed public indignation might have made a difference in New York. But the media ignored the reality of union sweatshops. Not only did the union face no pressure to enforce its contracts, it was allowed to go on posturing about its profound concern for exploited third world workers by singling out celebrity violators like Kathie Lee Gifford. Why not? Celebrity bashing was not only iconoclastic good fun, it was essential to the media's survival. Old celebrities must die if new ones are to be born.

LIVING WITH THE LUCCHESES: FROM DIO TO DEFEDE

Besides cheap, undocumented, unskilled immigrant labor, UNITE leaders relied on another unmentionable source of support: the mob. Gangsters in the garment union were an old story. When forced to deal with them at all, historians have described them as colorful *gonifs*— "Dopey Benny" Fein, who allegedly would have just as soon worked for the union as for management; Arnold Rothstein, who fixed the "Black Sox" World Series (Mayer Wolfsheim in F. Scott Fitzgerald's *The Great Gatsby*); and Rothstein's garment center aide, the soft-hearted but indomitable "Legs" Diamond, who wouldn't die despite being shot with seventeen bullets. In fact, the sensitive "Legs" liked to torture people with a red-hot iron. The pro-union "Dopey Benny" wound up a garment boss, and Rothstein made his millions in the garment district—not putting money in the workers' pockets, but taking it out.

Yet that's not the picture that has come down. The old mobsters, it's said, weren't really anti-union. Much in the way anxious athletes take steroids to bulk up, to give themselves an edge, garment union leaders, historians argued, used tacit alliances with organized crime to build up factional strength. Another alleged reason was that the union needed mercenaries to fight the bosses' goons.[50]

The mob, with the Luccheses as the lead family, now controlled the key trucking, cutting, and sewing locals, including the largest in the union, Local 23-25. Mobsters could pick the organizing targets, and the union leaders complied. They went along because the mobsters had the leverage to shut down shops. Mob-affiliated leaders had the delegates to determine who filled top union offices. But the union had drifted far from its initial purpose. It was no longer a means for members to obtain fair treatment and exploit collective bargaining power. It had become a shakedown tool. If an employer didn't want to pay union scale or union pension and welfare benefits, he paid the mob. The union still sent out officials to engineer piece rates in the factories. It was the mob, though, that often determined the real wage rates.

In many respects, the city's garment unions were very similar to its construction unions, where rule by Mafia families was pervasive and often taken for granted. There were two big differences, though. Construction unions retained a substantial stratum of workers who still benefited from high wages. The low-wage construction workers in the city were mostly non-union immigrants, so the leadership was able to keep a political base among the membership. In the construction unions, the membership and the leadership looked like each other. But increasingly, the low-wage garment union had no real ethnic base in the shops. It expressed its own "gorgeous mosaic": Italian crime family members who dominated Jewish union leaders who ruled over Chinese immigrant workers.

The other big difference was denial. Construction leaders didn't pretend to be crusaders against organized crime. But just as Dubinsky's successors evaded responsibility for U.S. sweatshops by campaigning against third world sweatshops, he himself distracted attention from the mob penetration of his own union by crusading against its presence in other unions.

At the AFL's 1940 convention in New Orleans, Dubinsky put forward a sweeping resolution against gangster unionism—designed, he said, to provoke the building trades and the Teamsters. The ploy worked. Dubinsky's stance even earned him a near poke in the mouth from crooked Operating Engineers boss Joey Fay—the prime suspect in the assassination of a dissident labor leader. Fay swung wildly and missed Dubinsky, hitting only his cigar and winding up in the lap of the *New York Times*'s Abe Raskin, who was sitting next to Dubinsky's daughter. Raskin wrestled for a while with the drunken Fay, and then filed a story about the altercation. The front-page account of his tussle with the sinister Fay gave Dubinsky the cover he needed to rejoin a federation that he himself described as dominated by thugs and thieves.[51]

It was the kind of protective coloration Dubinsky needed when a credible witness testified before the Senate Committee on Permanent Investigations in 1957 that Dubinsky had hired Lucchese mobster "Johnny Dio" Dioguardi to organize a garment plant in Roanoke, Virginia. This was really front-page news. Dubinsky and Dio were quite an item. Dubinsky was practically the embodiment of progressive labor in America. Dio, on the other hand, was a captain in the Lucchese crime family at the peak of his notoriety. He'd been indicted the previous year by a grand jury for arranging to have labor journalist Victor Riesel blinded in a sulfuric acid attack. It was an old intimidation tactic that Dio had learned organizing under Louis "Lepke" Buchalter in the ILGWU's trucking local in the 1930s.[52] Dubinsky insisted that the union was 100 percent Dio free. He'd never so much as spoken with Dio.

The problem of mob control went far deeper than Dubinsky's hiring a bad guy to scare a boss in Virginia. The mob was inside the union—in the all-powerful trucking union, Local 102. The trucking local controlled pickups and deliveries. Without trucking service, a contractor couldn't survive. In 1957, the entire leadership of Local 102 was convicted of labor racketeering. Veteran manager Sam Berger was convicted along with his brother Joseph, who was charged with being a "close associate of Johnny Dio and others reputedly engaged in racketeering activity." On the indictment of the Bergers and the rest of the Local 102 leadership, Dubinsky issued a statement declaring that he was "seeking to ascertain the facts."[53]

In his autobiography, Dubinsky finally acknowledged that his trucking members were controlled by mobsters. It was a practical matter, he explained. "We wanted control over nonunion work."[54] But by ceding control to the mob to get control over non-union work, Dubinsky risked losing control over the union. It's doubtful that Dubinsky could simply issue an order and make the mobsters go away.

Dubinsky's successor, Sol Chaiken, never even tried. His public statements about mob control over Local 102 had a kind of helpless, wistful character.[55]

In the 1990s, the Manhattan district attorney's office launched law enforcement's most recent attack against the mob's garment trucking cartel.

Eliot Spitzer, then an assistant D.A., succeeded in imposing big financial penalties on the fashion industry's mob moguls Tommy and Joseph Gambino. They were forced to sell many of their companies. A court-appointed monitor was put in place to regulate the industry. But Local 102 itself and the parent union emerged unscathed from the process. If Local 102 was mobbed up, apparently it didn't mean that the union could be held accountable.

Local 102 seems never to have been much more than a useful adjunct of organized crime. Local 23-25 has had a very different history, one that sadly illustrates the transformation of the union from a workers' movement to a mob tool.

Two years before the Triangle Shirtwaist Fire, the "Uprising of the 20,000" broke out. At the Leiserson factory, where Clara Lemlich worked, employers responded to the news that a few of their employees had joined Local 25 by locking out all 500 workers in the shop. The action had the opposite effect: workers streamed into Local 25.[56]

By the late 1970s, though, it wasn't conflict with employers that brought workers into Local 23-25. It was cooperation. The downtown contractors encouraged their workers to join. What motive could employers possibly have to encourage workers to join the union? Mostly, it was because the union controlled the work. The manufacturers would give work to contractors designated by the union. When Jay Mazur was manager of Local 23-25, Chinatown sportswear contractors made his career by bringing thousands of their workers up to Local 23-25's Seventh Avenue headquarters to buy union cards.[57]

By this time, though, the largest and most hallowed local in the union had been mob run for decades. Evidence comes from Joe Valachi's famous revelations. According to Robert F. Kennedy, the Senate testimony of Valachi, a relatively low-ranking crime family member, constituted "the biggest intelligence breakthrough yet in combating organized crime." Besides being the first mafioso to break with *omertà*, Joe Valachi was also in *schmatas*—the rag trade. When one of his loan shark customers failed to pay off, he wound up owning a dress factory just off Bruckner Boulevard in the South Bronx. His first order of business was to make sure he had no trouble with the union.

"So I go downtown to the garment district to see Jimmy Doyle, right name Plumeri, or one of the Dio brothers, Johnny or Tommy. They are in Tommy Brown's Family [Tommy Brown Lucchese] and they are supposed to straighten out any trouble with the union, I think it was Local 25."[58]

Not long afterward, Valachi got a visit from two union organizers anyway. He chased them off with a pistol. Said Valachi: "Johnny Dio calls me an hour later and he is laughing as he has heard what happened. 'That's the way to handle them,' he says. 'They said there was a wild man up there and they were lucky to get out alive. Don't worry, they won't be back.'"[59]

By the late 1990s, Dio had died in prison, but the Lucchese crime family was still in place, providing historical continuity and direction for Local 23-25. In December 1998, the head of the family plus several associates pleaded guilty to running labor peace rackets involving Local 23-25 that had lasted for two decades. None of the six union officials alleged by the Office of Labor Racketeering to have participated in the schemes was indicted.[60]

SEWING UP THE GARMENT CENTER

In the U.S. attorney's press release announcing the indictments, the union's presence could at least be faintly glimpsed. Mary Jo White, U.S. attorney for the Southern District of New York, spoke of "the use of contacts with Garment Center unions." Unions? Which ones? Are there any garment unions in the garment center besides those affiliated with UNITE? In the *New York Times* story the next day, though, the union disappeared entirely: Businesses, it says, "were given protection and labor peace and, if they were not unionized, were allowed to remain so."[61]

In fact, UNITE played a far more active part, which the Office of Labor Racketeering affidavit describes quite baldly: "The Lucchese Family has controlled the Garment Center through the Family's influence over the ILGWU."[62] The whole rationale for the raid on Local 23-25 headquarters was the claim that Romney directed organizers to make demands on garment factories and then let the threat lapse after they made an agreement with an organized crime family.[63]

In the corruption of the garment center, the government points to dozens of actors—mobsters, associates, and top union officials and their aides. But five can be singled out who played different but mutually supporting roles. The first was Joseph DeFede, the acting boss of the Luccheses. "Most companies in the Garment Center," according to the Office of Labor Racketeering, "were associated with an organized crime family."[64] But the Luccheses were entitled to 50 percent of all the bribes collected from the companies. The Genoveses and the Gambinos shared 25 percent apiece. The Colombos got whatever they could earn on their own.[65] DeFede pleaded guilty to directing the enterprise. Prosecutors estimated that he made $30,000 to $40,000 a month.

The second was Stanley Lieberman, who served as the principal Lucchese associate in charge of day-to-day family interests in the garment district. Lieberman knew the industry well: he didn't just shake down companies, he owned them too. Most often, it was Lieberman who initiated the shakedown schemes. He was "the strong arm" of the family. If an owner had a problem with the union, Lieberman was the man to see. Through his family connections—and what the government describes as "control over the ILGWU"—Lieberman would ensure labor peace for a fee.[66] His role lessened only slightly after his 1994 imprisonment. The feds had convicted him of running a JFK Airport extortion ring involving Teamsters' "Goodfellas" Local 851. But Lieberman was still able to get messages out when he was visited by Irwin Schlacter, his mob lawyer.

Schlacter, the third of the five, was a seventy-three-year-old attorney from Yonkers with long experience in the garment district. Schlacter would get the name and address of the target company from Lieberman. "Schlacter, in turn, would forward the company name to Edgar Romney," the Office of Labor Racketeering claimed. Then Romney would send an organizer to threaten unionization. "At that point either Lieberman or Schlacter would step in to 'work out a deal.'"[67]

On the basis of wiretaps of Schlacter's office, the Office of Labor Racketeering concluded that he had the ability to influence Local 23-25. One business agent he spoke to was Freddy Menau, the business agent who claimed he hadn't realized that his 446 Broadway workers hadn't been paid for ten weeks. In a May 3, 1996, conversation, Schlacter told Menau that he (Schlacter) "needed to sit down with 'Edgar' to discuss a couple of firms connected to the Mafia."[68]

It's hard to imagine a more implausible Mafia associate than Edgar Romney. The bespectacled, highly literate veteran labor leader is an African American who is a member of Social Democrats USA and gives one of the best speeches in the New York City labor movement. Even his management adversaries describe him as quite knowledgeable, fair-minded, and a skilled collective bargainer. But the Office of Labor Racketeering charged that Romney would get the list of company targets from Schlacter, who had gotten them from Lieberman. The affidavit concluded with a substantial charge. "Romney directs Local 23-25 business agents and organizers," it said, "to put pressure on companies with the threat of unionization or strike and thereafter withdrawing the threat when an agreement with an organized crime family is made, thereby facilitating organized crime control of Garment Center companies."[69]

Based on evidence from cooperating witnesses, a judge had allowed the FBI to wiretap Schlacter's office. But while several conversations were picked up involving Romney's aides, Romney himself was never intercepted talking to Schlacter. As a result, the *Village Voice*'s William Bastone reported, investigators crossed Romney's name off the list of individuals whose conversations they wanted to intercept.[70]

The fifth principal was Jeff Hermanson, a tall, long-faced veteran of the 1960s who served as Local 23-25's top organizer. The Office of Labor Racketeering intercepted three conversations between Hermanson and Schlacter. One call came early in the morning on July 16, 1996. The star organizer needed Schlacter's help in getting a Korean-owned company unionized. Hermanson told Schlacter that he was going to offer the company "a special deal": he only wanted part of the company to be signed up with the union. But "Edgar" was happy about this, said Hermanson. "Whatever you can do for us," he told Schlacter.[71]

What Schlacter could do for the union was to cut off trucking deliveries to the garment center. A couple of hours after receiving Hermanson's request, according to the affidavit, Schlacter called an associate in a mob-influenced trucking company and asked him not to pick up or deliver to the target Korean company.

Many UNITE business agents—including those working for Local 23-25—took bribes. But Hermanson didn't dress or act like money was an object. He was a Marxist intellectual who had been active in the 1960s movements and labor support groups. Another Chinese-speaking UNITE staffer, he was highly regarded among immigrant worker rights advocates. Presumably Hermanson hadn't learned Mandarin to talk to the mob. Hermanson was never indicted. He now works at the State Department–funded American Center for Labor Solidarity in Washington, D.C. He didn't return messages left on his answering machine.

After the 1998 indictments, Hermanson left UNITE and went to work for the Carpenters—first with the New York City District Council of Carpenters and then with the Carpenters in Las Vegas. While Hermanson is captured on the tapes, it's hard to believe he worked with the mob to get bribes. He seems to have been trying to get organizing leverage. In a union where bribe taking is a behavioral norm, there's no evidence that any of the accused UNITE officials took bribes.[72]

Perhaps Hermanson had come to believe that getting the "special deal" was the best he could do under the circumstances. At least some workers could buy into the union's health plan. (After 700 hours of work, a member could buy into the family plan, which then cost about $180 a month.)[73] Hermanson didn't start out trying to work within the interstices of mob unionism, but many principled people found their way into UNITE on the basis of its aura of progressiveness. Some stayed well past the shattering of their illusions.

A former staffer may serve as a proxy witness for many who left and many who remain. Call him "Fred," because he's got a job at another union and fears, probably with good reason, that he would be fired if his name were used.

In his ten years as an aide under Mazur and Romney, Fred had ample opportunity to inspect the shops. He saw that health and safety conditions in the shops were appalling. "There were locked and blocked fire exits just like the Triangle Shirtwaist Factory. In one five-story factory there was one bathroom that worked. Child labor was pretty common—even the sons." Fred made the conditions known. Not that it did any good. "I was there when a reporter from the *Daily News* came in to talk to Jay [Mazur]. He simply denied everything."[74]

Theft was better regulated than safety. It was tolerated, but there were limits, at least at the lower levels of the enterprise. "There were huge amounts of corruption. In the ten years I was there, six or seven BA's [business agents] were canned—basically because they got too greedy. One of the BA's I'd known for years got fired. I took his place. At one of the shops the employer tried to put $100 in my hand. I refused. He tells me, 'I gave you guys money just last week.' There was a sliding scale, $50 to $100 once a month. It wasn't too bad for comparatively low-paid business reps that serviced fifty to sixty shops." Fred reported his experience in the field to his superiors. "I was told, 'We'll deal with it.' But it was just ignored."

So was the basic wage and hour agreement. "Craft minimum were fictions," says Fred, "a proverbial joke in the industry. Workers weren't even getting the minimum wage. We had copies of the contracts." The business agents were supposed to distribute the contracts to the shop stewards. Fred once complained to Edgar Romney that the contracts were a dead letter in the shops. "Edgar asked, 'What can we do if we enforce the contracts? The places will go out of business.' At least he said it openly."

What finally forced Fred to consider a career change was his routine reporting on safety conditions in the factories. "There was some violation in practically every one—from a little to a lot. But I thought I was doing a great job. I was bringing in thousands [in penalties] into the welfare funds. All of a sudden Edgar calls me and says, 'I've got some complaints from the shops. You're being disruptive. You have to start giving them better notice before you show up.' Sure enough, in the next collective bargaining, the management lawyer reads a list of demands. One was that the health and safety inspector must give two weeks' notice before coming to make an inspection. I nearly fell out my seat laughing. But then the union agreed to it. That's when I decided to leave."

THE LITTLEST GARMENT WORKER

Staying with UNITE would be a stern test for staffers who still tried to orient their lives by the lights of the labor movement's best traditions. Corruption, for them, could always be explained away as a few rotten apples, or the product of a corrupt American culture. Sweatshop stories were a wrench, but the conditions weren't the union's fault, they were the fault of globalization. Harder to explain away, though, was the short life of Quin Rong Wu. She was an eleven-year-old girl who had disappeared after breakfast one spring day in May 1997. Quin's parents were Cantonese immigrants. Her father worked in a noodle factory, and her mother was a UNITE member, Local 23-25. A few weeks later, Quin's body, clad in jeans and a sweatshirt, turned up in the East River. She'd been strangled.

Initial press reports described her as an ordinary happy schoolgirl who'd been enrolled at PS2. But as Ying Chan reported in the *Daily News*, Quin Rong Wu had spent her last days working in a UNITE garment factory: NBC Connections at 54 Canal Street. Her mom said she just played in the factory. But the coworkers interviewed by Chan reported that she worked at machine number 67 in the factory, which was owned by John Lam, Chinatown's most prominent garment manufacturer. "She was so small," a coworker told Chan, "she had to rest her chin on the machine."[75]

No evidence ever appeared to even suggest that Quin Rong Wu's death had anything to do with her job at NBC Connections. But her presence at the machine was neither all that uncommon nor so difficult to explain. Lam paid Quin Rong Wu's mother about $100 a week for her fifty hours' work. If the Local 23-25 contract had been enforced, there probably wouldn't have been family pressure for Quin Rong Wu to become an eleven-year-old garment worker.

There was a big Chinatown funeral; the Wu family collected over $100,000 from mourners and sympathizers. It was said that UNITE staffers mourned too. They "felt terrible" said one source. Otherwise, several years later, little seems to have been changed by the tragedy. In 2001, the *Daily News* still listed Quin Rong Wu's strangling as one of the city's top ten unsolved crimes. When last interviewed, the Wus continued to live in the same tiny Henry Street apartment. But work at the factory had slowed. Mrs. Wu was looking for another job.[76]

As far as the union was concerned, the big news was the leadership change. When Jay Mazur retired as president of UNITE, he was replaced, as expected, in July 2001, by Bruce Raynor, a University of Pennsylvania grad who had been the secretary-treasurer. Romney was chosen to replace Raynor as the union's no. 2 official—and he kept his job as manager of Local 23-25. Freddy Menau, the Local 23-25 business agent who didn't know that the 446 Broadway workers hadn't been paid for ten weeks, moved up to become the local's assistant manager.[77] But then, as private detective Jake Gittes is advised in the finale of the movie, "Forget it, Jake. It's China-town."

CHAPTER TEN

Ron Carey

MARTYR OR MOUNTEBANK?

"No Corruption. No Excuses. No Exceptions."

■

—Ron Carey's 1991 Campaign Slogan[1]

For many progressives, former Teamsters president Ron Carey is the St. Sebastian of organized labor.[2] According to medieval hagiographers, St. Sebastian was tied to a tree and riddled with arrows for fighting pagans and trying to prevent the Roman Emperor Diocletian from persecuting Christians. According to his supporters, Ron Carey was brought down for his good works: battling the mob and leading a militant strike on behalf of UPS Teamsters. The first arrow was the overturning of his 1996 election victory over James Hoffa; the second disqualified him from participating in the rerun election; the third banned him from the Teamsters for life. Finally, Carey was pierced by federal perjury charges: seven counts of lying to a grand jury.[3]

That the wounds were inflicted by obscure magistrates and unelected officials increased suspicions of an administration plot. That Carey subsequently beat the charges in a trial held in the shadow of the September 11, 2001, terrorist attacks confirmed them. "The social forces underlying all of this," explained Stanley Aronowitz, a longtime labor activist and now a distinguished professor of sociology at City University of New York, "is that when labor raises its head and begins to fight, they get beaten down."[4]

The belief in Carey's martyrdom gained strength from his leadership of the 1997 UPS strike, widely if wrongly portrayed as the greatest victory for organized labor since the great 1937 Flint sit-down strike. At Flint, General Motors, the world's greatest manufacturer, was forced to bargain with union men who had occupied its Fisher Body Factory. The United Auto Workers agreement led to the organization of manufacturing plants all through the Midwest. The gains from the UPS contract, so modest as to be almost undetectable, had been achieved only with the indispensable help of Bill Clinton. He refused UPS demands to invoke federal powers that would have postponed or canceled the strike. Now, though, it appeared that the administration was repenting for its support of Carey by indicting him.

The apparent irony was lost on Carey's supporters. Under his leadership, they believed, the magma of working-class revolt was finally bursting to the surface. His reform program had made militant class action possible. Carey had cut his own salary, grounded the Teamsters jet fleet, sold the stretch limousine of former president Jackie Presser, and trusteed dozens of mobbed-up locals. But no sooner had Carey had begun to get the crooks out of the union and the working class on its feet than a Clinton-appointed U.S. attorney tried to put him in jail. And Carey, they insisted, hadn't even done anything.

Carey didn't just beat the federal charges that he'd lied about participating in an $885,000 money-laundering plot. For most in the Teamsters reform movement, he got his reputation back. According to Ken Crowe, author of *Collision: How the Rank and File Took Back the Teamsters*, the acquittal completely vindicated "the unshakeable Ron Carey, the most distinguished labor leader of modern times."[5]

Still, for so distinguished a labor leader, one so celebrated as a champion of rank-and-file concerns, it was odd that when the trial began in Manhattan, only a single member of Carey's Queens Local 804 showed up.[6] If Carey was a rank-and-file reformer, where were the appreciative members? The dozen rank-and-file Teamster reformers to whom Crowe had dedicated his book were all once hard-core Carey supporters. Now the most prominent among them had publicly become Carey's enemies.[7]

To appreciate what it meant for them to change sides, you had to understand who these men were and what they risked by becoming politically active in their union. These were ready-mix concrete drivers, members of Local 282. One of the oldest locals in the city, Local 282 is often identified as New York's most strategically placed construction local in a $20 billion a year industry. That's because to control concrete deliveries to construction sites is to control the lever that can stop a costly job or keep it running. Whoever runs Local 282 rules a kingdom of shakedowns. It was a regime long controlled by proconsuls from the Gambino crime family. In the 1980s and early 1990s, the ruler was the Gambino underboss Sammy "the Bull" Gravano, the confessed killer of nearly three dozen people. Of Local 282, Gravano said, "I had control of the whole thing. The president, who was Bobby Sasso, the vice president, the secretary-treasurer, delegates, foremen. If I wanted a foreman in there, I'd tell Bobby, 'Put this guy to work.'"[8]

Starting in the 1970s, a few brave drivers in the local took the risk of founding FORE—Fear of Reprisal Ends. Men like Teddy Katsaros, Leon Olson, and Larry Kudla exposed the union's cozy ties with employers and protested dues increases, the dubious pension fund investments, and the nepotistic appointment of foremen—not in articles in *The Nation* but on the floor of their union hall, where the criticism came in the form of flying fists, kicks, and generalized stomping by Sammy "the Bull" loyalists. Eventually FORE ran an opposition ticket against the Gambino-supported slate. In their first try, they got nearly a third of the vote, earning them threats, more beatings, and disciplinary charges. But it also got them a segment on *60 Minutes*.[9]

Among working Teamsters in New York, they were the gold standard of reform. In Carey's first run for president, he wooed them energetically. FORE members responded by going over *en bloc* to his candidacy. The alliance lasted about a year—as long as it took for Carey, in their view, to side tacitly with the local's criminal establishment. Carey's handpicked trustee replaced the indicted Gambino associates who had been running Local 282 not with reformers but with relatives of the indicted officials. In September 1993, FORE leaders wrote to Ron Carey complaining that the Old Guard was still in power "unimpeded and unchallenged by the Carey administration during two periods of trusteeship."[10]

COUNTING ON CAREY

Above all, what truly distinguished Ron Carey was the way he served as the bearer of a generation's hopes. For the young progressives of the 1960s who had gone into the labor movement to change the world, Ron Carey was their last, best shot. It was their perspective on Carey that dominated the center-left opinion world. Most progressives didn't often get a chance to talk union politics with ready-mix drivers, UPS warehouse workers, funeral home workers, or garbage pickup drivers. Readers of *The Nation*, *LA Weekly*, *The Progressive*, and other journals of left and liberal opinion got their view of Carey either directly or indirectly from what may now be the last genuine AFL-CIO progressives still standing: Teamsters for a Democratic Union (TDU).[11]

After their experience as campus Trotskyists in the 1960s, TDU's founders had gotten jobs as truck drivers. They put out a scrappy broadsheet, and they outfought the other reform caucuses to emerge as the leading oppositionists in the Teamsters. Their demands were lower officer salaries, better contracts, and greater union democracy. Using their Berkeley-honed political skills, TDU'ers created a national labor paper and a broad national network of reformers in AFL-CIO unions; they reached out to nonprofits and to talented labor lawyers across the country; and they acquired assets in the foundation world. They'd had their moments, but at the twilight of the Reagan years, TDU wasn't growing. And by the 1990s, the leaders were hitting fifty. Yet the rationale for their project still seemed to make political sense. The Teamsters were the nation's biggest union; if you could change the Teamsters, you could change the AFL-CIO; if you could transform the labor movement, you could change America. Somehow, they thought they'd managed to convince Rudolph Giuliani, who had sued the Teamsters in 1988 as U.S. attorney, to force direct elections. Carey had become their candidate when he promised to fight the mob and stand up for the rank and file.

To sustain their hopes, aging progressives had to look past obvious geographical, biographical, and political facts. They chose to ignore the fact that Ron Carey was a Reagan Republican. Carey was a good speaker, he was conscientious, and he got better contracts than his predecessor.

Basically, though, Carey was a pretty ordinary guy from Queens, whose office was located in Long Island City, a couple of miles from where Archie Bunker, Edith, Gloria, and Meathead lived in Astoria. The sentiments in his newsletter were Bunkeristic: "If you want Uncle Sam to take care of you, that's Socialism. If you want Comrades to take care of you, that's Communism. But if you want to take care of yourself, that's American-ism."[12] Intellectuals gave Carey the willies no less than they did Archie Bunker.

For their part, the progressive intellectuals were happy just knowing that the TDU activists allied with Carey were out there in rank-and-file country doing the work of Eugene Debs and Clara Lemlich. They were sanguine about Carey's switch from the Republicans to the Democrats, who now controlled the Justice and Labor Departments. They saw it not as a matter of finding a powerful new protector but as a sign of Carey's growing political enlightenment.

It's true that few labor progressives actually liked Ron Carey personally. Even though TDU was credited with almost single-handedly engineering Carey's election victory, he always kept them at a great distance personally.[13] Still, they deeply believed in Carey's calling. It was a belief that became anchored by material interest. Much as Miners president John L. Lewis hired communists to do his organizing in the 1930s, Carey, in the 1990s, a couple of years after initially denying them the spoils of their elec-tion efforts, started hiring members of TDU—and lots of other former radicals. The more he hired, the more they believed. To question Carey's credentials was to deny their hopes and threaten their mortgages. Even those who privately ridiculed Carey's pretensions still felt that their own virtue—as paid organizers and middle-level staffers—could compensate for his failings.

Believers tend to develop a binary outlook. If you didn't believe in Carey's mission to save the labor movement, if you *publicly* questioned his essential virtue, you were allied with his adversaries—Hoffa and the Old Guard.[14] Statements about Carey's past dealings with mobsters or his choice of the Lucchese crime family's top asset to run the JFK Airport lo-cal could never be assessed primarily on the basis of their correspondence with the truth. Rather, all facts had to be judged on their political effect: did they advance the "New Teamsters" or the Old Guard?

Evidently, Ron Carey spent a career with corruption breaking out all around him, giving somewhat unbelievable accounts of how much he knew. In the end, when he got taken down, the dreams of hundreds of thousands—perhaps millions—went down with him. They saw him as their greatest hope. But given the reality of who Carey was—something they chose not to fully see—he appears, perhaps most sadly, as the most glittering mirage yet to deceive the travelers in labor's increasingly parched desert.

CONFRONTING THE LEGACY

The question of Ron Carey's bona fides probably couldn't have stirred such passions in any other union. Few cared about whether the heads of the National Education Association or the president of AFSCME were sincere in their vocations. Their unions were at least as large as the Teamsters. But the Teamsters occupied a special position in American labor history all out of proportion to their size. It was a violent and profoundly corrupt tradition that generated all sorts of extreme hopes and fears—like Attorney General Robert Kennedy's claim that whoever controlled the Teamsters controlled America. The Teamsters had turned their pension funds into investment pools for the mob. Teamsters cash bought U.S. senators and helped Richard Nixon pay off Watergate conspirators. Teamsters local presidents like Anthony "Tony Pro" Provenzano murdered their political opponents and got away with it. Carey's stature drew from the scale of the evil he claimed to confront.

Other than his ability to swim in the swampier precincts of Joint Council 16 for long periods without seeming to get muddy and a certain facility for echoing loudly and often what his hearers liked to hear, it's hard now to understand what people saw in Carey. Maybe it was his very Long Island City ordinariness. Mediocrity was interpreted as authenticity. But most likely, the sky-high hopes for Carey's presidency were held so tightly less because of who he was than because of what the Teamsters were.

Of course, many minimize the dimensions of Teamsters corruption. Hollywood as well as academic labor history have combined to portray concern with racketeering in the International Brotherhood of Teamsters as little more than middle-class moralizing or outright boss talk.[15] As Jimmy Hoffa himself explained to his members, "All this hocus-pocus about racketeers and crooks is a smokescreen to carry you back to the days when they drop you in the scrap heap like they do a worn-out truck."[16]

Both *Hoffa* (1990), written by Pulitzer-Prize-winning playwright David Mamet and starring Jack Nicholson, and Sylvester Stallone's *F.I.S.T.* (1979), show Jimmy Hoffa as a militant leader undivided in allegiance to his members. In his effort to gain muscle for a battle against goon-using Detroit employers, Hoffa enters into necessary, albeit fatal, alliances with mobsters. Mob domination of the Teamsters turns out to be a disaster not for the members, but for Hoffa, who dies as an almost Christ-like victim of America's most famous abduction.

Quite a transformation for a man who sold worthless underwater lots in Sun Valley, Florida, to his Local 299 members in partnership with "Colonel" Henry Lower, an alleged crime family associate who had escaped from a California prison. To pay off bad bank loans for Sun Valley, Hoffa started brokering pension fund loans to big-time mobsters like New Orleans boss Carlos "Kingfish" Marcello and Florida's Santos Trafficante. When Hoffa eventually got nailed, it was because he was swindling his members, not saving them.[17]

It was Hoffa, of course, who turned the Central States Pension Fund into the mob's bank. His practice of giving soft loans to tough guys made him a true author of the fund's present-day underfunding crisis.[18] Apologists insist that the sweetheart loans didn't matter; after all, didn't Hoffa pay out liberal pensions to the members? They overlook (a) that it was easy to pay out liberal benefits in the 1950s and early 1960s, because there were few who could qualify, and (b) that by the 1970s and 1980s, when members did begin to retire in big numbers, Central States diddled with vesting requirements so that many retirees got only a fraction of what they deserved.[19]

Still, when the 1986 Presidential Commission on Organized Crime described the Teamsters as "the most controlled union," it was probably an oversimplification. There was no question that mobsters chose Teamsters presidents—they testified that they did, and so did the presidents they chose.[20] But compared with, say, the Laborers, the Teamsters were much less of a mob monolith. The Teamsters had a longer period of mob-free existence. History and diversity combined to make them a lot more interesting, more violent, and more frightening.

In the late 1920s, when the Chicago Mafia's Murray "the Camel" Humphreys began kidnapping Teamsters officials, it wasn't a matter of turning the Teamsters toward corruption, but rather determining who would control the revenues from the rackets. A lot of nonmob labor racketeers fought back. Bullets flew and blood flowed. Whether you were an employer, a member, or a union leader, your life expectancy was a lot longer in the more completely mob-dominated Laborers than in the more tumultuous Teamsters.

Much of the mob violence in Teamsters life expressed the fact that it had a political life—however deformed. Presidential succession wasn't just a series of faceless, pharaonic mob dynasties, as in the Laborers. In LIUNA, political conflicts were little more than struggles between mob families. They could be settled at mob funerals. There was shouting, but no shooting. When Chicago told Secretary-Treasurer Terence O'Sullivan Sr. to go, he left and went into the insurance business. When New Jersey's Tony Provenzano told Hoffa to keep out of Teamsters politics, he wrote a book exposing Tony Pro's pension fund scams.[21]

Even David Mamet couldn't have done much with LIUNA's presidents Angelo or Peter Fosco—mush-mouth old dullards who merely did what they were told. Outsized figures like Jimmy Hoffa and Jackie Presser lent themselves to Hollywood treatment by bursting out of their assigned roles as mob puppets. Presser (*Teamster Boss: The Jackie Presser Story*, 1992, starring Brian Dennehy) double-crossed his mob minders by becoming an FBI snitch. As for Hoffa, at least three sources—two of whom say they loved him—insist that he asked them to kill mob bosses as well as his successor, general president Frank "Fitz" Fitzsimmons.[22]

For decades, there were no elections and no conventions in the Laborers. The larger, more diverse, more individualistic Teamsters were harder to control. Many industries in their jurisdiction—like UPS—didn't have hiring halls. Local elections were often real contests. Even the most well entrenched fiefdoms, like Local 560 in New Jersey, were not entirely secure. When Tony Provenzano got fewer votes for president than a certain Anthony Castellito, who ran on an independent ticket for secretary-treasurer, it made him anxious enough to have Castellito strangled with a nylon rope. As a reward, "Tony Pro" made the strangler, Salvatore Briguglio, a Local 560 business agent.[23] Briguglio, too, was murdered, not long after his 1976 indictment.[24]

But for all the mayhem and horror, Teamsters history revealed an aching gap between what could be and what was. You could see more clearly the giant energies that were being bottled up by petty hoodlums and greedy hacks. Teamsters history contains real social movements like the 1934 Minneapolis General Strike, a strike by Teamsters that ignited a citywide labor revolt. Well after World War II, the capacity for resistance remained. The 1970 wildcat strike shut down thirty-seven cities, illustrating the power of independent working-class action. Even the Chicago 1905 strike that produced twenty deaths in what was probably nothing but a giant shakedown illustrated the real tragedy of Teamster history: the ingenuity, the combativeness, the fearlessness, the capacity to mobilize entire communities—all being squandered on a phony cause.

And for all his swindles, something undeniably genuine clung to Jimmy Hoffa. He wasn't a lawyer, like his son or the Laborers' Arthur Coia Jr., another president who followed in the wake of a powerful father with mob ties. While still a teenager, Hoffa led "the Strawberry boys" in a genuine up-from-the-loading-docks successful revolt against Kroger, which netted them a good contract. But the notion that Hoffa remained true to his vocation, simply taking a modest cut of legal graft while improving the lives of the members, ignores the real Hoffa and the true betrayal at the core of Teamsters corruption—which continued in the Carey era and persists right up to Hoffa Jr.'s effort to sell out Las Vegas convention members to an organized crime–linked management.[25]

Almost by itself, the Test Fleet case destroys Jimmy Hoffa's credibility as a trade unionist. Test Fleet sent Hoffa to prison for jury tampering. But the substance of the case reveals the emptiness of the old argument "but he got good contracts." Yes, he did. But then he conspired with management to roll back the raises and the benefits while depriving the members of any meaningful contractual rights. In return, he was able secretly to take a huge slice from the profits of a corporation he controlled that was nothing more than an antiunion racket.

Test Fleet was created by Hoffa and crony Owen Bert Brennan, a Detroit local leader, presumably to haul new cars—although it's unclear whether it ever actually did. In the 1940's, the two Teamsters bosses set up the company secretly in their wives' names. Each spouse owned half the business. And a profitable business it was. According to the federal indictment, GM funneled $1,000,000 to Hoffa through Test Fleet. The money rolled in because Test Fleet enabled General Motors' affiliate, Continental Carriers, to break strikes, lower costs, and control dissident drivers in the car haul business. When labor trouble brewed, GM affiliates simply switched to Test Fleet.[26]

From the Test Fleet acorn planted in Michigan grew the oak tree of the nationwide but unjustifiably obscure Boffa operation. Eugene Boffa was a high-rolling mobster who had begun his "labor leasing" business in the late 1960s.[27] He operated under the protection of Tony Provenzano and Russell Bufalino, an even more influential mafioso whose territory included parts of New York State, Pennsylvania, New Jersey, and Delaware.[28] When Boffa's enterprise expired about a decade later, his customers included about thirty companies in thirty states, including Coca-Cola, JC Penney, and Continental Can.

Boffa, like Hoffa, offered corporate executives an opportunity to cut labor costs. The companies would fire their drivers and sign up Boffa's. But Boffa's drivers were simply the fired drivers—they remained members of the same Teamsters local, but now they worked under a substandard contract. If workers went on strike, explained one Teamsters participant, "we'd break the strike the same day—it was an illegal secondary boycott." Then the men would be hired back, except for the "troublemakers."

An important player in Boffa's racket was Frank "the Irishman" Sheeran. The genial Genovese hit man—the only Irish American who was also a member of the Mafia's Commission—was also the head of a Delaware Teamsters local. He got 2 percent from Boffa on each corporate contract negotiated in his local's territory. Sheeran also earned extra cash as a contract killer for both Russell Bufalino and Jimmy Hoffa.

Hoffa was extremely close to both Sheeran and Russell Bufalino—perhaps fatally so. According to the FBI, the two showed up in Detroit the day after Hoffa was abducted from Machus Red Fox restaurant in Bloomfield in cars that were gifts from Boffa. Although Sheeran and Bufalino remained top suspects, they were never indicted. But just before he died,

Sheeran admitted that on Bufalino's orders and at Tony Pro's urging, he'd put two bullets in the back of Hoffa's head. Notes Sheeran, "My friend didn't suffer."[29]

Hoffa thought he was going to convince his good friend Sheeran to kiss Tony Pro. He never suspected he was about to be kissed. No doubt, it was a great betrayal, but hardly Judas-like. It was just one of countless numbers of betrayals that had been set in motion long ago in the days of the ancestors—Driscoll, Young, and Shea—and would continue under Ron Carey.

THE MAN WHO NEVER KNEW

Without Steven Brill's portrait of him in *The Teamsters* as the lone honest official, Carey, an otherwise obscure leader of a medium-sized local in Queens, would probably never have gotten close to the Marble Palace.[30] The 1977 bestseller, written by a top-flight investigative journalist, may have been the definitive book on Teamsters corruption.[31] Nearly thirty years later, it's striking how much Brill seems to have gotten right about Hoffa's abduction. It's an editorial convention, though, that you can't have an exposé with no good guys. A nearly fifty-page chapter reveals Carey to be a non-golfing, non–pinkie ring wearing Teamsters leader who was in the truck barns at 6:00 a.m. to meet with his members. He lived in a modest two-family house in Queens, which he shared with his father, a retired UPS driver. Unlike some Teamsters presidents who made nearly as much as corporate presidents, Carey's salary wasn't more than a UPS driver with seniority.[32] He had five kids, and his wife worked at Macy's to make ends meet.

In 1989, when the government forced the Teamsters to hold direct elections, Carey was well positioned to get support from reformers looking for a candidate. On the basis of Brill's glowing, knowledgeable, and finely detailed portrait, thousands of activists thought they knew a lot about Ron Carey.

ALL IN THE FAMILY

Brill portrays Carey's extended family as uniquely close. After a stint in the Marines, Ron follows in the footsteps of his father, Joseph, becoming a UPS driver in Long Island City. In the 1950s, father and son chipped in $18,000 to buy a modest house in Kew Gardens. Twenty years later, the Careys had created an ideal 1950s domestic arrangement. Joe had retired from UPS and gone back to college, but he was still sharing the same house with Ron, Ron's wife, and the five kids. On the rare occasions when hardworking, abstemious Ron took a vacation, when it wasn't in his backyard, it was to his father's bungalow in New Jersey.[33]

Who would have thought that Joe Carey was a multimillionaire from his purchases of UPS stock? Not Ron Carey. Nor did the Teamsters president suspect that he stood to inherit a hefty sum from the estate when Joe died in 1992. How Joe Carey accumulated $2.1 million in UPS stock was particularly hard to understand, since UPS didn't allow nonmanagement employees to buy company stock. But it turned out that in important respects, Ron and Joe weren't all that close. According to Carey's official spokesperson, "His father never discussed in detail or gave an explanation of how he got [the stock] or how it increased in value over time."[34] Said Carey of his father, "He was a very private guy."[35]

After his election, Carey had exclaimed, "This is no longer a union that's going to be run by millionaires."[36] But even without his inheritance, Carey had become a stealth real estate millionaire. Besides his Kew Gardens duplex, he owned a duplex in Jamaica Hills, Queens, a couple of oceanfront condos in Florida, a condo in Scottsdale, Arizona, a "fixer-upper" in New Jersey, and a condo in Virginia—most of which he had purchased secretly by signing his wife's name. How had he acquired it all on a salary that he boasted was less than the Marble Palace chef's? Pressed by reporters from the *New York Times*, *Time*, and *BusinessWeek*, Carey explained that he got some of the mortgage money from his mother, some from his son, and the rest from his mistress, who had been a co-owner of some of the Florida real estate.[37]

And despite how close the Careys seemed to be, Ron Carey claimed to have lost track of his brother after Carlisle Carey married into the

Colombo crime family. Brother Carlisle wed Josephine Garofalo, the widow of Angelo "Fat Tony" Garofalo, a Colombo crime family associate. Carlisle served as an officer of a family-owned carting company and became the company's contact person with the Teamsters,[38] but only after a series of deaths in the Garofalo family.

With family assistance, Angelo Garofalo had founded a prosperous Long Island carting business. Josephine became eligible for remarriage when the 550-pound Angelo died in Sing Sing of a heart attack. When their son Ralph, who was also in the carting business, died, it was assumed that he'd had a heart attack too. He weighed 560 pounds. But the Suffolk County Coroner later decided that the heart attack was due to a shooting. Suffolk Police concluded, though, that the murder was not a mob hit.[39]

Still, people have been known to get whacked in the mob-dominated carting business on Long Island, where Teamsters Local 813 has jurisdiction. Mob guys owned the carting companies. They also owned the "stops"—the customers who paid to have their garbage picked up. Mob owners charged the stops what they wanted. Without the union, the cartel wouldn't have run so smoothly: Contractors who thought about undercutting the cartel would have labor troubles. Or worse, rebel carters like Robert Kubecka and his brother-in-law would be murdered, allegedly for cooperating with law enforcement officials.[40]

Would Ron Carey be less inclined to trustee the carting local because of his brother's involvement in the carting industry? Carey said he never even met the Garofalos—except for Josephine—and he'd lost contact with his brother. Yet Barbara Carey, Ron Carey's wife, had her car registered at Carlisle Carey's address. And the Garofalo family lawyer handled the probate of Carey's father's estate. Carey explained that he had registered the car at his brother's house "for security reasons."[41]

WITNESS FOR THE DEFENSE

It never occurred to Carey's supporters that, in telling ways, Carey's leadership would be shaped by the necessary alliances, promises, and practices for advancement in a corrupt institution. For decades, Carey kept stumbling into associations with crooks—particularly from the Lucchese and DeCavalcante crime families. They would do bad things, like kill Teamsters business agents and use Carey's local to break strikes and sign sweetheart contracts; the Local's dental plan was run by the DeCavalcantes, who were also able to use Local 804's pension funds for loan sharking. Somehow, while Carey was Teamsters general president, the Lucchese crime family got to name one of its own to trustee Local 295, the JFK Airport local, made infamous in Martin Scorsese's *Goodfellas*. No one denies that these things happened. It's just, they say, that Carey didn't realize who the bad people were or what they were doing until too late.

When Carey testified in the spring of 1975 as a character witness for a local member, John Conti, he told the federal jury in Manhattan that Conti was "peaceful and decent guy, a regular guy."[42] The feds had accused Conti of being part of a Lucchese crime family crew that ran a murderous labor peace racket in the garment center.

In a deposition years later, Carey said that he didn't remember serving as a witness for Conti.[43] It was only when the trial transcript was shown to him that he was able to recollect the circumstances. Carey thought he was testifying in a "union matter." He did so regularly for members who got in trouble. In a typical contortion, Carey's supporters pointed out that at the time Carey testified for Conti, Conti was only a Lucchese family *associate*. Only about two years later was he formally inducted into the family with the full ceremony and oaths.[44] Carey, they say, was helping a member in trouble, but his goodwill effort was twisted to aid a criminal conspiracy.

WITNESS FOR THE PROSECUTION

Somehow Carey never knew that his local had become part of a full-blown criminal enterprise that operated for a decade under the control of the DeCavalcante crime family. Starting in the late 1970s, Carey's second in command, Secretary-Treasurer Johnny Long, did what mob patsies do—he handed over the local's pension funds to the mob and helped the family create a dental plan for Local 804 members. Long also persuaded the heads of other Joint Council 16 locals to create dental plans run by the DeCavalcantes. At the behest of the mob, Local 804 broke strikes, offered employers sweetheart contracts, and arranged for mob-connected companies to get contracts with UPS. In exchange for his services, Long received hundreds of thousands in bribes from Jesse "Doc" Hyman, a dentist–loan shark who worked under the control of Vincent "Vinnie" Rotondo, a made guy in the DeCavalcantes' organization.[45]

Notwithstanding the dead Teamster who was found in the trunk of Hyman's car, the enterprise thrived until 1985. Then Hyman got caught. Under pressure from Rudolph Giuliani, then U.S. attorney, Doc Hyman gave up Long, who was then charged in December 1987 with bribe taking. The exposure seems to have discredited Hyman's mob handler, Vinnie Rotondo, who was found dead less than a month later with a bag of rotting fish in his new Lincoln Continental. "Fish," explained the *New York Times*, "are used to designate an informer or a mob member who has dishonored himself."[46]

How was Local 804 transformed into a mob enterprise without Carey ever finding out? More specifically, how come Carey never inquired about the investments Long was making? These were the local's biggest investments, and Long couldn't have moved a nickel without Carey's signature. According to Carey's defenders, he was the victim of a plot hatched by Long and Doc Hyman. They made it seem as if the money was going into interest-bearing certificates of deposit. Carey signed off on the loans, but he never grasped who was actually getting the money.

In 1985, Giuliani had subpoenaed all Local 804 records relating to Hyman. Yet on finding out how in 1987 the union's funds were actually being used, Carey's professed shock and outrage seem far-fetched. He'd written out checks that went to Hyman, and Hyman had gone to trial and been convicted. When asked by investigative journalist Jeffrey Goldberg about this gap, Carey at first claimed that he didn't remember the subpoena. Then he acknowledged the possibility that he might: "It could have been brought to my attention," conceded Carey. "Obviously it was brought to my attention, and I was told it was being taken care of. It would not have led me to consider that this had anything to do with John Long."[47]

When Giuliani offered Carey immunity to testify against Long, Carey took it. To meet Giuliani's terms, Carey also had to promise to work with the FBI. But why, asked his adversaries, if Carey had nothing to hide, did he go for Giuliani's deal? Carey says he didn't want to ask for immunity. He claims his lawyer coerced him into signing. Carey couldn't help it. He was in a tight spot. His attorney gave him an ultimatum. Either ask for immunity or get a new lawyer. Under duress, Carey signed. But he says he later regretted it.[48]

The Long affair expresses Carey's career-long penchant for doing the wrong thing and blaming subordinates. It also foretells his future behavior. The hundreds of thousands in union money that wound up in Doc Hyman's hands got there under circumstances that strongly resembled those surrounding the $885,000 that went into campaign money laundering ten years later, in 1996. In both cases, Carey approved the expenditures, and in both cases, he explained that trusted subordinates had betrayed him. In both cases, he said he thought the money was being used for a worthy purpose. In 1996, it was helping environmental causes, getting out the vote, aiding the elderly, promoting the use of medical marijuana, and so on. A decade earlier, it was getting good, safe returns for his members. And all the time, the list of people who took advantage of Carey's good will and good intentions kept lengthening: It's his lawyer, it's the consultants, it's his secretary-treasurer, it's his campaign manager. Nothing is ever his fault.

A GOODFELLA FOR THE GOODFELLAS' LOCAL

Moviegoers packed the theaters in 1990 to see Martin Scorsese's *Goodfellas*, starring Robert DeNiro and Joe Pesci. The film showed how a Queens-based Lucchese family crew pulled off the $6 million Lufthansa heist at JFK. The Lufthansa heist set world robbery records, but, as the movie makes clear, it was only the culmination of a series of airport robberies, heists, and hijackings that had been made possible by crime family control of the JFK Teamsters—members of Local 295.[49] So you can imagine General President Carey's embarrassment when two years later he discovered that the Lucchese crime family's ranking asset in the Teamsters—William Genoese—had been appointed to be the trustee of 295—the *Goodfellas* Local.

Carey explained how his fingerprints were found on the appointment documents. Soon after his inauguration, he told Independent Review Board investigators, he got a call from Joint Council 16 boss Barry Feinstein pressing him about the Local 295 trusteeship. (Feinstein, whose own local had been accused of being one of the Luccheses' New York fiefdoms, would soon be banned for life from the Teamsters because of embezzlement charges.)[50] Carey said that he immediately handed off the assignment to Eddie Burke, his campaign manager and principal aide. Carey said he knew that Local 295 was mobbed up. But he gave the job to Burke, who claimed he was unaware of any mob problems in the JFK local.

Burke acknowledged that he badly bungled the job. He couldn't handle the intense pressure from Feinstein and from Genoese himself, who constantly bugged him about the job. But he didn't think he'd done anything wrong. Neither Feinstein nor Genoese had ever said anything about a mob problem in Local 295. So he "saw no harm" in trying to "ease political tension in the union."

No sooner did Genoese get the job than Judge Frederick B. Lacey took it away. He explained why in a 1992 memo: the Genoeses' appointment, he declared, "would directly and indirectly further and contribute to the association of the [local] to with the La Cosa Nostra or elements thereof."[51]

After Judge Lacey's reversal of the Genoese appointment, Burke took full responsibility. He apologized to Carey, confessing, "I screwed up."[52]

Carey had handed Burke a rubber sword, and Burke fell upon it. The ritual satisfied the Independent Review Board, a federally imposed three-person panel with the power to investigate and expel Teamster officials. On the other hand, if Carey was really so intent on wiping out mob influence, why give so crucial an assignment to someone who wouldn't have known the Godfather from a grandfather clock?

TALES FROM THE LAUNDROMAT

After his apparent second-term triumph in 1996, Carey exulted, "This victory sends a message to every mob boss in America: Our treasury and our pension funds will never again be the piggy bank for organized crime."[53]

By this time, though, Teamsters officials no longer controlled investments in the two giant Teamsters pension funds, so there was much less opportunity to get the mob involved. But treasury looting was still a possibility, and in 1996, there was a plot to loot the treasury. Carey was the beneficiary, since the money was secretly funneled into his campaign. But was he to blame? Not at all, insisted his supporters. There were two big conspiracies, but Carey was the victim in both of them. First, he'd been victimized by a band of greedy consultants who took advantage of his goodwill and concern for public policy issues. Then the government took advantage of his apparent transgression to punish him for his reform leadership of the New Teamsters, particularly his militant handling of the 1997 UPS strike.

As left-wing conspiracy theories go, this was one of the least compelling in a long time. Why would a Democratic administration want to indict one of its biggest campaign contributors? Even more obviously, why would the Clinton Justice Department go after top Democratic Party officials, like Terry McAuliffe, who were also implicated in the plot? And how could the outside consultants and junior-level lawyers who ultimately did get convicted acquire enough leverage over Carey that he would approve their tapping the Teamsters treasury for nearly $900,000—at a time when the union was going broke? How much weight could Carey's claim that he couldn't concentrate because of bad knees really hold?[54]

For almost twenty years, Teamsters reformers had stayed in the contest almost solely on the basis of their credibility. A 1991 poll had shown that TDU was more trusted than any of the candidates. But when they spun stories about Carey's innocence and victimhood against all grain of probability, they seemed like just another bunch of clients who backed their boss no matter what. True, Carey's corruption never rose to the level of Hoffa's in the Test Fleet case or the Boffa Affair under Fitz, but Carey was being judged by higher standards. By standing by their man, Teamsters reformers lost their moral capital. A decade later, they hadn't got it back.

Naturally, the Republicans jumped all over Carey and the Teamsters money laundering scandal. In many ways it was even juicier than Coia's relationship with the Clintons. Being able to show that the White House was on good terms with a mob asset like Coia was helpful. But there was nothing illegal about the relationship. In the case of Carey and the looting of the Teamsters treasury, it looked as if the top AFL-CIO leadership as well as the DNC's top fund-raising figures could all be indicted.

As stubbornly partisan as the issue became, some facts were not in dispute. In 1996, there was definitely a Teamsters presidential election money-laundering plot. Union officials are prohibited from using the union treasury to run for office. The purpose of the plot was to tap the Teamsters treasury without seeming to. Several organizations—Clinton-Gore, the Democratic National Committee, the AFL-CIO, and Citizen Action—were in on the various schemes. Carey officials would send them big checks from IBT campaign funds. Then the recipients—after taking what amounted to a money-laundering cut—would persuade one of their own donors to send a smaller check to the Carey campaign.

The 1996 Teamsters swaps scandal never got quite the media exposure of Al Gore's Buddhist Temple affair or Clinton's Lincoln Bedroom scandal. Those stories had stronger legs because they involved the men at the top of the ticket—and perhaps because the transgressions involved violations of sacred space. The swaps scandal, however, exposed, as nothing ever had before, the terms of the relationship between the Democratic Party and the AFL-CIO, its biggest single supporter.

IN PURSUIT OF CAREY'S MILLIONS

Midway through July 1996, the Carey crisis was a national story. It was all over the *Washington Post* that he'd suffered a series of surprising defeats by the Hoffa forces at the Teamsters convention in Philadelphia and that the Carey administration was broke going into the union's fall election. This meant a crisis not just for Carey but for the national Democratic Party and the AFL-CIO. In the short term, Carey's cash flow crisis crimped Democratic Party fund-raising efforts for the election in November, especially in the congressional and state races. In the long term, a Carey loss to the right-leaning Hoffa might drain many millions a year from Democratic Party coffers—and also put the leadership of the AFL-CIO in play.

Carey's predicament and its impact on his Democratic Party allies resembled a famous scene in Shakespeare's *Twelfth Night*, where Sir Andrew Aguecheek's freeloading companions discover that he's running out of money. The ringleader, Sir Toby Belch, tells the lame-witted Sir Andrew that he has a plan to help him recoup his fortune. In the meantime, though, Sir Toby suggests to Sir Andrew, "Thou hadst need send for more money."

One actor well suited for the role of the wily Sir Toby was Harold Ickes, the White House deputy chief of staff. Attorney Ickes knew the Teamsters. Barry Feinstein, the boss of Joint Council 16 who had "generated" the Genoese appointment, had been Ickes's client. So had Local 560, run by the murderous Provenzano family for the Genoveses. Ickes had also been the attorney for Local 858, one of the two *Goodfellas* locals at JFK controlled by the Lucchese crime family. Ickes's alarming client list had delayed his White House appointment, but eventually Ickes managed to reach the West Wing, serving as what he called the White House "point person" for organized labor.[55]

The White House viewed the Teamsters as a broken ATM that needed fixing before the midterm elections. As early as 1995, staffers had brought the problem of Carey's faltering cash flow to Ickes's attention. After an auspicious start, the Teamsters had stopped paying up. In 1992, Carey had given $2.4 million. But since then, according to a White House memo entitled "Teamster Notes," he'd tapped out. Carey himself was hard to reach. He seemed "distracted" by his internal opposition. The White House put Ickes on the "Get Cash from Carey" project.

White House staffers seem to have realized that Carey's internal opponents were making it hard for him to spend freely on political campaigns. They kept leaking the amounts of his contributions to the press. Many

Teamsters thought the expenditures were a waste of dues money. By appealing to the issues they thought mattered to Carey, though, the West Wing aides hoped to rekindle Carey's enthusiasm for check writing. There were some national issues he seemed to care about, but "parochial" issues seemed to count a great deal too.

Ickes tried to soften up Carey by appealing to items on his "parochial" agenda. He had a deputy trade secretary make calls to the boss of Diamond Walnut, a California company the Teamsters had been striking for over two years; the impression left was that trade matters might run more smoothly if Diamond Walnut settled with the Teamsters. Ickes arranged to have someone lean on the Japanese who chose FedEx instead of UPS for a slot in the Japanese package delivery market. The administration helped the Teamsters win their organizing campaign at Pony Express in part, it seems, by fixing it with the Labor Department.[56]

But Ickes, the big fixer, didn't fix the larger problem. Carey didn't send off for any more money. Conceivably it may be because Ickes wasn't seen as pushing very hard—that's what Attorney General Janet Reno said in denying the request for a special prosecutor to investigate Ickes. More likely, though, Carey didn't give because he was financially strapped and politically exposed. That may also explain why when Bill Clinton kept inviting him to the White House for breakfast, Carey kept turning him down. Few people like to be hit up for money, especially before breakfast. If you know the POTUS is going to ask for money and you don't have any, keeping your distance may be the best strategy.

Avoidance worked only so long. The DNC kept sending what amounted to invoices. But the Teamsters' DRIVE—Democratic Republican Independent Voter Education, their political action committee and its legal source of funds—was empty.

SWAPS AND TOPS

That was the beauty of the particular swaps plan that Martin Davis had come up with. It didn't require legal funds from the Teamsters' PAC—it was broke. Instead it relied on illegal funds from the general treasury that the union could channel back to itself. Davis, a Teamsters campaign consultant who would eventually be convicted of money laundering, was at age thirty-six a veteran political operative with a top-flight client list. In 1991, at age thirty, he'd run Carey's direct-mail campaign. A consultant's job with the Democratic National Committee followed. Now, in 1996, he devised a magic pole to vault over the formidable money obstacle. Everyone would get paid. It wouldn't cost the principals anything. Both of his primary clients—the Teamsters and the DNC—would have their financial needs satisfied simply by exchanging checks. And with the Teamsters' needs satisfied, Davis would get paid—and he could get the cash for the direct-mail campaign Carey urgently needed to combat the surging Hoffa.[57]

Davis called his swaps plan "leveraging." It sounded something like the pitch National Public Radio uses in its fund-raising marathons. If you give, your contribution will be matched by a wealthy donor. Davis's idea was for wealthy DNC donors to give to the Teamsters; then the Teamsters would match their donation "and much more" by giving to the DNC. The difference, of course, between NPR fund-raising and Davis's "leverage" method was that the key donors weren't wealthy at all—they were ordinary Teamsters who were putting up the matching funds involuntarily. The money was coming directly out of the Teamsters treasury.

Davis's money-laundering efforts can be divided into two types: those that failed and those that didn't. At least semisuccessful were the pledges from three of labor's biggest honchos: SEIU's Andy Stern, AFSCME's Gerald McEntee, and AFL-CIO secretary-treasurer Rich Trumka. Each promised to contribute $50,000. But it's illegal for labor leaders to contribute to each other's campaigns. When Trumka was questioned about his contribution before an election officer, he took the Fifth. Stern's lawyer admitted that he'd given $16,000 illegally for his client. A top McEntee aide acknowledged that he'd kicked in $30,000–$35,000 for his boss, who'd had come up with the money by leaning on a union vendor.

In the failed money-laundering efforts, Davis tried to exploit the contacts of his DNC boss, Terry McAuliffe. Working through a deputy and party bigwigs like California senator Diane Feinstein and Nebraska senator Bob Kerrey, McAuliffe tried to hit up wealthy contributors to the DNC. The idea was that instead of contributing to the DNC, the big money throwers could contribute instead to Teamsters for a Corruption-Free Union (TCFU)—and the DNC would consider it a favor. (Especially since the DNC would get a huge money-laundering fee from the Teamsters: Davis promised the DNC $1 million if they could come up with $100,000.) Among those approached with requests for $100,000 contributions were a Waco, Texas, insurance executive and Judith Vasquez, a wealthy Filipina businesswoman who had recently given money at a Diane Feinstein soirée. Vasquez, described in a DNC memo as "the richest woman entrepreneur in the Philippines," initially accepted Davis's offer to contribute, but she reneged after consulting with her lawyer. He had some problems with the idea. After checking out TCFU, he observed, "It wasn't a charity." What's more, "Vasquez wasn't a citizen. She didn't even have a green card. And she was an employer."

Davis didn't give up. He tried to coax McAuliffe back into the swaps arena. To make sure McAuliffe understood how much Carey appreciated the efforts of the world's greatest campaign fund-raiser, Davis asked the Teamsters president to call McAuliffe personally to tell him how grateful he was. Carey never spoke directly to McAuliffe, but he admitted to leaving a message.[58] Presumably McAuliffe got it, because he now reached out to involve Bob Kerrey on behalf of TCFU. The Nebraska senator and war hero was serving as the head of the Democratic Senatorial Campaign Committee. Kerrey turned for cash to Bernard Rapoport, an insurance millionaire from Waco, Texas. Despite his red-state residence and the unlikely provenance of his fortune, Rapoport must have seemed like he had the right credentials to give to a left-wing Teamsters campaign. In April 1996, he had told *Mother Jones*, "My father was a Russian Jewish revolutionist. The first candidate I supported was a socialist."[59] Kerrey asked Rapoport if he would like to contribute to TCFU. "What do you think of it?" asked Kerrey. "I don't like it," answered Rapoport. Kerrey confessed, "I don't either." Rapoport was later asked why he wouldn't give to TCFU. "I'm not a lawyer," he testified, "but I didn't think it would smell good."

Failing to get the desperately needed money through DNC channels, Davis decided to go Citizen Action—a get-out-the-vote nonprofit organization that he'd already swapped with. He contacted Ira Arlook, head of Citizen Action, and urged him to ask the Teamsters for $150,000. Arlook would write a $100,000 check to Davis's company, the November Group, for nonexistent services. Davis would put the money into mailings for Carey. And Citizen Action could keep a $50,000 swap fee.

It sounded just fine to Arlook. He wrote up a request to the Teamsters political director, Bill Hamilton. But Hamilton responded with a "Dear Ira" letter. Hamilton, prosecutors later suggested, was concerned with the suspicions that might be raised if anyone were to find out. Only a week before, the Teamsters had cut a check to Citizen Action for $475,000. At a time of great financial stress, it would seem suspicious for the Teamsters to follow up a check they've written for $475,000 with one for $150,000 a week later. "As much as I'd like to," Hamilton wrote Arlook, "I can't do another request."

But Hamilton's previous approval to Citizen Action and other nonprofits had already done enough to earn him a future jail sentence and to get his boss expelled from the Teamsters.

WHAT DID CAREY KNOW?

When U.S. District Court Judge Julius Edelstein appointed Judge Kenneth C. Conboy to be the Teamsters election officer, Conboy was the third in as many years. His predecessor, Barbara Quindel, had been forced to resign because of her ties to a swaps activist. She denied that she'd ever dated Michael Ansara, a small-fry Teamsters consultant who was finally convicted of conspiracy, but she acknowledged that her husband had an affiliation with one of the swapping organizations. Quindel never did actually uncover the plot herself.

Skeptics wondered how Quindel could possibly have missed the deception whose discovery led inexorably to Carey's disqualification. It was so obvious and grotesque. By far the largest single contributor to either Carey or Hoffa was the ubiquitous Teamsters for a Corruption-Free Union, which served as the principal conduit for the swaps. It had only six members. The biggest contributor of the six was a college student— who turned out to be the wife of Teamsters direct-mail consultant Michael Ansara. Money from the Teamsters' treasury went to organizations that agreed to give not to the Teamsters but, instead, to Teamsters for a Corruption-Free Union—TFCU would put the money into the Carey campaign. Somehow, TFCU got by Quindel, with all her staff and expertise. It took John Murphy, a Hoffa aide, digging in unprocessed piles of documents in Quindel's office, to raise TFCU's national profile.[60]

Judge Edelstein's appointment of Judge Conboy signaled that he had reverted to his initial skepticism about Carey's reform vocation. Conboy had a reputation for coming down hard on corruption. In addition to serving as a federal judge, Conboy had been a former New York City commissioner of investigation in the scandal-marked years of the Ed Koch administration. During Conboy's tenure, eighty-seven Koch officials were indicted, convicted, or forced to resign. While Carey's claims of ignorance produced only measured skepticism in Quindel, they prompted in Conboy a kind of indignant incredulity. He found Carey's various denials "unbelievable," "not credible," "difficult to believe," "completely untenable," and "directly contradicted by the documentary evidence."

Carey's defense is familiar: "If there is a victim here," he grumbled, "I certainly am the victim." He didn't know what his aides were doing. Carey simply had no idea that the $475,000 he'd authorized to go to Citizen Action was going to come back to him in the form of desperately needed campaign funds.

According to Conboy, Carey's motive for promoting the treasury plunder was plain. He was afraid he was going to lose to Hoffa. He was slipping in the polls; campaign funds were low; and he'd been told he needed a last-minute direct-mail campaign to turn the tide. So the run on the treasury was his last desperate hope.

Carey admitted to Conboy that he went to LaGuardia Airport in October for a meeting with his attorney and his campaign manager, Jere Nash. There Nash, who would later plead guilty to fraud, read him the bad news from the latest polls. His lead over Hoffa—once a seemingly insurmountable 25–30 points—had slipped to a statistical tie. Something had to be done. Carey also admitted to authorizing a huge, million-dollar direct-mail effort to beat back the Hoffa surge. He also conceded that three days later he had authorized sending a $475,000 check to Citizen Action. The check to Citizen Action was eighty times larger than any previous Teamsters contribution to the group. DRIVE, the Teamsters' PAC, was tapped out. Why give so much money to Citizen Action, Conboy asked, when you're broke?[61]

Carey didn't deny that the union was broke; he only denied that he *knew* the union was broke. At this point in the October 1996 deposition, Conboy whipped out a document. It was a loan request Carey had made in October to Crestar Bank for $500,000 to replenish the empty DRIVE account.

> Conboy: On page 7 of this document, is that your signature?
> Carey: Yes.
> Conboy: In which you approve, specifically approve, these monies being borrowed?
> Carey: That's correct.
> Conboy: And the next page, is that again your signature?
> Carey: Yes.
> Conboy: Does this refresh your recollection as to whether DRIVE borrowed $500,000 from Crestar Bank at the beginning of October 1996?
> Carey: It doesn't refresh my recollection, but it appears that we did.

Carey's final version of the real reason he decided to give nearly half a million dollars to Citizen Action while the union was going broke was not that Citizen Action was going to kick the money back into his campaign, but because "they were out there on issues that were important to us, Medicare, get out the vote, get people educated about the issues that would confront them."[62]

In the past, professions of good intentions and wide-ranging ignorance had always been enough to earn Carey a pass. This time, though, he had to surmount a problem of scale. The sheer number of illegal schemes, schemers, and discussants at work—many of them top figures in the AFL-CIO and Democratic Party establishments—perhaps Bill Clinton himself—raised the question: How could officials from the Clinton-Gore campaign, the Democratic National Committee, the Democratic Senatorial Campaign Committee, the Democratic Congressional Campaign Committee, U.S. senators Bob Kerrey and Diane Feinstein, plus various big campaign contributors—how could they all know about the swaps while Carey, the beneficiary of all the schemes, remained utterly oblivious for the entire five months the frantic finagling was going on?

Rather than accept that Carey knew, his supporters insisted that he was the victim of a Clinton administration conspiracy. His most passionate journalist supporter, former *Newsday* labor reporter Ken Crowe, writes: "Carey partisans, some pro-labor academics and Carey himself suspect a linkage—as paranoid as that may seem to others—between his UPS triumph, his aggressive leadership of the Teamsters turning the union into an activist force."[63]

If it's not paranoid, it's certainly self-serving and politically naïve. Setting aside the way the strike's results were overhyped, if it hadn't been for the Clinton administration, there would never have been a UPS strike. UPS, the Congress, and much of the media demanded that Clinton invoke Taft-Hartley—which probably would have postponed strike action indefinitely—and Clinton refused. And Quindel later acknowledged that she'd withheld the results of her swaps investigation so as not to interfere with the strike. Short of signing up for picket duty at a UPS package center, what more could government officials have done to help?

The clearest sign of a political movement that has lost its way is not that it suffers a defeat but that it's incapable of taking responsibility for it. Instead of reexamining their strategy—becoming Carey's clients—the AFL-CIO left looked for the culprits at the highest levels and the lowest levels. They pointed their fingers at hired consultants like Martin Davis and outside attorneys—mostly in their twenties and early thirties—who had somehow wormed their way into the campaign and bamboozled their superiors. And, of course, they looked at the Establishment, for whom their transgressive project was just too radical.

CRIMES, PUNISHMENTS, AND IMMUNITIES

Perhaps even more implausible than charging the Clinton administration with seeking to carry out an antilabor vendetta against Carey because of the great UPS victory was the labor left's notion of the manner of attack—biting its own tail, exposing the money maneuvers of the DNC, Clinton-Gore, top party funders, and so on.[64]

Some vendetta. By the time Clinton left office in January 2001, no one who mattered—none of the top union officials, Democratic Party officials, or marquee labor lawyers—had been indicted. As in the Abu Ghraib prison scandal, it was low-level "rogue operators" who were sanctioned. And even the rogue consultants got mostly fines and probation. Only after the Bush administration took control of the Justice Department did Mary Jo White, a Clinton holdover, indict Carey.

Succeeding Rudolph Giuliani as U.S. attorney for the Southern District of New York, White automatically had jurisdiction over the Teamsters cases, following the 1989 consent decree. As the scandal gathered media momentum, White took charge of the swaps investigation and began the slow process of accumulating evidence, using the traditional tactics of getting one conspirator to give up another.

White didn't make it very far up the conspiratorial ladder, though. Her office failed to turn up much new evidence. What facts had been uncovered by previous investigations grew stale. Of course, there were indictments, guilty pleas, and convictions, but they were almost entirely restricted to those whom real estate heiress Leona Helmsley famously designated as "the little people."

Among those charged were consultants Mike Ansara and Martin Davis, together with Charles Blitz, a Californian who'd helped them raise money for TCFU. They all pleaded out, receiving fines and probation, but no jail time. The testimony provided by Davis & Co. implicated Jere Nash, Carey's campaign manager. But Nash escaped prison by giving up Bill Hamilton, the Teamsters political director, who'd only been with the Teamsters about a year.

Hamilton actually did get a three-year prison sentence. But with him, the ratting-out process reached a low and final plateau. Hamilton was apparently never offered a deal. Lacking any incentive, when he appeared as a witness for the prosecution in the Carey trial, Hamilton's testimony was so damaging to the federal case that the U.S. attorneys had to put on another witness to rebut it.

That leaves the central figure in the campaign scandal, whose position all the others were trying to save. Did Ron Carey suffer martyrdom? He was removed from office, banned for life from the International Brother-hood of Teamsters, and then, like so many of his predecessors as Teamsters president, indicted on federal charges. But with the trial in 2001 at the Pearl Street Federal Courthouse in Lower Manhattan, Ron Carey's path began to diverge sharply from St. Sebastian's.

Both had suffered grievous wounds. But after being pierced with a hail of arrows on the orders of Emperor Diocletian, St. Sebastian suffered a second martyrdom. After the removal of multiple arrows from his body, Sebastian returned to the emperor's court to berate him for oppressing Christians. This time Diocletian sentenced St. Sebastian to be beaten to death with clubs and his body thrown in the Cloacae Maxima (Rome's great sewer).

After his five-week trial, Ron Carey got to go home.

Most who attended the proceedings felt the verdict was only fair. The trial had been interrupted by the September 11 attacks, and when the ju-rors were called back in early October, Carey's alleged crimes seemed friv-olously slight beside the murder of thousands just blocks away. A common sentiment seemed to be "What are we doing here?"

Certainly the prosecution gave the jury no powerful reasons to convict. Attorneys for the government argued a case so convoluted that it was all but impossible to follow even by those thoroughly familiar with the events and personalities. The contrast between their presentation and that of Carey's attorney, the clear and always persuasive Reid Weingarten, was all the more striking. He convinced the jury that Carey had been so distracted by agonizing pain in his knees that his client simply couldn't keep track of the scheme concocted by subordinates. The campaign aides weren't trying to win the election; they just wanted to get paid so they could build their consulting business.

What about Carey's remark that SEIU's Andy Stern "wasn't delivering" on his illegal $50,000 pledge? It had been misinterpreted. Carey was dis-appointed that Stern wasn't delivering *for his members*.

Finally, there was no reason for Carey to be concerned about the huge sudden outflow of cash he'd approved—$475,000 to Citizen Action and $150,000 to the AFL-CIO within a week—because the Teamsters were not nearly broke, as had been frequently alleged. Actually, the organization was flush with cash. The accountants called on by the prosecutors to refute the defense testified at mind-numbing length in the jargon of their trade—apparently convincing the jurors that if the case against Carey was so devilishly complex and so hard to follow, there must be room for reasonable doubt that Carey knew what was going on.

After more than a thousand years, the Catholic Church now says that the miracles attributed to St. Sebastian—surviving the arrows and walking around with his head in his hands after his final martyrdom—are no longer necessary articles of faith. In Carey's case, given that only a few years have passed, perhaps it's understandable that the progressive faithful still believe that he cleaned up the Teamsters, kicked out the mob, and brought UPS to its knees and that his only fault was that he tried to do too much too fast, prompting a ruling-class backlash that vitiated many of his achievements. After the trial they urged him to come out of retirement and lead them again in battle against the Old Guard. Carey himself expressed a desire to return to office. "It's been in my blood for forty years," he said.[65]

Unlike St. Sebastian, however, Carey decided finally not to risk giving the authorities another shot. Besides his legal vindication, he had ample reason to feel content with his situation. Carey had no legal bills—attorney Reid Weingarten had waived his fee. He had homes in Florida and New York and a small fortune derived from the sale of his UPS stock. And, like the Old Guard bosses he'd condemned to such great effect, Ron Carey retired on four Teamster pensions.

PART 4
The Failure of Reform

CHAPTER ELEVEN

Teamsters for a Democratic Union

HOW BOTTOM-UP REFORM HIT BOTTOM

Chartered over ninety years ago by the United Hebrew Trades, Teamsters Local 138 was one of those New York labor unions that expressed the darker side of the immigrant experience. In Local 138, which may have had nearly 3,000 members at its peak, the American Dream was realized not by those who worked hard and played by the rules, but by gonifs who battened on those who did. For generations, the warehouse and delivery truck union based in Queens and Long Island was run by crooked officials, first a Jewish dynasty that lasted through the 1950s and then an Italian dynasty up through the 1980s. Whatever the ethnic differences, classic labor racketeering techniques prevailed: the shakedowns, the labor peace scam, and stealing from the boss with the right hand and from the members with the left.

What distinguished Local 138, though, was the sheer amount of blood flowing from its normal operations. Every few years, it seemed, an assassination would claim one of the officers. In the 1930s, Manhattan district attorney Thomas Dewey made the local a special target. In the 1940s, *Gangbusters,* one of the country's most popular radio shows, aired a segment on bloody, gangster-ridden Local 138. After World War II, the union was allegedly taken over by the Colombo crime family.

Astonishingly, though, it wasn't until the coming of the Teamsters reform movement that Local 138 reached its full destructive potential. In 1986, the mob-backed officials were challenged by a seven-man slate of candidates. All but one were members of the Teamsters for a Democratic Union, the nation's premier labor reform organization. With the help of top TDU staff, the TDU good guys outpolled the Colombo-backed bad guys.

In the euphoria that followed, no one realized that the new president, John Georgopoulos, had twelve prior convictions on drug and larceny charges. Still less could the celebrants have imagined that Georgopoulos and his closest mates had no intention of wiping out corruption. They just wanted to take over the old rackets themselves—which they divided up at their very first postelection meeting.

What would actually destroy Local 138 was not the shift of the rackets to new hands. It was a disastrous strike in the early 1990s against White Rose, New York's largest independent wholesale food distributor. The eighteen-month job action was broken by the recently elected reform president, Ron Carey, TDU's patron. He approved a shameful settlement that transferred 425 of the local's jobs to a mob-controlled Teamsters local in New Jersey, where the wage rates were a fraction of those paid to the striking Local 138 members. Soon afterward, wages began to plummet throughout the East Coast warehouse division.

Later it was discovered that during the White Rose strike, the top TDU officers had been stealing strike pay. Although suspended from office, they managed to keep on receiving salaries illicitly, which led to their eventual ejection from the union. Then in 1997, the top officers were charged by the U.S. attorney with running labor peace rackets. After appealing a jury conviction all the way to the Supreme Court, three top officials, including Georgopoulos, finally went off to prison. The incarcerations—celebrated by former Local 138 members who had lost their jobs—furnished a suitable climax to one of the shadiest and least known stories in the history of union reform.

TDU supporters had made its initial victory in Local 138 a pivotal part of *Rank-and-File Rebellion*, the organization's semiofficial history.[1] But there would never be any public mention of Act II, the role of their patron, Ron Carey, in destroying the local, or Act III, the imprisonment of the local's TDU leadership.

Although the former Local 138 officials had begun their prison sentences in 1998 completely unnoticed, the year nevertheless marked a sharp turning point in the fortunes of TDU. Up to that time TDU had reigned as the nation's top union reform organization, perhaps the most influential since the AFL-CIO was founded in 1955. The tiny, cash-starved Detroit-based organization had been credited with winning "one person, one vote" elections for the Teamsters presidency and with putting Ron Carey into the Marble Palace and then using their rank-and-file influence to help him in his reform crusade—wiping out the Mafia, grounding the Teamsters jet fleet, and lowering bloated official salaries. In 1997, TDU got much of the credit for winning the UPS strike with its promise—never really fulfilled—of full-time jobs for part-timers.

Then in 1998, James P. Hoffa was elected Teamsters president. He replaced Carey, who'd been forced to resign because of his alleged involvement in a money-laundering scandal. The Hoffa ascendancy, along with Carey's disgrace, produced a sharp decline in TDU's membership and influence. But TDU continued to serve as the North Star for labor radicals and for much of the progressive media.

In fact, TDU's accomplishments had been vastly exaggerated, and its failures mostly unexamined.[2] By 1998, it represented less the pole star than a stellar black hole, an evolutionary end point, the last burst of energy of the dying Old Left in the AFL-CIO. Several charter members, including Ken Paff, the national organizer of TDU, had begun as Trotskyist revolutionaries. They had accomplished far more than most who had started out in the leftist sects, but like so many who dedicated their lives to building a reform movement in the AFL-CIO, they had ultimately become just another union faction, clients dependent on a boss. Much of the moral energy of TDU in New York sputtered out in the ruins of Local 138. To appreciate where they ultimately wound up after a lifetime of activism, it's essential to grasp the initial dimensions of their improbable dreams.

FROM CAMPUS TO CARBARN

As the year 1969 wound down, the twilight of the student protest era was clearly visible in the thinning crowds passing through Sproul Plaza at the University of California, Berkeley. Fewer students stopped to listen to political speeches. The Marxist sects had trouble staffing their literature tables. Instead of throngs of protesters marching through the Sather Gate, hundreds of stray dogs ran wild in baying packs through the plaza. For myriad aging student radicals at Berkeley, the mother ship of the 1960s campus revolution, it was time to trim beards, shave legs, cross the Bay, and start a professional career.

For Berkeley's biggest student revolutionary group, the nearly 100-member International Socialists (IS), the judgments were the same. Yes, the student movement was over, the Shangri-la of campus revolutionism would have to be abandoned, and professionalism beckoned. But for the Trotskyist vanguard IS, professionalization didn't mean a law or banking career on San Francisco's Montgomery Street. It meant "industrialization."

Members of IS—disproportionately Jewish graduate students in their middle and late twenties—decided to transform themselves into unionized blue collar workers. At the urging of their leader, Hal Draper, a UC Berkeley librarian who was one of America's top Marxologists,[3] they would fan out from Berkeley in two's and three's, finding jobs in America's industrial heartland—joining the Steelworkers in Gary, Indiana, the Autoworkers in Detroit, the Teamsters in Cleveland. And just as rear-echelon troops support those on the front lines, it was the task of those who didn't industrialize to support those who did.

After more than thirty years, Steve Kindred, an early industrializer who joined the IS off the University of Chicago campus, still recalls the almost intolerable wave of anticipation he felt. "I remember Hal Draper saying, 'Comrades, it's time to begin the colonization of selected comrades in industry.' I was so fucking excited, I couldn't stand it. It just made sense to me." What made sense to Kindred was the idea that the 1960s movement could be prolonged; if students were opting for careers, the workers couldn't be bought off; it was among them that there remained a potential for revolution.[4]

The IS'ers included some of the most gifted social science grad students in the country. What were they thinking they would accomplish by their cross-country trek? To begin with, in sectarian parties, industrialization had been a traditional rite of revolutionary passage. Just as adolescent tribal warriors undergo painful circumcision rituals, for generations, young Marxist-Leninist intellectuals in America were supposed to show their bravery and readiness for class combat by taking jobs in factories, particularly in the Midwest. As serious readers of Marxist texts, they had discovered that the secret of capitalism was control of its "commanding heights"—i.e., heavy industry. And the core of the country's manufacturing industry wasn't in California. (Unfortunately, the Marxist texts didn't reveal that that the "commanding heights" were about to be transformed into the Midwest Rust Bowl and that California would replace it as no. 1 in manufacturing.)

Once IS'ers were entrenched in the heartland factories, the plan was to convert millions of unionized industrial workers to the ideal of socialist revolution, sweep aside the AFL-CIO "bureaucrats," and then, from the party's base in the unions, overthrow the capitalist state, replacing it with a workers' state—along the broad lines explained by Leon Trotsky. The best official estimate was that it would all take about ten years.

Predictably, the IS offensive against the AFL-CIO had about as much impact as a cloud of gnats attacking a cannon ball.[5] In the eight or so main targeted unions where Trotskyist cells were implanted, there was only one where industrialization would pay any returns at all.[6] That was in the Teamsters, where Paff, the former Berkeley physics student who was now based in Cleveland, had formed something called Teamsters for a Democratic Contract.

Tall, thin, narrow-faced, and thin-lipped, Paff bore an uncanny physical resemblance to another organizational wizard who got his start in Cleveland, John D. Rockefeller. Paff also had Rockefeller's ineffable sense of mission, self-confidence, and ability to dominate others. In 1975, he took charge of a loose network of Teamsters activists.

Gradually, Paff would shape the organization into the best-known labor reform group in the United States. He began by rallying highway and local drivers across the country in a campaign to reject a proposed National Master Freight Agreement. He excoriated the "sell-out" and demanded that members have the right to vote on the contract. Paff started a lively muckraking paper, *Convoy*, that exposed the misdeeds of the corrupt, overpaid Teamsters hierarchy. He jousted with Ralph Nader, who had formed a rival Teamsters reform group. Paff won, merging Nader's organization into his own, which was now called Teamsters for a Democratic Union—TDU. For more than a quarter century, TDU's Detroit headquarters has served as a guiding light for the American labor left.

But by the end of the 1970s, Paff & Co. had become missionaries without a mother church. The IS had imploded. The party's top ideologist went off to become a millionaire commodities trader in Chicago. Others found their way back to academia.

Of the comrades who made the heartland trek from Berkeley, only Ken Paff stood out. Paff, who came from a Polish working-class background, was perhaps the toughest physically and among the least theoretically inclined. Abstract questions about the nature of the working class troubled him little; he cared about nuts-and-bolts organizational questions—like how to organize a rank-and-file meeting. Paff and the TDU'ers wound up dumping first Trotskyism, then Marxism, and finally all the remains of the socialist baggage they'd brought from campus. By the end of the 1970s, they'd split with more orthodox and still campus-bound IS'ers and become unqualified blue collar democrats.

It was easy to see why. It was one thing to be a Trotskyist sitting at a table in Berkeley's Sproul Hall Plaza, where the reddest of Trots faded into the kaleidoscope of radical political sects on campus. In Akron, you stood out as a target for Jackie Presser and his goons from BLAST—the Brotherhood of Loyal American and Strong Teamsters. The ideological attacks were more threatening than the physical sallies. In response to red-baiting attacks from BLAST, Paff said defensively, "TDU is not about socialism or dual unionism. It is about returning our union to the rank and file."[7]

TDU's pioneers were taking great risks, living austerely, and challenging the most violent, entrenched apparatus of corruption in the AFL-CIO. Paff had joined local 407, the largest local in Cleveland, and began organizing throughout Ohio, confronting BLAST with nonviolent tactics.

Meanwhile, Steve Kindred, who'd been so stirred by Draper's call to industrialize, was moving around the country as a TDU organizer, preaching the gospel of union reform, living on movement wages, sleeping on people's couches. He got badly beaten by Fitzsimmons's goons at the 1976 convention in Las Vegas. As the years slipped by, as his fellow alumni from the University of Chicago got tenure, became partners in law firms, or stepped out of chauffeur-driven limos, Kindred left TDU and started earning his living as a limo driver.

But TDU members weren't just romantic Berkeley rebels "putting their bodies on the line." TDU offered a serious, if ultimately flawed, strategy for cleaning up the Teamsters and, by example, transforming the entire American labor movement. Radicals should narrow their focus: go light

on anti-imperialism and gay liberation, and concentrate on union issues—especially union corruption, union democracy, and sell-out contracts. Step 1, use these issues to build a rank-and-file TDU caucus. Step 2,
use the caucus to run for local office. Step 3, win enough local offices to
capture control of the Marble Palace. Win the Teamsters, and you might
just take over the labor movement.

Now the ex-Trots in the Teamsters had gone from extreme internation-
alism to extreme localism, from world revolution to making the Teamsters
less corrupt and more democratic. They'd transformed themselves from a
revolutionary sect into a reform faction.

God knows, the Teamsters needed reform. And the TDU'ers' shared experience in IS gave them a cohesiveness other reform factions—like DC
37's Committee for Real Change—could have used. On the other hand,
old habits die hard. Sects promote strong internal discipline, but they
don't tolerate true dissent; their world is sharply divided into members
and outsiders. Their leaders tend toward infallibility. Not for nothing was
Ken Paff called "the Pope of Detroit." When Paff decided to put all the political capital the organization had accumulated in its rank-and-file campaigns behind Ron Carey's candidacy for the Teamsters presidency, the
organization swung totally and irrevocably behind Carey.

THE CAREY OPTION

In 1989, huge possibilities for a new kind of radical labor offensive had
opened up. The International Brotherhood of Teamsters (IBT) leadership settled the government's massive racketeering suit by allowing free
elections for national officers. Two years later, Carey won with the help of
TDU. The victory turned the organization into something between a junior partner and a secret mistress in the administration of Carey, the ex-
Marine and Reagan Republican.

As Paff explained in a confidential memorandum, TDU had backed
Carey because it had no choice. "If we had not backed Carey, TDU would
have become irrelevant." Its bottom-up strategy wasn't working. "TDU
could not succeed by growing one by one until we got to some point and

knocked the top officials out of the Marble Palace." The point from now on was to "make the most of what history dealt us."[8]

But Carey's prominence raised TDU's profile. Soon books were being written about TDU.[9] The organization became a pole of attraction for thousands of union reformers around the country, many of whom gathered each year in Detroit for the TDU-backed *Labor Notes* conference. U.S. District Judge David N. Edelstein, who supervised the 1989 consent decree that forced the IBT executive board to give up much of its power, actually complained about all the credit TDU was getting in the national media for having cleaned up the Teamsters.

To exploit the new strategic opportunities, TDU's strategy evolved from its strict reliance on bottom-upism. The old populism would have to be replaced by a new style of leadership that relied less on what the members thought was important. Instead of the old habit of servicing grievances and nurturing member complaints, it was time to reach out to the unorganized and "forge new community alliances." Predicted Paff: "We will likely find members complaining that the IBT leadership hasn't solved their problems." But "very clearly that kind of criticism points in a negative direction."[10]

As it turned out, Carey's election proved to be a false dawn. TDU's total embrace of the incumbent represented the final stage in the organization's adaptation to the AFL-CIO's political culture. Building independent local strength gave way to supporting the chief occupant of the Marble Palace. It was a slight, but TDU learned to suffer setbacks quietly. They grumbled only in confidential memos when Carey pursued an olive branch strategy toward the mob.[11] There was no protest when Carey purged nearly all the TDU members from his executive board, nor even when he replaced them with gangster-influenced bosses like Boston's George Cashman.[12]

Carey simply used TDU, adopting the old John L. Lewis strategy toward leftists. Criticized for his use of reds as field reps and in-house staffers, Lewis replied, "Who gets the bird, the bird dog or the hunter?"[13] TDU settled for the bird dog's role because they had little alternative. There were no other local victories over the mob as in Local 138. In fact, although Carey essentially gave TDU a local by appointing a TDU sympathizer as its trustee, the organization didn't independently win another local election in the New York–New Jersey region. Its growth among rank-and-file Teamsters had stalled. Detroit claimed as many as 15,000 members for the organization. But you could be a member of TDU by simply filling out a coupon and sending it in with thirty bucks. As Ken Paff himself pointed out, that level of commitment didn't mean too much in building an oppositional movement. In terms of "chapter" activity in the locals, TDU was never able to expand much beyond its first car haul and national master freight campaigns in the late 1970s. The peak number of real activists— Teamsters who regularly participated in yearly national conventions— probably never exceeded 700 or 800. TDU had never achieved more than token political power in the IBT. In the 1980s, after more than a decade's work, it could still elect only a couple of dozen delegates out of nearly 2,000 who voted at conventions.

Still, by the end of the Carey regime in 1997, TDU members had accumulated dozens of Teamsters staff jobs in the Washington, D.C., headquarters and on the national staff. They were a power in numerous UPS locals, flight attendants locals, and even some trucking locals. What TDU appeared to lose, though, was what had made it unique in the Teamsters: its political independence.

TDU had the soft power that came with trust and credibility. It had launched successful rank-and-file campaigns to defeat national contracts. It still regularly put out the feisty *Convoy-Dispatch*, which had a circulation of 40,000. Where else could members find out about the Teamsters officials in the $100,000 salary club, the sell-out contracts, the safety issues, the mob? The polling firm hired by Carey's opponent in 1991 discovered that TDU, with a 40 percent name recognition, was better known than any of the candidates and, with an approval rating of over 30 percent, substantially more respected.[14]

After Carey's election, however, TDU gradually adapted to the AFL-CIO value system, which prizes loyalty above all.

In Detroit, TDU assumed the client position. There could be no second thoughts about the commitment to mobilize for Carey & Co. "We need to be a support team for the new crop of leaders," Paff wrote to his seven-member International Steering Committee. "We need to be the troops on the ground, and we need to expand that leadership crop, especially in local elections."[15]

Paff's priorities provoked bitter debate, dire warnings, and continuous independent opposition—especially from working Teamsters. Pete Camarata, a cofounder of TDU, wrote to the steering committee, "Carey's performance on limiting corruption . . . as far as I know the score is ZERO." Camarata noted that in his own local, the historic Detroit Local 299, Carey had appointed a union trustee from the old BLAST crowd— the goon squad Jackie Presser had organized to beat up TDU'ers.[16]

In New York, TDU lost the support of FORE—Fear of Reprisals Ends— perhaps the most well known and most respected rank-and-file caucus in any Teamsters local. The men of FORE were not college boys who had industrialized. They were the real article, genuine working-class heroes who'd stood up to Gambino underboss Sammy "the Bull" Gravano. They'd joined TDU in the 1970s, and now they were disgusted and leaving *en masse*. At the 1993 TDU Convention, concrete truck driver Lee Olson, from Local 282, explained why. Carey had merely replaced one set of mobsters with another. In Local 282, Carey's personal representative had chosen a slate of officers to replace the mobsters who just been indicted; the new bunch was all indicted within six months after being installed. And Carey had been warned. Olson demanded that TDU face up to its uncritical support for Carey. "There was an issue which TDU has avoided for far too long," he said, "and it is time for discussion because it directly affects our credibility, our identity, and our integrity. The failure of the Carey administration to act more forcefully against corruption at the local union level, and their adoption of some of the customs and practices of the old guard: when—if ever—is TDU going to speak out?"[17]

GOODFELLAS AND REDFELLAS

Call it the Roach Motel syndrome. The leftists go in but they don't come out. They enter as revolutionaries determined to create a social movement. Those who survive the ordeal of industrialization become plain and simple union reformers. But eventually, if they build a base or move up in the hierarchy, it's because they've adjusted pretty thoroughly to the demands of a corrupt patron-client system.

After a decade or more of following AFL-CIO norms and rules, it sometimes gets hard to distinguish between the inveterate crooks and the erstwhile Marxist revolutionaries. The head of Joint Council 16 in New York, which was arguably the most mobbed up of all the joint councils in the Teamsters—was Bill Nuchow. Nuchow, who died in 1993 after only two months as joint council chief, was either a secret member or a fellow traveler of the Communist Party USA. His private papers show the extent of his sympathies.[18] As a student at Empire State College in the 1970s, one of Nuchow's instructors observed, he had a hard time seeing events except from a party perspective.[19] Besides serving as a placeholder for the mob, Nuchow ran his own crooked local.

In New York, Communist Party members had been prominent in Teamsters Joint Council 16 at least since the days of Jimmy Hoffa. As one former CP'er with a sixty-year involvement in the New York City labor movement recalls, the CP's influence began when the party-run grocery clerks union became part of the Teamsters. More informally, there was also something called the B'nai B'rith Teamsters Lodge. Membership included Jewish communists and former CP'ers who were active in Joint Council 16. The votes of Joint Council 16 CP'ers helped put Hoffa in as IBT president in 1957.

Teamsters locals run by people in the CP or close to it weren't the most corrupt. But the party actively supported Teamster bosses like Anthony "Tony Pro" Provenzano, who with his brother "Sammy Pro" ran what was commonly considered to be the most murderous unit in the IBT: Local 560. Tony Pro was a Genovese captain with a long mob vita. He served as cohost of the 1957 Apalachin, New York, organized crime conference. For killing local political opponents, Tony Pro was imprisoned in Lewisberg, where he served with Jimmy Hoffa—whom he is also alleged to have had killed.[20] In 1959, when Tony Pro was being challenged by a reform faction, he got party support. Even in the late 1990s, party members continued to scoff at the idea that "the mob" was a force in Hoffa's Teamsters. George Meyers, chair of the Labor Department of the Communist Party USA, describes Hoffa Sr. as "an outstanding fighter for his members."[21]

TDU was able to place "dozens" of members on staff at the Marble Palace and in national organizing positions.[22] But relations were not warm. Carey agreed to address TDU's St. Louis convention in 1992, but he essentially parachuted in and got airlifted out. His entire appearance lasted about thirty minutes.[23]

Bill Nuchow's Local 840 wasn't nearly as bad as Tony Pro's Local 560. There was never any rough stuff—just talk. In terms of integrity, among the fifty or so locals in Joint Council 16, it was about average—which means that it was pretty crooked. At Nuchow's funeral, everyone called each other "comrade."[24]

For generations, leftists have gotten trapped in the tar pits of local union office. They are often useful to the higher-level bad guys. Leftists know how to speak to the members in progressive accents. They have the enormous energy that comes from having a calling, and at the same time they're easily controlled because they have no independent base. Even top leftist theoreticians remained unaware of the institutional dangers faced by progressives in the AFL-CIO.

In the 1970s, Hal Draper, the Berkeley mentor of the IS, defended his party's strategy for Teamsters reform against campus skeptics who doubted that the notorious union could be cleaned up by student revolutionaries. But for Draper, it didn't matter whether the Teamsters leadership was corrupt or not. Ultimately, he insisted, the Teamsters "bureaucrats" had to act in the interests of the members. "The class character of an organization does not depend on its ideas," explained Draper, "it depends on its objective role and function in society."[25]

Draper knew a lot more about the rhyming devices of Heinrich Heine—Draper was his American translator—than he knew about Jimmy Hoffa and his stratagems. It's unlikely that he had read much U.S. labor history. What was there to know? If the union members could get truly revolutionary leadership, they would respond militantly. "No Marxist group," he declared, "has ever carried on any systematic revolutionary work in trade unions." Draper had probably never heard of Local 138. He seemed unaware of the problems faced by his Trotskyist predecessors in the Teamsters. But generations of socialist reformers had broken their teeth in an effort to crack its corrupt carapace.

BORING FROM WITHIN: THE EARLY YEARS

It was December 1939, and young Farrell Dobbs, the Trotskyist leader of the Minneapolis General Strike, the man who'd taught Jimmy Hoffa how to organize truck drivers and who'd probably brought as many members into the union than anyone else before or since, had called long-serving Teamsters president Dan Tobin for an appointment. When Dobbs arrived at Teamsters headquarters in Indianapolis, he announced his resignation right away. Tobin refused to believe what he was hearing. It was just a tactic, he thought, to get more money or a higher position. So Tobin promised he'd make Dobbs the highest-paid organizer in the IBT if he'd stay. Dobbs recalls Tobin predicting, "There were no limits to how high I could rise in the organization."[26]

But there was no dissuading Dobbs. He was a Trotskyist first and a Teamster second, and he'd been ordered by the party's top boss to give up his role as union organizer and become an antiwar organizer.[27]

Tobin regarded Dobbs almost as a son. If money wasn't an issue and Dobbs wanted to fight for socialist ideals, he argued, the trade union movement was the best place to be. Tobin explained that he'd been a socialist too, but he'd found that the best way to advance workers' goals was through the union and within the Democratic Party. By raising lots of campaign cash for FDR, Tobin had gotten leverage for the Teamsters within the administration. As Dobbs grew older, Tobin predicted, he would realize that the unions, with all their faults, were the only game in town for the labor left.[28]

If Dobbs had stayed, it's conceivable that he'd have wound up like the ex-socialist Tobin. It's easy to be contemptuous of Tobin—his lies, his evasions, his desperate need to hold on to the trappings of office even while actual power was slipping into the hands of mobsters. But ultimately, Tobin wasn't to blame for the fact that rampaging warlords controlled many provinces in his kingdom. He lacked the troops, the treasure, and the authority to resist effectively. Still, credit Tobin with having tried. He'd taken great risks, and he'd literally been beaten more than once in the struggle for union reform.

Still, Tobin failed utterly in his efforts to clean up the IBT. It is true—although, strangely, you'd never know it from reading Dobbs's memoirs—

that by the late 1930s, Dan Tobin's Teamsters had gained a reputation as the most corrupt union in America.[29] Tobin, though, had to find out that his union was gangster-run by listening to *Gangbusters*. At least that's what he told the members in the spring of 1940. He had tuned in to the popular weekly radio show and discovered that the evening's episode was about his own union. Said Tobin: "I was almost paralyzed when I heard a description of how an officer of our local Union No. 138 was persecuted and penalized by gangsters."[30] It was a pretty steep penalty. Morris Diamond, Local 138's business manager, was heading toward his Brooklyn subway stop to begin his morning commute to union headquarters. It was broad daylight on the morning of May 26, 1939, when a gunman stepped out of a car and shot him five times. Diamond died about an hour later. Tobin insisted that he was totally uninformed about the problems in Local 138. "We in the International Office, as I have stated before of course knew nothing about what went on in this local union."[31]

It's hard to believe that Tobin had only just gotten the news that racketeers were in charge of Local 138. Five years before Diamond's slaying, there was the even more sensational assassination of the local's president. One late summer night in 1934, on the Lower East Side, President Billy Snyder was negotiating for striking Local 138 members in a well-known Jewish restaurant. Snyder, who'd been seated with his back to the door, refused to suspend the strike. Finally, Local 138's vice president, Wolfie Goldis, got up and left the meeting. He opened a window in the adjoining room, and in crawled Goldis's younger brother, Morris. The twenty-seven-year-old assassin burst into the negotiations and shot Snyder in the back. Snyder died two hours later. Succeeding him as president was the next highest ranking officer of Local 138, who just happened to be Wolfie Goldis. It was Goldis who called off the strike.[32]

Snyder was murdered in 1934, and Diamond in 1939. How could Tobin not have known until the *Gangbusters* broadcast in 1940 that something had gone terribly wrong in Local 138? Especially since the odor from the Snyder affair persisted well after his burial. Thomas Dewey made the murder the centerpiece of his successful campaign for Manhattan district attorney. Local 138 became his personal project. He sent four officers to jail for extortion. Then he put away both Morris and Wolfie Goldis. In fact, the reason Local 138 business agent Morris Diamond was murdered was that he was caught going to see Dewey. The D.A. had been using Diamond to build a case against the Goldis brothers.[33]

As Dewey and mob assassins depleted the ranks of Local 138 officers, Tobin sent his personal troubleshooter out from Indianapolis to try to recruit new, more honest officers. The trustee wrote back to Tobin that the situation was as futile as it was scary. "This is a rotten mess. One of the worst I have ever handled, and I will be well pleased after the installation of the officers to get out of the picture, because I haven't much hope for their future."[34]

The pessimism was warranted. Local 138's corruption—which began no later than the 1920s and probably dates from 1915, when it received a charter from the United Hebrew Trades—would easily outlast Uncle Dan Tobin's presidency.

Early-twentieth-century labor radicals of Tobin's generation called their strategy for winning the workers to socialism "boring from within." The plan was for socialists to get union jobs; appeal as fellow workers to the downtrodden membership; get elected to local office by ousting the corrupt business unionists; and, once in office, turn the Federation into a progressive force and America into a workers' paradise. No one pretended it would be simple—learning a trade or performing common labor could be hard on mostly well-educated Marxists. But the political attractions were clear: the AFL was America's biggest, richest, and most powerful labor organization; the leftists didn't have to start from scratch to build an organization. And as elected officials or staffers, boring from within—unlike many other radical trades—provided you with a paycheck.

Such change as did take place in union governance was less a matter of rank-and-file empowerment than of ethnic succession. The Irish and the Jewish gangsters were mostly displaced by Italians. After the electrocution of Lepke in 1944 for murdering a truck owner, Local 138's leadership changed from Jewish gangsters operating out of Brooklyn to Italian gangsters operating out of Brooklyn.

A REVOLUTION IN LOCAL 138?

For the next forty years, Local 138 remained a sleepy province in the Colombo crime family domain. But the membership changed. The flour truck drivers delivering flour to bakers disappeared. By the 1980s, the 2,200-member union represented chiefly warehouse workers and drivers who were employed by big grocery retail and wholesale chains like Key Foods, White Rose, and Waldbaum's. Union leaders and grocery executives often shared a mob culture: one grocery bigwig who owned fourteen supermarkets and served as a director of Key Foods was charged with being a captain in the Gambino crime family.[35] There were also about three dozen smaller employers—too many to give the members of Local 138 much common interest.

The president of Local 138 in 1986 was the long-serving Frank "Butch" Ribustello. Ribustello ran a classic labor peace racket. The union had negotiated an excellent basic wage and benefit package for warehouse workers—mob unions often do—but the workers didn't all necessarily get what was in the contract. Employers paid off corrupt leaders so they could hire non-union workers at a much lower wage. Allegedly, the Ribustello team cut the employers all kinds of other breaks and took back cash.[36]

From a small office in industrial Long Island City, Ribustello was quietly carrying on Local 138's proud traditions when he was abruptly challenged by the new generation of Teamsters Trotskyists. TDU arrived on the Long Island warehouse scene in 1984 and began to reach out to dissatisfied warehouse workers. A small nucleus of TDU supporters formed at Key Foods. They held meetings and put out a newsletter, *The Free Key Press*. A network of activists and allies was established in the main warehouses.

The avatars of Farrell Dobbs aimed to replace Ribustello and the Old Guard in the fall 1986 election. Local union factions try to avoid seeming like factions by giving themselves broader, more civic sounding names. The TDU'ers called their ticket "New Beginnings."

TDU's authorized historian, Dan La Botz, begins his story of the Teamsters reform movement at this moment. Ribustello didn't like a leaflet TDU'er Mike Ruscigno was circulating. It accused Ribustello of giving

Key Foods employers whatever they wanted. There was quite a disparity in the age and physical condition of the two men. Ribustello was sedentary and nearly seventy; Ruscigno was a husky ex–merchant seaman from Brooklyn, a six-footer just over thirty years old. Still, in the fall of 1986, the aged but outraged union boss went looking for Ruscigno in a Long Island warehouse. When Ribustello found him, he let fly a punch.[37]

Ribustello managed to open a cut on Ruscigno's face that required two stitches to close, and he bellowed incoherently for about fifteen minutes. "The guy responsible for me blowing [losing] my job," ranted Ribustello, "he better fucking watch out and watch his fucking back."[38]

Ruscigno just happened to have a tape recorder on his person. He also was working with Dan Clifton, a top New York City labor lawyer who would significantly influence the outcome of the Local 138 story. Lawyers are more important than leaflets in modern union reform struggles, since frequently it's judges, not members, who make the key decisions. From Ruscigno, Clifton got a complete transcript of the incident, and he used it as the basis for a half million dollar federal suit. A federal judge issued an injunction against Ribustello "from infringing the free speech rights of Michael Ruscigno and any other candidate for union office in Local 138 by attacking, harassing or threatening these individuals." The savvy legal maneuver drew attention to the TDU challengers. A few weeks later, when election day arrived, the New Beginnings slate defeated the Old Guard slate overwhelmingly. Of the seven victors, all but one were TDU'ers.[39]

In fact, the biggest share of the electorate was the nonvoters: only a third of the members bothered to cast ballots. But it was enough of a mandate for TDU's authorized historian to declare, "Within the empty shell of the old union, a new union was born."[40]

By the early 1990s, Ruscigno could look back on years of accomplishment: "We've given them representation, which is one thing they never had. We're down in the shops. We're giving them a voice in their union. We want the union to work for the members, and we're trying to educate them that they are the union, that we work for them now." About the 1986 takeover, he concluded, "It was a kind of 'revolution.'"[41]

One of the oldest and most cynical clichés about revolutions is that "like Saturn, they wind up devouring their children." But in Local 138, the outcome of the TDU victory was fodder for even greater cynicism. New

Beginnings never became corrupt. It was always a scam. Literally from day one—at the first meeting of the newly elected Local 138 executive board—the main item of business, according to subsequent trial testimony, was how to divide up the Old Guard's rackets.

It needs to be said at the outset, though, that no TDU staffer and no member of TDU's steering committee ever took a penny from a Local 138 employer. Ruscigno, who stood closest to Detroit TDU and who has served for more than twenty years on the organization's International Steering Committee, was kept out of Local 138's inner sanctum because the thieves thought he might turn them in. Just before he ran for office in 1992, president John Georgopoulos kicked Ruscigno off the New Beginnings slate. "He said it was because I let the members know too much," said Ruscigno. He ran anyhow and won by a few votes.[42]

Eventually, though, in 1998, Georgopoulos and two other top officers of Local 138 were convicted of taking bribes from employers. Despite appeals all the way to Supreme Court and legal assistance from Ralph Nader's Public Citizen, each wound up serving federal prison terms. But imprisoning the Georgopoulos crew couldn't undo the extraordinary damage they'd done. By sentencing time, Local 138, one of the oldest Teamsters locals in America, was history. It had been destroyed and officially dissolved.

In a way, the destruction of Local 138 could be understood as the mob's revenge. As long as a local was run by a crime family, its jurisdiction was respected by other crime families. Once Local 138 lost its mob leadership, it was fair game. All the members who'd worked for White Rose, the local's largest employer, had their strike broken by a Genovese-controlled Teamsters local in New Jersey.[43]

The union had struck White Rose because the new owner, Arthur M. Goldberg, the Wall Street takeover artist, demanded givebacks. Goldberg wanted to freeze warehouse workers' pay at $18 an hour (about $25.40 in 2005 dollars), and he insisted on health insurance copayments. But in fighting White Rose, the members had to wage a two-front war, against the employer and their own union. It was the IBT itself that provided White Rose's new boss with strikebreakers.[44]

Strikebreaking means giving aid to an employer during a strike. Commonly it involves crossing a picket line formed by the strikers or providing a struck company with supplies. Practically unheard of, though, would be for one local in the same union to accept the terms being rejected by strikers in another local so they could take away their jobs.

That's exactly what caused 500 members employed by White Rose in Farmingdale, New York, to lose their jobs permanently, thanks to the pact worked out between Goldberg and Local 97's Arnold Ross. Under the terms of the deal, the new hires in New Jersey would get about $11 an hour instead of the approximately $18 received by Local 138 members. (In 1993, Ross would be banned permanently from the union by the Independent Review Board, charged with being under the influence of organized crime.)[45]

It's understandable why businessman Goldberg would shop around for the cheapest Teamsters warehouse local in the region; you could also see why mob associate Arnold Ross would like to have 500 new members. What doesn't make sense is why newly elected reform president Ron Carey signed off on the deal. No genuine trade unionist, much less a genuine reformer, would have found it acceptable.

Even for the Teamsters, it was an extraordinary sell-out. Generally, only non-union workers take union members' jobs. More rarely, it happens with members of different AFL-CIO unions. But members of the same international union? Why even have a union if one local scabs on the strike of another—which is exactly what Carey permitted by authorizing the New Jersey workers to do the work of the New York strikers for 60 percent of their pay?

The only concession for the 500 fired workers was that they got $1.5 million in severance pay. It sounds like a lot of money, but it worked out to three weeks' pay per worker. An attorney for White Rose estimated that the members had lost over $20 million in wages in the strike—and that's a conservative estimate. Still, local president Georgopoulos was quoted as saying, "There is a lot of hope built into this agreement."[46]

In fact, Local 138 itself went down with its members. It became the Poland of Teamsters locals. In the same way that Russia, Austria, and Germany historically divided up Poland, stronger locals favored by higher officials at the international level now gobbled up 138's territory. Local 97 in New Jersey as well as Local 707 in Queens got a piece of Local 138. Georgopoulos protested, but Carey's chief aide wrote to Georgopoulos that he must withdraw charges against Local 707—the grocery handlers local that historically belonged to the Colombo crime family.[47]

Key Foods later performed the same New Jersey shuffle as White Rose. Local 138 members were the victims again. In 1996, the IBT decided to dissolve Local 138. Members who hadn't lost their jobs in the White Rose strike were transferred into Local 802. Key Foods officials then went after them, threatening to move the company's New York City warehouse operations to ever-friendly Local 97 in Elizabeth, New Jersey. Management demanded that wages be reduced from $18.25 to $16.25 an hour. Most members accepted the reductions. But 100 workers lost their jobs anyway.[48]

By the end of the decade, wage concessions hadn't stopped the flow of jobs across the Hudson. Around the country, in the 1990s, the total number of Teamster and warehouse jobs had increased by 25 percent. In New York City, the total had fallen by about a third, from 33,000 to 22,600.[49]

The New York–New Jersey warehouse locals were competing in submissiveness. Frightened Local 707 workers overwhelmingly accepted a union-busting deal from Waldbaum's. Their revised contract created a two-tier scale, with new hires getting $11 an hour.[50]

TDU could have exposed the White Rose deal, putting pressure on Carey to deny his approval. They'd put all their energy into electing Carey. Seven TDU members were now on the Teamsters international executive board. They had less than a third of the votes, but they could have made some unwanted noise. Besides, Local 138 was their local. It had just been designated the cradle of the Teamsters revolution; there was even a member of TDU's steering committee—Ruscigno—who was losing his job. And at the most elementary level, it was just a rotten deal.

Yet TDU's newspaper, *Convoy Dispatch*, always vigilant at spotting sell-outs by the Old Guard, barely even managed to notice what happened, much less to call for strong countermeasures.

TDU had become part of the Teamster patronage system. They were Carey clients.

TDU would also remain silent about the nearly nine-year skein of corruption in Local 138 after the candidates it supported won election and re-election. Georgopoulos would allow small employers to hire as many as three-quarters of their employees non-union. And as the big chains like

Key Foods and Waldbaum's followed White Rose in gaining concessions, starting warehouse wages fell from about $15 an hour in the early 1990s to something like $11 at the end. Even today, few members of the reform team wants to take responsibility.

Former Local 138 attorney Dan Clifton, who now works for UNITE and the Laborers, among other unions, refused to be interviewed. "I have to maintain lawyer-client confidentiality," he insisted.[51]

Ruscigno blamed Wall Street investor Arthur M. Goldberg, who bought the company and handled the strike. (Goldberg died in 2001.) "The members understood," he said, "it was Goldberg who cost them their jobs."[52]

Not everyone felt that Goldberg deserved all the blame. A letter from a former Local 138 member to Judge Hurley asking that no clemency be extended to Georgopoulos and his two cronies insisted that the damage they had caused lay not in the crimes they were convicted of but in the outcome of the White Rose strike. "Over 500 members lost their jobs at White Rose Foods, many with over 25 years on the job," he observed. "Unfortunately, only the taking of bribes is a crime. The impact these three had on over 1,000 members in Local 138 is tremendous. Therefore I implore you, no plea bargaining and the harshest sentence possible under the law."[53]

Steve Kindred, at the time of the White Rose strike, was the chief organizer for New York–New Jersey TDU and admits error. "We should have said something," he acknowledged.

One could argue that the cover-up was justified because keeping Carey's reputation clean was vital to the cause of Teamsters reform. Sometimes you have to destroy the village to save the country. But what does it say about the possibility of rank-and-file reform if the fiercest advocates of bottom-up movements ultimately side with their patron against the rank and file in the one local where they'd been able to claim a clear-cut victory over mob corruption?

FROM CLEAN-UP TO SHAKEDOWN

"Where would we be without TDU?"

■

—Local 138 Leaflet

The Local 138 story helps make sense of why Teamsters reform, often seen as the spearhead of the most significant effort to transform American unions in the postwar period, was blunted by the late 1990s. It helps explain why Hoffa Jr. beat the reformers. Of course, it wasn't primarily a matter of TDU's failure in Local 138. That was just symptomatic of deeper reasons. Carey wasn't who he said he was. Reform wasn't really happening. Carey's trusteeships of mob strongholds in the eastern region were often phony. Gradually, this became known among the members in the locals. TDU, in outward appearance completely unified, was in fact hopelessly factionalized, unable to develop a coherent approach to reform.

Within the original New Beginnings caucus, there was a four-person inner group of small-time thieves. New Beginnings' leader, John Georgopoulos, was a 350-pound veteran warehouse worker with eleven arrests on his record, mainly from the 1960s, for drug dealing[54] as well as grand larceny and auto theft. No one seemed to know about his criminal background. He was well read, spoke effectively, and radiated a kind of quiet authority. But soon after the election, Georgopoulos and his crew took bribes for almost a decade, mainly so bosses could hire non-union workers.

Georgopoulos's first order of business was to develop guidelines for getting bribes from employers. Within three months, officers were getting birthday money and vacation money and arranging for regular cash pick-ups.

Why did Georgopoulos & Co. take the employers' bribes and embezzle the members' strike funds? The simplest answer wouldn't be altogether wrong: because they were crooks. Georgopoulos spent much of the 1960s as a drug dealer operating under half a dozen aliases. He was a pre-Rockefeller era drug addict who supported his habit by stealing cars. (In 1973, Governor Nelson Rockefeller enacted harsh mandated sentences for drug possession.) You have to wonder how someone with his rap sheet could hold union office. But in fairness, he did seem to turn his life around when he got a job with White Rose as a warehouse worker. He got married and had kids, and after his wife died, he raised his two daughters by himself. He got involved in union politics, got elected to shop steward, and served on negotiating committees.[55]

But Georgopoulos's hold on honesty was precarious. At best, it was the honesty of thieves. As one of the big four on the witness stand recalled, "John said if we were going to take the money, it would be split four ways and not for anybody to go out and be a cowboy. Don't go out on your own and do you own thing. Everybody bring everything [the bribes and the shakedown money from the employers] back."[56]

With Georgopoulos there were ambiguities. Not so with Patrick Lauer, his colleague from the White Rose warehouse who was elected recording secretary in the New Beginnings sweep. As the defense emphasized in the 1998 trial, in which Lauer testified for the prosecution, he still had drug and alcohol problems. Lauer admitted that he regularly stole $400–$500 a week in goods from his employer as a grocery truck driver. "I would steal from one stop and sell it at the next," he explained. "You try to beat the guy out of the cases." Eventually, Lauer explained, he quit the leadership because he could make more money stealing from the employer than from the union.

Taking money from the bosses was on their minds from the beginning. Trial testimony revealed that when the newly elected New Beginnings officers met for the first time on January 1, 1987, they discussed bribes. They agreed that if anyone got offered a bribe, they would return to the union hall to discuss it, "primarily with John, him being the president," explained one board member, and then they would decide how to proceed.[57]

Ultimately it wasn't anyone from TDU who brought down the Georgopoulos regime, but an unaffiliated member named Robert Cox, who ran for secretary-treasurer of Local 138 and won. Cox soon discovered that the employers routinely bribed the officers. Rather than be associated with labor racketeers, Cox testified that he resigned his paid position and went back to driving a truck. He also decided to cooperate with the U.S. attorney.

MICROCOSM

How typical of TDU's corruption-fighting efforts was their battle against Local 138's Old Guard? "What happened in Local 138," observes TDU historian Dan La Botz, "was a microcosm of a fight for union democracy that is taking place throughout the Teamsters union." It all depends on what's meant by "microcosm." If it means "representative," then Local 138 is no microcosm. There's simply no population of which it could serve as a representative sample. TDU's strength was in UPS, the flight attendants, brewery workers, and over-the-road trucking locals, which, comparatively speaking, weren't all that corrupt.[58] TDU never had much success in other mob-controlled locals. In the Gambino-controlled Local 282, the concrete drivers, there was a strong faction allied with TDU, but they turned on the organization when TDU supported Carey's appointment of new officers who were all allied to the previous leadership and who would be indicted six months later. In the JFK *Goodfellas* local in the early 1990s, TDU had exactly one member.[59]

But if "microcosm" means smaller bodies operating according to the same principles as the larger ones—and the little ones revolving around the big ones as satellites—there's a good case for seeing Local 138 as microcosmic. The most important operating principles shared by the macro and micro worlds were patronage and protection.

Naturally, as a practicing labor racketeer, Georgopoulos would show homage to Carey. He found the firing of all his White Rose members "hopeful." What else was he going to say about the results of Carey's intervention? The truth? That Carey had made it possible for the mob to sell out his members?

What the White Rose strike showed was that IBT officials, at every level—local, joint council, conference, and international—and from every political persuasion, had moved in harmony to allow warehouse workers' wages to be cut drastically. The TDU leadership was now part of the macrocosm apparatus, so they moved with its gravitational pull. But it didn't take much prescience to see that other employers would follow Goldberg in demanding the same deal and that the political fallout would be as substantial as the economic impact, since the warehouse division was the biggest in the IBT.

Still, Ken Paff is unrepentant. He observes: "Left-wing critics say, 'You backed Georgopoulos and Georgopoulos was a crook.' I say—so fucking what? All sorts of things happen in a movement. Some campaigns work and others don't. TDU has done more for reform in the labor movement than any organization in America. The Teamsters are more democratic today, [and] there is less corruption than ever before. I like to measure my accomplishments against what other people have done. What have left-wing critics accomplished?"[60]

Not much, either. In the most arid fields, even the tallest cornstalk doesn't rise above shoe-top level. A century of "boring from within" has reduced the AFL-CIO left to measuring progress in terms of each others' failures.

CHAPTER TWELVE

Eyes off the Prize

REFORM'S REBUFF IN DC 37

After World War II, the United States bombarded the atoll of Bikini in the South Pacific with a dozen H-bombs as part of its nuclear weapons testing program. The tiny island was completely flattened. But within a surprisingly short time after the bombings were stopped in the 1950s, plant and animal life returned—different individuals, of course, but the same species. Today Bikini is just the target of tourists. They're warned not to eat the coconuts. Otherwise, though, they can engage in all the old pastimes—fishing, hunting, and swimming—just like the previous inhabitants.

The devastating law enforcement attack on DC 37 ultimately played out in similar fashion. Between 1996 and 2000, Manhattan district attorney Robert Morgenthau took out over two dozen DC 37 officials on corruption charges. The days of immense salaries, nepotism, thievery, and kickbacks seemed over for good. Yet, within a few months, after an AFSCME-imposed trusteeship was lifted in 2001, life in the district council began to move back to normal—and for the same reasons as on Bikini. Only individuals had been wiped out. The basic ecology of the institution hadn't been altered.

Although heavily promoted as a struggle between reformers and the Old Guard, the familiar battles soon resumed between DC 37's ins and outs. Each side fought fiercely for the prizes the institution could bestow: yearly compensation packages of a quarter million dollars plus; the status that comes with ruling the city's largest municipal union; control over hundreds of millions in dues money and benefit funds; the power to hire your relatives and reward your clients; and regular all-expenses-paid trips to convention spots like Las Vegas, Bermuda, and Honolulu.

The reformers loudly claimed the political high ground. They said they stood for "one person, one vote"—direct elections for the union's highest offices. In practice, though, they preferred to take power through private lawsuits, press leaks, and quiet power-sharing arrangements greased with cash from the DC 37 treasury.

Arthur Z. Schwartz, the veteran Greenwich Village–based attorney for the reformers, acknowledged making an offer of $150,000 in spring of 2004 to get Lillian Roberts, DC 37's seventy-eight-year-old executive director, to resign and hand over the union to his clients. She and her alliance of regulars had just beaten the reform candidates, who were led by Social Service Employees Union president Charles Ensley and Park Workers president, Mark Rosenthal. Schwartz explained that his offer was made in the context of settling private lawsuits.

It was only one of his many legal maneuvers on behalf of the reformers. Schwartz had also sued Roberts to gain control over DC 37's $171 million benefits funds.[1] He charged that she'd hired her son's firm to handle the fund's legal work. Roberts replied that Ivan Smith wasn't her son, he was her nephew, and that his firm was well qualified for the job.

For her part, Roberts was suing the reformers for age discrimination. The reformers controlled the union's executive board, and it was the board that decided how much DC 37's top officers could make. After losing the election for the top executive offices, the board decided to reduce Roberts's $250,000-a-year executive director's salary to a more proletarian $175,000. Lopping off $75,000 from Roberts's compensation package was payback for her campaign against Mark Rosenthal, the former dissident park worker who was running for treasurer on the opposition ticket. In Roberts's campaign literature, she portrayed Rosenthal, who made nearly $250,000 a year, as indifferent to the plight of welfare moms who had work-experience assignments as park workers. Rosenthal responded by having Schwartz sue Roberts for anti-Semitism.[2]

By 2004, the long march of reform in DC 37 had ended in a contest reminiscent of ethnic food fights for control over seats in the high school cafeteria. But the crusade to fix DC 37 had started off in a completely different spirit. In 1997, social workers (Local 371) president Charles Ensley tried courageously to expose the union leadership's brazen vote fraud. Reform gathered momentum in 1998, when Rosenthal was elected president of Local 983, ousting the mob-linked leadership of his local. As the principal critics of the administration, Ensley and Rosenthal became prophets when district attorney Morgenthau indicted top officials in the ballot stuffing case. Rosenthal, profiled in the *New York Times* as "big, bold, brash, and bent on change," also wound up on *60 Minutes* and was featured in *Readers' Digest*.

But change presented Rosenthal with a challenge. Essentially, he was being offered a quarter of a million dollars to join the new administration. Why did a reformer need to earn so much money—especially when some of his members earned only a little over $8.00 an hour? Rosenthal answered that he couldn't give part of his salary back, as some of his supporters had urged. It would embarrass his new allies.

It wasn't long before the former park worker became a DC 37 player, taking calls every day from the likes of Hillary Clinton and Mayor Mike Bloomberg. Rosenthal's office was lined with photographs of Rosenthal with celebrities, including diet diva Suzanne Sommers. He'd been overweight for some time, but since his election as Local 983 president, Rosenthal had swollen to over 400 pounds, making it hard for him to walk more than a block or so at a time. He couldn't take the subway; he had to be chauffeur-driven everywhere.

Rosenthal's appetite for celebrity and recognition was as large as his craving for Chinese food. When his *60 Minutes* episode ran, Rosenthal threw a screening party at Nadine's in Greenwich Village. Hundreds of well-wishers dropped by. He talked to novelist Jimmy Breslin about writing his life story. Rosenthal wanted to have a documentary movie made, too. To gather material for it, during his first six months in office as president of Local 983, he had himself almost constantly videotaped.

Still, Rosenthal made time to co-found, with Ensley, the Committee for Real Change. What made the CRC highly unusual in AFL-CIO circles was that it was an organization funded by local leaders who promised to transfer power to the members. "One person, one vote" was their slogan. They promised to hold direct elections so the members could choose the local's top officials. In the existing system, DC 37's bosses were chosen by delegates, who were effectively chosen by, at most, five or six officers of the bigger DC 37 locals, and often by as few as two.

The reformers waited until 2002 before they scrapped their reliance on the bottom-up approach and entered into a power sharing deal with the very Old Guard they'd pledged to oust. Instead, the two factions united to oust the trustee, Lee Saunders, who had been sent out in November 1998 from AFSCME headquarters in Washington, D.C., to restore credibility and loyalty to one of the government employee union's largest sources of cash flow.

Somehow, Saunders had managed to unite DC 37's two warring factions against himself. First he alienated the reformers, whose most well known figure was Rosenthal. Saunders kept him off the executive board—an $18,000-a-year perquisite. Then he sent the results of an internal audit on a Rosenthal ally, local president Al Cannizzo, to the Manhattan district attorney. Cannizzo, a member of the reform wing's Committee for Real Change, charged the union $15,000 for 215 visits to the Golden Gate Motor Inn, a Brooklyn "short-stay" motel. He also ran up a $45,000 cell phone bill.[3] Rosenthal's reaction was to attack Saunders for being inconsistent. What about the Old Guard's most prominent member, Helen Greene, whom Saunders had supported for international vice president? She'd embezzled too, Rosenthal charged, but Saunders let her pay back the money and didn't turn her over to the D.A.[4]

At the same time that Saunders was protecting Helen Greene, the tall, attractive head of a health service workers local and the Old Guard's choice for DC 37 executive director, he also managed to antagonize many of her Old Guard peers. Historically, the DC 37 Old Guard had never been as scary a bunch as the Teamsters' Old Guard. They could embezzle on their American Express cards, steal an election, and take kickbacks from turkey and sandwich vendors, but serious labor racketeering, like shakedown strikes, were well beyond their scope. And the big money—the benefit funds—was controlled not by local but by district council officials.

Still, even if many were only petty chiselers, they were used to being handled like peers of the realm. Saunders treated them like spoiled teenagers who'd overspent their allowance.

From a survivalist standpoint, Saunders's biggest mistake was to cross the Old Guard's biggest baron, Veronica Montgomery-Costa, who had taken over the 27,000-member school aides local from the larcenous Charlie Hughes.[5] Saunders very publicly quashed Montgomery-Costa's effort to double her own salary. It grated her that she wasn't even allowed to earn six figures—while Hughes had earned a quarter million. Montgomery-Costa put out feelers to Rosenthal, who was also aggrieved. In factional terms, they became an item.

The spirit of common grievance spread. The regulars also reached out to the social workers president Ensley, the most powerful and respected member of the reformers. A veteran of the 1960s civil rights movement, he limited himself to a modest $88,000 a year in salaries. Of all the local leaders pledged to reform, his local had the most delegates in the 327-member assembly that chose the executive director. By early 2002, a deal was worked out—a compromise that would send Saunders back to Washington, D.C., and allow the two factions to share power.

The capstone of the agreement was the replacement of Saunders with Lillian Roberts, a highly respected figure from DC 37's golden age. Roberts had started her organizing career while still in her teens in Chicago in 1945 as a nurse's aide. When Victor Gotbaum, the man who built DC 37, got the call to run the struggling institution, he'd brought her with him to New York, where he'd put her in charge of the crucial Harlem Hospital organizing campaign that made DC 37 the default choice for all nonuniformed, nonteaching city workers forever after.

Although seventy-five when she took over, Roberts had aged marvelously. She was slim and beautifully dressed, corsaged, and coiffed—she looked twenty years younger than her age. Not only did she have a striking presence, but she could also evoke pioneering days of public sector unionism—the great organizing drives, the illegal strikes, the nights in jail. It was obvious when she spun tales from the 1960s to a Barclay Street crowd that hundreds of DC 37 women in the audience practically adored her.

As understood by the reformers, the agreement between the two factions called for Roberts to be a caretaker executive director while Rosenthal got to step up to the treasurer's job. After Roberts's anticipated retirement in 2004, Ensley would succeed her. In the meantime, as Roberts herself acknowledges, she promised Ensley an AFSCME international vice presidency.[6]

"It was either Lillian or McEntee," explains Ensley of his decision to commit the reformers to Roberts. Ensley says that Gerald McEntee, the AFSCME president, wanted to install his own satrap so he could rule directly from Washington. Neither the reformers nor the regulars wanted to lose their autonomy. He got an invitation from the regulars to meet them at the Marriott. "They asked me," he recalled, "'How would you feel if Lillian Roberts were to be the executive director?' Eddie [Rodriguez, the boss of Local 1549] was there. Veronica [Montgomery-Costa of Local 372] was there. Between them, they had 44,000 votes. I could count."[7]

From the reformers' standpoint, Roberts's strong qualifications were her ancient arteries and an understanding that she would leave soon. Ensley believed that he'd follow Roberts. Rosenthal was definitely convinced that he'd follow Ensley. It also helped make up Rosenthal's mind that Roberts offered him DC 37's treasurer's job, which paid over $180,000 a year plus expenses. By virtue of his new position, Rosenthal became chair of the trustees of the benefit funds trust.

In a post-Roberts era, the reformers' public scenario called for full-strength democracy to prevail. They would institute "one person, one vote." This meant that the lions—the heads of the big locals—would step aside to allow the member-lambs to choose the occupants of DC 37's top offices.

There was little precedent for such a repeal of the AFL-CIO laws of nature. All local unions in the United States have direct elections, but only because federal law requires it. Above the local level, direct elections are rare. The leadership of the Teamsters and the Laborers decided to have them. Their alternative was to go to trial and face federal RICO charges.

For direct elections to take place in DC 37 without Justice Department intervention, the reformers would have had to transform their mostly paper organization—the Committee for Real Change—into a responsible, mass-based political party—one with genuine members and a leadership that appealed to them on the basis of a shared program. In other words, the reformers would have to stop acting like an office-seeking cabal.

But real change was hard for the reformers too. They were mostly good, well-meaning barons who criticized genuinely bad barons, but they had no intention of giving up their own perquisites or sharing power with the powerless. As they became insiders, the temptations to play a classic inside game became overwhelming. Now they had jobs and perquisites to give out too.

The political debts the reformers had run up also created limits to how much real change was possible. Besides embezzlement, the core of corruption in public service unions revolved around the award of vendor contracts. And reformers, who as candidates for office had no money and no contracts to offer, acquired heavy obligations to professionals, lawyers in particular. Lawyers helped reform candidates navigate election laws; they filed protests; and they gave authority to their clients' corruption charges. They found legal reasons to file civil suits against the incumbent adversaries. If an attorney had helped you get into office, didn't he or she deserve the most lucrative retainers the union had to give out? Perhaps. But a spoils system wasn't truly compatible with the on-the-merits approach the reformers were supposed to uphold.

DANCE MACABRE

There's a picture in *The Chief Leader*, the weekly civil service paper, of Mark Rosenthal and Lillian Roberts dancing together. Given Roberts's advanced age and Rosenthal's considerable size, no one expected a Fred-and-Ginger partnership. But the two union officials did put on wan smiles and performed a little dip for the camera. When and why did the music stop?

For Lillian Roberts, it was about eight months after she'd taken office. "Mr. Rosenthal contacted my nephew. He offered to pay me $150,000 if I would go away. I was very upset. I was highly insulted. It was as if I'd done nothing. They had used me to bring the union out from the trusteeship. And now he wanted to push me aside and take over."[8]

Actually, Roberts's nephew, Ivan Smith, remembers getting four calls that dangled the $150,000-a-year consultancy, which would be for either two or three years. Rosenthal, he says, called three times, and then Rosenthal's lawyer, Arthur Schwartz, called, just after the February 2004 election. "The members had spoken," said Smith. "If they really cared about union democracy, they would have backed off."[9]

Rosenthal denies ever having made the offer himself. "If Arthur called her, that's something different," he said. "She's a disaster—I'd support any way of getting rid of her."[10]

Schwartz insists that his cash proposal to Roberts on behalf of the reformers needs to be put in its proper context. "It was made all in the course of a discussion of the settlement of litigation," he says. "To say we offered her $150,000 to go away is really a very crass mischaracterization. There were many elements in the proposal, including a unity ticket everybody would agree to when she left, you know, carving out places for people on both sides."[11]

In 1999, Schwartz had made Gus Bevona, the powerful boss of SEIU's Local 32BJ, disappear by this method. First he sued Bevona on behalf of reformers. Then, in exchange for dropping the suit, Bevona agreed to retire with a $1.5 million settlement (see chapter 13).

But unlike Bevona, Roberts refused to roll over. She says that the offer just stiffened her resolve to run for reelection.

INDESTRUCTIBLE ICON

Roberts appeared to present a broad and inviting target for reform attack. The reformers portrayed her as a classic nepotist. She'd hired her son's firm to serve as counsel to the benefit funds. When DC 37's ethics counsel ruled that she'd violated the ethics code, Roberts argued that her "son" was really her nephew. Then, when the ethics counsel didn't buy the claim, Roberts forced the resignation of the ethics counsel. Her opponents also say she hired her boyfriend, Oliver Gray, who had no experience in labor unions, as associate director.

But the conflict-of-interest charges not only failed to wound Roberts, they may have actually helped her. Going into the 2004 election, Roberts had to carry the burden of having signed a widely criticized contract with Mayor Bloomberg's administration. Ivan Smith, who was also Roberts's campaign adviser, conceded, "Without those stories to stir up our base, we might have been in big trouble."[12]

An AFSCME member for fifty-eight years, Roberts was a genuine living fossil, returned from the days when the struggles of the civil rights movement and public sector unionism were still intertwined. She was as close as anyone in town to being the embodiment of Black History Month. Yet, week after week, the union's African American female union leaders and staff would read stories in *The Chief Leader* describing their boss as "an empty suit" or "the queen of denial." They reacted with a seething hostility that made it uncomfortable for *The Chief Leader*'s beat reporter to walk 125 Barclay Street's corridors.[13]

A certain immunity attaches to established leaders of long-excluded, much-oppressed groups, especially if the attacks originate from outsiders. DC 37 was now made up predominantly of black women—by one estimate, 80 percent were women and 60 percent of those were black. Ambitious and young, the black female trade unionists no longer deferred to black male union leaders. By replacing septuagenarian figures like Charlie Hughes and Jim Butler, they were creating a new Old Guard led by black women. And what gave them added legitimacy was the pioneering Roberts.

At the same time, Roberts's less celebrated experience as a top HMO executive and as a seasoned expert in DC 37 infighting made her a much more formidable opponent than she seemed. She might not have gotten good contracts, but there were few political shots anywhere on the court that she couldn't return. As Mark Rosenthal finally acknowledged, "I got beat by a seventy-seven-year-old grandma."

During the trusteeship, Roberts, who'd once gotten as high as DC 37's no. 2 spot, had returned after a twenty-year absence to work as a consultant. After only a few months, she emerged in January 2002 as the regulars' candidate for the no. 1 job. She was able to entice the reformers with the promise—or the prediction, depending on who is telling the story— "You'll be next."[14]

Explaining his decision to back Roberts in 2002 for the executive directorship, Charles Ensley, her 2004 opponent, told the *New York Times*, "We thought Lillian would be the perfect transition candidate. She brought no baggage."[15]

Actually, as DC 37 insiders knew full well, Roberts brought a veritable baggage train. She had a penchant for violently expressive personal feuds—it was her irrepressible conflict with Local 420 president Jim Butler over control of the city hospitals that drove her out of the union. Eventually, although he denies it, Victor Gotbaum tired of her—pretty radically. Roberts accused him of throwing an ashtray at her at an executive board meeting before she left the union in 1982.[16] Countered Gotbaum, "I was the one who had the ashtray thrown at me."[17]

No matter who hurled the ashtray, Roberts wouldn't end up succeeding Gotbaum. But the Barclay Street rumbles didn't prevent her from reaching a higher perch as state labor commissioner under Governor Hugh Carey. She lasted six years, until Carey's successor, Mario Cuomo, sent a "fourth-level aide" to tell her to clear out her desk.[18]

Then it was on to the private sector for Roberts. She became executive vice president at Total Health—a now-defunct HMO. In 1988, the city Department of Investigation charged that she had handed out payments to DC 37 officials, who then urged DC 37 members to choose Total Health as their HMO. Roberts acknowledged that she'd paid them $30,000 to $40,000, but it wasn't clear that she'd broken any laws. The affair proved once again that Roberts knew how to organize. In the period when Roberts was directing the operation, Total Health gained more members than any other HMO. But the city's Department of Investigation's inquiry put a halt to the campaign.[19]

The Total Health affair produced no indictments. The short-lived company, which never made any money, was merged into Equitable shortly after exposés in *Newsday*.[20] Roberts retired from the HMO business in 1992. But the mini-scandal suggests that rather than not having any at all, Roberts's baggage had been screened and waved through by both the reformers and the Old Guard.

Total Health established her credentials in the world of vendor politics—a capability that certainly wouldn't have hurt Roberts with the union's regulars. And there was no more regular figure than AFSCME's president, Gerald McEntee. McEntee was quietly playing vendor politics in DC 37, too. A drug benefit manager company, National Prescription Administrators, Inc. (NPA), had a $120 million no-bid contract with DC 37's funds. McEntee had been present at the company's creation. His ex-wife and his daughter were employed in executive positions. It must have been a relief to McEntee to know that Lillian Roberts understood the rules of the great game.

Although it had been twenty years since she'd left DC 37, it hadn't really changed all that much—at least not in numbers, strength, or structure. Membership continued to fluctuate around 120,000. DC 37 workers regularly took the brunt of city layoffs, and they were still the city's lowest paid—averaging less than $30,000 a year. An agreement with Mayor Bloomberg signed by Roberts in 2004 ensured that modest raises were paid for by a 15 percent cut in the pay of new hires.

The latest kerfuffles at the top had reshaped the public image of the union. From the 1960s through the early 1980s under the executive directorship of Victor Gotbaum, DC 37 had been admired as a source of progressive policy initiatives and innovative member services. In the 1990s, when Stanley Hill was in charge, DC 37 was reviled as a junket-obsessed den of thieves. Now, in the new millennium, as the reformers challenged Roberts's rule, DC 37's cast of characters seemed drawn from a comic opera—perhaps Gilbert and Sullivan's *Princess Ida*—only without the romantic ending. In the Gilbert and Sullivan classic, Princess Ida turns her fiefdom, the Castle Adamant, into a fortress ruled by philosophic feminist warriors. No men are allowed. Not even chessmen. The Princess and her female entourage stand ready with battle-axes to repel male invaders. But the project is eventually subverted when Princess Ida falls in love with a prince and turns over Castle Adamant to him.

In DC 37's revival of *Princess Ida,* Roberts plays the lead role, surrounding herself with female barons, whom she nurtures and mentors just like as the princess does in the opera. The new DC 37 production captures the latest phase of ethnic succession in the council. African American women now permeate the old ruling clique of black men—which had replaced the white male leadership. Since 1999, these women have run several of the big locals—but not very differently.

Veronica Montgomery-Costa, who took over from her former boss, Charlie Hughes, runs the largest and in many ways the worst local in the union. Her members are the lowest paid and the among the least politically active. And hardly had Montgomery-Costa taken office when she doubled her salary, only to have the action overruled by trustee Lee Saunders.

As executive director, Roberts put restoring Montgomery-Costa's salary at the top of her priorities. Almost immediately, she restored the increase Saunders had taken away. When Montgomery-Costa won reelection by 475-28—out of 27,000 members—DC 37's house organ didn't mention the less-than-2-percent turnout but proclaimed a victory by an "overwhelming majority."[21] Roberts then awarded Montgomery-Costa a place on the regulars' ticket as president of DC 37—a job with no real duties—and when the ticket won, she got another salary: an extra $50,000 a year, in itself more than double the yearly income of her average member. Notwithstanding the novelties of race and gender, this is the stuff of which political machines have always been made.

Compared with the way Princess Ida ran her realm, Lillian Roberts was much more steadfast. She certainly wasn't about to relinquish control to the males—whatever their race. Instead of turning over the realm to a prince, Roberts turned her close friend, Oliver Gray, into her prince consort. She awarded him the job of associate director of the union, which guaranteed her a loyal no. 2. But Gray had never negotiated a union contract or represented workers in arbitration. For DC 37 insiders, like former executive director Victor Gotbaum, who had been Roberts's mentor, the appointment was completely unacceptable. Recalls Gotham, "I told her you can't give Oliver the number two"—the job he'd once given to Roberts. "Okay, Lillian," I said, "if you have thirty-six jobs to give out, you can give him one of them. But the second-highest job in the union? It's outrageous." Roberts replied that she wasn't all that close to Oliver. "But then she makes him the associate director!" marveled Gotbaum.[22]

Roberts denies that Gotbaum even discussed the issue with her. "He's senile," she roared. "It's racist and sexist," she added, that anyone should even ask about her relationship with Gray. "Here I am a seventy-eight-year-old woman and I have to answer questions like that?"[23]

THE FUND FIGHTS

In 2002, before their great falling-out, Roberts had put Rosenthal in charge of the benefit funds. It was like putting the hen in charge of the henhouse. As a shrewd and gutsy rank and filer, Rosenthal had been very good at ferreting out corruption in his local. He grasped easily what it meant when his union's officers paid $90,000 for a Christmas party that lasted just a few minutes and featured bologna sandwiches served to a handful of members. But as Local 983 president, Rosenthal displayed a lack of supervisory skills. His own treasurer, Fernando Rodriguez, an accountant, turned out to be an ex-convict who pleaded guilty to attempted grand larceny. Allegedly, according to DC 37, he wrote checks to himself from the local's account and signed Rosenthal's name.[24]

It was during their honeymoon period that Rosenthal had approved Roberts's May 2002 decision to give a $180,000-a-year no-bid contract to her nephew's law firm to serve as the benefit funds' legal counsel. What eventually smoked out the alleged conflict of interest was a report written about six months later by Barbara C. Deinhardt, DC 37's ethical practices officer, who ruled that Roberts had violated the union's ethics code.[25]

Rosenthal, who had previously supported Roberts's decision, now went on the attack. What had changed? He says he grasped now what he hadn't before: that Ivan Smith would profit from the deal because he was a partner at the firm. Rosenthal explained that he had simply not known that law partners share in law firms' profits. But there was a simpler explanation. Rosenthal opposed the deal when he became an outsider, not when he was on the inside.

When Rosenthal was still on the inside, he was angling for his own candidate to get the benefit funds contract. His candidate was his attorney, Arthur Schwartz. A meeting took place at Docks Oyster Bar just after Roberts's election, attended by Roberts, Smith, Rosenthal, Schwartz, and Schwartz's law partner, who made a pitch for the benefit funds job.

As long as Rosenthal was allied with Roberts, he bowed to her decision to hire Smith's firm instead of Schwartz's. But when he and Roberts fell out, the deal became an odious conflict of interest. What seems to be going on is less a battle between reform and corruption than a battle between cronyism and nepotism.

In Lewis Carroll's "The Walrus and the Carpenter," the two talk of many things, of cabbages and kings. But the real issue is who's going to get the oysters.[26] Just as Roberts wanted the job to go to her son's firm, Rosenthal was supporting Schwartz, his legal mentor. Schwartz was also the attorney for Charles Ensley's local as well as for the reform-controlled executive board. He could be expected to become the attorney for DC 37 if the Ensley-Rosenthal forces ever get control of the union. So the battle between the reformers and the regulars couldn't be entirely divorced from the multimillion dollar struggle between the lawyers for fees from the council, its locals, its funds, and its executive organs.

Arthur Schwartz may not look formidable, but he is. A portrait in *City Limits*, a progressive urban affairs monthly, described his tousled hair and untrimmed mustache as "making him look like a Wheaten terrier in a drip-dry suit."[27] But when this legal terrier sinks his teeth into an adversary's ankle, the pain has just begun. The attack escalates in a flurry of lawsuits and biting newspaper leaks. It often ends with the mangled union leader limping off into retirement and Schwartz's client in his place.[28]

Schwartz has spent a lifetime representing union dissidents against some of the biggest figures in the labor movement. Early in his career, nearly a quarter of a century ago, he represented a dissident Laborers union member in a suit that led to the fall of Ronald Reagan's labor secretary. But unlike Bert Hall, Schwartz's deceased former mentor—who practically lived in a closet and owned only one suit—Schwartz's work never created fundamental changes in case law, like Hall's *Salzhandler v. Caputo*, the case that established free speech rights for union members,[29] or *Hall v. Cole*, a case that Hall argued before the U.S. Supreme Court that established the precedent for awarding attorney fees in union democracy cases.[30]

Thanks to the abstemious Hall, though, Schwartz can represent union dissidents and at the same time own a Greenwich Village townhouse. ("A building I bought a long time ago," says Schwartz.)[31] The dissidents can tap Schwartz's canny legal counsel, media connections, and political savvy. Once in power as union presidents, they gratefully unlock the union treasury. The dissident route has enabled Schwartz to pick up retainers from such unions as SEIU, the union that represents the employees of Key Span (formerly Brooklyn Union Gas Co.), the Transport Workers Union, Professional Staff Congress, AFSCME District Council 1707, and, in DC 37, Rosenthal's Local 983, Ensley's Local 371, and the DC 37 executive board. Altogether Schwartz's firm represents forty unions.[32]

THE ROY COMMER STORY

One union president Schwartz no longer represents is Roy Commer, former president of DC 37's Civil Service Technical Guild—Local 375.

After Commer was ousted from the presidency of the 6,000-member organization, Schwartz dropped him as a client.

Commer's ouster and isolation—despite strong and repeated support from his members—is perhaps the most telling sign of how the DC 37 reform movement ran aground. There was no more consistent, outspoken, and determined foe of corruption than Commer. Running twice on an anticorruption program, he'd been elected president of the local twice by his members. Yet in the demonology of DC 37, Commer occupies a place somewhere between the Brooklyn Dodgers' Walter O'Malley and the Book of Revelations' seven-headed beast. AFSCME president Gerald McEntee took a personal interest in seeing to it that Commer would be expelled from the union for life. Al Diop, the orchestrator of the 1996 vote fraud, didn't get kicked out of AFSCME for life.

But besides co-founding the Committee for Real Change and standing up at AFSCME's 1998 Honolulu convention and attacking McEntee to his face for corruption—what had Commer, a forty-nine-year-old Staten Island Boy Scout leader, actually done wrong?

Nineteen formal charges were filed by his local enemies—including that he advocated "dual unionism," the worst imaginable sin in AFSCME theology, since it consists in publicly asserting that another union might be preferable to AFSCME. Eventually, Commer beat all charges but two: having sent out an unauthorized postcard announcing an upcoming election in his local, and then apparently compounding the crime by refusing to pay the fine that had been levied by his adversaries on the local's executive board. An AFSCME judicial panel, appointed by McEntee, ruled that Commer must go.[33]

Serving as his own lawyer in 2000, Commer appealed his removal to the U.S. District Court. In his private chambers, veteran jurist Robert W. Sweet allowed, "Roy, you've been fucked, but there's nothing that can be done about it." Judge Sweet doesn't affirm or deny making the observation but insists that if he did, "I shouldn't have."[34]

Commer's real crime was that after his 1998 election, he had wanted to have a look at the books of his union's funds. He'd heard rumors. But his political opponents argued that his motives were partisan and corrupt. They said he only wanted to cast suspicion on them and install his own attorney to run the funds. Commer's requests for audits of the funds were rejected by the local's hostile executive board, and the board soon initiated charges in the purloined postcard affair.[35]

Commer's appeal to the union came to the floor of the summer 2000 AFSCME convention in Philadelphia. McEntee was presiding. He was wearing a fixed smirk. His expression may have been the product of the effort it took not to appear like he was savoring the avalanche of obloquy that was descending on Commer from AFSCME delegations from all across the country. Commer's only defenders came from the Committee for Real Change. Their arguments—that he shouldn't be expelled because he'd been twice elected by his members and that DC 37 really did have a corruption problem—had absolutely zero effect on the delegates.[36] Almost unanimously, 6,000 green-shirted delegates gave full-throated approval to Commer's banishment.[37]

It had always been easy to dismiss Roy Commer. But you couldn't ignore him. Shaggy-bearded, wide-shouldered, an Orthodox Jew standing well over six feet tall and weighing over 300 pounds, he wore a big wide-brimmed black hat that served as a kind of yarmulke. But Commer lacked all Talmudic subtlety. He was more Maccabean. It never occurred to him to ally with the little crooks to drive out the big ones. In Commer's view, they should all be expelled from the temple. His members agreed. But the first time he won the presidency, the ballots disappeared from DC 37's locked security office. DC 37 ruled that the election had to be rerun. Commer won again. The ballot thieves were never found, although there wasn't much of a search.

But it didn't make a great deal of difference how often the members voted, or for whom. Several of those who ran on Commer's slate turned against him when he refused to give them full-time paid staff jobs. It cost him the majority on the union's executive board. Then too, of all the locals in DC 37, his most closely resembled an ongoing caucus of the Mad Hatter's tea party. One of Commer's biggest critics, the union's political director, had moved from the city because the SPCA wouldn't permit him to keep crocodiles in his Brooklyn apartment.[38]

After his expulsion at the Philadelphia AFSCME convention, Commer went back to his city job and sank beneath the waves of controversy. But in 2004, he reemerged as a prophet without honor in his own union. Local 375's bookkeeper confessed to stealing $2.4 million from union and benefit funds. The thirtieth DC 37 official bagged by district attorney Robert Morgenthau had stolen more than any other thief in DC 37's kleptocratic history.[39]

For over a decade, Lloyd Clarke, the crooked bookkeeper, had been building a stealth real estate empire in the Bronx with the millions he stole from the funds. Clarke had been able to get away with the long-running embezzlement until he was caught in 2003 in part because his supervisor, the union's treasurer, with whom he shared a small office, had never bothered to check the books. He just signed the checks. It also helped that the administrator of the legal services fund never noticed that hundreds of thousands of dollars were going from the legal services funds directly into Clarke's private accounts. He'd never thought to check either. Both officials had been fierce critics of Commer's anticorruption campaign.[40] Eventually, both the Local 375 treasurer and the head of the legal services fund resigned their positions. But they weren't kicked out of the union like Commer.

KADDISH FOR REFORM

As a plausible reform strategy, neither Rosenthal's posture of greater flexibility nor Commer's unbending adherence to principle seems to have budged DC 37 from its familiar ways. If Commer had given patronage jobs to his allies, he could have controlled his local's executive board. Instead, relying on his election mandate from the membership, he rewarded competence. It cost him his career.

The Ensley-Rosenthal path recognizes the severe limitations of a strategy that relies on principles. "It would have done absolutely no good to appeal to principles with the delegates," Ensley observes. "They're simply in it for the perks, the trips."[41] Fair enough, but trying to outbid or simply buy out the incumbents proved no royal road to office either.

Rosenthal was a great whistle-blower, but he turned out to be a poor reformer. He started out proclaiming "one person, one vote" and wound up offering $150,000 and no vote.

Roberts, who will be eighty by the time of the next election in 2007, intends to run again, "if the members want me." Warned Roberts, "I'm not going to be a lame duck. Nobody's going to run me out of the union I helped to make."

For his part, Ensley intends to take another shot at Roberts. But whoever prevails, the overall plight of the members doesn't seem likely to change much. A spokesperson for DC 37 says that the average member's yearly salary is under $30,000. But as Ensley observes, the median is probably a good deal less. In the union's two largest locals, the median may be under $25,000. Seven years after the turkey conspiracy shook DC 37, low-wage members are still lining up for free turkeys at Thanksgiving time.[42] Of course the turkeys aren't free. They're paid for by the members who don't make it to the head of the queue.

The original architects of the Barclay Street edifice built solidly. You see how deeply the institutional foundations of DC 37's political culture have been sunk when Victor Gotbaum, the retired former executive director, gave a February 2005 speech to forty or so fellow retirees from Local 371.[43] The speech itself was over in a few minutes. But the attentive audience kept him on his feet for more than an hour of questions and answers. Many questions dissolved into heartfelt statements of how much they missed Gotbaum. One African American woman waved her hand, insisting that the meeting not break up until she'd been heard. A contemporary of the octogenarian Gotbaum, her praise of his personal gifts lasted a couple of minutes. Finally she got to the end of her encomium. She would never forget Gotbaum and will always be in his debt. "Without you, Victor," she said with eyes shining, "I would never have gotten to Hawaii."

CHAPTER THIRTEEN

Andy Stern's Dead Souls

"I have seen the future of progressive leadership in
America and its name is Andy Stern."

■

—Arianna Huffington[1]

The year 2005 was the Golden Jubilee year of the American labor movement, the fiftieth anniversary of the marriage between the CIO and
the AFL. It also marked the passage of a decade since John Sweeney's New
Voice movement, promising to revive the AFL-CIO, achieved power. But
organized labor's steady and seemingly unstoppable membership hemor-
rhage, the failure of Sweeney's organizing strategy, the collapse of a major
southern California grocery strike, the fiasco of the Iowa Democratic
Party presidential caucuses (in which labor's top two candidates finished
a distant third and fourth), and the persistent odor of corruption in many
of the classic venues as well as some novel ones—like the Ullico insider
trading scandal—all combined to dampen any gala mood. Under the circumstances, an exuberant national party commemorating Sweeney and
the AFL-CIO would have run the risk of resembling a ceremonial honor-
ing of President Rick Wagoner and the top management of General Motors, which also hit a postwar market-share low. Instead, the twin
anniversaries were clouded by recriminations and threats to split the Federation if it didn't mend its ways.

The threats were plausible because of a caucus of union officials formed
and led by Andy Stern, a fifty-five-year-old former social worker from
New Jersey. Stern headed the 1.8 million–member Service Employees International Union, the largest and fastest-growing affiliate in a federation
that was steadily shrinking. Not only did Stern have more members, he

also had more energy, more ideas, more money for political action, and more chutzpah than anyone in the higher circles of organized labor. Although he spent a record $85 million on Democrats in the 2004 election cycle, Stern didn't put his mouth where his money was. Instead, he expressed doubt that the labor movement could survive a Kerry victory. "It's a hollow party," Stern said, adding that "if John Kerry becomes president, it hurts' chances of reforming . . . organized labor."[2]

Stern was also the only high official willing to point to the dinosaur in the room: organized labor itself. "Our employers have changed," he said in "Andy Stern's Journal," his personal blog in November 2004, "our industries have changed, and the world has certainly changed, but the labor movement's structure and culture have sadly stayed the same."[3]

Stern's idea of union reform, however, had nothing in common with the classic corruption-fighting, democracy-widening program of the AFL-CIO left. Although he'd probably done more to root out corruption than any top official, he never referred to his successes except in the most oblique way. Stern was openly disdainful of union democracy. He battled it on his own blog, taking on union adversaries who perhaps wisely chose to remain anonymous.

Good ideas about how to run unions trickled down from the top, he believed. And Stern's coalition brought together like-minded officials drawn from Ivy League backgrounds. They called themselves the New Unity Partnership and drafted a program for a radical restructuring of the AFL-CIO.

Stern's program had to be a rude provocation to John Sweeney, his old boss and immediate predecessor as SEIU president. Stern wanted to cut Sweeney's AFL-CIO budget by 50 percent. The dues would be rebated to the more growth-oriented affiliates so they could add more members. He also wanted Sweeney to persuade the forty or so smaller affiliates—whose lesser size showed they'd lost the fitness contest for survival—to find a merger partner among the bigger, more successful organizations. By the time the Executive Council was to meet in Las Vegas in early 2005, Stern and his combative ideas had made the covers of *BusinessWeek* and the *New York Times Magazine*.

If genius is the ability to hold two contradictory ideas at the same time while extracting the latent power of both, Stern's membership-building strategy certainly qualifies. What he's done is no less than to connect the radical organizing tactics of Saul Alinsky, Chicago's Back-of-the-Yards philosopher, with the conservative organizational principles of former General Motors president Alfred P. Sloan. Although too young to participate at the time, Stern is a child of the 1960s, when every Ivy League campus radical who wasn't a Marxist was attracted to Alinsky's ideas. When Hillary Clinton was at Wellesley, she wrote her undergraduate thesis on Alinsky. Stern reportedly attended the Alinsky-inspired Midwest Academy, founded by Heather and Paul Booth—now a top AFSCME staffer.[4]

From Alinsky, Stern got the idea to transform every battle over local economic issues into a crusade for social justice. Alinsky, too, had pioneered the notion of deploying confrontational tactics on behalf of moderate, but still tangible, goals: mounting direct action campaigns—not just with conventional pickets and signs, but using imaginative stunts like embarrassing the powers-that-be by showing up at their private meetings, exposing the contrast between the powerful and the powerless while mobilizing community sympathy on behalf of the latter. These tactics were all on display in the early 1990s Justice for Janitors campaign that produced the great L.A. triumph, which was made into a Hollywood movie, *Bread and Roses*, in 2000.

What made Stern different and successful in the trade union field was his ability to supplement Alinsky with Sloan. Stern's ideas on how unions should be structured—as opposed to how members can be recruited—are distilled from Sloan's *My Years with General Motors*, written back in the 1940s, but still a management bible. It is telling that the L.A. Justice for Janitors campaign, while it was sold to the public in terms of social justice, was originally conceived in Washington, D.C., in corporate terms as a "market recovery program." The Central American radicals who took the police beatings during the campaign and won the sympathy of Westside L.A. were eventually hustled off the stage—given buyouts and replaced by a Stern aide from SEIU headquarters. The potential for local revolt was further reduced when the L.A. local itself was dissolved and replaced by a huge statewide organization with its headquarters in Sacramento. All across the country, Stern liquidated locals, replacing them with regional organizations that functioned as part of Sloan-style managerial divisions.

Ultimately, Sloan's principles trumped Alinsky's. By the end of the 1990s, the use of Alinsky-style tactics tended to be mostly pro forma. What was really driving membership growth was SEIU money and lobbying: huge contributions to state and local politicians. They allowed Stern to bring in members who were not strictly workers at all but beneficiaries of entitlement programs. Essentially, Stern was able to organize hundreds of thousands of new members in the home care and day care fields because he understood welfare programs and how to play the welfare system. Family members were turned into each other's "clients." All across blue-state America, Stern was able to persuade state and local politicians to create agencies that acted as the employer for these family care providers. That their condition improved by their becoming union members is probable, although most received less than a thousand dollars a month because their hours were few, their pay was very low, and their SEIU dues surprisingly high. That SEIU's organizing campaigns had much relevance to problems of organizing members in either private or public sector unions is highly unlikely.

Because Stern's organizing techniques never got the scrutiny of his organizing results, he could appear as the inheritor of the great CIO leaders of the 1930s. As hostilities increased during the run-up to the July 2005 convention in Chicago, labor experts foresaw a possible reenactment of 1935. In October of that fateful year, nine union leaders, led by the Miners' fist-swinging boss, John L. Lewis, stormed out of an Atlantic City convention to form the Congress of Industrial Organizations. In San Francisco, at the SEIU's 2004 convention, Stern told the delegates that it was time to "change the AFL-CIO or build something stronger." According to one account, "the floor erupted, delegates stood and whooped for a full minute." Wrote Harold Meyerson, editor of the *American Prospect*, breathlessly, "If Stern and company don't prevail, the same door John L. Lewis left through is always gapingly wide."[5]

The Stern-led New Unity Partnership never got as far as Chicago. While the CIO leaders had withstood veritable armies of Henry Ford's goons during the great 1937 River Rouge organizing campaign and the blazing shotguns of the Chicago police at Little Steel, the Partnership collapsed after the first few months of intra-AFL-CIO sniping. The AFL-CIO wasn't yet ready for Stern-style reform. The New Unity Partnership's dissolution was announced in January 2005.

Still, Stern refused to back down. He scrambled to put together a new, looser coalition. He even succeeded in adding the Federation's largest private sector union—UFCW. Pro-Stern unions amounted to nearly 40 percent of the AFL-CIO membership.

Basically, the unions loosely arrayed on Stern's side represented the nation's bottom-feeding unions: the UFCW, SEIU, UNITE-HERE, the Teamsters, and the Laborers. These unions control the weaker, lower-paid AFL trades. Yet a couple of them—SEIU and the UFCW—have grown quite substantially. SEIU is now the largest AFL-CIO union, and the UFCW is the Federation's largest private sector union.

Both have adapted by going with the flow—the outflow of jobs now called "foreign outsourcing"[6] and the inflow of immigrant and undocumented workers, nearly half from Mexico. Both trends feed a burgeoning low-paid service sector and, to a lesser extent, a growing cheap-labor food-processing industry. By offering only modest demands, the union is rewarded by the employer who adds workers at factories, stores, and office buildings that meet market discipline. Essentially, the unions making up the Stern axis offer the employer low wages and try to make up in volume what they lose on price.[7]

Besides wage flexibility, the Stern axis is dominated by organizations noted for their elasticity on questions of ethical practice. Of the four unions cited by the President's Commission on Organized Crime as the most seriously mobbed-up in America, three are in the Stern coalition—the Teamsters, the Laborers, and HERE. Not one of their current bosses—James Hoffa Jr. of the Teamsters, Terence O'Sullivan Jr. of the Laborers, or John Wilhelm of HERE—could have reached his pinnacle without denying that mob rule existed in their organizations. Stern's reticence about acknowledging his own highly effective corruption-fighting record may be a consequence of his new alliances.

Stern's adversaries—particularly the Machinists, AFSCME, the Steelworkers, the Miners, and the Communications Workers—represent the old AFL and CIO unions still trying to maintain the American labor standards that have been slipping since the 1970s. They can't organize millions of workers at wage rates equal to those of their current members. The temptation is to buy new members by accepting low-wage "tiers." Of all the old CIO unions, the autoworkers have gone the farthest in that direction, cutting wage rates almost in half in their agreements with parts manufacturers. Most have held the line, but a slowly disappearing salient it is.

In 1935, the split in the AFL took place because for the industrial unions, the organizing prospects were so promising, with thousands of workers occupying plants demanding to be organized and the government urging millions more to join unions. In 1955, the merger between the AFL-CIO took place because, in organizing terms, all the low-hanging fruit had been picked. In 2005, a new split threatened the AFL-CIO not because 1930s-style organizing opportunities had returned, but because the 1955 disarmament treaty turned huge swaths of the country into no-fly zones for union organizers. The only territory left for the unions to conquer is each other's. But Stern seems confident that he can win the battle against rival leaders. It's an assurance that seems justified given his most outstanding but least widely known accomplishment—wresting control from SEIU's corrupt barons.

THE LEGACY OF "TWO GUN" LOUIE

Unions that start out corrupt usually stay that way. There are Teamsters locals in Chicago, Boston, and New York with a 100-year history of gangster rule.[8] It's also not uncommon for unions that start out honest to become corrupt. The teachers union and AFSCME started out as social movements. Many locals in these two organizations have wound up as havens for high-living embezzlers, benefit fund thieves, and mob wannabe's, abetted by the leadership in Washington. The SEIU is an anomaly: a union that began as a Capone family enterprise, run by pimps, bombers, assassins, and professional strikebreakers but has actually managed to overcome its debilitating legacy. In part because of the requirements of his new alliance and in part because of the taboo on mentioning corruption in the present-day AFL-CIO, it's a feat Stern can only allude to indirectly. He talks about unions "ruled by various families"—he doesn't say "various crime families."[9]

Stern obscures his own achievement through an exercise in false nostalgia. "For SEIU's first sixty years," he explained to the 2004 convention, "our conventions were basically family affairs. The delegates to our first convention in 1921 were from seven janitor unions, and the convention's sole purpose was for those local union leaders to create a new national union with a simple founding principle—local union independence and autonomy."[10] It's unlikely that the leaders would have been so concerned with abstract principles of governance when they'd been indicted and were about to stand trial. In 1922, the top ten officers of what was then known as the Building Services Employees International Union—including president William Quesse—were found guilty of extortion and conspiracy to bomb. The "labor terrorists" were convicted by a jury that deliberated six hours.[11]

Certainly, the founding BSEIU fathers were no social workers, like Stern. According to the Dailey Commission, set up in 1921 by the Illinois state legislature to investigate union corruption in Chicago, the use of explosives and extortion was commonplace in organizing for the building services.[12] Quesse said as much. Quesse's successor, his chauffeur, Jerry Horan, had beaten a murder indictment; he was accused of killing two cops.[13] In Chicago, those credentials, plus the presidency of the Flat Janitors Local No. 1, qualified Horan to serve on an elite three-man clemency committee for Al Capone organized by the Chicago mob.[14]

Under Horan, conventions had become family affairs indeed. In attendance at the 1935 convention at the Bismarck Hotel in Chicago were mobsters from the leading crime families in the nation. They held a secret convention within the convention. From the organization that would eventually evolve into the Genovese crime family came "Little Augie" Pisano. Brooklyn was represented by Joe Adonis, who ran the waterfront in New York. From Capone's Chicago came Frank "the Enforcer" Nitti—known to TV watchers as Eliot Ness's chief adversary on *The Untouchables*. There were lone operators too, like "Baby Face" Nelson and "Machine Gun" Kelly. Also among the criminal luminaries was the BSEIU's own Louis "Two Gun" Alterie, president-for-life of the Chicago Theater Janitors union. Alterie was credited with twenty murders. But just months after the Bismarck convention, Alterie was entering his automobile when he was struck by twelve bullets that pierced his steel vest, killing him before he could reach his union office. Because Alterie had just been questioned in the killing of a rival union leader, police theorized that his murder might have been mob related.[15]

An even more fantastic figure than the misnamed "Two Gun" Louie Alterie—who actually carried three guns and performed his rubouts with machine guns—was George Scalise. Scalise dressed conventionally and spoke politely, but he may have been the only head of an international union whose sole prior experience was as a professional gangster. Scalise's first trade was managing prostitutes. After his release from federal prison in 1915, he turned to labor racketeering. Scalise founded Sentinel Services, hiring goons to threaten employers and then offering to protect the employers against his own operatives. Jerry Horan, at the request of the Capone gang, made Scalise head of the BSEIU's eastern district. The announcement of Scalise's appointment was actually made from the offices of Sentinel Services. But as a labor leader, Scalise continued to operate in much the same fashion as he had in the private sector. Manhattan district attorney Thomas Dewey demonstrated this in a case that won them both national notoriety. Besides bribes from employers, Scalise plundered the BSEIU treasury, with half the spoils going to the Capone gang. Yet had it not been for the investigative reports of right-wing journalist Westbrook Pegler, Scalise might well have gone down in SEIU history as one of its greatest organizers, along with Horan, the two who had, respectively, doubled and tripled the union's size.[16]

Men with less notorious credentials replaced Scalise, and the union was renamed the SEIU, but these developments scarcely changed the character of the representation provided by the union's leadership. The Chicago Outfit continued to be influential at least through the 1960s.[17]

William McFetridge, president of SEIU and head of Chicago's Local 1, was the right man to continue the tradition. He was the nephew of William Quesse, the first president, who had made McFetridge a union steward in Local 1 at age ten. In a civil suit, McFetridge was charged by the union's secretary-treasurer, George Fairchild, with embezzlement. He was also charged in a civil suit with the same offense that led to his uncle's going to jail—taking bribes from landlords.[18] In his deposition, McFetridge was asked about having taken bribes from a long list of building owners; for each name on the list, he took the Fifth. His determination to use SEIU funds to finance Marina City, the landmark Chicago residential towers on the Chicago River, impaired the benefit funds and provoked the most serious split in the union's history. McFetridge may have accumulated the greatest fortune of any labor leader in American history. When he died, a causeway leading to Soldiers Field was named after him.

The SEIU was no less corrupt in New York than in Chicago. The founder of the union's largest local, New York's James Bambrick, went to jail for sharing the union treasury with George Scalise (who split his share 50–50 with the Capone gang). But Local 32B, which had the New York City Janitors' jurisdiction, was generally able to conduct its business without murdering anyone.

Not so Local 32E, founded by George Scalise himself, whose territory included the Bronx and Westchester. It was a bloody battle between the Teamsters and the Janitors for control of Yonkers Raceway that led in 1953 to the gunning down of Tommy Lewis, Local 32E's president, one sunny summer day in the Bronx.[19] The mayor's Bronx campaign manager was questioned in the assassination, although the crime was never really solved, in part because the assassin himself was killed almost immediately after the shooting.[20]

Governor Thomas Dewey urged that 32E's charter be revoked, but president William McFetridge demurred, insisting that a cleanup would suffice, and he installed new officers. By 1966, however, almost the entire clean team he put in place had been convicted of labor racketeering, including the president, Henry Chartier.[21] After serving their sentences, a slate of convicts headed by Chartier was allowed by Thomas Donahue, a top international SEIU official, to run for office with no opposition.[22] Donahue would later become the AFL-CIO's acting president. It was also Donahue who had arranged, just a few years before, for John Sweeney to become a top staffer at Local 32B.

But in 1966, Donahue managed to preserve 32E's traditions for another generation. For over fifty years the only real change in 32E was dynastic, as Robert Chartier replaced his father. Under the regime of Robert Chartier, at least five officers were convicted of taking bribes. In 2000, Stern ousted Chartier a few weeks after Chartier tried to take the 8,700-member local out of the SEIU.[23]

By similarly wiping out Boston and Detroit fiefdoms, as well as those in Chicago and New York, Stern was able to impose his principles on the entire union. As far back as the early twentieth century, the old AFL barons had explained they weren't really corrupt, they were just practicing American business principles. But in Andy Stern, genuine business unionism had finally emerged.

SLOAN RULES AT SEIU

"Trade unions are more and more being based on
business principles and more and more being
managed by business-minded leaders who operate
according to business methods."

■

—*Union Herald*, Atlantic City, 1901[24]

In his 2004 San Francisco convention speech, Stern closed with the conventional imagery from *Solidarity Forever*. His speech rolled with Biblical references and the call and response rhythms of the black church. There was cheering that could have come from a high school pep rally. But despite the populist rhetoric and religious forms, what 3,000 union delegates really cheered were the premises of mainstream American management philosophy.[25]

The unacknowledged hero of the 1960s and 1970s movement veteran who now runs the SEIU is not Marx or Debs, or even Walter Reuther, but professional management icon Alfred P. Sloan. It was Sloan who saved General Motors from the chaos and near-death caused by its financier founder, William Crapo Durant. In the early 1920s, Sloan, working for the new owners of GM, the DuPont family, brought Durant's sprawling fiefdoms under centralized control. He developed a plan for reorganizing GM that would express the principles of good corporate management for the next two generations. They're still canonical throughout much of the business world, including at Microsoft; Bill Gates says that Sloan's *My Years with General Motors* is the "best book to read if you want to read only one book about business." Sloan's rules have also become the matrix of SEIU management philosophy.

Above all, Sloan provides managers with an identity. For him, the manager is a professional. "Like any other profession," the professional manager has a "client"—in this case the corporation. Sloan's client was GM; Stern's is the SEIU—the institution, that is, not the members.

Second, Sloan stressed the importance of structure. Management, he emphasized, is not just a matter of leadership. Stern makes the same distinction. The problem with the AFL-CIO, he says, is not John Sweeney—"a good man"—it's the AFL-CIO, "a structure that divides workers' strength by allowing each union to organize in any industry."

Proper structure demands a balance between centralization and decentralization. Under Sloan, GM reined in Durant's independent companies, turning them into divisions of the larger corporation: Buick, Chevy, Pontiac, Olds. At the San Francisco convention, Stern announced "long-term plans to create truly national unions in each of our four divisions—hospitals, long-term care, public service, and building service."

Finally, the point of administration is to realize the highest possible market share. Sloan liquidated many of Durant's enterprises because a strong market share wasn't possible for them. It's this principle that helps inform Stern's crusade against "general" unionism. Dominant market shares can't be achieved that way. Just as Sloan argued that the stockholders can't profit from markets where the company has a low market share, Stern insists that only through increased market shares can workers earn more money.

The SEIU leadership didn't pick up these classic managerial principles haphazardly or from their AFL-CIO colleagues sitting around the pool at Bal Harbour. MIT industrial relations professor Michael Piore studied SEIU in the early 1990s. He seems to have been the first to notice that SEIU's organization and philosophy were strikingly different from those of the rest of the AFL-CIO—self-consciously so. The SEIU saw itself as an organizational success, reports Piore, and the rest of the labor movement as a failure. The AFL-CIO had failed not just because of employer resistance, but because it was poorly structured, he argued. The 1960s and 1970s movement veterans who had filtered into SEIU were different from the ex-Trotskyists who formed TDU. The SEIU officials reacted against bottom-up movement principles, but also against traditional local union organization. They opted for business principles and business structure. "Their single most important source was probably the *Harvard Business Review*," says Piore. "The union hired the American Management Association to do staff training."[26]

Still, translating business school principles into union doctrine wasn't easy. Ever since 1932, when Adolph A. Berle and Gardner Means exposed the separation of ownership and control in their classic *The Modern Corporation and Private Property*, students of business management have been trying to fathom exactly whom corporate executives are working for. Some say the customer while others insist it's just the stockholder. Nor is there agreement on what managers should be aiming at: Return on investment? Sales? Overall enterprise expansion?

The puzzle is only magnified when unions try to adapt business principles. Unions don't have stockholders. No one owns them. Their members don't select the top leaders. The top leaders are selected by secondary leaders who owe their positions to the top leaders. (In the Stern model, this is even more true, as local autonomy has almost vanished.)

What policies should business-oriented union leaders pursue? Bargain for low wages and expand the union? Or raise wages at the cost of expanding membership? The antagonism between Old Guard and reform factions in the SEIU played out along these lines. The Old Guard locals, like Gus Bevona's Local 32BJ, the old Flat Janitors union in Chicago, and the Chartier dynasty in the Bronx and Westchester, had high wages and stagnant or declining membership. Stern-appointed managers replaced them all.

Nothing solidified Stern's hold over the union more than his purge of Bevona. Many 32BJ members were disturbed by Gus's CEO-level salary and the rumors of mob ties. But they saw their wages and benefits—by far the highest in the nation and nearly double those in virtuous L.A.—as coming from Gus. Stern-backed reformers had never gotten more than a third of the vote. Stern could never have gotten rid of Bevona through the ballot box. But in achieving his objectives, Stern had never relied much on direct elections. He had other means.

HOW GREEDY GUS GOT THE GATE

What stopped the smooth succession of the various corrupt SEIU dynasties around the country was the 1995 elevation of John Sweeney to the AFL-CIO presidency and his replacement by Andy Stern. Stern won the SEIU presidency by beating Old Guard leader Richard Cordtz, the longtime boss of the Detroit fiefdom known for sweetheart contracts, low wages, and big spending on officer perks.[27] Cordtz in turn was backed by other Old Guard figures, like Gus Bevona in New York, said to be the highest-paid union leader in America, and Ed Sullivan Jr. in Boston.[28] Sweeney backed Stern. But Stern used his office very differently from Sweeney.

"When I became president, there were at least 15 major local unions ruled by various families that passed the union on like a small business," Stern observed in his blog, "Fight for the Future."[29] Stern wasn't bragging. Nor was he posing as a corruption fighter. He was simply defending himself against critics who accuse him of suppressing democracy in the SEIU by getting rid of local autonomy. He was asking, What was so democratic about the old corrupt, decentralized SEIU?

A point well taken, perhaps. But Stern accomplished his purges not through open, principled campaigns involving the membership, but managerially. In 2001, when Boston's Eddie Sullivan was caught driving under the influence in a union car without a license, he was simply ousted. In the ousting of the far more powerful Gus Bevona, Stern eased him and his retainers out with golden parachutes.

Stern was in a position to arrange these ousters because the union's Washington, D.C., leadership had managed to wrest control of the Old Guard forces through organizing. The new health care, home care, and day care locals could outvote the old East Coast and Midwest janitors locals. In the new health-based locals, officials owed their positions not to local patronage machines, but to the international union, which put them in charge. Stern selected lifelong staff members, college graduates, and progressives to serve as trustees of the big janitorial locals; then they got elected to the presidency—Mike Garcia, from Local 1877 in California, Mike Fishman, from Local 32BJ in New York, and Tom Balanoff, who became president of Local 1 in Chicago.[30]

Sweeney had never sought to eliminate the Old Guard enclaves. Rather, he served as a mediating figure between the crooked and the reforming factions. He supported SEIU's janitorial services organizing campaign, Justice for Janitors, but he also had a cozy relationship with Gus Bevona, his successor as head of 32BJ (formed from the merger of Locals 32B and 32J). Bevona gave Sweeney $400,000 over thirteen years to serve as his adviser, and Sweeney appointed Bevona to a job as the SEIU's $90,000-a-year eastern regional director.[31]

According to Al D'Arco, the FBI's top informant, who at one time served as acting boss of New York's Lucchese crime family, Bevona was a Genovese family associate; his dad, Peter, was alleged to be a made guy. The union had long been a Genovese fiefdom, D'Arco testified.[32] Bevona denounced the accusations as nonsense. But the 32BJ president was a bizarre figure—over 400 pounds, a penthouse-living loner. His salary topped $400,000—more at the time than the president of the United States, and Bevona was only president of a janitors local. What had Sweeney seen in the young Bevona to crown him as his successor? Or did Sweeney have much to say about the appointment?

Stern suffered from no such encumbrances. When Bevona lost a civil suit against two dissidents that threatened to bankrupt him, Stern worked out a four-sided deal that gave everyone something—at member's expense. The two plaintiffs, a doorman and a janitor, got staff jobs.[33] Their attorney got a retainer from the SEIU. The members picked up Bevona's legal bill. In addition, Bevona, along with his brother and his wife, who were also on the payroll, all promised to go away. Gus himself got $1.2 million, and his top staff got $5.6 million.

But Stern wound up with control of a 75,000-member local. He made one of his top subordinates, Tom Balanoff, the trustee, though he eventually replaced him with an SEIU staffer, Mike Fishman. Then Stern turned on Robert Chartier's Bronx-based Local 32E. It was simply dissolved and put under Fishman's control.

Union presidents commonly trustee their political adversaries, claiming to be corruption fighters. But they tend to ignore corruption when their own allies are caught. Teamsters president Ron Carey was a classic case. So is Jim Hoffa today. Stern may well be an exception. So far, at least in one high-profile case, his people stood up for what was right.

Business agents from 32BJ still get mixed up in mob plots to replace the $17-an-hour members with lower-paid maintenance workers—but they don't get any support from the top leadership. When two Genovese crime family members sat down with an associate steeped in 32BJ history to figure out how to help a Brooklyn landlord get rid of the union, they got a lesson in comparative history. With Gus and his people, "you can go and have conversations," explained the labor adviser to the Genoveses. "Now you go and talk to them, you could just figure they are going to be wired, OK? Let me explain it to you. . . . You cannot talk to 32B [sic], take them off the table, you can't talk to them because they're rats, okay?"[34] Considering the source, this was high praise.

By waging a successful campaign against the Old Guard, Stern was not, as so many other international presidents were, a weak ruler dependent on strong vassals. He won the war because his reform faction had essentially organized a new health care union within the SEIU that vastly outnumbered the members in the old janitorial core.[35] The Justice for Janitors organizing campaign also gave the reformers a toehold on the Old Guard territory.

BREAD AND ROSES?

From the days of William Quesse, through Capone man George Scalise, and right up to managerially minded Andy Stern, SEIU leaders have always been good at adding members. At least Stern can say he's growing the union without the benefit of either the bombs favored by Quesse or the even bloodier mob backup exploited by Scalise & Co. What Stern can't say, though, is that working under an SEIU contract will lift a member out of poverty.

The 1990 Justice for Janitors campaign in L.A., launched when Stern was still an aide to Sweeney, was successful beyond all measure—unless you count wages. The drive added thousands of new members and projected the union as a force for social justice in the immigrant community—there was even that movie based on the effort—but its success came at the cost of maintaining the labor standards that had been achieved in the 1980s. At that time, unionized janitors, mainly African American, had been making about $12 an hour. They were replaced by non-union Central American immigrants who earned $4. Focusing on Century City, Justice for Janitors began the recruitment of Central American janitors. When the L.A. police beat peaceful Latina demonstrators right in front of local TV cameras, the campaign gained media traction. The Century City contractors settled, and 8,000 janitors joined the union. If Hollywood called it "Bread and Roses," Stern would use it as a prime example of what he called his "market recovery program." Yet the starting wage was only $4.25 an hour.[36]

Since then, subsequent pacts have raised the official wage floor. Yet SEIU, like its New Unity Partner UNITE, seems to have great difficulty enforcing its contracts. In 2005, the union won a class action suit against Von's and two other grocery chains. SEIU had a contract with the companies, but the companies disregarded the terms. The court affirmed SEIU's charge that the companies had been hiring janitors through subcontracts for as little as $2.47 an hour. For most workers, according to the director of a union-funded monitoring group, "the pay is a little better, they're still working six or seven days a week."[37] A $21 million penalty imposed on the grocery chains by the court represented a legal victory for SEIU, but it can't disguise the weakness of the union: Stern's SEIU is good at bringing workers into the union, but not at representing them once they've become members.

Poor contracts and lack of enforcement weren't the only problems with SEIU-style organizing. There was also the lack of democracy. The Central American insurgent janitors whose demonstrations shook Century City power brokers tried to take over their own union by electoral means. Their Multi-Racial Alliance won twenty-one of twenty-five seats on the local union's executive board, but the defeated incumbents refused to allow them to take over. The locks were changed. A hunger strike followed. To settle the dispute, SEIU headquarters in D.C. sent in a trustee, who simply dissolved the union, making it part of a statewide local headquartered in Sacramento.[38] The new boss was Mike Garcia, a former Chicano studies major who'd served on Stern's national organizing staff.[39]

All of Stern's considerable energy, ingenuity, and passion go to building SEIU's membership rolls. The half million members he's added in less than a decade represents a total unmatched in labor history. But to what end?

Perhaps Stern, who runs what is essentially the largest health care union in America, shares the motivation of some health care industry managers. In the declining city of Buffalo, the demand for hospital beds keeps shrinking, but, as the New York Times reports, the CEOs keep trying to grow their individual hospital empires anyhow. Explained one CEO, "We're kingdom builders as a group: 'I've got to have more beds than you do. I've got to have more hospitals than you do. I've got to have the biggest empire.'"[40]

Organized labor's two biggest empire builders clashed just before the end of the 2005 AFL-CIO executive committee meeting in Las Vegas. A shouting, cursing spat broke out between Stern—who ruled over 1.8 million members—and AFSCME's Gerald McEntee—1.5 million. Allegedly, McEntee called Stern a "hypocrite," and Stern responded by calling the AFSCME president a "motherfucker."[41]

The row was reported as just a symptom of the tensions between the two sides in the debate over AFL-CIO reform.[42] And it's also true that Stern and McEntee have been fighting for years, partly because their jurisdictions overlap, and partly because they compete for top status in the Federation. But the substance of their battle shouldn't be ignored either: 49,000 child care workers in Illinois.

"Mine," claimed Gerald McEntee. He objected to the way Stern had tried to corral the day care workers. Stern's alleged penchant for cheap labor, bad contracts, and raiding were all points raised by McEntee.[43] "We are the largest child care union in the United States," he told the *Los Angeles Times*. "That is our core industry."[44] Besides, McEntee argued, Stern's wage package—which maxed out after four years at $9.34—undercut AFSCME members in the same industry.

"No, mine," said Stern of the child care workers. He insisted that McEntee had stepped between him and the potential members, contesting an election that ought to have been just a formality. After all, he had already bought and paid for the child care workers when he gave Illinois Governor Rod Blagojevich $800,000 in campaign contributions. In return, the good governor agreed to support SEIU's organizing drive.[45]

It was the type of deal Stern had been pulling off for years, most notably in the 1999 campaign to organize the 74,000 home health care workers in California.[46] The union gives money to politicians, and the politicians agree to recognize the union. Sometimes "recognition" means only that the union gets to collect dues; sometimes it means full collective bargaining rights. Rarely does it mean a wage that exceeds the poverty level.[47] SEIU home care workers in Maryland earn $50 a day. They haven't had a raise since 1986, and they get no health care benefits, sick days, or retirement benefits.[48]

In a contest in which about a third of members mailed in ballots, SEIU got 80 percent of the votes.[49] But an examination of the path to victory revealed a surprise—just how much "organizing" had changed since 1937, when autoworkers occupied Fisher Body plants No. 1 and No. 2, demanding union recognition. The terms "worker," "employer," and "union representation" have lost much of their meaning.

Local 880 had won the right to bargain with the employer, but the day care workers didn't really have an employer in a conventional sense. Parents—who are generally former welfare recipients—drop their kids off at the homes of the day care providers—also often former welfare recipients. But the parents aren't the employer; they can't afford to pay, and they're subsidized by the state. The state, however, doesn't hire the workers or receive the service. It just pays for it—about $8 per day per child. Typically the day care providers watch about three kids each. It's the union's job now to try to get Springfield to raise the rates.

The status of Local 880's 37,000 home care workers is similar, but their path to representation is stranger. Illinois home care patients don't pay for their care either. The state does. SEIU "represented" them for nearly twenty years without ever getting a collective bargaining agreement. The agreement came in 2004, after Governor Blagojevich—who'd gotten the $800,000 in SEIU cash ("our guy," says Local 880's organizing director, Keith Kelleher)—delivered collective bargaining rights. In the bargaining, some 20,0000 workers got a raise—a dime an hour; they were still only making $7.25. But the contract called for two dollars more an hour by 2007.[50]

SEIU claimed a great victory. Beyond the money, at least now the workers had a contract. In 1990, Blagojevich's Republican predecessor, Jim Thompson, had given Local 880 dues check-off rights but no collective bargaining rights.[51]

What were the members paying union dues for during all those years? AFL-CIO unions justify making nonmembers pay dues on the grounds that otherwise they're freeloading on the dues-paying members, who must shoulder the full cost of the collective bargaining services. But why should workers pay dues when they *don't* receive collective bargaining services?

Forcing workers who earn poverty-level wages to pay dues to a union that doesn't even legally represent them has to be questionable even within the norms of the AFL-CIO. Some unions waive dues until they've actually got a contract. SEIU collects dues when it doesn't even have collective bargaining rights.

Organizing as lobbying. "With Wal-Mart setting the pace," observed Andy Stern in the *Forward*, a New York–based Jewish weekly, "one in four workers in America now makes less than $9.00 an hour—far too little to support a family."[52]

It's sad but true. An even sadder truth, perhaps, is that none of the 124,000 members in SEIU's largest unit—Los Angeles–based Local 434b, representing home care workers—earns anything close to Wal-Mart's pace-setting $9.00 an hour. Most SEIU home care members don't work enough hours to qualify for health benefits. But when Local 434b won the right to represent 74,000 home care aides in February 1999, SEIU publicists proclaimed it labor's biggest organizing victory since February 11, 1937—the historic "Gettysburg of the CIO," when over 100,000 autoworkers forced General Motors to recognize the United Auto Workers after eighteen separate sit-down strikes beginning in the winter of 1936.[53]

Andy Stern likes to address the rest of the labor movement from the mountaintop of his own historic organizing achievements. He rarely misses a chance to point out that he's brought 900,000 workers into SEIU in nine years—while the rest of the AFL-CIO has been stuck in reverse. The difference, he explains, is that the rest of the labor movement is divided, while the SEIU model enables workers to "unite their strength."

In assessing Stern's claims that he found the formula to "restore the American Dream," surely it's relevant to note that it's a deeply discounted dream. When Local 434b's L.A. members got a raise in 2005, their pay rose to $8.15. Since fewer than half work more than eighty hours a month, we're talking about workers who earn about $650 monthly, from which taxes and union dues still must be deducted.[54] The 2005 federal poverty level for a one-person household is $9,570 a year—$1,800 higher than the gross income received by the average unionized home care worker in L.A.[55]

Actually, though, as it turns out, the poverty-level wages earned by SEIU's newly organized members affect the attractiveness of the Stern organizing model less than other, even more fundamental, problems. First of all, many or even most of the members he's bringing into the labor movement aren't really workers at all. They're chiefly beneficiaries of welfare programs who are being paid to care for family members and close friends. Second, SEIU's organizing can't legitimately claim descent from the great CIO organizers of the 1930s. Rather, Stern, a former welfare bureaucrat himself, has learned how to game the welfare system.

"Organizing" implies an appeal primarily to workers. But Stern lavishes millions on state and local power brokers. At his behest, they create public authorities that act as employers set up just for the purpose of recognizing the union. Disguised by the holding of representation elections is what amounts to a raid on public entitlement funds.

Local 434b's Web site describes home care providers as "women of predominantly Latino, African-American, Armenian, and Asian descent." Even with the slight exaggeration of the Armenian membership to fill out the ethnic rainbow, it's not much of a stretch. But describing the home care recipients as "clients" is.[56] The dictionary defines a client as someone who uses professional services. If the home care recipients were really "clients," the providers would be workers. But is an elderly mother the client of her adult children? Is a father the client of his disabled child? The union acknowledges that "some" providers are family members,[57] and the head of the home care agency that serves as their nominal employer says that "many" providers are family.[58] But according to court papers and Los Angeles County officials, *most* home care providers choose to be taken care of by someone in their immediate family or by very close friends.[59]

For most of them, home care is not a full-time job. Only about 10 percent work forty hours a week or more.[60] Nor has the union been able to make much progress organizing home care aides who work for a conventional employer, like those employed by private agencies.

Most SEIU home care workers are like Jesus Moreno, a former fruit picker from Oxnard, California: they take care of just one person and the person is someone very close to them. In 2001, Moreno's wife died, so he quit his job in the fields to take care of his fifteen-year-old son Jesus Jr., who has an incapacitating spinal injury. Mr. Moreno bathes and feeds the boy, brushes his teeth, and drives him to doctor's appointments. Recently, the union won a pay increase, so Mr. Moreno now gets $8.00 an hour. He clocks the maximum hours allowed—283 hours a month, the equivalent of seven 40-hour weeks—but he still finds it hard to make ends meet. "The cost of living continues to go up," Mr. Moreno explained to the *Los Angeles Times*.[61]

Patricia Guajardo, like Moreno, is also taking care of a son with a spinal problem. She has been caring for Francisco, now twenty-six years old, ever since he was a few months old. She quit her cafeteria job to become a home health care worker. "We just decided to take care of Frankie ourselves," she told a *Los Angeles Times* reporter.[62]

The issue here is not welfare policy or whether home care really saves taxpayer money—a debate that's raged for years—but rather, what example does Stern's organizing model provide for the rest of labor to follow? What lessons does he have for the autoworkers or the carpenters or the steel workers union? Stern can point to tens of millions of potential home health care and day care providers who can be organized. Most now provide their services for free to family members. It's not implausible that hundreds of thousands more—if not millions—will decide to become home health care aides and wind up paying dues to the SEIU, like the Morenos and the Guajardos. But how can other unions outside the health care field tap this growing dues flow—other than to fight SEIU for the members?

Lobbying against the old and the sick. The model Stern provides seems closer to welfare rights organizing than labor organizing. The difference, though, is that the old welfare rights groups of the 1960s that tried to improve benefit levels for recipients were voluntary, bottom-up organizations run by recipients. They used the weapons of the weak—sit-ins, disruptions, and occupation of welfare offices. SEIU often gestures in these directions, but with SEIU's home care organizing drive, the action was primarily staff-directed and cash-driven. Within a year of its founding in 1988, Local 434b got the right to collect dues from members. Notes the union's official history: "This paved the way to stabilize membership dues and finance activities of the union's growing membership and increase the union's resources."[63]

But Local 434b didn't get the extraordinary privileges of SEIU's Local 880 in Illinois, which got dues check-off without being able to represent anyone. The L.A. home care local also didn't have the right to collect dues automatically from nonmembers, who formed the vast majority of L.A. home care workers. The union had no collective bargaining rights. And the courts had decided its members weren't workers, but rather independent contractors.

So a ten-year legal and lobbying campaign began in order to create an employer who would then recognize the union and allow it to impose dues check-off on all providers, union or not. (Imposing dues on non-members is allowed under the "agency shop" rules.) But with the voluntary dues money serving as political capital, the union was able to win allies, both at the mayoral level and within the Los Angeles County Board of Supervisors. The SEIU has poured millions into their campaigns.[64] In fact, the union had big checks for all cooperative incumbents. In the 2005 campaign alone, the leading contributor to Mayor James Hahn's losing race was the union made up of desperately poor home care providers. From Local 434b Hahn got nearly $450,000—more than 10 percent of all the independent contributions to all the candidates in the mayoral race.[65]

In 1998, with influential supervisor and chief Local 434b ally Zev Yaroslavsky in the lead, the supervisors agreed to create something called the Personal Assistance Services Council. The PASC agreed to be the employer for the home care aides and abide by the results of a representation election held a few months later.

SEIU staffers made 35,000 home visits to persuade the workers to mail in ballots supporting the union. The staffers told them that voting "yes" meant a raise plus health care benefits. In results heard 'round the country if not the world, workers voted 8 to 1 for the union. It was a famous victory indeed. But despite the media resonance, one of the loudest sounds was silence: three-quarters of the home health care workers never made it to the mailbox.[66]

But so what if Stern's modus operandi can't be compared with classic labor organizing? If, instead of benefiting the conventional working class he's actually helping the indigent, that's not an inconsiderable accomplishment. By unionizing the recipients of entitlement programs, Stern puts money in their pockets, and he's allowing some members to have health benefits who would otherwise lack them.

It's far from clear, though, that Stern's lobbying and influence-peddling helps poor people or the indigent sick across the board. At best, it's targeted assistance, aiming to preserve pay and benefits for his people. At worst, SEIU cynically blocs with private nursing home care employers against indigent patients' rights. It's happened in Florida and Texas, but it was in California that SEIU's tactics drew the loudest protest from patient advocates.[67]

When nursing home orderlies across California began to trundle thousands of indigent sick and confused elderly patients from their nursing home beds, forcing them to remain in the blazing noontime sun for two hours in August 2004, it may have seemed like a typical Alinsky-inspired direct action protest. Organizers explained to TV and newspaper reporters, who had been alerted in advance, that the action was a nursing home funding crisis drill. Lack of state money, they warned, might soon force owners to shut down nursing homes. Don't be cruel, they pleaded—spare our fragile patients further turmoil.[68]

The novelty of this particular Alinsky-style demo was that it was organized by the powerful against the powerless. SEIU and nursing home operators had agreed to merge resources and Rolodexes into something called California United for Nursing Home Care, the alliance that staged the media event. Their aim was to get the legislature to pass Assembly Bill 1629.[69]

The bill, which eventually sailed through both houses, certainly defused the funding crisis, if there ever was one. Called the "Nursing Home Quality Care Act," AB 1629 gave an estimated $3 billion windfall to the nursing homes over five years. In the event that costs rose, the bill contained an unprecedented guarantee of company profits. At the same time, the version of AB 1629 that eventually passed gutted the original patients' rights sections.

Then, having got AB 1629 passed, the nursing home operators and the SEIU joined again to crush the Nursing Home Residents Bill of Rights. This measure had been promoted by a consumer coalition including AARP and California Advocates for Nursing Home Reform. One provision would have increased the fine levied on a nursing home if one of its employees rapes a patient. Instead of just $1,000, it would have to pay $20,000.[70]

The SEIU proclaimed that its alliance with nursing home owners was designed strictly to help workers and improve patient care. But e-mails from an SEIU lobbyist in Sacramento, obtained by *SF Weekly*'s Matt Smith, revealed the actual terms of the union's deal with management. In exchange for the union's support, the nursing home operators agreed not to block SEIU organizing attempts. Such political sweeteners are a staple of SEIU's private sector organizing repertoire. Health care industry executives agree to recognize the SEIU in exchange for its support for more funding in the statehouse. What SEIU brought to the alliance in this instance were its ties to Sacramento Democrats. In 2003, SEIU had made $600,000 in campaign contributions. The e-mail obtained by Smith detailed how the SEIU lobbyist would lean on the union's Democratic allies to defeat patients' rights and nursing home accountability.[71]

California nursing home operators fear genuine legislative reform the way Dracula fears the cross. According to the Department of Health Services, most of the state's 1,200 nursing homes are substandard, failing to meet the most basic safety standards. Patients regularly die of dehydration, bedsores, and urinary tract infections. There is no adequate inspection system. The threat of lawsuits is almost all that exists to restrain the rapacious operators. Even this feeble remedy would be abolished by SEIU-sponsored "tort reform."[72]

Nursing home advocate Pat McGinnis, of California Advocates for Nursing Home Reform, who'd walked picket lines with SEIU in the past, battling company abuses, expressed bafflement as well as indignation. "Why would SEIU enter into a deal which did nothing to improve pay or staffing for its members?" she asked.[73]

But the incentives were ample enough, if you appreciate Stern's obedience to Sloan's management rules and values. In his testament, *My Years with General Motors*, Sloan was very clear about how he wanted his legacy to be judged. He never mentioned increases in workers' well-being or wages. What he notes, rather, is the huge increase under his watch in GM's sales and profits.[74]

Stern doesn't boast about wage improvements either—which have been negligible at best. But even the legendary GM executive can't come close to matching the SEIU's growth rates. Between 1993 and 2004, SEIU revenues increased 600 percent. Political contributions—the key to Stern-style growth—increased from a million a year to probably 100 times that figure.[75]

CONCLUSION: SEIU'S DEAD SOULS

At times Stern's single-minded quest for growth seems to suggest, more than faintly, the fable of Pavel Ivanovich Chichikov in Gogol's classic nineteenth-century satire *Dead Souls*. Chichikov conceives a plan to buy from the landlords their deceased serfs, who are still being carried on the official tax rolls as if they were alive. By selling them to Chichikov, the landlords can reduce their tax liability, and Chichikov in turn can take the deceased serfs to the bank: he can get a mortgage on them so that he can acquire the capital to become a real landlord with a huge estate.

Of course, Stern's home health care members are alive, not dead. And Stern had to pay a lot more to the politicians than the nominal sum Chichikov gives the landlords. But the addition of purely nominal members with little real voice or impact on the institution that supposedly represents them raises some of the same issues of integrity, motive, and hypocrisy as well as the fundamental premise of the institution.

If there's something suspect, something faintly corrupt, about selling a dead serf, is the sale of a live one much more valid? Of course, you couldn't really sell serfs—at least not one at a time. They simply came with the estate. They were bound to the land and couldn't leave—just as nominal union members come with the territory. A key provision of the Stern plan for renewing the labor movement, the transfer of millions from the small unions to the large unions without their explicit consent, evokes the sale of great Russian estates—in which the serfs simply went with the land. Rather than a reform, it merely express the fundamental lack of worker sovereignty in American unions. It's past time to challenge the very basis of the American labor movement—which remains, after more than a century, its fundamental lack of consent.

Conclusion: Solidarity for Real

"Unity House—created in 1951 with dues from members—was Rutledge's dream of a labor temple."

■

—Obituary, Arthur Rutledge, *Honolulu Star Bulletin*, September 23, 1997

"Unity House, Inc., the hybrid labor organization created more than 50 years ago by union patriarch Arthur Rutledge, was seized yesterday by federal agents investigating criminal charges against Rutledge's son and grandson."

■

—*Honolulu Advertiser*, December 15, 2004

A bout a hundred years ago, at the height of the Progressive period, "new labor" unions began to form. Labor radicals created the Industrial Workers of the World. Muckrakers like Upton Sinclair exposed working conditions in Chicago's meatpacking houses. And, most mysteriously, ordinary union members began to build labor temples in cities all around the country. Workers in the separate trades—cigar makers, carpenters, bricklayers, hod carriers, tinners, bakers, painters, car builders—apparently felt a need to break down jurisdictional barriers so they could meet, discuss, and just share each other's company.[1] There were hundreds, and perhaps over a thousand, temples. But little or nothing in the standard labor history books suggests why they were built or whom they served or what they meant. There are dozens of books in print about Egypt's pyramids, and not one about America's labor temples. I first heard about them from my father. He told me about the one in his hometown of Omaha, Nebraska, when he was growing up in the 1930s. "I used to go to hear the Trotskyites speak," he recalled.

Nowadays, to hear a Trotskyist speak you would have to visit an elite campus. To find a labor temple, you would have to visit a Web site. From the evidence available, though, it seems that labor temples were more like a fraternal Shriners' temple than a church or a synagogue. They were financed from donations and often built by volunteer labor. According to one Web site, the San Jose Labor Temple was established informally between 1901 and 1903 by Harry Ryan, an early San Jose labor leader, and Jack London, the author of *The Call of the Wild*. London finished the last chapters of his novel there.[2] The San Jose Labor Temple might also have been one of the places where London delivered a famous speech, "War of the Classes," in which he commented, perhaps too optimistically, "The working class is no longer losing its strongest and most capable members. These men denied their ambition in the capitalist ranks remain to be the leaders of the workers."[3]

London was probably thinking of men like Big Bill Haywood and Gene Debs, not Pinhead McCarthy or Sam Parks.[4] As it turned out, London was no great prophet. But the American workers movement meant a great deal to him—as it did to Upton Sinclair, Frank Norris, and Carl Sandberg. Where are their successors in today's literary world? Few contemporary poets or novelists could even name a modern labor leader, much less distinguish among them. It's hard to imagine a place in today's culture for the labor temple: a venue where ordinary American workers could come to hear novelists like Jack London address their hopes and concerns. It's also hard to imagine finding novelists who felt compelled to do so. The San Jose Labor Temple lasted until the time of the AFL-CIO merger, when it was demolished.

It wasn't just a structure that was destroyed. Consider the passion, belief, energy, and commitment that must have been involved in the initial volunteer construction. Building a labor temple was a very different kind of project from building a modern union headquarters, which houses the staff and officers. Today's union headquarters are financed by the members, but rarely welcome them. "There was a time," recalls Harry Kelber, a ninety-year-old labor movement veteran, "when all major cities had Labor Temples where members would gather to spend time together. That's all but gone. Union officers don't want members hanging around and disrupting their office routine."[5] Some contemporary union headquarters have been built because officers can get kickbacks from approving the contracts.

As mainstream American labor hardened into today's recognizable forms, the temples in some cities were taken over by individual unions. In others, Central Labor Councils became tenants in the labor temples. But it wasn't the same: the Central Labor Councils were made up of officials who got paid to attend. Rarely were meetings attended by workers who came of their own accord.

The labor temples seem to have been an integral part of the Progressive effort to reinvent the old American civic religion. The core belief in the civic religion of the republican founders—what gave rise to their determination to separate from England—was the conviction that the worst civic sin was "corruption"—dependence on the will of another. The political culture of the revolutionaries, according to historian J.G.A. Pocock, was based on a civic and patriotic ideal wherein a man's character was founded on economic independence, "perfected in citizenship, but perpetually threatened by corruption." Patronage, faction, standing armies, established churches, and the promotion of a moneyed interest were identified as the principal sources of corruption, and corruption was deemed irreversible if action was not taken immediately.[6]

The highest republican virtue was freedom—not in the sense of freedom from all outside restriction but freedom in the sense of autonomy, living under laws of your own making. And the only way to achieve autonomy was through individual participation in politics—the highest civic duty—along with service in the militia. As industrialization spread, the possibility of ordinary people achieving individual autonomy had been narrowed to the point of meaninglessness by the rise of institutions like the Standard Oil Trust, the railroad empires of the robber barons, patronage pits like Tammany Hall, the exclusive craft unions, and the increasing power of Wall Street. The labor temples were monuments to the faith that American workers could restore the salience of the old American civic religion in an age of giant corporations and political machines.

Of course they failed. The AFL, as it emerged at the twilight of the Progressive Era, raised wages for some workers in part by excluding others. The regimes of the labor czars, who ruled with fists, clubs, and dynamite over the new exclusionary realms, represented a grotesque distortion of labor movement ideals. The unions buried their civic republican values, reviving old forms of dependence and inventing new forms of corruption—the labor union racket.

Many argue that the era of organized labor movements is behind us. You might as well, they say, try to organize a landless peasant movement. Or bring back the Grange. Those who urge us to "move on" include the believers in the new economy, who see the importance of consumption dwarfing the significance of labor; the prophets of deindustrialization, who see no problem with a U.S. economy based largely on nonexportable services; and the postmodernists in academia, who fear that a revived labor movement would stir up latent American populism, threatening gains won by gays and minorities.

Bill Clinton used to say that what's wrong with America has to be fixed by what's right with America. Clinton's apothegm contains a kernel of truth: those who seek to change their country can't begin by thoroughly despising it. But the maxim might be better turned around. If you want to see what's gone wrong with America, start by looking at the countervailing institutions that have been created to correct what's wrong. Above all, the unions.

One value of the debate on Andy Stern's proposals for AFL-CIO reform and New Unity Partnership is that for the first time in a generation, someone in official labor has acknowledged the full depth and breadth of the crisis facing organized labor. In the 1970s, when the alarms first began to go off, president George Meany famously insisted that it didn't matter if the labor movement shrank. "I used to worry about the membership," he admitted, "but quite a few years ago, I just stopped worrying about it."[7] Meany's successor, Lane Kirkland, showed more concern. In the mid-1980s, he put out a white paper that actually confronted some of the AFL-CIO's failings.[8] But Kirkland's practical response to a shrinking AFL-CIO membership was to take back the mobbed-up Teamsters, whom Meany had expelled. In the 1990s, John Sweeney insisted that a change in leadership and more resources plowed back into organizing were really all that was needed to get the Federation back on course. Now, as the AFL-CIO appears to list helplessly, Stern acknowledges that without substantial repairs, the AFL-CIO may not survive.

Union "structure," not just leadership, must change. Stern wants to examine only parts of the structure: the relationships between the large and small affiliates, between the AFL-CIO headquarters and its affiliates, and between the headquarters of the affiliates and their locals. Exempt from his scrutiny are the atrophied relationships between the members and their elected leaders.

Long ago John Stuart Mill identified the root of the problem. "Representative institutions are of little value," he wrote, "and may be a mere instrument of tyranny or intrigue, when the generality of electorate are not sufficiently interested in their own government to give their vote, or if they vote at all, do not bestow their suffrage on public grounds, but sell them for money or vote at the beck of some one who has control over them, of whom for private reasons they desire to propitiate."[9]

AFL-CIO locals, as they stand—and have for some time—are just the kind of representative institutions Mill is talking about: where apathy reigns too widely and a connected stratum of members simply delivers their vote in exchange for jobs and job security.[10] It's no wonder that yesterday's reformer is today's felon.

For too long "union democracy" has served as a kind of political Hamburger Helper in AFL-CIO reform circles: it pads out a program that's too thin to truly revive the labor movement but provides the appearance of an agenda and an excuse for action. No amount of "democracy" can alter the fact that the AFL-CIO is rooted in compulsion, exclusion, and monopoly.

Among those who recognize the depth of the problem, there will be differences not just on tactics but on strategy. One of the chief questions is whether the main energy should be spent trying to restructure the AFL-CIO or whether reformers should create new labor unions based on alternative principles. But reformers require agreement on goals, and goals imply principles. Five principles might serve as a starting point: consent, solidarity, accountability, participation, and autonomy.

BASE UNION MEMBERSHIP ON CONSENT

In the Western world, American unions like the Teamsters, the Long-shoremen, UNITE, and the Laborers are the last refuge of premodern despotism. In governance terms, they resemble Afghanistan and Somalia more than Sweden and Finland. More than any single factor, what turns them into realms governed by petty warlords is a lack of consent.

The most fundamental principle of modern democratic political organization is "consent": no consent, no legitimacy.

Nonconsent—compulsory union membership—has always been justified in fascist and communist labor movements on the grounds of a need for national or class unity. In America, the justification has been more purely pragmatic. Only unions that have the power to compel membership and exclude rivals can flourish. But how well have American unions really done in the last generation? Compare them with labor movements that require consent, such as those in Italy, France, Scandinavia, and South Korea. Where have workers made the best gains? Which movements have been the best at defending workers against austerity?

Consent does more than confer legitimacy. The power of a union is measured in the numbers of its members willing to make individual sacrifices for the common good and to take action. Action and sacrifice flow from commitment, and commitment implies consent.

In other spheres of society, lack of consent is identified for what it is: forced labor is slavery; forced marriage is concubinage; forced sex is rape. Few acknowledge that forced unionism—unionism without consent—is despotism.

The practical problem with despotism is that it makes people stupid and passive. Only the despot thinks and acts. Everyone else simply follows orders. Subjects are too busy competing for privileges and favors from the despot/warlord to imagine real autonomy, while the sovereign gradually loses contact with a reality that artificially bends to his will.

American workers must be allowed the freedom to join whatever union they wish, or none at all if they so choose.[11]

REPLACE SOFT CORRUPTION WITH GENUINE SOLIDARITY

Unions aren't philanthropic institutions. They must defend the material interests of the members. But they can't be based simply on those interests, or they become corrupt. If self-interest runs completely unchecked, if there's no effort to identify a broad common interest, self-interest becomes narrower and narrower; there's more and more fine-tuning of the contract to benefit a minority of the members, and only the elite members who pay the most dues and who have the most job security have the ear of the business agents. These members are at best indifferent to those less well situated in the union, and they're even less concerned about the interests of members of the same trade in a different jurisdiction, members of other trades, and working people in general. The real slogan of many American unions might as well be "An injury to one is an injury to one."

Without solidarity, without real social bonds between more powerful and less powerful workers, unionism withers and democracy degenerates into formalities that ultimately effect a transfer of wealth from the many to the few.

Unions must become stronger communities, not more efficient corporations. For corporations, only immediate, individual self-interest counts. Thus, whenever it's profitable to do so, it's not just okay, it's mandatory for managers to shut down plants and liquidate corporate assets and distribute them to the stockholders. But union members owe what they have to the sacrifices of those who came before. They cannot justly agree to eliminate retiree benefits or write off the interests of future members by accepting multitier agreements. Solidarity forbids it.

MAKE UNION LEADERS TRULY ACCOUNTABLE TO MEMBERS

No one disputes the idea that leaders should be judged by some set of standards and should answer to someone. Even England's divine right monarchs, like Henry VIII, acknowledged that they were accountable to

God. "Democracy" eventually became the universal solution to the problem of accountability.

Today, union reformers are all "union democracy" advocates who say they want above all the principle of "one person, one vote" to prevail. Delegated voting doesn't work, they argue, because the delegates aren't free to vote their choice; they would lose their jobs if they didn't vote for the candidate preferred by the union boss.

But "one person, one vote" can't solve the accountability problem either: there is already "one person, one vote" at the local level, and the locals are the primary source of corruption. The problem, particularly in the AFL trades, is that the members tend to vote for the officials who provide them with jobs. The business agents are able to allocate jobs insofar as they cultivate good relations with contractors. Ultimately, "one person, one vote" has the perverse effect of making the members dependent on the officials and the officials dependent on the employers. Even in unions without a business agent system, officials create powerful machines—based on patronage—that turn voting into a job fair.

In 1996, the Laborers elected their general president for the first time by "one person, one vote," and the candidates were the two representatives of the two major crime family factions in the union. By the time of the second direct election, both candidates had been charged with mob association and convicted of felonies.

To make accountability real, there must be a twenty-first-century reprise of the tactics developed by early-twentieth-century progressives in fighting urban machines. Dry up the sources of patronage, promote the recall, and create a broad civic agenda in place of narrow political patronage politics.

REPLACE THE PATRONAGE SYSTEM WITH MASS PARTICIPATION

With over 13 million members, the AFL-CIO is still America's largest organization. That it counts for so little in American life seems amazing until you realize that the activism is mostly limited to the approximately 85,000 officials and staff. In direct union elections, participation often falls into single digits.

In fact, low turnout is the aim. Union machine politics operate by the same mechanisms and produce the same deadly results as urban machine politics: a politics of intense self-interest among the few, and a politics of apathy among the many. Only the politics of mass participation can break the cycle.

Voluntary participation strengthens the union by raising the political level of the rank and file; they learn through doing, becoming more knowledgeable and better equipped with speaking, writing, and negotiating skills. Again, this is why incumbent officials so often fear mass involvement.

Participation creates commitment. Members care about something they've put their energy into or taken risks for. It gives them an investment in the union cause.

Participation promotes solidarity. By becoming active, members encounter others with different points of view and learn to think about interests other than their own and the need to liberate only themselves. Members learn how to situate their concerns and frame them in the common interest.

"Participation," as Benjamin Barber explained in *Strong Democracy*, "enhances the power of communities and endows them with a moral force that non-participatory rulership rarely achieves."[12]

MAKE THE LEADERSHIP DEPENDENT ON THE MEMBERSHIP INSTEAD OF VICE VERSA

Autonomy means more than freedom from interference. It means the right to live under laws you help make. For the eighteenth-century republican founders of the United States, corruption was the worst political sin because it deprived citizens of autonomy.

In the nineteenth-century revolt against industrial capitalism, unions were created to restore the autonomy that workers had lost when they entered the workplace. Naturally, workers wanted more money and benefits and less work and insecurity. But there was also a powerful desire to regain their dignity, to be able to look the boss in the eye. Unions were invented in no small part to enable workers, in David Montgomery's words, "to straighten their backs." By the beginning of the twentieth century, however, union members found themselves cringing and scraping in the very institutions they'd created to win workplace autonomy.

Trading autonomy for a job—either a staff job or a job out of the hiring hall—has been an essential part of union commerce since the days of Sam Parks. It was simply an extension of the Tammany Hall patronage system to trade unionism. The more effective the union in monopolizing markets, the longer the line of members seeking to become clients of the boss, lining up in work clothes to smile deferentially and shake the hand of their business agent, dressed in a tie and suit.

Without individual member autonomy, solidarity is forced charity, participation is compulsory labor, and accountability is a dream.

INSIDE THE BOX REFORMS

The odds against transforming the AFL-CIO from within are steep. The radicals go in, but they don't come out. At least not as radicals. There is no left versus right in the AFL-CIO—just ins versus outs. It's not just that the struggle against incumbents is so unequal and the temptations of power so overwhelming. There is also the almost complete lack of values beyond immediate self-interest to which reformers could appeal.

Still, despite the unfavorable terrain for solidarity evangelism in the AFL-CIO, there remain 13 million members. And the effort doesn't have to be completely successful to be meaningful. The first generation of abolitionists failed. So did the original campaigners at Seneca Falls in 1848 for women's rights. The goals should be simple and achievable, comprising measures that would make members more autonomous, less dependent on leaders. And the organizing focus has to be on where the problems are: the locals.

Here are seven proposals:

Make leadership a sacrifice, not a sinecure. There's no good reason why the difference between union leaders' pay and members' pay in the United States should be many times greater than in European countries. When UNITE president Jay Mazur retired, his total compensation of over half a million a year dwarfed the median yearly earnings of Local 23-25 members—about $7,000.

Cut the number of officials. In Sweden, there are about 1,200 members for every full-time official. Here, it's closer to 250. How do the Swedes manage? With volunteers.

Free the union press. The circulation of the AFL-CIO press runs into the tens of millions. Union papers rarely run ads. Copies are given away "free" to members—who of course pay for it out of their dues. What they get are stories about the greatness, dedication, and achievements of their leaders. In some ways, the American trade union press appears even more slavish, more sycophantic than the media in the former Soviet Union. Even under Stalin, *Pravda* never ran the Great Leader's picture on every page. And frequently letters critical of lesser government officials were printed.

"*America@Work* [the official publication of the AFL-CIO] has never printed a critical letter in its entire history," notes Martin Fishgold, president of the International Labor Communications Association, an organization representing union journalists. "There's very little dialogue or dissent in union media."[13]

Why not allow dissent? Because it would be undemocratic, explains Peter Gilmore, editor of *UE News*, the paper of the United Electrical, Radio, and Machine Workers of America. "We would rather devote space to what members are doing rather than give up valuable space for one member to sound off."[14]

The routine stifling of members' voices is a perfect reflection of a regime based on force and not on argument. The best remedy would be to give control of the budget for the paper to the members. Let them allocate the funds to competing news groups based on circulation. Next best would be the Scandinavian solution. In countries like Sweden, the labor press is independent—union leaders can't control what's written. Union members pay for the press, but they hire independent professionals to write and edit the stories. As a result, the labor press can cover stories without fear or favor; it's lively, and it's read by the membership—none of which is true in America.

Political campaign contributions: let the members decide. Unions are surprisingly competitive with big corporations when it comes to campaign contributions. Of the largest soft money donors to national political parties in 2002, five of the top eight contributors were unions. Beating out giant corporations like AT&T (no. 12), Philip Morris (no. 14), and Microsoft (no. 15) were AFSCME, SEIU, the Carpenters, the Communications Workers, and the American Federation of Teachers.[15] To stay competitive, unions have to devote a huge portion of their resources to political campaigns. How come they keep on contributing when no one thinks their legislative agenda has a chance?

More plausibly, public sector union leaders contribute money to buy help for this contract or that budget item. It's mostly a zero-sum game. Especially in a time of fiscal crisis, unions with more money wind up getting benefits at the expense of workers with smaller treasuries and less clout. In New York state, SEIU, which is by far the largest campaign contributor, got raises for its health care workers. But in the general austerity movement provoked by fiscal crisis, school aides, represented by the teachers union, got laid off.

A huge reason why union leaders contribute is generally left unstated: the contributions benefit them. Big campaign gifts buy them influence and access. After Teddy Maritas, boss of the New York City District Council of Carpenters, raised $100,000 for Ed Koch's run for the mayoralty and put 300 of his men at the candidate's disposal, he found himself a player not just at Gracie Mansion but also in D.C. Maritas, a Genovese crime family associate, bragged, "Hey, I go to the White House, I meet with the Governor, I'm with this one, I'm with that one. I can't be seen hanging out with wiseguys."[16]

Big money keeps the big union bosses out of jail. Laborers president Arthur Coia had been indicted for benefit fund fraud and had been described as a mob puppet by the Justice Department (recall the 212-page complaint against his union). Eventually, Coia went down on felony tax charges, but at least he stayed out of Club Fed. Is it surprising that he would have donated millions of the members' money to buy Get Out of Jail Free cards from Democratic Party politicians? Or that the mobbed-up International Longshoremen's Association would have provided New Jersey governor James McGreevey in 2003 with campaign cash and a suite at the Caribe Hilton in San Juan, Puerto Rico?[17]

Members need to subject their leaders' campaign expenditures to some kind of oversight. At the very least, they should be able to find out how

much of their money has been spent and who got it. At best, union political expenditures should be based on members' preferences. A poll of the
members should determine which candidates get union support.

Term limits. The argument against requiring top officers to step down
after completing a single tour of duty is derived from an analogy with the
military. Unions are said to be armies, and armies require experienced
generals. (Why these generals are so often seen socializing with the enemy,
giving and receiving awards, and insisting on the need for labor-management cooperation is left unexplained.) The Roman Republic may have
been one of the most successful states in history. Certainly its military
power was incomparable. Yet the highest office in the Roman government
was the consulship, which was divided between two men who ruled in al-
ternate months and could hold office for only one year. The legendary
consul Cincinnatus went from digging a ditch on his small farm to commanding the Roman legions and then back to his farm. When the senate
prepared to reelect him, he refused.[18] Why can't union leaders model
themselves after Cincinnatus and retire after one term?

Of course, everyone knows why: union leaders don't want to go back to
the bench, the keyboard, or the cab of a truck. But it could happen—at
least on a modest scale.

Plug the information gap. When Dade County Teachers boss Pat
Tornillo needed a little breather, he liked to stay at the Mandarin Oriental
Hotel on Brickell Key. One eight-night stay there cost the members
$20,138.53.[19] If Tornillo knew that the members would find out what he
spent, he might have found a cheaper alternative. But Dade County teachers knew next to nothing about what was going on in their union. Altogether, Tornillo's secret extravagances, along with those of his cronies,
wound up costing them over $2 million.[20]

Every union should have a Web site, and many do now. But none have
information that would hold officers accountable: Web sites should post
the federal documents that reveal official salaries as well as those that detail pension and benefit fund expenses. And they should post contracts,
union vendors, all officers' expenses, and the union constitution. Make it
a two-way Web site, with members able to post comments that other
members can read.

Do leave home without it: abolish union credit cards. D.C. Teachers

Union president Barbara Bullock made over $4.6 million in unauthorized charges to her American Express card during a seven-year shopping spree that ended in 2002. Just the thirty-five handbags she charged—from Fendi to Louis Vuitton—added up to $35,000. The union treasurer, James O. Baxter II, was in on the deal, and so was her chauffeur. Baxter approved the expenditures, then he rang up $537,0000 in credit card charges for art, clothing, and theater and sporting event tickets. Besides helping each other, Baxter and Bullock had help from the chauffeur, whose $90,000-a-year salary was paid in part to compensate him for his union money-laundering duties. Altogether D.C. Teachers officials stole $5 million.[21]

It's hard to resist embezzling the members' money. It's so easy. The union provides officers with company credit cards. The remedy is to require that union leaders carry their own credit cards and apply for reimbursement from the union. It won't stop embezzlement by determined thieves, and certainly the mob won't be deterred, but it would block the easiest avenue for less avid crooks.

OUTSIDE STRATEGIES

The time to reform an established institution is during its first fifty years. After that it may disintegrate, like Soviet communism, or be overthrown, like the divine right monarchy in France. Well-rooted, venerable institutions rarely change much because of internal opposition. Martin Luther would probably not have gotten far if he kept his protest within the Roman Catholic Church.

Warlord systems are especially well adapted to resisting change. For centuries, ruling Afghan and Somalian clans have controlled the good bottomlands, trade routes, smuggling operations, and so on. These resources enable them to recruit selected fellow clan members as clients—chiefly as fighters. Those who aren't in the clan are deprived by the system. They don't vote. To include them would be an attack on the entire system.

Our own union warlords are ultimately much more vulnerable. AFL-CIO local governance may resemble Afghanistan, but the rest of America doesn't.

The Federation is vulnerable to the pull of an alternative union model. Yes, despite corruption, disaffection, and apathy, there are millions of satisfied AFL-CIO members and a hard core of perhaps as many as 100,000 staff and officers who are deeply attached to its survival. But there remain well over 100 million American workers outside the AFL-CIO's reach.

The point is not to fight for each tiny island, but to harvest the sea. Focus on the 90 percent of American workers in the private sector who remain outside the AFL-CIO. Workers want unionism.[22] In 2002, Peter Hart Research Associates, which analyzes attitudes for the AFL-CIO, found that in their sample of about 800 workers, just over 50 percent would vote for a union if an election were held at their place of work. That's up from 43 percent the previous year.[23]

The percentages would be a lot higher if the public held American labor leaders in higher esteem. As Rutgers professor Charles Heckscher observes in his contribution to the Century Foundation's Task Force on the Future of Unions, "Essentially, the polls show that people want unions but not the unions we have now."[24]

Why not try to design unions that workers want? Here are seven ways to bring about changes that could never be accomplished within the AFL-CIO framework. These seven measures are not reforms. They're revolutionary proposals designed to liberate the energies of millions of working people entrapped in a dead organization.

Abolish exclusive jurisdictions. The system of exclusive jurisdictions explains, more than anything else, why our unions become fiefdoms. If it's legal for a single union to monopolize a territory, if workers are legally compelled to join the union that's in place, the resulting institutions, mentality, and behavior are quite predictable. Jurisdictional monopolies produce both the powerful but uncritical adhesion of the insiders to their union boss and the weak sense of union identity on the part of the remainder, who become purely nominal members. The jurisdictional system explains the limitation of union power to the boundaries of the jurisdiction and the temptation of the ruling minority to turn union office into a sinecure.

Territorial limits not only produce weak, corrupt mini-states, they cut off members from the concerns of others beyond their jurisdiction. Workers have little incentive to support broad efforts to improve minimum wage, safety, health coverage, and pension benefits for those outside their jurisdiction. Historically, the AFL opposed universal health insurance, unemployment insurance, workmen's compensation, and the eight-hour day for federal workers.[25] Today the AFL-CIO formally stands opposed to single-payer forms of health insurance, and energy and enthusiasm for any broadening of the coverage is strictly limited. The leaders aren't out of step with the members, who tend to be interested in the benefits that accrue from their own contracts in their own jurisdiction.

Workers have legitimate local interests. Many issues are best dealt with at a local level. But the locals don't have to be the exclusive territories of a single faction. Let the locals take care of workers' shop-floor grievances, while ceding bargaining, organizing, and public policy to higher-level organizations.

Make union membership voluntary. What we have now is a labor movement built around the closed shop—not literally and not exclusively, but essentially. The closed shop is illegal. Unions can't require membership as a condition of employment. But in most states, they can force an employee to join within thirty days (the so-called union shop).

The closed shop serves two opposite functions. First, it's a prophylactic, protecting the members against those they'd rather not compete with— historically, blacks and women. It still serves to keep out women, who thirty years ago formed less than 3 percent of the membership in the trades; the percentage is about the same today. Black progress in the skilled trades is better—about 7 percent twenty years ago and significantly more today, but discrimination still reigns.

The second function of the closed shop is as a crutch. Union experts think that if you end the closed shop, American unionism won't be able to stand. That's why, they say, conservatives promote it and genuine trade unionists oppose it. Nevertheless, the evidence doesn't show that unionism is impossible without the closed shop. Not only does the United States organize a smaller percentage of the workforce than Europe, but Europe out-organizes us without having to impose the closed shop. In the United States, the fastest-growing union membership is in Nevada—an "open shop" state.

The point is not to demand that old, arthritic AFL unions throw away their crutches, but rather to show that unions can be built on a voluntary basis. There's no reason to assume that American workers are uniquely in need of the goad of compulsory unionism. They should be allowed the freedom of choice, like workers everywhere else in the advanced industrialized world.

Throw out the exclusive bargaining clause of union contracts. The first clause of every labor contract reads something like this: "The Employer recognizes the Union as the exclusive collective bargaining representative for all employees engaged in the following operations . . ." It's the contractual foundation of monopoly unionism, and it means ultimately and perversely that the employer has the right to determine what union represents the workers.

Bosses have a duty to promote the best interests of their stockholders. It's in their interest to have as their negotiating partner a patsy, a corrupt enterprise that will exchange weak contract enforcement for dollars. Why did the Teamsters grow so fast in the 1930s? It wasn't just Jimmy Hoffa's innovative organizing techniques. Much of the reason was that the Teamsters offered bosses substandard contracts at a time when they were threatened by more militant, less corrupt CIO organizers. A union should owe its status as a workers' agent not to the bosses' preference, but to the workers' preference. That preference not just whether to join a union, but also which union to join.

A real choice would allow unions that effectively represented their members to grow at the expense of those that didn't.

Make union dues voluntary. The main legal argument for involuntary dues is that since members get the benefit of the contract, they should pay for the costs of servicing it. But that claim raises the question of whether you want the services you're being charged for. Or whether the service provider is simply imposing unwanted services on you.

The editors of *Labor Notes*, the main journal of AFL-CIO reformers, offer many arguments to show that automatic dues check-off is superior to voluntary, face-to-face efforts. It's more efficient, less time consuming, and less vulnerable to corruption. Might not the union stewards who collect the dues simply steal them? But the most insidious feature, they argue in a pamphlet entitled *Democracy Is Power*, is that a voluntary system encourages an "individualist and consumeristic approach." Permit voluntary dues, they warn, and "people could decide whether to pay dues or not based on whether they personally received services they felt were worth the money."[26]

Yes, they could. And they probably would. But those who would deny them that opportunity need to ask themselves what "democracy" means if not the power of the people to decide for themselves whether an organization is worth supporting.

Finally, there's the practical argument. In any group, there are always free-riders. When the California Nurses Foundation lost its automatic dues check-off, 20 percent of its revenue disappeared. For patronage-dispensing, perk-giving union bosses, a loss of 20 percent of their revenue would be a severe blow. But a leaner type of operation that relied more on genuine volunteers might do very well on a fraction of what the big AFL-CIO locals spend.

Compared with American models, French unions are severely understaffed; their top officials are paid less than the expense accounts of American trade union leaders. French union dues are completely voluntary. Yet this seemingly haphazard system doesn't stop French workers from regularly pulling off countrywide general strikes whose scope and effect is unimaginable here. (Recall the 1995 general strike that brought down a conservative government and led to the establishment of the thirty-five-hour week.)[27]

The problem with American unions is not lack of cash. It's a lack of calling. As Stephen Lerner, the AFL-CIO's former assistant director of organizing, has observed, for many locals, "their primary reason to exist is to keep on existing and to provide employment for officers and staff."[28] Automatic dues check-off is the lifeblood of these zombie locals.

Citywide operation of hiring halls. Open a book about trade unions. If it contains a discussion of hiring halls, continue reading.[29] If not, as the philosopher advises, "consign it to the flames." Not all unions have hiring halls, but the classic AFL trade unions do—the construction unions, the Teamsters, the musicians, longshore. In these institutions, it's often the union, not the employer, that decides who works. Employers, particularly small employers, don't maintain year-round labor forces. They rely on the union to provide them with trained and qualified workers.

In allocating jobs, the trade union bosses have historically refused to create fair hiring systems. Instead, they've used their power to give out jobs to hold on to their own and to exploit the desperation of those out of work. The classic longshore shape-up system portrayed in *On the Waterfront*, in which workers placed a toothpick behind their ear to indicate that they'd pay bribes to work, was only the most notorious. The system still exists today on both sides of the Hudson, only it's been brought indoors and the jobs sometimes pay six figures. In craft unions, hiring halls have seldom operated equitably. While favored ethnic groups work, women and disfavored minorities tend to sit on the bench. Beside them sit the dissidents.

Why should the mob risk killing dissidents when it can just starve them out? Hiring must be depoliticized by taking it out of the hands of business agents. A simple rule can replace discretion—first out of work, first out of the hiring hall. Hiring halls could be run by local civil service commissions. Hiring hall rules could be established by citywide union referenda, with voter eligibility determined by work status. The rules and the out-of-work list could then be posted on the Internet.

Federalize pension fund investment. Perhaps the saddest single fact about the American labor movement is that, by and large, the average worker is more likely to get a pension from funds controlled by their bosses than by their own union leaders. This is partly because of the union pension fund trustees' penchant for delaying vesting as long as possible and limiting payouts to the most senior workers. Excessive administrative costs and simple corruption add to the toll.

Naturally, the funds have attracted organized crime. Labor leaders lack expertise in money laundering and the ability to coordinate the money-losing schemes so essential to funding pilferage. That's why in the really large fund scandals, the mob almost always tends to be involved.

Fund manipulation is well organized. It robs the members of their life savings, and it takes place routinely at local, intermediate, national, and even the AFL-CIO level, as the Ullico scandal showed. Since the AFL-CIO has proven itself untrustworthy at every level, fund management should be taken out of its hands. Government regulation has failed too. It's the old story: the regulators have come under the influence of the regulated. What's required is not better government oversight of pension fund investors but government investment of the funds.

The government agency entrusted with the money must be able to withstand political pressure. So why not apply funds earned from collective bargaining to special accounts within the Social Security trust fund system? Invest union funds the same way as the standard Social Security funds: in Treasury bills. That way, at least workers could be sure they would get back more than they invested—which is true of only a minority of workers in union-run contribution plans today. Federal rules should forbid special plans for union leaders and staff; such plans almost always enable the union big shots to emerge with larger retirement incomes than those who pay their salaries; their salaries are far higher, and the plans are managed more efficiently.

Guarantee workers the right to form unions. The right to form unions and bargain collectively is internationally recognized as the bedrock of workers' rights. The United States is a signatory to various international agreements and covenants that affirm it, such as the 1949 Treaty of the International Labor Organization. The United States gave workers the right to form unions before any international body proclaimed it. The Wagner Act of 1935 states plainly: "Employees shall have the right of self-organization, to form, join or assist labor organizations, to bargain collectively through representatives of their own choosing and to engage in concerted activities, for the purpose of collective bargaining or other mutual aid and or protection."

But under Stalin, the 1936 Soviet constitution guaranteed the people all the rights that citizens in bourgeois countries could exercise: freedom of speech, press, and assembly, the secret ballot, even the right to hold protest demonstrations. The rights, of course, remained on paper. And so it is, for the most part, with American workers' rights to union representation.

The sweeping language of the Wagner Act is qualified by election procedures that make the rights almost impossible for ordinary workers to exercise. The law makes it easy not just for employers to deny workers the right to form unions, but also for unions to collude with employers, so that the organization recognized by the employer is not a true agent of the employees. Nor does the law confront the monopoly of representation by the AFL-CIO. Workers whom the AFL-CIO doesn't want to represent have a hard time finding any representative.

The result is that employers have rights; unions have rights; but ordinary workers have precious little in the way of rights that employers or unions are bound to respect.

The right to engage in concerted action extends well beyond the right to join organizations whose representatives help set the terms and conditions of employment. The horizon of concerted action ought to extend beyond a once-in-your-life signing of a mail-in ballot.

Dead unions and a comatose party system hooked up to the IV's of political action committees can't provide the institutional support for a genuine republic. For there to be citizens as opposed to mere consumers, there have to be some institutions in which concerted citizen action and deliberation take place, particularly workplace-based institutions to generate countervailing power in the vacuum left by the collapse of the AFL-CIO. Who is going to stop corporations from shifting more millions of manufacturing jobs to China? Who is going to bring back the forty-hour workweek? Or block the repeal of the overtime provisions from the 1938 Fair Standards Labor Act? Who can arrest the lumpenization of the hardworking bottom fifth of the American workforce?

Every employee in America ought to have not just the formal right to act in concert but the substantive right.

Guaranteeing such rights in America would be unprecedented. Yet it's common and well established in other advanced industrialized countries. It was back in 1891 that Germany established the Law for the Protection of Labor, which mandated elective bodies in firms with more than twenty workers.[30] Today, throughout the European Union, employers must permit the formation of works councils.[31] Even famously non-union U.S. multinationals are covered. The employees elect the councils, and the employers are required to recognize them for a range of purposes.

In America, works councils were set up in the 1920s by management to preempt real unions. In Europe today, the legislation in some countries requires works councils to seek accommodation with management. In others, the councils are presided over by the employer. But rules can be written so that American works councils don't fall under management authority. For example, the law could require that the councils be employee-only organizations.

The AFL-CIO would be faced with having to run candidates in council elections or leaving the field to uncontrollable elements. Not since the AFL-CIO merger in 1955 have American labor leaders had to explain why their union model is the best. Yet nothing would do more to make AFL-

CIO unions accountable than having to compete again in contests where the issue couldn't be settled by strong-arm or sleight-of-hand methods. Competition in works councils could promote the rise of a new AFL-CIO breed with a democratic style of work.

The point of creating works councils, though, is not just to raise the level of democracy in the AFL-CIO, but also to offer a new political horizon for American workers. To accomplish that, works councils at a firm level would have to have a way to connect with each other. They would offer workers an opportunity to discuss, debate, and act on issues of common concern. Higher-level city and regional organizations could represent workers' interests not just in the terms and conditions of labor, but in a whole range of urban issues—housing, education, civil rights, the environment, crime, transportation, zoning, and city planning.

No one can foretell the future, but at least two alternative directions seem possible for the American labor movement. In the first scenario, the trends of the last generation continue. U.S. unions, weak, fragmented, and corrupt, whether or not their numbers increase, remain unable to resist the main drift: the steady slippage back toward the Dickensian nightmares of early American industrialization—the disintegration of the social safety net, the elimination of work protections such as minimum wage and safety laws, the fade-out of unemployment compensation and pension benefits—all the residual forms of social democracy.

At the same time, the AFL-CIO continues to provide an essential political prop in the maintenance of the advanced world's most expensive, inefficient, and irrational health care system. Work itself continues to grow increasingly contingent and part-time; a growing labor force, bulked up by the elderly who can't afford to retire, supplies ever more hours per year, causing aggregate wages to fall or stagnate.

Inequality continues to widen, producing grotesque concentrations of wealth that defy efforts to find common interests between the top and bottom income earners. On the one hand, there are the top twenty-five hedge fund operators, who, according to a survey published by Institutional Investor's *Alpha* magazine, earn an average of $250 million a year. The top manager, Edward S. Lampert of ESL Investments, earned $1.02 billion.[32] On the other hand, there are the members of the bottom fifth of the U.S. population. According to a 2001 survey by the Federal Reserve, they had an average after-tax income of $8,761.[33] Mr. Lampert earns in an hour about what a member of the bottom fifth would earn in forty years.

To maintain their plutocratic advantages, the wealthy subvert the political system so that elections become more and more like auctions. The legislative process regularly delivers upward redistribution of wealth along the lines of the 2005 repeal of the estate tax and the bank-favoring bankruptcy bill.

At some point in this scenario, America ceases to be a democratic republic in anything but name. Freedom becomes simply freedom to obey market forces. And equality—the political foundation of the Declaration of Independence—is effectively redefined in terms of the "opportunity society."

In an alternative scenario, perhaps after a hard landing, the recognition grows that America's most serious problem is not its trade balance or its balance-of-payments deficit—as alarming as they may be—but its solidarity deficit.

Republics are best defended not by advanced missile systems, but by citizens who form common bonds. Without those felt ties—without solidarity—the pursuit of common interests is impossible. But sentiments without institutions to promote them are vacuous. Where can cohesiveness grow and flourish if not in a revived labor movement? Certainly not among the Forbes 400 or in the corporate and real estate worlds. Not within sectarian religious movements or within the precincts of the American party system. And certainly not within the AFL-CIO of Sweeney, or in the rival group led by Stern and Hoffa.

The periods of creativity and growth in the American labor movement have always come when the trade unions were challenged from outside—in the 1930s with the rise of the CIO, in the Progressive Era by the Wobblies, and, above all, during the era of the Knights of Labor in the mid- to late nineteenth century. Each period saw not just increased numbers but a revival of labor's republican potential.

Perhaps it's not too late for one more great effort to reclaim the promise of American labor for American society. The outcome depends on a historic compromise: corporations must give up their resistance to worker representation, and unions have to give up their right to monopoly representation. With such a settlement in place, works council elections could be a model for more than just the labor movement. And who knows, the upsurge might also bring a rebuilding wave of the lost labor temples that once flourished in the "red states" of the American heartland.

NOTES

PREFACE

1. http://www.randomhouse.com/wotd/index.pperl?date=19991220
2. Unions were viewed negatively by 61 percent of union households and 69 percent of working adults. Unions were viewed even more negatively than corporations. Pollsters didn't include a question about corruption. Harris Poll 68, August 31, 2005, http://www.harrisinteractive.com/harris_poll/. See also Zogby International, "Nationwide Attitudes Toward Unions," February 26, 2005, Table 6, http://psrf.org/info/Nationwide_Attitudes_Towards_Unions_2004. pdf. "Corruption" was the reason most often given by union members to explain why they opposed unions.
3. Office of the Independent Hearing Officer, LIUNA In re: Trusteeship Proceedings No. 97–30T, Hearings, Midland Hotel, 172 West Adams Street, Chicago Illinois, July 18, 1997, see esp. 654–659. See also Order and Memorandum, 51–54. Neither man was ever charged. Palermo, however, got thirty-two years on a gambling charge and died in jail. Guzzino received a thirty-nine-year sentence for racketeering and is still in prison. See "Local Mob Boss Dies in Prison," *Northwest Indiana Times*, April 19, 2005.
4. Although "Tough Tony" spelled it "Anastasio" and Albert called himself "Anastasia."
5. *U.S. v. Anthony M. Scotto and Anthony Anastasio,* Nos. 1121,1132, Dockets 80–1041, 80–1044. U.S. Court of Appeals, Second Circuit, May 20, 1980, argued; September 2, 1980, decided. Cuomo denied any knowledge of the contribution.
6. In 2005, Louis Valentino was identified as a Gambino crime family associate and named an unindicted co-conspirator in the government's RICO case against the ILA. See U.S. District Court, Eastern District of New York, *U.S. v. International Longshoremen's Association,* Complaint, Civil Action CV–05, 23.
7. John Kenneth Galbraith, *American Capitalism: The Concept of Countervailing Power* (Boston: Houghton Mifflin, 1956).
8. U.S. District Court, Eastern District of New York, *U.S. v. International Longshoremen's Association,* Complaint, Civil Action CV–05.

CHAPTER 1: THE CURSE ON THE HOUSE OF LABOR

1. John Sweeney, *America Needs a Raise* (Boston: Houghton Mifflin, 1996), 121.
2. Among them were Mike Bane, for example, an alleged crime family associate whose father "took a bullet" for Hoffa's father, and Larry Brennan, Jim Hoffa's former employer, whose father Bert was Jimmy Hoffa's closest partner.
3. Stephen Franklin and Todd Lighty, "City Teamsters Linked to Chain of Corruption; Quashed Probe Uncovers Charges," *Chicago Tribune*, October 17, 2004.
4. Pavlak wasn't killed, but he got fired from his union job. "I still believe in unions," he told the *Chicago Tribune*, "but I don't believe in a corrupt union." Stephen Franklin, "Mob-Control Allegations Rise Among Teamsters: Union's Internal Probe Collapses," *Chicago Tribune*, November 7, 2004.
5. Ibid.
6. *U.S. v. Anthony Accardo*, U.S. S.D. Fla. No. 81–23 O-CR-ALH 18 USC.51962(d).
7. *Utica Observer-Dispatch*, February 10, 1998.
8. Relationship confirmed by telephone interview, May 3, 2004. Rando's secretary spoke with him. He gave her the message that he couldn't come to the phone, but that yes, Frank was his brother.
9. Quoted in Jonathan Kwitny, *Vicious Circles* (New York: W. W. Norton, 1979), 275.
10. Ronald Sullivan, "Prosecutors' Aides in Passaic Called in a Union Inquiry," *New York Times*, September 8, 1971.
11. "Five Indicted in Embezzlement of Union Funds in Newark," *New York Times*, March 3, 1972.
12. Joseph P. Rizzo was charged in 2000 with having taken bribes amounting to $200,000–$350,000 from employers in return for favorable treatment on wages and benefits. He pleaded guilty to conspiracy. Associated Press, October 22, 2001.
13. Thomas Ginsberg, "Union Compensation Shows a Wide Gap," *Philadelphia Inquirer*, November 21, 2004.
14. Telephone interview, Gloria Niccollai, March 16, 2005.
15. U.S. Attorney, Southern District of New York, press release, "U.S. Charges Acting Boss, Acting Underboss, and Top Leaders of Gambino Crime Family with Racketeering and Other Crimes," March 9, 2005, http://www.usdoj.gov/usao/nys/Press%20Releases/March05/Squitieri%20Indictment%20PR.pdf.
16. Telephone interview, March 16, 2005.
17. Telephone interview, March 16, 2005.
18. Jo-Ann Mort (ed.), *Not Your Father's Union Movement* (New York: Verso, 1998), 44, 52.
19. CNN/*USA Today*/Gallup Poll, November 14–16, 2003.
20. See Michael Pierce, "The Populist President of the American Federation of Labor: The Career of John McBride, 1880–1895," *Labor History* 41, 1 (2000): 5–24.

21. John Hutchinson, *The Imperfect Union: A History of Corruption in American Trade Unions* (New York: E. P. Dutton, 1970), 124–126.

22. George Meany, Tom Donahue, and John Sweeney.

23. Bambrick went to jail for giving Scalise $10,000 in union funds. See Hutchinson, *The Imperfect Union*, 406–407.

24. Malcolm Johnson, *Crime on the Union Front* (New York: McGraw-Hill, 1950), 522.

25. Steven Greenhouse, "Chief of Building Workers' Union Leaves with $1.5 Million," *New York Times*, February 2, 1999.

26. Jonathan Mahler, "The Boss: Gus Bevona's Labor Pains," *New York Magazine*, February 9, 1998.

27. Robert Fitch, "Sweeney's Labor," *Nation*, November 25, 1996.

28. "Union Officer Is Seized," *New York Times*, July 21, 1941. Abrams lasted only three years before he was indicted for extorting $100,000 from Bronx landlords. He was followed by Tommy Lewis (assassinated) and Henry Chartier (convicted of extortion). See Charles Grutzner, "Union Plans Clean-Up of Racket Local," *New York Times*, September 11, 1966, 78.

29. Burton Hall, "Labor Insurgency and the Legal Trap," in *Autocracy and Insurgency in Organized Labor*, edited by Burton Hall (New Brunswick, NJ: Transaction Books, 1972), 259–260.

30. Information from Donatella Della Porta, chair of the Department of Sociology, European University Institute, 2004, e-mail response to questions.

31. Herbert Asbury, *Gem of the Prairie* (New York: Alfred A. Knopf, 1930), 313.

32. Henry S. Faber and Bruce Western, "Round Up the Usual Suspects: The Decline of Unions in the Private Sector, 1973–1998," Princeton University, Industrial Relations Section, Working Paper No. 437, 36. The authors assume current rates of employment growth (0.05) and new organizing (0.001).

33. AFL-CIO, "The Silent War: The Assault on Workers' Freedom to Choose and Bargain Collectively in the United States," Issue Brief, June 2002, 2. In 2004, the civilian labor force numbered over 145 million (U.S. Census Bureau, *Statistical Abstract of the United States*).

34. David Brody, "Labor and the Great Depression," *Labor History* 13 (Spring 1972): 237.

35. Richard Bensinger, "When We Try More, We Win More," in Jo-Ann Mort (ed.), *Not Your Father's Union Movement*, 27–43.

36. See Internal Review Board, "Proposed Charges Against International Representative Dane Passo and International Representative and Joint Council 25 President William T. Hogan, Jr.," May 23, 2001; Stephen Franklin, "Union Panel Votes Out 2 Teamsters for Life," *Chicago Tribune*, May 31, 2002, 1.

37. Judge Atlas's opinion quoted in Debbie McGoldrick, "Anti-Irish Bias Acquits Carpenter Union Leader," *Irish Voice*, May 11, 2005.

38. Bureau of Labor Statistics, "Major Work Stoppages (Annual)," Table 1, "Work

Stoppages Involving 1,000 or More Workers, 1947–2004," http://www.bls.gov/news.release/wkstp.toc.htm.

39. Jim Fuquay, "UPS Strike a Major Win for Labor, Reich Says," *Fort Worth Star Telegram*, August 20, 1997; Steven Greenhouse, "Gains Put Unions at Turning Point, Many Experts Say," *New York Times*, September 1, 1997; quotes from Leo Troy, "The UPS Strike: Labor Tilts at Windmills," Heritage Foundation, Backgrounder No. 1165, March 20, 1998.

40. Bureau of Labor Statistics, "Major Work Stoppages (Annual)," Table 1.

41. See Robert Fitch, "Dead Men Leading: Why Our City Labor Leaders Need French Lessons," *Village Voice*, April 16, 1996. A milder, more recent version of the 1995 strike took place in France when efforts by another conservative government to change pension laws drew nationwide protests by teachers, hospital workers, scientists, and firefighters that preceded the transfer of power in French regional elections. See Craig S. Smith, "French Veer Left in Regional Vote," *New York Times*, March 29, 2004. Some may ask, "But don't job actions by European workers jeopardize their competitive status?" Perhaps. But at least they have organizations that endow them with the power to choose whether or not to take that risk.

42. "Sciopero generale, piu di 50 manifestazioni," *Corriere della sera*, March 26, 2004.

43. "Journée de mobilisation nationale pour les salaries et l'emploi," *Le Monde*, March 10, 2005.

44. Jacob Antoine, "Le secteur privé au Danemark est touché par une grève massive," *Le Monde*, April 29, 1998; Dietmar Henning, "Danish Government Ends Strike," World Socialist Web Site, May 12, 1998, http://www.wsws.org/workers/1998/may1998/den=m12.shtml.

45. Denis Hughes, president of the New York State AFL-CIO, quoted in Steven Greenhouse, "Bitter Strike at Domino Sugar Finally Ends," *New York Times*, February 27, 2001.

46. Letter from Joe Crimi, http://www.labournet.net/docks2/0103/domino1.htm, February 28, 2002. The remaining workers got a 5 percent raise.

47. Tim Golden, "U.S. Sues Longshoremen's Locals, Charging Decades of Mob Control," *New York Times*, February 15, 1990.

48. See Jerry Capeci, "Red Sings the Waterfront Blues," This Week in Gang Land: The Online Column, November 21, 2002, http://www.ganglandnews.com/column305.htm.

49. In Saddle Brook, New Jersey, 400 UFCW workers who earned as little as $5.25 an hour after five years of employment were on strike against Arrow Fastener Co. See Kevin G. Demarrais, "Strikers Have Company," *Bergen Record*, October 26, 2004.

50. Even the SEIU, which had made the most serious efforts to improve wages, was mostly a low-wage union.

51. Robert Fitch, "The Union from Hell," *Village Voice*, January 20, 1998.

52. Daniel Bell, *End of Ideology* (Cambridge, MA: Harvard University Press, 2000; originally published 1960).

53. Congressional Budget Office, "Administrative Costs of Private Accounts in Social Security," March 2004. See also Form 5500 for Local 814 (EIN [Employer Identification Number] 11–6234358). The filings are available online at freeERISA.com.

54. For Bonanno control over Local 814, see U.S. Court of Appeals for the Second Circuit 879 F 2d 20; 1989 App. LEXIS 9364, March 13, 1989, No. 88–6289.

55. Mary Williams Walsh, "Teamsters Find Pensions at Risk," *New York Times*, November 15, 2004.

56. Richard B. Freeman and James L. Medoff, *What Do Unions Do?* (New York: Basic Books, 1984), 68–69. The authors acknowledge that union plans have "less liberal" vesting rules than non-union plans. Why? Because "union policies are determined by all members and thus are more influenced by the desires of older, more stable workers." Ralph and Estelle James's study of the Teamsters' pension fund operation was based on attendance at meetings and access to minutes. They argued that vesting rules were determined mainly by considerations of public relations—i.e., to make Hoffa look good—and also to conserve assets so that they could be lent to Hoffa's dubious allies. Freeman and Medoff can't explain how it was in the interest of members to deny themselves benefits if they simply switched from one local to another. See Ralph James and Estelle James, *Hoffa and the Teamsters* (Princeton, NJ: Van Nostrand, 1965), especially ch. 24, "Manipulating Pension Benefits."

57. AFL-CIO, press release, "Remarks by John J. Sweeney, President of the AFL-CIO On the Wall Street Rally," July 30, 2002.

58. Along with George Bush Sr. and Democratic National Committee chair Terry McAuliffe.

59. "New Leaders Stabilize ULLICO and Try to Put Scandal in the Past," *Engineering News-Record*, May 31, 2004, http://www.enr.com.

60. Employee Benefits Security Administration, press release, "Labor Department Removed Plumbers' Union Pension Fund Trustees, Collects $10.98 Million for Workers' Retirement," August 3, 2004.

61. Steven Greenhouse, "Union Chief to Return $200,000 from Stock Deal Under Inquiry," *New York Times*, November 1, 2002.

62. Nancy Cleeland, "Organize or Die," *Los Angeles Times*, March 10, 2002.

63. Jeffrey L. Rabin, "Lawsuit Alleges Mishandling of Pension Funds," *Los Angeles Times*, January 19, 2000, 1.

64. PR Newswire, March 6, 2002, Communications Workers of America. Cited in Kenneth F. Boehm, Testimony Before the Subcommittee on Capital Markets, Insurance, and Government-Sponsored Enterprises, Committee on Financial Services, U.S. House of Representatives, May 1, 2002.

65. Communications Workers of America, press release, June 16, 1999.

66. NPR, "All Things Considered," February 12, 2002.

67. Aaron Bernstein, "A Black Eye for Labor," *BusinessWeek*, April 8, 2002; see also "Union Movement Launches 'No More Enrons' Campaign" on the AFL-CIO Web site. The AFL-CIO Executive Council called for reform of corporate governance, admonished corporations for promoting a culture of greed, and called on directors to allow workers to have a greater voice in pension plans.

68. Who was also a participant in the Ullico insider trading scandal. For the Ironworkers embezzlement cases, see U.S. Department of Justice, press release, May 2, 2003.

69. John E. Mulligan and Dean Starkman, "Coia Votes May Decide AFL-CIO Presidency," *Providence Journal-Bulletin*, October 24, 1995.

70. Fortune Archive, "The 50 Biggest Mafia Bosses," 1986 list, http://www.fortune.com/fortune/mafia.

71. Transcript of Chicago hearing available at http://www.laborers.org/Coia_Test.html.

72. Draft Civil RICO Complaint, *U.S. v. Laborers International Union of North America, AFL-CIO, et al.*, November 11, 1994, U.S. District Court, Northern District of Illinois.

73. "Gore's Guys," *Wall Street Journal*, February 11, 2000.

74. Office of the Independent Hearing Officer, Laborers' International Union of North America, In the Matter of Arthur A. Coia, Docket No. 97–52S, Order and Memorandum, section V, paragraph 22.

75. The New York firefighters are battling the New York City Police Department for control of emergency response situations. The SEIU's and the Teamsters' political priorities cancel each other out: the SEIU wants more Mexican immigrants in; the Teamsters want Mexican truckers off American roads. The big priority for the International Brotherhood of Electrical Workers is more money for Amtrak; it's less so for the UAW. Carpenters want tariffs on softwoods from Canada; Laborers lobby for free trade. And so it goes. It's not exactly sixty different affiliates pulling sixty different ways. But it doesn't add up to strong, univocal progressivism either.

76. Linda Chavez, *Betrayal* (New York: Crown Forum, 2004), 18, 97.

77. Davis's political target was lapsed Trotskyists—like *Dissent* editor Irving Howe and Democratic Socialist leader Michael Harrington. They argued that the Democrats would already be a European-style social-democratic party—or on the cusp of becoming one. See "Voices From the Left: A Conversation Between Michael Harrington and Irving Howe," *New York Times Magazine*, June 17, 1981, 24. See also Harrington's *Socialism* (New York: Bantam Books, 1973).

78. Dan La Botz, *Rank-and-File Rebellion* (London: Verso, 1990), 191.

79. The official history of the Teamsters for a Democratic Union, La Botz's *Rank-*

and-File Rebellion, which appeared in a series edited by Mike Davis, savages Presser but treats Jackson as a valued supporter.

80. F. C. Duke Zeller, *The Devil's Pact: Inside the World of the Teamsters Union* (Secaucus, NJ: Carol Publishing Group, 1996), 409. Zeller was the communications director of the Teamsters for fourteen years.

81. Ibid.

82. In 1986, he surrounded himself with as many presidential candidates as he could. At one rally, Presser snagged four, including Illinois Democrat Paul Simon. For the Cincinnati rally, see James Neff, *Mobbed Up* (New York: Dell, 1989), 463.

83. President's Commission on Organized Crime, Report to the President and the Attorney General, "The Edge: Organized Crime, Business, and Labor Unions," 1985, section 4, see especially p. 86, fn 13.

84. Monica Davey, "Unions Finance Jackson Staffers: 'Work Isn't Quid Pro Quo,' He Says," *Chicago Tribune*, March 26, 2001.

CHAPTER 2: THE HIDDEN COST OF CORRUPT UNIONS

1. Richard Rorty, *Achieving Our Country* (Cambridge, MA: Harvard University Press, 1998), 77.

2. CBS News Polls, "Poll: Economy Remains Top Priority," CBSNews.com, May, 13, 2003, http://www.cbsnews.com/stories/2003/05/13/opinion/polls/main55 3730.shtml.

3. David Brooks, "Our Sprawling, Supersize Utopia," *New York Times*, April 4, 2004.

4. See *Magnan v. Anaconda Industries, Inc.*, 479 A.2d 781, n.8 (Conn. 1984). "Scholars and jurists unanimously agree that Wood's pronouncement in his treatise, *Master and Servant . . .* , was responsible for nationwide acceptance of the rule."

5. In the 2002–2003 recovery, corporate profits got an unprecedented share of the growth in national income, 41 percent, while labor got 38 percent. See Bob Herbert, "We're More Productive. Who Gets the Money?" *New York Times*, April 5, 2004, citing Andrew Sum, "The Unprecedented Rising Tide of Corporate Profits and the Simultaneous Ebbing of Labor Compensation: Gainers and Losers from the National Economic Recovery in 2002 and 2003," Center for Labor Market Studies, Northeastern University, 2004.

6. Richard B. Freeman, "How Labor Fares in Advanced Economies," *Working Under Different Rules*, edited by Richard B. Freeman (New York: Russell Sage Foundation, 1994), 22.

7. Ibid.

8. Ibid.

9. David Brooks, "Fear and Rejections," *New York Times*, June 2, 2005.

10. Ibid. It's odd. The more the United States hollows out its once-mighty industrial base, the less competitive it becomes in international trade; the deeper in debt it goes to foreign nations, the more its productivity rates soar. For decades, America's productivity growth rates remained mired around 1 percent yearly—less than Europe's. Since the mid-1990s, though, there's been a reversal of fortunes. The secret? Some think it "hedonics." Inventive U.S. macreconomists now measure output to take quality improvements into account. Instead of just measuring increases in physical output, productivity measures now include increases in satisfaction, too. (The extra button on your new blender makes you happier, increasing its value, therefore embodying more productive labor.) Certainly the effect of this new measurement mode must be satisfying to American corporate leaders, since it tends to lower inflation, thus keeping wages and benefits down. And at the same time, it improves U.S. competitiveness on paper, adding prestige to the U.S. model of enterprise.

11. Thomas Meyer, "The Transformation of German Social Democracy," in *Looking Left: European Socialism After the Cold War,* edited by D. Sassoon (London: I. B. Tauris, in association with the Gramsci Foundation, 1997), 126.

12. Sheri Berman, *The Social Democratic Movement* (Cambridge, MA: Harvard University Press, 1998).

13. Unemployment fell sharply, confounding the economists who predicted "national suicide." In 2004, when the conservatives tried to take the thirty-five-hour week away, they lost in nearly every one of France's twenty-six regions.

14. Werner Sombart, *Why Is There No Socialism in the United States?* (White Plains, NY: International Arts and Sciences Press, 1976; originally published 1906), 106.

15. Ibid., 74.

16. Samuel Gompers, *Labor in Europe and America* (New York: Harper & Brothers, 1910), 62.

17. *Industrial Worker,* August 19, 1909, cited in Philip S. Foner, *History of the Labor Movement in the United States,* vol. 3, *The Policies and Practices of the American Federation of Labor, 1900–1909* (New York: International Publishers, 1964), 148.

18. Ibid., 260.

19. Angus Maddison, *The World Economy: A Millennial Perspective* (Paris: Development Center of the Organization for Economic Cooperation and Development, 2001), Table E-7, 351.

20. Marcel Van der Linden and Jurgen Rojahn, *Formation of Labor Movements, 1870–1914* (Leiden: E. J. Brill, 1990), 260.

21. See Maddison, *The World Economy*, Ibid.

22. Lawrence Mishel, Jared Bernstein, and Heather Boushey, *The State of Working America, 2002/2003* (Ithaca, NY: Cornell University Press, 2003), 425.

23. Paul Ginsborg, *Italy and Its Discontents* (New York: Palgrave Macmillan, 2003), 58.

24. The first six are Finland, the United States, Sweden, Taiwan, Denmark, and Norway.

25. Marvin Harris, *Cannibals and Kings* (New York: Vintage, 1977), 274.

26. It would be necessary to increase the distance between the classes so that the bottom feeders would be invisible to the *übermensch*. See Friedrich Nietzsche, *The Gay Science* (New York: Vintage, 1974), 91.

27. William Graham Sumner, "The Forgotten Man," *Capitalism Magazine*, September 11, 2000.

28. Given how much harder Americans work, you'd think they'd be a lot richer than Europeans, but in per capita terms, they're not. Using market exchange rates, half a dozen countries are richer and another half a dozen are only slightly less rich. Lawrence Mishel, Jared Bernstein, and Sylvia Allegretto, *The State of Working America, 2004/2005* (Ithaca, NY: Cornell University Press, 2005), 385.

29. Ibid., 401–404.

30. Ibid., 102, 124. Or, to put it more provocatively, it's the increase in the amount of labor that Americans furnish that helps explain why their wages fell. That's what generally happens when the supply of something increases: the price falls. The behavior of American workers makes sense in individual but not in collective terms. It's like the crowd arriving early to beat its own rush.

31. Mishel et al., *The State of Working America, 2004/2005*, 62.

32. "The Rising Tide," *Forbes*, March 15, 2004.

33. Nigel Holloway, "In Praise of Inequality," *Forbes*, March 17, 2003.

34. The Gini index measures income or wealth concentration. It tracks the percentage of national income earned by different domestic income groups. A perfectly equal society would be expressed as a curve with a forty-five-degree angle. A perfectly unequal society would display a curve that would lie flat until the very end, when it would shoot upward. The curve for United States bends further upward from the forty-five-degree angle than that of any other advanced economy.

35. "Spreading the Yankee Way of Pay," *BusinessWeek*, April 18, 2001; "Executive Pay," *BusinessWeek*, April 18, 2001.

36. Roger Doyle, "Income Inequality in the U.S.," *Scientific American*, June 1999.

37. Mishel et al., *The State of Working America, 2002/2003*, 168.

38. Mishel et al., *The State of Working America, 2004/2005*; see especially 205–212, "The Technology Story of Wage Inequality."

39. CNN Money, "Jurors See Tape of Kozlowski's Party," October 29, 2003; LouAnn Lofton, "Kozlowski Faces the Music," *Motley Fool*, September 29, 2003; Art Weinberg, "Tyco's Kozlowski Sets Sail," *Forbes*, June 3, 2002; Andy Kessler, "Winnick's Voyage to the Bottom of the Sea," *Wall Street Journal*, March 21, 2002; Jon Swartz, "Homes of the Rich and Infamous," *USA Today*, July 14, 2002; "WorldCom's Woes," *Forbes*, August 9, 2002.

40. Harris Poll, no. 72, December 4, 1999.

41. Lars Osberg and Timothy Smeeding, "An International Comparison of Preferences for Leveling," paper prepared for the Twenty-eighth General Conference of the International Association for Research in Incomes and Wealth, Cork, Ireland, August 22–28, 2004.

42. In Germany, though, Klaus Zwickel, the chief of IG Metall, the nation's largest union, was forced to resign after he was implicated in what was known as the Mannesmann affair. Zwickel was accused of connivance in a merger that essentially gave the directors a 130 million euro bribe in exchange for approving the deal. Because of *Mittbestimmung*, the presence of unions on the board, Zwickel could have stopped the looting with his single vote. He wasn't charged with sharing in the "bonuses" (see "Geld-Geber," *Die Zeit,* July 2003). Eventually the case against the executives collapsed.

43. Alan Reynolds, "Marginal Tax Rates," *The Concise Encyclopedia of Economics,* http://www.econlib.org/library/ENC/MarginalTaxRates.html. No advanced economy has as low a rate as the United States; the country with the lowest rate is Bolivia (10 percent).

44. M. Carley, European Foundation for the Improvement of Living and Working Conditions, "Industrial Relations in the EU, Japan, and the USA, 2002," 11–12, Table 3, 2004.

45. Silvia Ascavelli, "CEO Compensation Surges in Many European Countries," Wall Street Journal Online, July 26, 2004.

46. Alexis de Tocqueville, *Democracy in America*, vol. 1 (New York: Alfred A. Knopf, 1944), 3.

47. James Poterba, "The Rate of Return to Corporate Capital and Factor Shares," National Bureau of Economic Research, Working Paper No. 6263, April 1999.

48. Mishel et al., *The State of Working America, 2002/2003*, ch. 2.

49. David Card, Thomas Lemieux, and W. Craig Riddell, "Unions and Wage Inequality: A Comparative Study of the U.S., U.K., and Canada," National Bureau of Economic Research, Working Paper No. 9473, September 2003.

50. See *Economic Report of the President*, 1999, "The Experts Consensus on Earnings Inequality" (Washington, DC: U.S. Government Printing Office, 1999), 175, Box 5–3.

51. "Reducing the Cost of New Housing Construction in New York City," New York University Center for Real Estate and Urban Policy, 1999, http://law.nyu.edu/realestatecenter.

52. Mark Brenner, labor economist at Association for Union Democracy construction trades conference, cited in Carl Biers, "New Voices at AUD Construction Trades Conference," *Union Democracy Review* 145 (January/February 2003).

53. Union officials justified their favoritism toward their own relatives, saying, "We need them to be good people who'll build the union." Ronald D. White,

"With Deluge, Longshore Jobs Become Long Shots," *Los Angeles Times,* August 18, 2004. See also "An Inside Job on the Docks," *Los Angeles Times,* August 29, 2004.

54. Mac Daniel, "Audit Targets Payroll at Docks," *Boston Globe,* June 10, 2005; Ralph Ranelli and Mac Daniel, "Unions Alleged to Pad Payrolls with Children," *Boston Globe,* June 9, 2005.

55. Dan Weikel, "Anything But Casual About Dock Work," *Los Angeles Times,* May 9, 1999, 1.

56. For the classic trade union argument for wage cutting to accommodate market forces, see David Dubinsky and A. H. Raskin, *David Dubinsky: A Life with Labor* (New York: Simon and Schuster, 1977), chapter 5.

57. U.S. Department of Labor, Form LM–2, File number 517–385.

58. Ibid.

59. Robert Fitch, "Deadmen Leading," *Village Voice,* April 16, 1996.

60. Ibid.

61. Ibid.

62. Gosta Esping-Anderson, *The Three Worlds of Welfare Capitalism* (Princeton, NJ: Princeton University Press, 1990), Table 3.1.

63. Seymour Martin Lipset, *American Exceptionalism* (New York: W. W. Norton, 1996). For idealization of nineteenth-century poor relief, see Marvin Olasky, *The Tragedy of Compassion* (Washington, DC: Regnery Publishing Co., 1992). Olasky, the prophet of "compassionate conservatism," specifically invokes nineteenth-century charitable practices, which in New York City required applicants to chop wood or scrub clothes for a certain number of hours. In New York, private relief controlled by charity societies replaced "outdoor relief." The private societies were run by landlords, who would otherwise pay a disproportionate share of relief.

64. Lipset, *American Exceptionalism,* 294.

65. Gary Langere, "Health Care Pains," ABC News, October 20, 2003, http://abcnews.go.com.

66. Pew Research Center, "Bush Failing in Social Security Push," http://people-press.org/reports/display.php3?PageID=926.

67. Cited in Ruy Teixeira, "Happy with Health Care?" *American Prospect* 11, 3 (December 20, 1999).

68. Esping-Anderson, *The Three Worlds of Welfare Capitalism,* 27.

69. Ed Garsten, "GM Health Care Bill Tops $60 Billion; Cost Adds $1,400 per Vehicle, Hurts Competitiveness," Detnews.com, March 11, 2004, http://www.detnews.com/2004/autoinsider/0403/11/a01-88813.htm.

70. William H. Dawson, *Bismarck and State Socialism: An Exposition of the Social and Economic Legislation of Germany Since 1870* (London: S. Sonnenschein & Co., 1891).

71. In France, for example, a general strike brought the Popular Front to power in

1935. The following year, the Blum government enacted a forty-hour workweek and a two-week vacation. In 1995, a similar scenario played out, with a general strike bringing down a conservative regime, although some of Premier Juppé's reforms in tax and health care fields were continued, against union opposition.

72. Kathleen Jones, *The Making of Social Policy in Britain, 1830–1990,* 2nd ed. (London: Athlone Press, 1994), 101, 140.

73. Lipset, *American Exceptionalism,* 92.

74. CBC, "The Greatest Canadian," http://www.cbc.ca/greatest.

75. Aziz Choudry, "Childcare: A Workers' Issue," *TIE Asia,* May 2001; also author interview with Dan Clawson, a sociology professor at University of Massachusetts, Amherst, who organized a child care conference involving AFL-CIO officials in 2000.

76. Esping-Anderson, *The Three Worlds of Welfare Capitalism,* 50, Table 2.1.

77. Theron J. Schlabach, *Rationality and Welfare: Public Discussion of Poverty and Social Insurance in the U.S., 1875–1935,* ch. 5, p. 3, http://www.ssa.gov/history/reports/schlabach6.html.

78. "Insurance Companies See Aid to Health in Golf," *New York Times,* February 11, 1922, 10.

79. David Brian Robertson, *Capital, Labor, and State* (Lanham, MD: Rowman & Littlefield, 2000), 239; data from U.S. Commissioner of Labor, "Workmen's Insurance and Benefit Funds in the United States, Twenty-third Annual Report" (Washington, DC: Government Printing Office), 23, 31.

80. "Report Condemns Social Insurance," *New York Times,* January 14, 1917, 12.

81. Schlabach, *Rationality and Welfare,* ch. 6, p. 5, http://www.ssa.gov/history/reports/schlabach6.html. The AFL Executive Council had already warned, "The workers should be on their guard against provisions of this nature which are only disguised methods of eliminating workers."

82. Robertson, *Capital, Labor, and State,* 240, 243ff.

83. *New York Times,* January 31, 1920, 3.

84. Cited in Schlabach, *Rationality and Welfare,* ch. 6, p. 6.

85. Robertson, *Capital, Labor, and State,* 153; see also 160.

86. Schlabach, *Rationality and Welfare,* ch. 6, p. 6. The AFL had 2 million members in 1916 and paid out a total of $3 million in benefits that year.

87. *New York Times,* July 15, 1917, 13. A report coauthored by Stone went on in the same vein: "self-respecting workmen resent pampering . . . such laws are an invasion of industrial rights which labor will not tolerate—that local health insurance societies become labor unions." During World War I, Stone joined August Belmont Jr., a subway tycoon and the head of the National Civic Federation, in opposing monthly benefits for wounded veterans or death benefits for their survivors. It was better, the two agreed, just to give them a lump sum.

88. See Brotherhood of Locomotive Engineers and Trainmen, "History," http://www.ble.org/pr/history/page4h.html.

89. William Z. Foster, *The Wrecking of the Labor Banks: The Collapse of the Labor Banks and Investment Companies of the Brotherhood of Locomotive Engineers* (Chicago: Trade Union Educational League, 1927).

90. "Labor and Capital Honor W. S. Stone," *New York Times*, June 16, 1925.

91. Martin Plissner, "A Health Care Bill Fantasy," *Slate*, June 5, 2001.

92. Marie Gottschalk, *The Shadow Welfare State* (Ithaca, NY: ILR Press, 2000), 71.

93. For the unions' position in the policy debates, I've relied mostly on Gottschalk, *The Shadow Welfare State*, 68–75, although my interpretation differs from hers.

94. Steffie Woolhandler, Terry Campbell, and David U. Himmelstein, "Costs of Health Care Administration in the United States and Canada," *New England Journal of Medicine* 349, 8 (August 21, 2003): 768–775.

95. Reports Marie Gottschalk, "Some union officials grumbled that Georgine's position with ULLICO explained why he refused to throw the weight of the building trades behind any health-care reform proposal to eliminate or greatly reduce the role of insurance companies in providing health care." Gottschalk, *The Shadow Welfare State*, 51.

96. Merrill Goozner, "Health Care Debate Splits Union Ranks," *Chicago Tribune*, February 18, 1991, 1.

97. Charles Lewis, *The Buying of the President 2000* (New York: Avon, 2000), 41.

98. Gottschalk, *The Shadow Welfare State*, 151, citing Georgine's congressional testimony.

99. Ibid.

100. Ibid., 109.

101. "Transcript of the Debate Between Bush and Kerry, with Domestic Policy the Topic," *New York Times*, October 14, 2004, A23.

102. World Health Organization, *World Health Report*, 2000, statistical appendix. Senator Kerry didn't try to refute Bush's attack on government-run systems. He failed to point out that the health care status quo rests on tax expenditures of $145 billion a year to support the private insurance–run system. He just looked straight into the camera and insisted that the government didn't have a role in his proposed system. As a candidate he didn't have much choice: there is simply no organized support for changing the system, even though a wide majority rejects it as inadequate. Certainly Kerry would get no support for fundamental change from the AFL-CIO.

103. Ross Clark, "How Labour Is Turning Britain into a Land of Paupers," *Spectator*, October 16, 2004.

CHAPTER 3: THE REVOLT AGAINST SOLIDARITY

1. Of all Hoffa Jr.'s predecessors, Shea is the only one who was not awarded a portrait and a place on the wall in the Teamsters' Washington, D.C., Marble Palace headquarters. (Even FBI informant and mob associate Jackie Presser has a portrait.) Shea does make an important appearance in David Witwer's *Corruption and Reform in the Teamsters Union* (Urbana: University of Illinois Press, 2003).

2. For the composition of the board and for what is still the best treatment of the ULP, see Walton Bean, *Boss Ruef's San Francisco: The Story of the Union Labor Party* (Berkeley: University of California Press, 1967). Eugene Schmitz, of the Musicians Union, not McCarthy, was the ULP mayor of San Francisco in the paint-eating period. Nevertheless, McCarthy and his administration, drawn more exclusively from the construction trades, nearly matched their predecessors in corruption.

3. Lincoln Steffens, *The Shame of the Cities* (New York: Hill and Wang, 1992; originally published 1902).

4. Robert Kennedy, *The Enemy Within* (New York: Da Capo Press, 1994; originally published 1960), 239.

5. *New York Times*, December 18, 1963, 47. Under pressure from the unions, the city's Human Rights Commission backed down. In the Hunts Point affair, unions went back to work; the blacks agreed to take a test administered by the union. They failed the test and never became Local 2 plumbers. See Roger Waldinger, *Still The Promised Land?* (Cambridge, MA: Harvard University Press, 1996), and especially Herbert Hill's classic study, "The New York City Terminal Market Controversy: A Case Study of Race, Labor, and Power," *Humanities in Society* 6, 4 (1984): 351–391.

6. Alice Kessler Harris, "Comment on Howard Kimmeldorf's 'Bringing Unions Back In,'" *Labor History* 32 (Winter 1991).

7. See Julie Greene, *Pure and Simple Politics: The American Federation of Labor and Political Activism, 1881–1917* (Cambridge, England: Cambridge University Press, 1998), especially her sources in chapter 1, "Building the Federation." Greene notes that the best account is still Norman Ware, *The Labor Movement in the United States, 1860–1890* (New York: D. Appleton, 1929).

8. Harris, "Comment on Howard Kimmeldorf's 'Bringing Unions Back In.'"

9. David Montgomery, *The Fall of the House of Labor* (New York: Cambridge University Press, 1987). Montgomery's argument is that workers' sentiments, customs, and culture create union principles and bylaws (see p. 23). Mine is the opposite. In the struggle for power within the union, the leadership passes a constitution and bylaws that create the norms of the workplace culture.

10. Montgomery, *The Fall of the House of Labor*; Herbert Gutman, *Work, Culture, and Society in Industrializing America: Essays in American Working Class Social*

History (New York: Vintage, 1977); Rick Halpern and Jonathan Morris, eds., *American Exceptionalism? U.S. Working Class Formation in an International Context* (New York: St. Martin's Press, 1997).

11. Robert Michels, *Political Parties* (New York: Free Press, 1962). American sociologists tended to see American unions through the eyes of European critics (see below).

12. Engels, excerpt from Letter to Schlutter, January 29, 1891, in *Marx and Engels on the Trade Unions,* edited by Kenneth Lapides (New York: International Publishers, 1990), 142. By 1891, the Knights were almost completely dead. Engels was well informed about the American labor scene, but his fixed ideas about the course of the labor movement prevented him from properly assimilating the material he was given. Shortly after his letter to Schlutter, Engels was urging everyone to work with Gompers and the AFL as the only practical response. Because Marx and Engels exaggerated the importance of inexorably unfolding economic laws, they necessarily scanted the question of which type of organization could better enable workers to reach their goals. Engels's prescription of "boring from within" the AFL would be followed by the next four generations of Marxists.

13. Cited in Bruce Laurie, *Artisans into Workers* (Champaign: University of Illinois Press, 1989), 174. The author describes Powderly's tirade as "bigoted." A bigot is "intolerant of others' beliefs or behavior." Why *should* Powderly have tolerated the nascent labor czars?

14. William Haywood, "The General Strike," in *Rebel Voices: An IWW Anthology,* edited by Joyce L. Kornbluh (Chicago: Charles H. Kerr Publishers), 49.

15. Bernard Mandel, *Samuel Gompers* (Yellow Springs, OH: Antioch Press, 1963), 89; Department of Labor, LM–2 000–106, 2004.

16. Laurie, *Artisans into Workers,* 165.

17. Ware, *The Labor Movement,* 264. The term "tenement house scum" came from Gompers's mentor, Adolph Strasser, boss of the Cigar Makers International Union.

18. Ware, *The Labor Movement,* 262–263.

19. Selig Perlman, in John R. Commons, *History of Labour in the United States* (New York: Macmillan, 1918–1935), vol. 2, 396–397. Perlman's point was that the AFL's victory was inevitable given the mentality of American workers, who were job conscious rather than class conscious. Perlman ignores the possibility that the labor institutions of the period, i.e., the AFL trade unions, mightily promoted job consciousness.

20. Haywood, "The General Strike," 50.

21. While John Dos Passos devoted a section of his novel *1919* to the incident, most modern labor historians pass over Centralia as quickly as possible. Montgomery devotes not a word. An older account that presents both the defense and prosecution arguments while siding with the IWW is Louis Adamic's *Dy-*

namite: The Story of Class Violence in America (New York: Viking Press, 1931), 292–305. See also Philip S. Foner, *History of the Labor Movement in the United States*, vol. 8, *Postwar Struggles, 1918–1920* (New York: International Publishers, 1988), 214–225.

22. Roland McMaster quote in Dan E. Moldea, *The Hoffa Wars* (New York: Charter Books, 1978), 33.

23. Matthew Josephson, *Union House, Union Bar* (New York: Random House, 1956), 230.

24. The principal murder witness was the union's secretary, Jack Rubenstein, who, as Jack Ruby, would assassinate Lee Harvey Oswald in Dallas.

25. Richard Lester, *As Unions Mature: The Evolution of American Unions* (Princeton, NJ: Princeton University Press, 1958).

26. Nelson Lichtenstein, "Introduction to the Illinois Edition," in C. Wright Mills, *The New Men of Power: America's Labor Leaders* (Champaign: University of Illinois Press, 2001; originally published 1948), xx.

27. In 2004, the United Mineworkers had 100,000 members (LM–2 000–063), the Steelworkers 525,000 (LM–2 009–094), and the Autoworkers 654,000 (LM–2 000–149). All figures can be found on the Department of Labor Web site, http://www.dol.gov/esa.

28. That's even if you include rumored candidates—like HERE's John Wilhelm.

29. Daniel Bell, *End of Ideology* (Cambridge, MA: Harvard University Press, 2000; originally published 1960), 223. Meany, as labor's boss, far outlasted Bell's career as a labor journalist. He retired as AFL-CIO boss in 1979.

30. Hoffa's lawyer thought he became more and more criminally deranged. His last day, July 30, 1975, was spent in the parking lot of Machus Red Fox restaurant waiting for Detroit mobster Anthony Giacalone, who is thought to have killed him. Hoffa's murder may have been in retaliation for his having allegedly ordered that the car of Teamsters local president Richard Fitzsimmons be bombed a few weeks earlier. Fitzsimmons was the son of Teamsters general president Frank Fitzsimmons. See Frank Ragano and Selwyn Raab, *Mob Lawyer* (New York: Charles Scribner's Sons, 1994).

31. *Commonwealth v. Pullis* (aka *Cordwainers*), Mayor's Court of Philadelphia (1806), cited in William B. Gould IV, *A Primer on American Labor Law*, 3rd ed. (Cambridge, MA: MIT Press, 1997), 9.

32. In *Commonwealth v. Hunt* (1842), 45 Mass (4 Met.) 111 (1842), cited in Gould, *A Primer on American Labor Law*, 10.

33. John R. Commons, *Trade Unionism and Labor Problems* (New York: Augustus M. Kelley, 1967; originally published 1905), vii.

34. See J. J. Rousseau, *The Discourses and Other Early Political Writings* (Cambridge, England: Cambridge University Press, 1977), 198; Niccolò Machiavelli, *Discourses on Livy*, book 1 (London: Penguin Press, 1970), 153–164; J. J. Rousseau, *Social Contract*, (Harmondsworth: Penguin, 1968), ch. 4; Thomas

Jefferson, "Notes on the State of Virginia," in *The Portable Thomas Jefferson* (New York: Penguin Books, 1975), 165–166.

35. Montgomery, *The Fall of the House of Labor*, 5.

36. American unions would even celebrate this inequality as "the union difference." See AFL-CIO Web site, http://www.aflcio.org/joinaunion/why/union difference/index.cfm. Richard B. Freeman and James L. Medoff, in their chapter on the union wage difference in *What Do Unions Do?* (New York: Basic Books, 1984), never mention one of the most obvious reasons for it: the power of unions to exclude their competitors from the market. Instead of explaining how union monopoly power works—by exclusion—they resort to a tautology: "The smaller the response of employment to wages, the greater is the ability of unions to raise wages without incurring significant losses of employment" (50–51). But this is simply the definition of inelasticity, when what is required is an explanation of why the market is inelastic.

37. "For corruption of this kind," wrote Machiavelli in the *Discourses*, "and ineptitude for a free mode of life is due to the inequality one finds in a city, and, to restore equality it is necessary to take steps which are by no means normal" (Book 1, Discourse 17).

CHAPTER 4: THE FALL OF SAM PARKS

1. *New York Times*, September 8, 1903, 5.

2. Ray Stannard Baker, "The Lone Fighter," *McClure's*, December 1903, p. 196.

3. Ibid.

4. "Pre-hire" agreements that required workers to be union members before being hired were made illegal by the 1947 Taft-Hartley Act. But "post-hire" agreements, which required the worker to join the union within thirty days, remain legal in most states.

5. R. Emmett Murray, *The Lexicon of Labor* (New York: New Press, 1998), 130.

6. Derek Bok, "Comparative Labor Laws," *Harvard Law Review* 94 (1971): 1396–1397.

7. Philip Zausner, *Unvarnished* (New York: Brotherhood Publishers, 1941), 75.

8. Lincoln Steffens, *The Shame of the Cities* (New York: Hill and Wang, 1992; originally published 1902).

9. Scholars who think the media invented the title are probably wrong. It wasn't journalist Harold Seidman's *Labor Czars* (New York: Liveright Publishing Corp., 1938) in the 1930s that constituted the first use of the term. Much earlier, it was Russian Jewish immigrants: "To make it brief," read one petition to Samuel Gompers, "our president assumed the role of a Czar and practiced Czarism throughout the entire proceedings." AFL correspondence, August 6, 1904, cited in Philip S. Foner, *History of the Labor Movement in the United*

States, vol. 3, *The Policies and Practices of the American Federation of Labor, 1900–1909* (New York: International Publishers, 1964), 156.

10. Albeit a comic opera, by Lucius Hosmer.

11. See Luke Grant, "The Walking Delegate," *Outlook,* November 10, 1906, 616.

12. Thomas Jefferson, cited in Richard K. Matthews, *The Radical Politics of Thomas Jefferson* (Lawrence: University Press of Kansas, 1984), 39.

13. Robert A. Christie, *Empire in Wood* (Ithaca, NY: Cornell University Press, 1956), 62–63.

14. Ray Stannard Baker, "The Trust's New Tool—The Labor Boss," *McClure's,* November 1903, 31.

15. John Hutchinson, *The Imperfect Union: A History of Corruption in American Trade Unions* (New York: E. P. Dutton, 1970), 31.

16. Baker, "The Trust's New Tool," Ibid., 31.

17. "The Real Sam Parks: An Interesting Study," *New York Times,* September 6, 1903, 21.

18. Ibid.

19. Hutchinson, *The Imperfect Union,* 35.

20. See below. In the 1905 Chicago Teamsters strike, the trucking contractors, even under enormous pressure from the city's business establishment, decided officially to remain neutral, but their sympathies were with the unionists.

21. Plus those contractors excluded from the cartel. Ray Stannard Baker thought he could explain Parks as a creature of the big new trusts. Parks worked for Chicago-based Fuller Construction. He came to New York when Fuller entered the New York market. From 1896, when Parks began as walking delegate, to 1903, when he went to Sing Sing, Fuller never suffered a major job action from the Ironworkers. District attorney Jerome charged that Parks was actually brought to New York for the purpose of calling strikes on the competition's jobs.

22. "Mr. Poulson Describes Dealings with Parks," *New York Times,* June 18, 1903.

23. Ibid.

24. "Murphy Gets Five Years," *New York Times,* August 1, 1903, 12. See also "The Murphy Defense," *New York Times,* August 1, 1903, 6. Commented the *New York Times,* "A conspiracy of plunder more daring and more shameful than anything lately revealed has been made public, with great circumstantiality of detail."

25. Kenneth Jackson (ed.), *The Encyclopedia of New York City* (New Haven, CT: Yale University Press, 1995), 330.

26. "Parks Is Rearrested on Other Charges," *New York Times,* June 10, 1903, 1.

27. Ibid.

28. "Labor Day Parade a Fizzle," *New York Times,* September 8, 1903, 5.

29. Sidney Fine, *"Without Blare of Trumpets": Walter Drew, the National Erectors Association, and the Open Shop Movement, 1903–1957* (Ann Arbor: University of Michigan Press, 1995), 20.

30. Richard Freeman and James L. Medoff, *What Do Unions Do?* (New York: Basic Books, 1984), 214. See also Derek C. Bok and John T. Dunlop, *Labor and the American Community* (New York: Simon and Schuster, 1970), 69.

31. Royal E. Montgomery, *Industrial Relations in the Chicago Building Trades* (Chicago: University of Chicago Press, 1927), 21.

32. William T. Haber, *Industrial Relations in the Building Industry* (Cambridge, MA: Harvard University Press), 346–349; John R. Commons, "The New York Building Trades," in *Trade Unionism and Labor Problems* (New York: A.M. Kelley, 1967), 65–68.

33. Commons, "The New York Building Trades," 69; Baker, "The Lone Fighter," 38. In fact, as the Brotherhood would show, from the regime of Jake "the Bum" Wellmer to the assassination of District 9's Jimmy Bishop by the Lucchese crime family, it would be only the beginning.

34. Lockwood Committee, Intermediate Report, 1922; Final Report, 1923. See Seidman, *Labor Czars*, 68–93.

35. Cafaro, testimony to Nunn Committee, cited in Stephen Fox, *Blood and Power* (New York: Penguin, 1990), 406.

36. In strictly numerical terms, the growth of the American labor movement continued through World War I, but after the wartime artificial demand for labor slackened, even the strongest movements, like the San Francisco craft unions, gave way to the open shop movement. By 1930, union density was about what it was in 1910.

CHAPTER 5: DYNAMITE ORGANIZING

1. Robert Gottlieb and Irene Wolt, *Thinking Big: The Story of the Los Angeles Times* (New York: G. P. Putnam's Sons, 1977), 85.

2. *Engineering News-Record*, "Poor Health May Save Union Leader from Jail Time," October 20, 2003; U.S. Attorney's Office, District of Columbia, press release, August 7, 2002.

3. My understanding of the connection owes much to Sidney Fine, *"Without Blare of Trumpets": Walter Drew, the National Erectors Association, and the Open Shop Movement, 1903–1957* (Ann Arbor: University of Michigan Press, 1995).

4. Michael Kazin, *Barons of Labor* (Urbana: University of Illinois Press, 1989), 205.

5. Facsimile front page for September 2, 1911, in W. W. Robinson, *Bombs and Bribery* (Los Angeles: Dawson's Book Shop, 1969).

6. Cited in Ray Ginger, *Eugene V. Debs: A Biography* (New York: Collier, 1962), 323.

7. Cited in Louis Adamic, *Dynamite: The Story of Class Violence in America* (New York: Viking Press, 1931), 234.

8. Robert Gottlieb and Irene Wolt, *Thinking Big* (New York: G. P. Putnam's Sons, 1977), 23.

9. Fine, *"Without Blare of Trumpets,"* 94.

10. Kazin, *Barons of Labor*, 205.

11. See Gottlieb and Wolt, *Thinking Big*, 86.

12. Cited in Philip S. Foner, *History of the Labor Movement in the United States*, vol. 5, *The AFL in the Progressive Era, 1910–1915* (New York: International Publishers, 1980), 30.

13. Adamic, *Dynamite*, ch. 6. Significantly for Adamic's thesis of dynamite as a class weapon, there is no mention of Parks's coercive use for corrupt purposes. Even Capone's use is assimilated into the class struggle model.

14. It was his last desperate battle. In December 1903, Parks deployed the "wrecking crew" to complement his entertainment committee. The wreckers were irregular troops in Parks's struggle with the Building Trades Employers Association, a newly organized militant contractors group. It tried to break Parks's hold on the ironworkers by recognizing a competing local. Two buildings where the competing union members worked were blown up. To stop assaults by Parks's wrecking crew, New York City employers hired 200 security guards. A spokesman for the building trades owners claimed that Parks planned to blow up more steel structures and murder his rivals. Parks wound up convicted on other charges and died soon afterward. But the terror tactics allegedly attempted against New York contractors would be a model for the campaign actually carried out all across the country by the international union against the world's biggest corporation—the billion-dollar U.S. Steel.

15. Cited in Gottlieb and Wolt, *Thinking Big*, 94.

16. Whatever Buchanan was for, Parks was against. A business agent from Parks's Local 2 recalled that they had not given the agreement "one minute's consideration." Insisted Parks: "It should be thrown in the garbage." Fine, *"Without Blare of Trumpets,"* 23.

17. Fine, *"Without Blare of Trumpets,"* 29.

18. Wall Street Journal, *A History of Organized Felony and Folly* (New York: Wall Street Journal, 1923), 20–21.

19. Fine, *"Without Blare of Trumpets,"* 98–99.

20. Grace Heilman Stimson, *Rise of the Labor Movement in Los Angeles* (Berkeley: University of California Press, 1955), 385.

21. Ibid., 384.

22. Tveitmoe was appointed by Mayor Eugene Schmitz from the musicians union. It wasn't until after Schmitz was indicted that the building trades took over the Union Labor Party. Initially, McCarthy, a top official in the Democratic administration of James Phelan, was opposed to the party's running candidates. On Tveitmoe, see Kazin, *Barons of Labor*, and especially Adamic, *Dynamite*.

23. Stimson, *Rise of the Labor Movement in Los Angeles*, 334–335.

24. Fine, *"Without Blare of Trumpets,"* 97. McManigal also reported that John Mc-Namara said, "That wild San Francisco bunch did this."

25. Fine, *"Without Blare of Trumpets,"* 98. McNamara's other presents—the Baker Iron Works, the *Times* auxiliary plant, the Alexandria Hotel, and the L.A. Hall of Records—couldn't be delivered because of tactical problems. Gompers blamed the L.A. bombings on conspirators who sought to undermine the unions. He also claimed that the bosses were blowing up their own factories and bridges to make the labor movement look bad. (And presumably city officials blew up their own city halls.) Even on its face, though, the accusation made no sense. The bombings of non-union contractors would frequently be followed by signed contracts. Why didn't the non-union contractors simply sign the contract offered by the Ironworkers, instead of blowing up their projects first? It was certainly an unorthodox negotiating tactic.

26. Fine, *"Without Blare of Trumpets,"* 110.

27. Adamic, *Dynamite*, 236.

28. Ibid., 237.

29. Fine, *"Without Blare of Trumpets,"* 127.

30. Kazin, *Barons of Labor*, 207.

31. A trade union critic of the ULP regime wrote, "A 'Union Labor' Government which is worse than any other government is a crime against union hopes." Kazin, *Barons of Labor*, 137. The best source on the ULP regime is Walton Bean, *Boss Ruef's San Francisco: The Story of the Union Labor Party* (Berkeley: University of California Press, 1952).

32. Fine, *"Without Blare of Trumpets,"* 129.

33. Seidman, *Labor Czars*, 22.

34. Foner, *History of the Labor Movement in the United States*, vol. 5, 19.

35. W. W. Robinson, *Bombs and Bribery: The Story of the McNamara and Darrow Trials Following the Dynamiting in 1910 of the Los Angeles Times Building* (Los Angeles: Dawson's Book Shop, 1969).

36. Fine, *"Without Blare of Trumpets,"* 110.

37. Ibid., 82.

38. Foner, *History of the Labor Movement in the United States*, vol. 5, 27.

39. Stimson, *Rise of the Labor Movement in Los Angeles*, 418.

40. Foner, *History of the Labor Movement in the United States*, vol. 5, 27.

41. William J. Burns, *The Masked Man* (New York: George H. Doran Co., 1913).

42. Karl Marx and Frederick Engels, *The Communist Manifesto* (London: Verso, 1998; originally published 1848), 61.

43. Foner, *History of the Labor Movement in the United States*, vol. 5, 29.

44. The chief objective of the Militia was set forth in section 3 of its constitution and charter laws: "This shall be henceforth the proper dominant note of the Militia of Christ: to cultivate the aspirations of the workers to better their conditions through organization in conservative trade-unions, through collective

bargaining and trade agreements, conciliation and arbitration of industrial disputes."

45. The other main bombers, Ortie McManigal and George E. Davis, were former ironworkers.

46. See Fine, *"Without Blare of Trumpets,"* ch. 4.

47. Ibid., 92–93.

48. Ibid., 94.

49. Ibid., 88–89. Sometimes, though, the threat had to be carried out before a company would sign. Pan American Bridge refused to sign a closed shop contract for a job in Peoria. Its plant in New Castle, Indiana, was dynamited. After Pan American capitulated, officials were told that they wouldn't need to post guards at their plants anymore.

50. Wall Street Journal, *A History of Organized Felony and Folly*, 20.

51. Fine, *"Without Blare of Trumpets,"* 93.

52. Ibid., 92.

53. Ibid.

54. See *New York Times,* October 2, 15, 17, 18, and 23, 1925. Also Fine, *"Without Blare of Trumpets,"* 313.

55. Adamic, *Dynamite*, 202.

56. Kazin, *Barons of Labor*, 187.

57. Ibid., 178.

58. *Organized Labor*, December 8, 1906, and March 10, 1900, cited in Alexander Saxton, *The Indispensable Enemy* (Berkeley: University of California Press, 1975), 244, 247.

59. Kazin, *Barons of Labor*, 166.

60. American Federation of Labor, *Some Reasons for Chinese Exclusion: Meat vs. Rice: American Manhood Against Asiatic Coolieism; Which Shall Survive* (Washington, DC, 1901). In a 1908 reissue, the title page bears the names of Gompers and Herman Guttstadt. See Saxton, *The Indispensable Enemy*, 275.

61. Howard Zinn, *A People's History of the United States* (New York: Harper Perennial, 1995), 341–346.

62. U.S. Senate Committee on Education and Labor, Report of the Committee of the Senate on the Relation Between Labor and Capital, 4 vols. (Washington, DC: Government Printing Office, 1885), vol. 1, 340, cited in David Brian Robertson, *Capital, Labor, and State* (Lanham, MD: Rowman & Littlefield, 2000), 65.

CHAPTER 6: SOLIDARITY FOR SALE, CHICAGO, 1905

1. For a current management perspective on labor's continuing jurisdictional wars, see Steven D. Atkinson, "Jurisdictional Wars Continue," http://www.aalrr.com/CM/AtkinsonsAnswers/AtkinsonsAnswers222.asp.

2. David Montgomery, *The Fall of the House of Labor* (New York: Cambridge University Press, 1989), 312–313.

3. "Cost and Scope of the Big Strike," *Chicago Tribune*, July 22, 1905, 2.

4. See Jeffrey B. Perry (ed.), *A Hubert Harrison Reader* (Middletown, CT: Wesleyan University Press, 2000), 97. See also Edward Robb Ellis, *Echoes of Distant Thunder: Life in the United States, 1914–1918* (New York: Coward, McCann, and Geoghegan, 1975), 416. Another major race riot that grew out of an AFL strike was the 1919 meatpacking strike, which also took place in Chicago. On East St. Louis, see Elliott M. Rudwick, *Race Riot at East St. Louis* (Carbondale: Southern Illinois University Press, 1964).

5. Irish gangs in the Back of the Yards neighborhood kept blacks from going to work in the meatpacking district. Federal troops were called in to escort blacks past striking white workers. A particularly strong documentary movie, *The Killing Floor* (1984), helps make sense of the tangle of racial and labor conflicts.

6. John R. Commons et al., *History of Labor in the United States* (New York: A. M. Kelley, 1966), vol. 4, 628. As immediate memories of the strike dimmed further, the Chicago action grew to heroic proportions. Until recently, when powerfully challenged in David Witwer's doctoral dissertation ("Corruption and Reform in the Teamsters Union, 1898 to 1991," Ph.D. diss., Brown University, 1994), it has been seen almost universally by labor historians as one of the AFL's noblest chapters. As noted, Montgomery speaks of Chicago 1905 in the same breath as the 1905 St. Petersburg strike that toppled the czarist autocracy in Russia. Why? Certainly not because of the consequences—admittedly, they were disastrous—but because it was a moral victory, one that showed that our AFL was capable of solidarity too. Philip S. Foner treats the Chicago strike as a straightforward labor vs. capital struggle. Of course, in a real sense it was: many members viewed it that way. But the presence of corrupt motives and racial antagonism can't simply be ignored. Philip S. Foner, *History of the Labor Movement in the United States*, vol. 3, *The Policies and the Practices of the American Federation of Labor, 1900–1909* (New York: International Publishers, 1964), 310–311. Foner insists, against the preponderance of evidence, that the strikebreakers were white (244).

7. John R. Commons, "The New York Building Trades," in *Trade Unionism and Labor Problems*, edited by John R. Commons (New York: Augustus M. Kelley, 1967), 66–69.

8. John R. Commons, in *Quarterly Journal of Economics*, May 1905. See the postscript that follows the reprint of the essay in *Trade Unionism and Labor Problems*, 64.

9. John R. Commons, "The Teamsters of Chicago," in *Trade Unionism and Labor Problems*, 64.

10. Ibid., 53.

11. Arthur S. Henning, "Cornelius P. Shea, the Teamster 'Boss' of Chicago," *Harper's Weekly*, June 17, 1905, 862–863.

12. Ibid.
13. Witwer, "Corruption and Reform in the Teamsters Union," 18.
14. Ray Stannard Baker, "Capital and Labor Hunt Together," *McClure's* 21, 5 (September 1903).
15. Commons, "The Teamsters of Chicago," 47–53.
16. Witwer, "Corruption and Reform in the Teamsters Union," 47–48.
17. See Commons, "The Teamsters of Chicago," 58.
18. Witwer, "Corruption and Reform in the Teamsters Union," 57, citing minutes of IBT convention.
19. Ibid., 58.
20. *Chicago Tribune*, April 24, 1905, 1. When the UGW pulled out, it left Shea without a rationale. Quickly, he devised one. He'd been lobbied hard, he pointed out, by the head of the Chicago Federation of Labor, Charles Dold. But Dold had little public credibility. Although they'd had a violent falling out, Dold had gotten the top CFL job through Martin "Skinny" Madden, boss of the Chicago Building Trades. Going back to the 1890s, Madden was notorious as the pioneer of the fake sympathy strike. Later he specialized in selling strike insurance against sympathy strikes. Madden's most notorious shakedown took place during the construction of the twenty-one-story Insurance Exchange Building, which is what finally got him indicted in 1909. Madden was charged with demanding $20,000 for strike insurance. The contractors came up with only $10,000, however, so work stopped at the tenth floor. Skinny's man in the Chicago Federation of Labor is not likely to have distinguished closely between genuine and fake sympathy.
21. *Chicago Tribune*, May 5, 1905, 2.
22. William Z. Foster, "The Great Steel Strike and Its Lessons," cited in Perry (ed.), *A Hubert Harrison Reader*, 83.
23. John Landesco, *Organized Crime in Chicago*, part 3 of the Illinois Crime Survey, 1929 (Midway Reprint; Chicago: University of Chicago Press, 1968), 141–142.
24. Ibid.
25. Herbert Asbury, *Gem of the Prairie* (New York: Alfred A. Knopf, 1930), 341.
26. *Chicago Tribune*, January 13, 1929, 16.

CHAPTER 7: TOTALLY MOBBED UP: DAILY LIFE IN THE LABORERS UNION

1. "I have always considered the Genovese Family to be the most powerful LCN [La Cosa Nostra] family in the United States," says Alphonse "Little Al" D'Arco, ex-underboss of the Lucchese family, the government's highest-ranking LCN informant. *U.S. v. Mason Tenders District Council of Greater New York*, Declaration of Alphonse D'Arco, 94 Civ. 6487 (RWS), 5. The others in the running were the Gambino, Columbo, Lucchese, and Chicago families.

2. See the Web site of the Mason Tenders District Council of Greater New York and Long Island, http://www.masontenders.org/lecet/gnylecet.htm.

3. *Daily News*, August 29, 1999, quoting Roger Madon, former attorney for Laborers International Union of North America Local 95, now dissolved.

4. All mob dialogue quoted here comes from exhibits from *U.S. v. Mason Tenders*.

5. In re Mason Tenders District Council and Trust Funds, (*N.S.A. et al v. Mason Tenders et al* 1:94-CV 06487 RWS), Statement of Frank Faro Lupo, August 9–11, 1994, 140 (hereafter "Lupo deposition").

6. In connection with the Diplomat Hotel (see chapter 1).

7. Just in 2004 in New York City, the top official of the Carpenters was convicted of taking bribes from the son-in-law of the DeCavalcante crime family; the Genoveses were charged with controlling the drywall unions; the Luccheses were indicted in connection with Laborers Local 66, the Bricklayers, and the Blasters, Miners, and Drill Runners (BMDRU); and the Genoveses and the Gambinos were charged in connection with Laborers Local 79, the Elevator Constructors, and the Operating Engineers.

8. President's Commission on Organized Crime, *The Edge: Organized Crime, Business, and Labor Unions* (Washington, DC: Government Printing Office, 1985).

9. These are two cases. *U.S.A. v. International Brotherhood of Teamsters* (No. 88. Civ. 4486); and U.S. District Court, Northern District of Illinois Eastern Division, *U.S. v. LIUNA*, Draft Complaint (1993).

10. Kenneth C. Crowe, *Collision* (New York: Charles Scribner's Sons, 1993), Appendix D, "Teamsters Charged with Ties to Organized Crime."

11. The DeCavalcantes think they're the model for HBO's *The Sopranos*. "Hey, what's this fucking thing, '*Sopranos*'? What the fuck are they . . . is that supposed to be us?" asked Joseph "Tin Ear" Sclafani. Replied soldier Anthony Rotondo, "You are in there, they mentioned your name in there." Rotondo went on to praise the acting and the verisimilitude in *The Sopranos*. See Jerry Capeci, *Gangland*, January 6, 2000. http://www.ganglandnew.com/co/vmn289.htm.

12. Robert Gearty and Tracy Connor, "Mob Boss Pleads to Killer Deal: Hit S.I. Man for Gotti," *Daily News*, September 6, 2003, 3.

13. As early as the 1870s, in Palermo, prosecutors indicted mafiosi for running what later would be called "a racket" in the grain milling business. Palermo mill owners and the carters who worked for the millers both paid a *pizzu*, or tribute, to the Mafia for protection. Prosecutors described a kind of "guild" called the *Mugnai della posa* (dues-paying millers). The organization aimed to regulate prices and keep competition from getting out of hand. What made it different from an ordinary—and legal—guild was the *pizzu* that millers paid to the Mafia, who "protected" the organization. In return, those workers whom the Mafia allowed to join got job security and a piecework wage. Carters were also compelled to pay the *pizzu*. The Mafia tied the carter's or-

ganization and the millers together: the millers agreed to accept grain only from carters who were a part of the association, and the carters worked only for millers who were part of the association. The Mafia-controlled grain business in Salerno uncannily resembles the Outfit-run gravel business in Chicago that grew up fifty years later in the construction industry. See James Fentress, *Rebels and Mafiosi* (Ithaca, NY: Cornell University Press, 2000), 163–166.

14. Humbert S. Nelli, *The Italians in Chicago, 1880–1930* (New York: Oxford University Press, 1970), ch. 3.

15. Curt Johnson, *The Wicked City: Chicago from Kenna to Capone* (New York: Da Capo Press, 1998), 87.

16. Nelli, *The Italians in Chicago*, 79–80, 149–150; Ovid Demaris, *Captive City* (New York: L. Stuart, 1969), 217–219.

17. John Landesco, *Organized Crime in Chicago,* part 3 of the Illinois Crime Survey (Chicago: University of Chicago Press, 1968).

18. Hod carriers mix cement for bricklayers and carry it to where bricklayers lay the bricks. Thus the term "mason tenders."

19. "Hearing Officer Affirms Trusteeship over Laborers Union in Chicago," *BNA Daily Labor Reporter*, March 4, 2004, A–14.

20. In his successful effort to impose a trusteeship on Local 2, general executive board attorney Robert Luskin charged in a complaint that "at least since 1985 Local 2 has been corrupted by the influence of organized crime." Office of the General Executive Board Attorney, Complaint for Trusteeship, April 23, 1999, http://www.ipsn.org/trusteeshipcomplaint.htm.

21. Michael Powell, "The Saga of Arthur Coia and His Union Is Straight Out of 'The Godfather,'" *Washington Post*, October 3, 1999.

22. Ron Fino to U.S. Attorney Patrick J. Fitzgerald, February 17, 2004, http://www.laborers.com/Fino_Fitz_2–17–04.htm.

23. U.S. District Court of the Northern District of Illinois, Eastern Division, *U.S. v. LIUNA*, Draft Complaint, November 4, 1994. (See chapter 1.)

24. U.S. Department of Justice, U.S. Attorney District of Massachusetts, Re: Arthur A. Coia Criminal No–00, January 27, 2000.

25. Diego Gambetta, *The Sicilian Mafia: The Business of Private Protection* (Cambridge, MA: Harvard University Press, 1993), 17.

26. Ed Barnes and Bob Windrem, "Six Ways to Take Over a Union," *Mother Jones*, August 1980.

27. Carl Sifakis, *The Mafia Encyclopedia*, 2nd ed. (New York: Checkmark Books, 1999), 141.

28. Lupo deposition, August 9–11, 1994, 46.

29. *U.S. v. Mason Tenders*, 22.

30. Ibid., 22–23.

31. The most recent book-length look at union corruption was written in 1970—

The Imperfect Union: A History of Corruption in American Trade Unions (New York: E. P. Dutton, 1970), by John Hutchinson, a business school professor at UCLA. The Mafia isn't mentioned. New York University law professor James B. Jacobs has provided the most insightful analysis so far, in *The Final Report of the New York State Organized Crime Task Force* (New York: New York University Press, 1990). No book conveys the scope of Mafia control better than Jacobs's *Gotham Unbound* (New York: New York University Press, 1999).

32. *Investigations Officer v. Barbaro*, 94 Civ. 6487 (RWS).

33. *U.S. v. Daly*, 842 F.2d 1380 (2d Cir. 1988), and *U.S. v. Gallo*, 671 F.Supp. 124 (EDNY) 1987.

34. In the case of the New York City concrete industry, where the mob controls the entire industry and can dictate what firms can bid on a project and how much, the contractors pay a 1 or 2 percent fee to the mob's "construction panel."

35. *U.S. v. Mason Tenders*, Government's Memorandum of Law in Support of Its Request for Permanent Injunctive Relief, No. 118, 17–18.

36. See Eric Hobsbawm, *Primitive Rebels* (New York: W. W. Norton, 1965), ch. 3.

37. See Declaration, Ron Fino (94 Civ. 6487) (RWS).

38. Lupo deposition, August 9–11, 1994, 39.

39. Kenneth C. Crowe, "Union Fund Showers Money on Dubious Real Estate Deals," *Newsday*, July 21, 1991, 69.

40. Lupo deposition, 66.

41. Davis was charged with racketeering; see *U.S. v. Mason Tenders*, 39–40.

42. Lupo deposition, 37.

43. Ibid., 36.

44. Ibid., 58–59.

45. Ibid., 60.

46. *Mason Tenders District Council Pension Fund et al. v. James Messera et al.*, Complaint, 95 Civ. 9341. See Racketeering Acts 148 and 149.

47. Lupo deposition, 133–135.

48. Fino to U.S. Attorney Patrick J. Fitzgerald, February 17, 2004.

49. See, for example, Jerry Seper, "Probe of DNC Union Pal Was Killed," *Washington Times*, August 7, 1997, and Rowan Scarborough, "Soft Deal for Union Termed a Success," *Washington Times*, July 25, 1996. Coia also availed himself of the help of White House counselor Harold Ickes, who later served as Hillary Clinton's Washington campaign manager in her 2000 Senate run in New York. In the critical late 1994 period, when the government seemed about to take over LIUNA, it was Ickes who served as the crucial intermediary between Coia and the White House. And appropriately so, since Ickes's law practice was weighted with several of the most notorious mob unions in America—including work for the New York–New Jersey regional Laborers' boss Sam Caivano, who'd been installed with the approval of the Genovese crime family.

50. Interview, Robert Luskin, July 2003.
51. Mike Stanton and John E. Mulligan, "Coia Agrees to Plead Guilty to Tax Fraud," *Providence Journal*, January 28, 2000.
52. Telephone interview, Ron Fino, April 3, 2005.
53. Ron Fino to Patrick J. Fitzgerald, February 17, 2004, http://www.laborers.org/Fino_Fitz_2–17–04.htm.
54. Ibid., and Statement, July 24, 1996, House of Representatives, Committee on the Judiciary.
55. Brian Lockett, "Mason Tenders in New York City Holds First Officers' Vote in Trusteeship," Bureau of National Affairs, December 15, 1997.
56. Juan Gonzalez, "Labor Movement Reborn, and Strong," *Daily News*, July 2, 1998. David Firestone, "Laborers Doing the Heavy Lifting for Unions," *New York Times*, July 8, 1998.
57. Ello was also the grandson of the Mason Tenders' founder.
58. Ello was one of the officials who took free gifts from secretary-treasurer Danny Kearney. See footnote 61.
59. Employers' trustee Paul O'Brien, who joined the board in 1991, was never charged.
60. LIUNA trustee Steve Hammond had his wife placed in a no-show job in the Mason Tenders' benefit office. When Louise Furio complained to court-appointed monitor Lawrence B. Pedowitz, he explained that Hammond's wife was "lonely" in Washington, D.C. (Pedowitz, of Wachtel, Lipton, later served as Martha Stewart's lawyer.)
61. Tom Robbins, "Laborers Looted," *Village Voice*, November 3, 2004. See also Report of Interview with Daniel F. Kearney, "Local 79 Misapplication of Funds," International Auditor John R. Billi, April 1, 2003, and April 2, 2003, http://www.thelaborers.net/LOCALS/LU79/kearney_confession.htm.
62. See Steve Hammond to David Elbaor, "Report and Recommendation," September 7, 1995, memorandum in author's possession. "For this Local, I would recommend Mike Pagano as the Business Manager. Although Mike has had his problems with his involvement in the District Council and implications by the U.S. Attorney, I find Mike to be one of the most knowledgeable people in the council" (p. 9). In 1997, Hammond was appointed Arthur Coia's special assistant.
63. Lawrence Giardina, "Notes on Michael Pagano, Jr." unpublished ms. Mike Pagano Sr. had also been an officer in Local 104 as well as a LIUNA international representative. Giardina, head of Local 23, had a genealogy similar to Pagano's.
64. In Albany, Pagano also found a lot of familiar faces—including Sal Lanza, his new boss at the funds. Lanza was the Genovese associate who had disrespected James Messera at Gaspar's funeral. He could get away with it, because he was protected by the top uptown Genovese boss, Liborio "Barney" Belommo. Like

Pagano, Lanza needed a job after being banned for life from the Mason Tenders. When Lanza was finally removed as Albany funds boss under government pressure, his colleagues awarded him a $250,000 golden parachute.

65. FEC filings. See FEC C00220566, http://query.nictusa.com/cqi=bin/dcder/forms/F.E.C.Image.20635001767, (1–82).

66. U.S. Attorney's Office, Eastern District of New York, press release, September 15, 2004.

CHAPTER 8: DC 37: A PROGRESSIVE KLEPTOCRACY

1. Bernard Bellush Papers, Series VII, Box 4, Folder 143, Robert F. Wagner Labor Archives, New York University.

2. "Average increases in compensation for municipal employees should be substantially below the expected rate of inflation," recommended Ray Horton, president of the influential Citizen's Budget Commission, in 1993. Charles Brecher and Raymond D. Horton, with Robert A. Cropf and Dean Michael Mead, *Power Failure* (New York: Oxford University Press, 1993), 261. The commission was founded in 1932 by J. P. Morgan, Jr. and John D. Rockefeller II.

3. Budget experts say that each 1 percent of pay increase costs taxpayers $600 million. If the contract had merely compensated for yearly increases in the cost of living in New York City—estimated at 4 percent—that would have cost $2.4 billion a year.

4. Bellush Papers, Box 4, Folder 159; interview, September 16, 1981.

5. Steven Greenhouse, "Voting System at City Union Is Tainted, Leaders Say," *New York Times*, November 28, 1998.

6. Robert Fitch, "Union for Sale," *Village Voice*, September 2–8, 1998.

7. Commer was guilty of sending out a postcard to the members announcing an upcoming election without the approval of his executive board. Commer agreed to pay back the costs of the mailing, and he did so, but officials claimed that he didn't. In 2004, a member of the executive board admitted that he had received Commer's check but simply didn't cash it.

8. I attended the convention.

9. H. Ron Davidson, "Harry Van Arsdale and the New York Fiscal Crisis," unpublished ms., August 1999, 13, citing *New York Times*, November 26, 1975.

10. Who knew what evil lurked in the minds of analytic philosophers? See Steve Fraser and Josh Freeman, eds., *Audacious Democracy* (Boston: Houghton Mifflin, 1997), 58.

11. Joe Calderone, "Beleaguered Labor Leader Quits HIP Post," *Daily News*, August 19, 1999, 36.

12. James Farmer, *Lay Bare the Heart* (New York: Arbor House, 1985), 180.

13. Robin Givhan, "A Failure in Flair: Teachers' Union Head Dressed by the Rules,"

Washington Post, January 24, 2003, C1; Allan Lengel and Neely Tucker, "Ex-Chauffeur Aids Union Probe," *Washington Post*, February 6, 2003, B1.

14. Tom Robbins, "The Mob Meets the Detectives," *Village Voice*, March 26, 2001.

15. Joe Mozingo, "Insurer Landed Schools Contract After Tornillo, Exec Took Trip," *Miami Herald*, August 24, 2003.

16. Public sector unions, with about 36 percent of the 7.25 million members, have fallen back to levels not seen in decades.

17. Robert Fitch, "The Big Fix: Corruption in DC37, Part Two: How the Union's Bosses Rule by Fraud and Intimidation," *Village Voice*, September 15–26, 1999.

18. Quote in Carl Biers, "Suspect Referendum in AFSCME DC 37, NYC," *Union Democracy Review*, April 1996, 6.

19. *The People of New York v. Al Diop and Martin Lubin*, No. 4053/99. Diop's defense attorney tried to argue that there'd been no ballot stuffing on the grounds that the vote totals in the local weren't all that different from 1991 to 1996. True, conceded assistant district attorney Jane Tully, but the membership had fallen from 38,000 to 23,000.

20. In 1997, shortly after the incumbent president of Local 375 had been declared the upset loser and the ballots suddenly disappeared from DC 37's locked security office, the declared winner petitioned federal court.

21. The source for this section is the trial record (*People v. Diop*).

22. Kroll Associates, "The Ratification Vote on the 1995 Economic Agreement: A Report to the General Counsel of AFSCME," September 30, 1999, 27.

23. Yes, there's the old iron law of oligarchy, Robert Michels's explanation of European trade union elitism. But Michels wasn't trying to explain labor racketeering. Massive vote fraud, organized crime domination, and stealing hundreds of millions simply hasn't been characteristic of European unions.

24. Interview, Mark Rosenthal.

25. *People v. Diop*, 540.

26. Carl Sifakis, *The Mafia Encyclopedia*, 2nd ed. (New York: Checkmark Books, 1999), 79–80. Vinnie Parisi, before he became boss of the blue collar division, drove Victor Gotbaum, who was DC 37's executive director before Hill. Interview, Sara Gotbaum, 1999.

27. Jesse Drucker, "Union Boss Hughes' Funny Money Mansion?" *New York Observer*, March 2, 1998.

28. Charles Lewis, "Investigative Report," Center for Public Integrity, October 24, 2000.

29. Dissident presidents and staffers told me about it in 1996.

30. Bellush Papers, Diop file.

31. Hill claimed he did respond. The petitioners disputed his claim. See Fitch, "Union for Sale."

32. See *The People of the State of New York v. Corrado Family Affair, Inc.*, Felony Complaint Docket No. 5387/2000.

33. District Attorney, New York County, press release, November 28, 1998; Steven Greenhouse, "For Unions, A Holiday Turkey Is Starting to Look Like an Albatross," *New York Times,* November 22, 1998.
34. District Attorney, New York County, press release, March 24, 1999.
35. See particularly the three *Daily News* stories by Tom Robbins, December 6, 7, and 9, 1998.
36. Interviews with Local 983 members; also Tom Robbins, "Mob Job," *Daily News,* December 6, 1998, 1.
37. Interview, longtime Local 983 staffer, who wishes to remain anonymous, September 1999.
38. Robert Fitch, "The Big Fix," *Village Voice,* September 15–21, 1999.
39. Robert Fitch, "Union Jacked: How DC 37 Became America's Most Indicted Union," *Village Voice,* August 25–31, 1999. See also Richard Steier, "Lessons from DC 37's Past," *Chief Leader,* August 25, 2000, and *Daily News,* June 1, 2001.
40. The presidency of DC 37 should not be confused with the executive directorship. DC 37's president draws a $50,000-a-year salary but, unlike the executive director, has no managerial responsibilities or executive authority.
41. Robbins, "Mob Job."
42. Ibid. The date of Cutolo's expulsion is from Kenneth C. Crowe, *Collision* (New York: Charles Scribner's Sons, 1993), 281. Cutolo remained a trade union leader until his dying day. Law enforcement authorities speculate that his 1999 disappearance was actually a murder carried out by another faction of the Colombo crime family. At the time of his disappearance, Cutolo was president of Local 400 of the Production Workers Union, which represented municipal workers.
43. A copy of the picture appeared in *The Chief Leader* in September 2000.
44. Interview, Charles Ensley, president of Local 371, August 1999. Ensley supported Zurlo and helped pass out the anti-Morelli leaflets.
45. Fitch, "Union Jacked."
46. Ibid. See also Maureen Fan and Tom Robbins, "Union Big Broke Bread with Alleged Mobster," *Daily News,* December 17, 1998.
47. Gotbaum insists that DiNardo contacted him for the meeting. "I didn't even know the fucking guy," he said. See Fitch, "Union Jacked."
48. Interviews with Local 983 members and officers.
49. Fitch, "Union for Sale."
50. Ibid.
51. Ibid.
52. Mark Meier, *City Unions* (New Brunswick, NJ: Rutgers University Press, 1987).
53. Ibid., 111.
54. Jack Schierenbeck, unpublished UFT study.
55. Community Service Society, "Who Needs a Living Wage," CSS Data Brief, April 1, 2002.
56. U.S. Department of Labor, Bureau of Labor Statistics, New York–Northern

New Jersey, Long Island NY-NJ-CT-PA, National Compensation Survey—April 2004, Bulletin 3125, December 2004.

57. Interview, Donna Silberberg, DC 37 communications director, June 7, 2005.

58. Ford Fessenden and Josh Barbanel, "Rise of the Six-Figure Teacher," *New York Times*, May 15, 2005.

59. Frank Lombardi, "Rudy Praises Embattled Union Big," *Daily News*, February 5, 1998.

60. Juan Gonzalez, "A Hard Look at Union Chiefs Who Got on Rudy Bandwagon," *Daily News*, December 8, 1998, 6. Besides DeCanio's $7,500, Diop kicked in $6,000, Hughes $5,500, and the District Council $5,000. See New York City Campaign Finance Board Web site, http://nyccfb.info/public_disclosure/index.htm.

61. Gonzalez, "A Hard Look at Union Chiefs."

62. *New York Times*, January 21, 2000. The leaked AFSCME report showed that there were thirty-five pending claims for reimbursement from the union's insurance company for embezzlement by officials within the previous year.

63. AFSCME International Executive Board Report, Summary of Bonding Claim Activity, October 1, 1999–November 22, 1999, Center for Public Integrity; see also Steven Greenhouse, "Cloud of Corruption," *New York Times*, January 21, 2000, 1.

CHAPTER 9: UNITE'S GARMENT GULAG

1. UNITE stands for Union of Needletrades, Industrial, and Textile Employees, and HERE stands for Hotel Employees and Restaurant Employees International Union.

2. Lester Velie, *Desperate Bargain* (New York: Reader's Digest Press, 1977); James Neff, *Mobbed Up* (New York: Dell, 1989); Jonathan Kwitny, *Vicious Circles* (New York: W. W. Norton, 1979).

3. John Dewey, *David Dubinsky* (New York: Inter-allied Publications, 1951).

4. Matthew Josephson, *Sidney Hillman: Statesman of American Labor* (Garden City, NY: Doubleday, 1952).

5. Irving Howe, *World of Our Fathers* (New York: Harcourt Brace Jovanovich, 1976).

6. A. H. Raskin, "Thug Hurls Acid on Labor Writer; Sight Imperiled," *New York Times*, April 6, 1956, 1.

7. Peter Maas, *The Valachi Papers* (New York: Bantam, 1968), 174–178.

8. David Dubinsky and A. H. Raskin, *David Dubinsky: A Life with Labor* (New York: Simon and Schuster, 1977), 153–154.

9. Howe, *World of Our Fathers*, 355.

10. Niebuhr was also wise enough to recognize the limitations of the myth-centered approach: "I think there ought to be a club," he wrote, "in which preach-

ers and journalists could come together and have the sentimentalism of the one matched with the cynicism of the other. That ought to bring them pretty close to the truth."

11. U.S. Department of Labor, "U.S. Department of Labor Compliance Survey Finds More Than Half of New York City Garment Shops in Violation of Labor Laws," press release 97–369, October 16, 1997.

12. William Bastone, "Feds Finger Labor Boss," *Village Voice*, October 20, 1998.

13. *U.S. v. The Premises Known and Described as the Office of Local 23–25 Unite*, Affidavit in Support of Search Warrant, April 3, 1997, James Vanderberg, Special Agent, Department of Labor, Office of Labor Racketeering, 22 (hereafter "Vanderberg affidavit").

14. See, for example, Annelise Orleck, *Common Sense and a Little Fire: Women and Working Class Politics in the United States, 1900–1965* (Chapel Hill: University of North Carolina Press, 1995).

15. Philip Foner, *History of the Labor Movement in the United States*, vol. 5, *The AFL in the Progressive Era (1910–1915)* (New York: International Publishers, 1980), 232.

16. Vanderberg affidavit, 24.

17. Ibid., 16.

18. Sharon Edelson and Arthur Friedman, "Probe into Mob Might Also Aim at Apparel Union," *Women's Wear Daily*, April 30, 1998, 1.

19. Bastone, "Feds Finger Labor Boss," 24.

20. *U.S. v. Joseph DeFede et al.*, 98 Cr. 373.

21. Robert Fitch, "The Union from Hell: How It Fails to Protect Garment Workers," *Village Voice*, January 20, 1998.

22. Ibid.

23. Testimony, U.S. House of Representatives, Committee on Education and the Workforce, The American Worker at a Crossroads Project, Confidential Witness, Government Worker #1, March 31, 1998.

24. James B. Jacobs, *Gotham Unbound* (New York: New York University Press, 1999), 24.

25. Fitch, "The Union from Hell."

26. Steven Greenhouse, "Lawsuit Accuses Fashion House of Running Sweatshops," *New York Times*, June 8, 2000.

27. David Von Drehle, *Triangle: The Fire That Changed America* (New York: Grove Press, 2003), 57–58.

28. Foner, *History of the Labor Movement in the United States*, vol. 5, ch. 12.

29. U.S. Department of Labor, Wage and Hour Division, *2001 San Francisco Garment Compliance Survey*, March 2002, http://www.dol.gov/opa/media/press/opa/SanFrancisco_survey.htm.

30. Dubinsky's autobiography mentions the role played by ILG-supported officials Irving Brown and Jay Lovestone. See Dubinsky and Raskin, *David Dubin-*

sky: A Life with Labor. Much more depth and dramatic detail are provided by Ted Morgan's *A Covert Life* (New York: Random House, 1999).

31. Marick F. Masters, *Unions at the Crossroads* (Westport, CT: Quorum Books, 1997), 78, Table 4.3.

32. Department of Labor, Form LM–2, Labor Organization Report, 000–381, 2001; see Schedule 9. Mazur earned $498,554 in salary and $21,775 in expenses, for a total of $520,329. The filing has a handwritten entry: "includes separation pay."

33. *The "I Hate Kathie Lee Gifford" Book*, by Gary Blake and Robert W. Bly (New York: Kensington Publishing, 1997), was published soon afterward.

34. Interview, Ellen Braune, National Labor Committee, December 1997.

35. In cost-of-living terms, the 43 cents an hour earned by Wendy Diaz was below average even in Honduras. However, according to Honduran consular officials here, it went a lot further than $4.30 an hour in New York City. Interview, Mario Lee, Consulate General's office, New York City, May 27, 2004.

36. U.S. Department of Labor, *2001 New York City Garment Compliance Survey*.

37. Donna Tam, "Garment Industry Survey Shows Improvement," *Asian Week*, April 19–25, 2002. Bush appointees removed the previous, more critical surveys done by the Wage and Hour Division from the department's Web site.

38. Jay Mazur, testimony, U.S. House of Representatives, Committee on Education and the Workforce, August 6, 1998.

39. Herbert Hill, the garment union's most profound critic, whose work has been a source of inspiration in many ways, was the first to explain low wages as a consequence of the union's membership retention strategy. See, for example, "The ILGWU: The Decay of a Labor Union," in *Autocracy and Insurgency in Organized Labor*, edited by Burton Hall (New Brunswick, NJ: Transaction Books, 1972), 147–160.

40. Dubinsky and Raskin, *David Dubinsky: A Life with Labor*, 120. Raskin, who died in 1992, was the *New York Times* labor editor for forty years. Dubinsky served for thirty years as ILGWU president. He died in 1982 at age ninety.

41. Jacobs, *Gotham Unbound*, 136.

42. Hill, "The ILGWU: The Decay of a Labor Union."

43. Robert Laurentz, "Racial/Ethnic Conflict in New York City Garment Industry, 1933–1980," Ph.D. diss., State University of New York, Binghamton, 1980.

44. Mike Myerson, "ILGWU: Fighting for Lower Wages," *Ramparts* 8, October 1969.

45. Laurentz, "Racial/Ethnic Conflict in New York City Garment Industry."

46. *Los Angeles Times*, January 12, 2003, B1.

47. Membership from LM–2's; garment industry employment from New York State Department of Labor (unpublished figures). U.S. Department of Labor, Form LM–2, Organization Annual Report, 043–961, 2003.

48. Michael Piore, "The Economics of the Sweatshop," in *No Sweat*, edited by Andrew Ross (New York: Verso Press, 1997), 135.

49. Interview, Dov Charney, 2003.
50. Rich Cohen, *Tough Jews* (New York: Vintage, 1999). This is a well-written example of the genre.
51. David Dubinsky on AFL craft unions: "Their thievery and thuggery became so brazen that it eventually threw a heavy blanket of filth over the whole AFL" (Dubinsky and Raskin, *David Dubinsky: A Life with Labor*, 156–157). Then why switch from the honest and progressive CIO? Dubinsky doesn't expect us to believe it, but his answer is because John L. Lewis insisted on a third term as CIO president.
52. The assailant allegedly hired by Dio was murdered. Three witnesses refused to testify, and Dio and the others in the alleged conspiracy got off.
53. "Extortion Is Laid to Dress Unionist," *New York Times*, March 19, 1957, 39.
54. Dubinsky and Raskin, *David Dubinsky: A Life with Labor*, 153–159.
55. See Jacobs, *Gotham Unbound*, chs. 5 and 12.
56. Foner, *History of the Labor Movement in the United States*, vol. 5, 229.
57. Interview with a former ILGWU staffer who wishes to remain anonymous, 1998.
58. Maas, *The Valachi Papers*, 174–175.
59. Ibid., 176.
60. These were Edgar Romney, Freddy Menau, Jeff Hermanson, Julio Ballester, Wilfredo Donnes, and "CW-3"—i.e., cooperating witness no. 3.
61. Benjamin Weiser, "Reputed Crime Family Head Indicted in Extortion Case," *New York Times*, April 29, 1998.
62. Vanderberg affidavit, 6. The claim was made on the basis of information provided by the former acting boss of the Luccheses, "Little Al" D'Arco—widely considered the government's best mob informant.
63. Ibid., 22.
64. Ibid., 6.
65. The fifth family, the Bonannos, weren't allowed to participate.
66. Vanderberg affidavit, 7.
67. Ibid., 7–8.
68. Ibid., 16.
69. Ibid., 22.
70. Bastone, "Feds Finger Labor Boss," 27.
71. Vanderberg affidavit, 17.
72. Dubinsky says he fired ninety-three officials for taking bribes from employers. But he insists that "perhaps that isn't a large number." Perhaps it is, considering Dubinsky didn't fire people until they were indicted (for example, the Berger case) (Dubinsky and Raskin, *David Dubinsky: A Life with Labor*, 147).
73. A big reason why the health plan delivered so little was the union's complicity in mob schemes to allow bosses to opt out of the plan in exchange for bribes.
74. Interview with former Local 23–25 aide who wishes to remain anonymous, 2002.

75. Ying Chan and Anne E. Kornblut, "Her American Dream Ended in River," *Daily News,* June 1, 1997, 13.

76. Patrice O'Shaughnessy, with Shirley Wong, "Chinese Girl's Slay Unsolved," *Daily News,* January 11, 1998; Michelle McPhee and Patrice O'Shaughnessy, "The City's Top 10 Unsolved Crimes," *Daily News,* May 6, 2001, 6.

77. Department of Labor, Form LM–2, Labor Organization Annual Report, 043–961, 2003.

CHAPTER 10: RON CAREY: MARTYR OR MOUNTEBANK?

1. Cited in James B. Jacobs, *Gotham Unbound* (New York: New York University Press, 1999), 166.

2. David Corn, "The Prosecution and Persecution of Ron Carey," *Nation,* March 19, 1998.

3. U.S. District Court, Southern District of New York, *U.S. v. Ronald Carey,* 01 Cr.; also Phil Hirschhorn, "Former Teamsters President Ron Carey Indicted," CNN.com, January 25, 2001.

4. Quoted in Ken Crowe, "The Vindication of Ron Carey," *Union Democracy Review,* December/January 2001–2002.

5. Crowe, "The Vindication of Ron Carey."

6. The trial's opening session was sparsely attended, and Tim Sylvester was the only member of Local 804 there. I spoke with Sylvester. He said he'd come alone. Ken Crowe suggests that the reason other Local 804 members stayed away was that the independent review board had put Carey beyond the pale (Crowe, "The Vindication of Ron Carey"). It was true that union members couldn't talk to Carey. But they could hold rallies, make signs, or at least show up at the courthouse—which no one but Sylvester did.

7. Leon Olson, speech at Teamsters for a Democratic Union conference, 1992. See International Brotherhood of Teamsters, Local 282, FORE (Fear of Reprisal Ends) records (1970–1997), Wagner 107, Box 1, Folder 7.

8. Peter Maas, *Underboss* (New York: HarperPaperbacks, 1997), 369.

9. *60 Minutes,* December 3, 1978, broadcast.

10. Letter from Leon Olson and Lawrence Kudla to General President Ron Carey, September 21, 1993, copy in author's possession.

11. Steve Early, writing under pseudonyms in *The Nation* and *The Progressive,* was a TDU member; he also described himself as TDU head Ken Paff's attorney. *Nation* columnist Alexander Cockburn seems to have been influenced by a next-door neighbor who happened to be Paff's brother. In *LA Weekly,* see, for example, David Moberg, "Teamster Tumult," November 28, 1997.

12. Steven Brill, *The Teamsters* (New York: Pocket Books, 1978), 180.

13. Frank Swoboda, "Turning Point for the Teamsters? Race to Head Union a Test of Reforms," *Washington Post,* July 14, 1996, H1.

14. Or you were literally insane. Prominent TDU'ers suggested that investigators like Mike Moroney and journalist Jeffrey Goldberg were actually, not just figuratively, crazy.

15. See, for example, Thaddeus Russell, *Out of the Jungle* (New York: Alfred A. Knopf, 2001).

16. Quoted in Charles Brandt, *I Heard You Paint Houses: Frank "The Irishman" Sheeran and the Inside Story of the Mafia, the Teamsters, and the Final Ride of Jimmy Hoffa* (Hanover, NH: Steerforth Press, 2004), 92.

17. Hoffa's attorney on the case was Frank Ragano, a Santo Trafficante associate who, with Selwyn Raab, wrote *Mob Lawyer* (New York: Scribner's, 1994).

18. The $16.5 billion fund is about $7 billion short of being able to meet its liabilities.

19. For an early but informed look at Hoffa's pension practices, see Ralph James and Estelle James, *Hoffa and the Teamsters* (Princeton, NJ: Van Nostrand, 1965); see especially ch. 24 for the sad saga of Teamsters vesting practices.

20. For General President Roy Williams's testimony, see James Neff, *Mobbed Up* (New York: Dell, 1989), 100–105; for Cleveland mobster Angelo Lonardo's testimony on politicking for the Teamster presidency, see 376–377.

21. James R. Hoffa, *Hoffa: The Real Story as Told to Oscar Fraley* (New York: Stein and Day, 1975).

22. Brandt, *I Heard You Paint Houses*, 214; Joseph Franco with Richard Hammer, *Hoffa's Man* (New York: Prentice Hall, 1987), 300–301; Ragano and Raab, *Mob Lawyer*, 268.

23. *The Teamsters: Perception and Reality*, prepared for International Brotherhood of Teamsters by Stier, Anderson & Malone, LLC, September 2002, ch. 19.

24. Brill, *The Teamsters*, 68–69.

25. Independent Review Board Report of Investigation of General President Ronald Carey, July 11, 1994. The Independent Review Board is a three-person panel established by a 1989 consent decree to investigate and take appropriate action to rid the union of corruption.

26. Ragano and Raab, *Mob Lawyer*, 103–104 (Ragano was Hoffa's lawyer in the Test Fleet case); also Dan E. Moldea, *The Hoffa Wars* (New York: Charter Books, 1978), 55–56; and John Hutchinson, *Imperfect Union: A History of Corruption in American Trade Unions* (New York: E. P. Dutton, 1970), 270.

27. In 1988, the Justice Department listed him as a member of the Mafia's "Commission."

28. According to *On the Waterfront* screenwriter Budd Schulberg, who was commissioned to do the screenplay, it was a letter from Bufalino that stopped Twentieth Century Fox from making a movie out of Bobby Kennedy's *The Enemy Within*. Letter cited in Brandt, *I Heard You Paint Houses*, 93.

29. Brandt, *I Heard You Paint Houses*, 257.
30. Brill did say that Carey wasn't the only honest Teamster, but he doesn't name any others.
31. As *the* book on the Teamsters, it bested Dan Moldea's *Hoffa Wars*, a much darker portrayal that ignored Carey and got many things right: he reported on Ken Paff, which Brill didn't; he wasn't taken in by Jackie Presser, and Brill was. Moldea's book got far less attention and had much less credibility because of his focus on the JFK assassination.
32. Brill doesn't try to turn Carey into a picture-perfect saint. Carey embodies just the right balance of virtue and practicality. When the son of "Joe T" Tretretola comes around to Local 804's union hall to sell insurance, Carey says, "We've got all we need." On the one hand, this was brave, because Joe T's dad was the mob-installed boss of Joint Council 16; you couldn't cross Joe T and survive. On the other hand, says Brill, Carey was polite. He didn't throw him out of the office.
33. Brill, *The Teamsters*, 159.
34. Joe Calderone, "Union Big Had Ties to $2 M in UPS Stock," *Newsday*, August 1, 1994.
35. Selwyn Raab, "Teamsters President's Real Estate Deals Are Questions," *New York Times,* May 2, 1994.
36. Edward Barnes and Richard Behar, "Rich Man, Poor Man," *Time*, April 11, 1994.
37. Independent Review Board Report, 53–65. The IRB report didn't clearly exonerate Carey, as his supporters insisted. The report concluded that if the information provided by Carey's private accountant was accurate, he could have purchased the properties as he claimed. Carey's accountant, however, turned out to be a crook who provided information to the IRB quite informally. See below.
38. Ibid., 44.
39. Tom Demoretcky and Scott Minerbrook, "Cops: Heart Attack Killed Shot Man," *Newsday*, June 3, 1984, 4.
40. Jacobs, *Gotham Unbound*, ch. 6.
41. The IRB backed up all Carey's claims and concluded: "There is no proof of any knowing association by Ron Carey with [the Colombo crime family]." Independent Review Board Report, 47.
42. *U.S. v. Joseph Natale, Frank Russo and John Conti*, 75 CR 291 (SDNY). See Carey direct, 427–429.
43. Carey had told Richard Behar, of *Fortune*, that while he remembered Conti, "he doubted" he ever would have testified on his behalf. Richard Behar, "The Trouble with the Teflon Teamster," *Fortune*, October 27, 1997.
44. Independent Review Board Report, 33–34.
45. See *U.S. v. John F. Long and John S. Mahoney*, Nos. 89–1227, 89–1392, U.S. Court of Appeals for the Second Ct. 917 f.2d 691; 1990 U.S. App. LEXIS 18498.

Long and Mahoney got the jury verdict reversed on a technicality. Long is now dead, and Mahoney works in the labor movement in New Jersey.

46. "Dock Union Organizer Is Found Slain in Auto," *New York Times*, January 5, 1988.

47. Jeffrey Goldberg, *New York Magazine*, July 31, 1995.

48. Kenneth Crowe, *Collision* (New York: Charles Scribner's Sons, 1993), 190.

49. Although the film never mentions the Lucchese family as such, it does identify top family members by name. If you missed the movie, it was all there in the bestseller on which the movie was based, Nicholas Pileggi's *Wiseguy* (New York: Pocket Books, 1987).

50. Michael Ledeen and Mike Moroney, "The White House Joins the Teamsters," *American Spectator*, November 1998.

51. In January 1993, after Genoese was charged with knowingly associating with Lucchese family members, Carey removed Genoese from his position as boss of Local 732, another airfreight handlers local.

52. Independent Review Board Report, 39.

53. Frank Swoboda, "Carey Claims Reelection Win," *Washington Post*, December 15, 1996, A25.

54. Peter Szekely, "Carey in Court: Lawyers Say Carey Unaware of Campaign Scandal," Reuters, January 20, 1998.

55. Senate Committee on Homeland Security and Internal Affairs, 105th Congress, 1997, Special Investigation in Connection with the 1996 Federal Election Campaign, "White House, DNC, and Clinton-Gore Campaign Fundraising Involving the International Brotherhood of Teamsters," 4–5.

56. Ibid.

57. The progressive left's case against Davis was that Carey never should have hired him in the first place. The campaign should have relied totally on grassroots energies and the progressive in-house staffers and local activists who could unleash them. But Carey turned to Davis precisely because reliance on the grass roots was leading to defeat. See Jim Larkin, "Labor Pains: The Teamsters: What Went Wrong? The Campaign Money Scandal of Teamster President Ron Carey," *In These Times*, December 14, 1997; and Alexander Cockburn, "The Teamsters and the Journal," *Nation*, August 11–18, 1997.

58. U.S. District Court, Southern District of New York, *Decision of Teamsters Election Officer Kenneth Conboy to Disqualify International Brotherhood of Teamsters President Ron Carey*, November 17, 1997, 11.

59. "The Mother Jones 400," *Mother Jones*, April 1996.

60. It prompts the question, Who thought up "Teamsters for a Corruption-Free Union" anyhow? Court papers show it was Cohen, Weiss—the law firm of Judy Scott, the Teamsters' general counsel. See Election Officer for the International Brotherhood of Teamsters, In re: Jeraldine Cheatem, et al, August 21, 1997, 67.

61. U.S. District Court, *Decision of Teamsters*, November 17, 1997, 20–22.

62. Ibid., 22. And again: "If there is an indication it would have benefited my campaign, that would have never happened" (28).
63. Crowe, "The Vindication of Ron Carey," 3.
64. See, for example, Lee Sustar, "The Trial of Ron Carey: An Attack on Our Unions," *Socialist Worker Online*, September 14, 2001.
65. Crowe, "The Vindication of Ron Carey," 9.

CHAPTER 11: TEAMSTERS FOR A DEMOCRATIC UNION

1. Dan La Botz, *Rank-and-File Rebellion* (London: Verso, 1990), 1–8.
2. For an example of such inflation, see Robert Fitch, "Revolution in the Teamsters," *Tikkun* 8, 2 (1993).
3. Hal Draper, *The Marx-Engels Chronicles: A Day-by-Day Chronology of Marx and Engels' Life and Activity* (New York: Schocken Books, 1985) and *Dictatorship of the Proletariat: From Marx to Lenin* (New York: Monthly Review Press, 1987).
4. Interview, Steve Kindred, September 26, 2002.
5. As late as 1976, the organization probably hadn't recruited more than one or two genuine workers. Attrition of the original participants was heavy. The IS leadership was able to keep the industrialization effort alive by recruiting newly radicalized students off campuses who would then be fed into factory jobs. Still, seven years after the beginning of "industrialization," IS had only about forty operatives among the AFL-CIO's 16 million members.
6. Trotskyists didn't call them "cells"—that was the Stalinist term; their cells were "fractions."
7. La Botz, *Rank-and-File Rebellion*, 188.
8. Ken Paff, confidential memo, "What We've Done and Where We're Going," March 21, 1992. Robert F. Wagner Labor Archives, New York University.
9. La Botz, *Rank-and-File Rebellion*; Samuel R. Friedman, *Teamsters Rank and File: Power, Bureaucracy, and Rebellion at Work and in a Union* (New York: Columbia University Press, 1982); and Ken Crowe, *Collision* (New York: Charles Scribner's Sons: 1993), which had chapters about TDU set in the wider context of Carey's presidential victory.
10. Paff, "What We've Done and Where We're Going."
11. "Where Are We Headed," a confidential report to the International Steering Committee (ISC), Association for Union Democracy Papers (AUD Papers), Walter Reuther Library, Wayne State University, Detroit, undated (probably 1993), probably written by Ken Paff.
12. For Cashman's alleged mob connections, see Jack Sullivan, "Teamsters Head Said to Retaliate for Probe," *Boston Herald*, April 27, 2001, 21.
13. This quote and the analogy were both suggested to me by Staughton Lynd.

14. David Wilhelm, The Strategy Group, to Dan Ligurotis, April 26, 1991, 3, AUD Papers.

15. Memo, "To the ISC" (not for circulation; n.d.), AUD Papers.

16. Pete Camarata, letter to ISC, April 13, 1993, AUD Papers. Detroit Local 299 was historic because it was the local of Teamsters presidents Jimmy Hoffa and Frank Fitzsimmons.

17. Lee Olsen, Teamsters for a Democratic Union Convention Speech, 1993, AUD Papers.

18. William Nuchow Papers (1946–1983), New York University, Tamiment/Wagner Archives.

19. Nuchow Papers, Folder 21.

20. Steven Brill, The Teamsters, ch. 4; Dan E. Moldea, The Hoffa Wars (New York: Charter, 1978), 113–114.

21. For the reform campaign against Provenzano, see Brill, The Teamsters, 134. For Meyers, see Fred Gaboury, "Rank and File Teamsters say, 'Probe Hoffa finances,'" People's Weekly World, October 24, 1997.

22. Interview, Ken Paff, June 8, 2005.

23. I attended the convention.

24. Tom Robbins, "Lefty Teamsters Battle," Village Voice, February 7–15, 2001.

25. Draper was paraphrasing Marx. But the argument that unions must express the interests of the working class is theological in form. St. Anselm (1033–1109) had argued similarly to prove that God exists. It was a syllogistic argument from essence that works as follows: (i) It is the essence of a perfect being to exist; (ii) God is a perfect being; therefore (iii) God exists. Substitute the working classes' essence for God's essence, and the conclusion follows—unions must express the workers' interests.

26. Farrell Dobbs, Teamster Power (New York: Pathfinder Press, 1973), 246–247.

27. Ibid., 127, 244–245. For the Trotskyists, there was no important political difference between the two imperialist camps—the Allies and the Axis.

28. Ibid., 247.

29. Harold Seidman, Labor Czars (New York: Liveright, 1938), 254.

30. David Witwer, "Corruption and Reform in the Teamsters Union, 1898 to 1991," Ph.D. diss., Brown University, 1994, 177, citing IBT News, December 1940.

31. Ibid.

32. Ibid., 248.

33. Ibid., 246–248, 350–252.

34. Ibid.

35. Murray Kempton, "Mafia Shoots Itself," Newsday, February 20, 1987.

36. Brill, in The Teamsters (185), explained the excellent contracts negotiated by mobsters in Joint Council 16 on the grounds that crooked leaders needed only a few sell-out contracts to make money. In fact, just as much or more money is

made on the excellent contracts by charging bosses to opt out of them. In addition, the better the contract, the more corrupt leaders gain patronage power by playing favorites.

37. La Botz, *Rank-and-File Rebellion*, 1.

38. Ibid.

39. Ibid.

40. Ibid., 1, 7.

41. Ibid., 8.

42. Interview, Mike Ruscigno, 2002.

43. Local 97 had been mobbed up since 1960, according to the Independent Review Board (IRB). See "Re: Proposed Charges Against Local 97 Member Thomas A. Plinio," Washington, D.C., August 26, 2003, 2.

44. Kenneth C. Crowe, "Union Ends Strike at White Rose; Workers to Divvy Up $1.5 M Fund," *Newsday*, July 24, 1992. See also Kenneth C. Crowe, "Dark Days at White Rose: Teamsters Strike Enters 13th Week," *Newsday*, April 28, 1991.

45. *U.S. v. IBT*, In Re: Application of the Independent Administrator, Opinion and Order 86 Civ. 4486 (DNE), July 13, 1993.

46. Crowe, "Union Ends Strike at White Rose," 47.

47. Memo, anonymous, AUD Papers.

48. Crowe, "Union Ends Strike at White Rose."

49. Ibid.

50. Ibid.

51. In a letter to the federal judge who presided over the 1998 criminal trial, Clifton didn't accept that Georgopoulos—who was actually convicted on racketeering, bribery, and extortion charges in *two* jury trials—was even guilty. Clifton to Denis R. Hurley, December 12, 1997, 3. See *U.S. v. John Georgopoulos and Robert Skeries*, 96 CR 401(S) (DRH).

52. Interview, Mike Ruscigno, 2002.

53. Robert Commike to Judge Hurley, January 5, 1997, court papers.

54. *U.S. v. Georgopoulos*, 96 CR401 EDNY.

55. Daniel E. Clifton to Honorable Denis R. Hurley, Re: John Georgopoulos, 96 Cr 401 (Eastern District of New York), December 12, 1997.

56. Trial transcript, *U.S. v. Georgopoulos*, 74.

57. IRB memo, April 15, 1997, 8.

58. See *Convoy Dispatch*, no. 138, "Why Did Hoffa Lose the Vote Among Every Group He Bargained For?" p. 4.

59. Interview, Steve Kindred, who was then a Local 295 BA.

60. Interview, Ken Paff, June 8, 2005.

CHAPTER 12: EYES OFF THE PRIZE: REFORM'S REBUFF IN DC 37

1. *Mark Rosenthal et al. v. Lillian Roberts and Oliver Gray*, 04 CV 5205 (DC).
2. *Mark Rosenthal v. District Council 37*, Docket No. M-R-X–04–1015773-E.
3. Tom Robbins, "Boss Billed Union for 215 Visits to Motel," *New York Daily News*, February 2, 2000, 3; William Murphy, "Local 1508 Taken Over," *Newsday*, January 29, 2000, A20.
4. District Attorney Robert Morgenthau charged that Greene had paid back about $5,000 of the $8,700 she'd stolen. Steven Greenhouse, "Municipal Leader Is Indicted in Embezzlement," *New York Times*, April 26, 2001.
5. Montgomery-Costa won her last election with the votes of only 1.7 percent of her membership. And just as Hughes's votes kept the old executive director, Stanley Hill, in power, Montgomery-Costa's buttressed Roberts's position. Meanwhile, the members—lunchroom workers and school aides employed by the Board of Education—continue to receive less than $18,000 a year while paying nearly $1,000 a year in dues. They are customarily the first city employees to be laid off during fiscal crisis.
6. Interview, Lillian Roberts, April 6, 2005.
7. Interview, Charles Ensley, February 23, 2005. Lillian Roberts says Rodriguez sent a representative. Interview, Lillian Roberts, April 6, 2005.
8. Interview, Lillian Roberts, April 6, 2005.
9. Interview, Ivan Smith, April 7, 2005.
10. Interview, Mark Rosenthal, April 12, 2005.
11. Interview, Arthur Z. Schwartz, May 20, 2005.
12. Interview, Ivan Smith, April 7, 2005.
13. Interview, Deirdre McFadyen, February 2005.
14. Interview, Ivan Smith, April 7, 2005; interview, Mark Rosenthal, April 12, 2005.
15. Steven Greenhouse, "Brickbats for Labor's Grand Dame," *New York Times*, December 29, 2003.
16. Bernard and Jewel Bellush Papers, Wagner Archives, New York University Bobst Library, Lillian Roberts file.
17. Interview, Victor Gotbaum, February 23, 2005.
18. Henry Gilgoff, "Ex-Labor Commissioner Embroiled in HMO Issue," *Newsday*, March 28, 1988, 3. See also Lillian Roberts testimony, "In the Matter of the Arbitration Between Carolyn Harper et al. and Lillian Roberts and Oliver Gray," January 13, 2005, New York Hilton Hotel, AFSCME Judicial Panel, Case No. 04–71.
19. Henry Gilgoff, "HMO's Recruiting Tactics Probed," *Newsday*, March 28, 1988, 11.
20. Alan J. Wax, "For 21 M, Equicor May Restore Total to Health," *Newsday*, June 29, 1989, 45. Roberts herself says that Total Health was merged into Cigna. See "In the Matter of the Arbitration Between Carolyn Harper," 72.

21. "Union Democracy in Action," *Public Employee Press*, July–August 2002, http://www.dc37.net/news/PEP/7_2002/costaensley.htm. *PEP*, DC 37's house organ, didn't mention the total vote figure. For these totals, see "For Union Democracy in Action, Watch NYC Public Employees," *Union Democracy Review*, August–September 2002, http://www.uniondemocracy.com/UDR/34-NYC%20Public%20Employees.htm.

22. Interview, Victor Gotbaum, February 15, 2005.

23. Interview, Lillian Roberts, April 6, 2005.

24. Jose Sierra to Collen Detroy, April 5, 2005, memo. Sierra is head of DC 37's blue collar division. See also Edward Wong, "Union Treasurer Charged with Cheating Immigrants," *New York Times*, October 19, 2000, B4.

25. Barbara C. Deinhardt, Esq., to Members, Ethical Practices Committee, Results of Investigation, Case No. 02–02.

26. "'O Oysters,' said the Carpenter, 'You've had a pleasant run! Shall we be trotting home again?' But the answer came there none. And this was scarcely odd, because they'd eaten every one" (Lewis Carroll, "The Walrus and the Carpenter").

27. Michael Hirsch, "Gunning for Gus," *City Limits*, September/October 1998.

28. A personal disclosure: nearly six years ago, Arthur Schwartz gave me free legal advice on my PublicAffairs book contract.

29. *Salzhandler v. Caputo*, 316 F.2d 445; 1963 U.S. App. LEXIS 5546. ·

30. *Hall v. Cole*, 412 U.S. 1 (1973) No. 72–630. Hall got $5,500.

31. Arthur Z. Schwartz, "Trying to Balance the Personal and the Political," *The Villager* 73, 22 (October 1–7, 2003).

32. In June 2005, Schwartz's firm, Kennedy, Schwartz, and Cure, split. Schwartz left the firm. Several of his trade union clients remained.

33. Bob Fitch, "DC 37 Crashes," *Village Voice*, November 24–30, 1998; interview, Roy Commer, May 25, 2005.

34. Interview, Robert W. Sweet, May 26, 2005.

35. Ibid.

36. This defense was made by Charles Ensley, who seemed somewhat uncomfortable as a Commer supporter but defended him on principle.

37. A campaign speech by Vice President Al Gore followed. Had there been as much AFSCME enthusiasm for electing Al Gore as for kicking out Commer, the Democrats might have seized the White House that year. (I attended the conference.)

38. Fitch, "DC 37 Crashes."

39. District Attorney, New York County, press release, December 22, 2003.

40. William Murphy, "Bookkeeper Admits Theft of $2.4 Million," *Newsday*, June 3, 2004, A20.

41. Interview, Charles Ensley, February 23, 2005.

42. Ibid. "In Mark's local too," he points out.

43. Local 371 is not located in 125 Barclay, but a few blocks south of Union Square on Broadway.

CHAPTER 13: ANDY STERN'S DEAD SOULS

1. Quoted by H. Carl McCall at the Drum Major Institute's "Marketplace of Ideas" roundtable discussion featuring Andy Stern, March 14, 2005, at the Harvard Club, New York City.
2. David S. Broder, "SEIU Chief Says the Democrats Lack Fresh Ideas," *Washington Post,* July 27, 2004, A13.
3. See http://www.purpleocean.org/blog/42, November 9, 2004.
4. Although no one at the academy now can confirm it, and Stern's office hasn't been able to find out.
5. Harold Meyerson, "A Global Vision for Labor," *American Prospect,* June 25, 2004.
6. It used to be called "globalization."
7. Dues are inelastic with respect to wages. Some of the lowest-paid workers pay the highest dues.
8. On Chicago, see Stephen Franklin, "Mob-Control Allegations Rise Among Teamsters; Union's Internal Probe Collapses," *Chicago Tribune,* November 7, 2004.
9. Andy Stern, "Democracy and SEIU Justice@Work," seiu.org/blog/index.cfm?b cat_id=9, March 17, 2004.
10. Andrew L. Stern, "Keynote Address to SEIU Convention," June 21, 2004, San Francisco, California. Actually, blacks created the first janitors' local, a flat janitors union in 1902. They had a federal charter from the AFL, but Samuel Gompers took it away.
11. "Chicago Janitors Guilty," *New York Times,* June 10, 1922, 18.
12. Illinois Building Investigation Commission, *Report to His Excellency Len Small, Governor, and the Fifty-third General Assembly,* Springfield, 1923, cited in John Hutchinson, *The Imperfect Union: A History of Corruption in American Trade Unions* (New York: E. P. Dutton, 1970), 398.
13. Jay Robert Nash, *World Encyclopedia of Organized Crime* (New York: Da Capo Press, 1993), 32; see also Edward Sullivan, *This Labor Union Racket* (New York: Hillman-Curl, 1936), 115.
14. Sullivan, *This Labor Union Racket,* 115.
15. "Chicago Foes Slay Gang War Veteran," *New York Times,* July 19, 1935, 11.
16. David Witwer, "The Scandal of George Scalise: A Case Study in the Rise of Labor Racketeering in the 1930s," *Journal of Social History,* Summer 2003.
17. SEIU Vice Presidents Collection, Walter P. Reuther Library of Labor and Urban Affairs, Box 3, Files 18–25.

18. Ibid., Box 5, File 19, "McFetridge Charges."
19. Meyer Berger, "Union Chief Slain; Assassin Shot Dead," *New York Times,* August 29, 1953, 1.
20. Emanuel Perlmutter, "Mayor's Manager in Bronx Queried on Labor Slaying," *New York Times,* September 1, 1953, 1.
21. Edward Ranzal, "Union Aides Held in Sell-Out Case," *New York Times,* February 6, 1964, 15.
22. Burton Hall (ed.), *Autocracy and Insurgency in Organized Labor* (New Brunswick, NJ: Transaction Books, 1972), 269.
23. "SEIU Replaces President of NY Janitors' Local," http://cleanfax.com/news.asp?mode=4&N_ID=18902, December 7, 2000.
24. Cited in Philip S. Foner, *History of the Labor Movement in the United States,* vol. 3, *The Policies and Practices of the American Federation of Labor, 1900–1909* (New York, International Publishers, 1964), 136.
25. Keynote Address to SEIU Convention by President Andrew L. Stern, June 21, 2004, San Francisco, California.
26. Michael J. Piore, "Unions: A Reorientation to Survive," in *Labor Economics and Industrial Relations,* edited by Clark Kerr and Paul D. Staudohar (Cambridge, MA: Harvard University Press, 1994), 528.
27. Leah Samuel, "High Official of Service Employees Runs a Problem-Plagued Local," *Labor Notes,* August 1999.
28. On Sullivan, see Cynthia Peters, "Janitors Prepare to Strike for Justice," *Labor Notes,* October 2002.
29. Andy Stern, "Democracy and SEIU Justice@Work," http://www.seiu.org/blog/index.cfm?startmonth=3&startyear=2004&archives=1, March 17, 2004.
30. Previously Balanoff had been president of Local 73. For a candid portrait of his tour of duty there by his communications director, see Suzan Erem, *Labor Pains* (New York: Monthly Review Press, 2001).
31. Robert Fitch, "Labor Pain," *Nation,* November 25, 1996.
32. Jeffrey Goldberg, "Yikes! Are the Clintons in Trouble," *New York Magazine,* July 8, 1996.
33. One eventually got fired and the other soon quit in disgust.
34. From FBI tapes cited by Tom Robbins, "Cleaning Lessons for Dirty Bosses," *Village Voice,* September 20, 2002.
35. Stern hadn't invented the SEIU reform movement. Credit for that probably belongs to Charles Hardy—the president before Sweeney—or perhaps even Hardy's father, George, who dared to face down Scalise. "Go jump in the lake," Hardy replied to the Capone man when asked by Scalise to fire a staffer. See Hutchinson, *The Imperfect Union,* 126.
36. Roger Waldinger et al., "Helots No More: A Case Study of the Justice for Janitors Campaign in Los Angeles," in *Organizing to Win: New Research on Union Strategies,* edited by Kate Bronfenbrenner et al. (Ithaca, NY: ILR Press, 1998);

Catherine L. Fisk et al., "Union Representation of Immigrant Janitors in Southern California: Economic and Legal Challenges," in *Organizing Immigrants*, edited by Ruth Milkman (Ithaca, NY: ILR Press, 2000).

37. Nancy Cleeland, "Von's Continues to Underpay Janitors," *Los Angeles Times*, January 25, 2005, C1.

38. Sonia Nazario, "Hunger Strike Marks Union's Split," *Los Angeles Times*, August 8, 1995, 1. Tellingly, only 11 percent of the members voted.

39. Nancy Cleeland, "Leader of the Revolutionary Pack," *Los Angeles Times*, August 13, 2000, 26.

40. Lisa W. Foderaro, "Half-Empty Hospitals in a Shrinking City," *New York Times*, April 25, 2005.

41. Reported on Jonathan Tasini's Web site, "Working Life," http://workinglife. typepad.com/daily_blog/2005/03/showdown_in_veg_2.html. Tasini, a former labor journalist, used to be a UAW local president. See also Nancy Cleeland, "Territorial Dispute at AFL-CIO Highlights Obstacles in Holding Federation Together," *Los Angeles Times*, March 4, 2005, and Steve Greenhouse, "Labor Chief Emerges from Meeting a Winner, But for How Long?" *New York Times*, March 4, 2005.

42. Cleeland, "Territorial Dispute at AFL-CIO."

43. Stephen Franklin, "2 Unions Feud over Illinois Workers," *Chicago Tribune*, March 4, 2005.

44. Cleeland, "Territorial Dispute at AFL-CIO."

45. Franklin, "2 Unions Feud over Illinois Workers"; Tracy dell'Angella, "Home Day Care Fights for Respect," *Chicago Tribune*, July 13, 2003, 1.

46. Dan Morain and Dave Lesher, "California and the West: California Elections," *Los Angeles Times*, October 8, 1998, 3.

47. In January 2005, a union-backed research project in New York put the poverty line cutoff at $8.95 an hour. See Restaurant Opportunities Center of New York, "Behind the Kitchen Door," January 25, 2005. Primary research support was furnished by the Urban Justice Center, the Brennan Center for Justice at New York University Law School, and the Community Service Society.

48. Associated Press, "Home Health Care Workers Seek Better Pay," April 8, 2005 (on MSNBC News, at http://msnbc.msn.com/id/7433493).

49. Stephen Franklin, "Service Workers Union Wins Child-Care Organizing Rights," *Chicago Tribune*, March 26, 2005, 1.

50. Christopher Hayes, "Healthcare Workers Win Raises," *In These Times*, January 21, 2004.

51. Interview, Keith Kelleher, Local 880 organizing director, April 25, 2005.

52. Andy Stern, "Restore the American Dream by Addressing the State of Unions," *Forward*, June 10, 2005.

53. Robert H. Zieger, *The CIO: 1935–1955* (Chapel Hill: University of North Carolina Press, 1955), 46–54.

54. Some SEIU home care aides in other California counties earned more—as much as $10 an hour. But the 50,000 day care workers in Illinois, organized by SEIU's Local 880 the same year, earned nearly a dollar an hour less. See below.

55. U.S. Department of Health and Human Services, "The 2005 HHS Poverty Guidelines," http://aspe.hhs.gov/05poverty.shtml.

56. SEIU Local 434B, "Who Are Homecare Workers?" http://www.seiu434b. org/homecare/what_is_homecare.cfm.

57. Ibid.

58. Maggie Belton, Panel Presentation, White House Conference on Aging, Los Angeles, April 7, 2005, http://www.whcoa.gov/about/des_events_reports/ Belton.pdf.

59. *Carla West et al. v. SEIU Local 434b,* U.S. District Court, Central District California, Western Division, Case No. CV 01–10862 CAS, August 20, 2002. See also Charisse Jones, "Providers of Home Care in Budget Pinch," *Los Angeles Times,* March 22, 1989, 1.

60. Michael R. Cousineau, "Providing Health Insurance to IHSS Providers (Home Care Workers) in Los Angeles County," June 2000, http://www.chcf.org/topics/ healthinsurance/index.cfm?itemID=12471.

61. Fred Alvarez, "Caregivers Get Raises; Benefits," *Los Angeles Times,* November 28, 2004, B1.

62. Ibid.

63. SEIU Local 434b, "Chronology," http://www.seiu434b.org/docUploads/Union %20History%20Dec04.pdf.

64. For the SEIU role in supervisors elections in the 1990s, see, for example, Richard Simons, "Huge Sums Go to Races for Supervisor," *Los Angeles Times,* October 27, 1992, 1.

65. See Los Angeles City Ethics Commission, http://ethics.lacity.org.

66. Steven Greenhouse, "In Biggest Drive Since 1937, Union Gains a Victory," *New York Times,* February 26, 1999, A1.

67. Matt Smith, "The Politics of Cynicism: SEIU Lobbies for Nursing Home Chains," *SF Weekly,* April 27, 2005, http://www.sfweekly.com/Issues/2005–04– 27/news/smith_1.html. See also California Advocates for Nursing Home Reform, "Nursing Home Operators Hit Jackpot with Taxpayers' Money!" http:// www.canhr.org/publications/newsletters/advocate/adv_200409.html.

68. Matt Smith, "Gutted," *SF Weekly,* August 25, 2005, http://www.sfweekly. com/issues/2004–08–25/news/smith.html.

69. Lynda Gledhill, "Nursing Homes on Verge of Cash Infusion," *San Francisco Chronicle,* September 18, 2005.

70. Smith, "The Politics of Cynicism."

71. Ibid.

72. "At the Mercy of Their Caretakers" (editorial), *San Francisco Chronicle,* May 15, 2005.

73. Interview, Pat McGinnis, June 14, 2005.

74. Alfred P. Sloan Jr., *My Years With General Motors* (New York: Currency Double-day, 1990), 191–216.

75. For 2003, see Marick F. Masters, *Unions at the Crossroads* (Westport, CT: Quorum Books, 1997), 97, 147; for 2004, see Department of Labor, Form LM–2, 2004 Report, 000–137.

CONCLUSION: SOLIDARITY FOR REAL

1. Molly Beck, "Sticking to the Union: The AFL-CIO Saves One of the Nation's Oldest Labor Temples," *Illinois Times,* July 17, 2003, http://www.illinoistimes.com/gbase/Gyrosite/Content?oid=oid percent3A2369. Beck describes the unions that made up the Jacksonville, Illinois, labor temple.

2. "Early 20th Century San Jose, Ca.," http://www.lullah.com/GEDC/early20th century.html.

3. Jack London, "War of the Classes," http://eserver.org/books/war_of_the_classes.html.

4. On London's sympathy with Haywood and the IWW, see Jack London, *The Iron Heel* (1907), ch. 17, "The Scarlet Livery."

5. Harry Kelber, "Corporate Unionism," September 27, 2004, http://www.labor educator.org/corpunion4.pdf.

6. J.G.A. Pocock, *The Machiavellian Moment* (Princeton, NJ: Princeton University Press, 1975), 507.

7. Cited in Nelson Lichtenstein, *State of the Union* (Princeton, NJ: Princeton University Press, 2002), 247.

8. AFL-CIO, *The Changing Structure of Workers and Their Unions* (Washington, DC: AFL-CIO, 1985).

9. John Stuart Mill, "Considerations on Representative Government," in *Utilitarianism; on Liberty, Considerations on Representative Government: Remarks on Bentham's Philosophy*, edited by Geraint Williams (London: J. M. Dent, 1993), 192–193.

10. Compare C. Wright Mills: "Democracy within the unions, as within the nation as a whole, is usually a democracy of machine politics imposed upon a mass of apathetic members." C. Wright Mills, *The New Men of Power: America's Labor Leaders* (Urbana: University of Illinois Press, 2001), 64.

11. Ultimately, the American model of unionism as we've known it—compulsory unionism, a structure that was already old before the Model T was invented—is never going to make it through the century. Either it will continue to disintegrate and unions will eventually disappear entirely, or there will be some effort to launch a new model. The prime features that have to be scrapped are all those

features that preempt consent: compulsory membership, exclusive representation, closed shop, "union security." Denial of consent creates the foundations of corruption, warlordism, and boundless political apathy and indifference. Consent builds the possibility of participation, accountability, and solidarity.

12. Benjamin Barber, *Strong Democracy: Participatory Politics for a New Age* (Berkeley: University of California Press, 1984), 8.

13. Telephone interview, Martin Fishgold, September 2, 2003.

14. Telephone interview, Peter Gilmore, September 2, 2003.

15. See http://www.opensecrets.org/softmoney. And union money doesn't flow only to national campaigns. The top soft money contributor by far to New York state campaigns is SEIU.

16. *U.S. v. Maritas*, Cr No. 81–122 (EDNY); see Tape 78, Box 2; "Carpenters for a Stronger Union," Robert F. Wagner Labor Archives, New York University.

17. *Newark Star-Ledger,* July 19, 22, and 23, 2003.

18. St. Augustine, *The City of God* (London: Penguin Books, 1984), 210.

19. Manny Garcia and Joe Mozingo, "Union Paid for Chief's Opulent Lifestyle," *Miami Herald*, May 18, 2003, 1A.

20. Manny Garcia and Joe Mozingo, "UTD Leaders Had Secret Pension Fund," *Miami Herald*, May 25, 2003, 1B.

21. Allan Lengel and Neely Tucker, "Ex-Chauffeur Aids Union Probe," *Washington Post*, February 6, 2003, B1; Justin Blum, "Audit Says Union Lost $5 Million to Theft," *Washington Post*, January 17, 2003, A1; Robin Givhan, "A Failure in Flair: Teachers' Union Head Dressed by the Rules," *Washington Post*, January 24, 2003, C1.

22. Richard B. Freeman and Joel Rogers, *What Workers Want* (Ithaca, NY: ILR Press, 1999).

23. Cited in Andy Stern, "Restore the American Dream by Addressing the State of the Unions," *Forward*, June 11, 2005.

24. Statement of Charles Heckscher, *What's Next for Organized Labor: The Report of the Century Foundation Task Force on the Future of Unions* (New York: The Century Foundation Press, 1999), 53.

25. David Brian Robertson, *Capital, Labor, and State* (Lanham, MD: Rowman & Littlefield, 2000).

26. Mike Parker and Martha Gruelle, *Democracy Is Power* (Detroit: Labor Notes, 1999), 50–51.

27. Critics of the French model point out that union density—the share of union members in the workforce—is even less in France than in the United States. But they ignore the fact that union *coverage* is over 90 percent—that is, more than nine out of ten workers are covered by union contracts.

28. Stephen Lerner, "Three Steps to Reorganizing and Rebuilding the Labor Movement," *Labor Notes*, December 2002.

29. Cell phones are gradually displacing the halls. Workers can wait in their homes,

or anywhere, for calls to work. But the members' dependence on the business agent hasn't changed.

30. Martin Baethge and Harald Wolf, "Continuity and Change in the 'German Model' of Industrial Relations," in *Employment Relations in a Changing World Economy*," edited by Richard Locke, Thomas Kochan, and Michael Piore (Cambridge, MA: MIT Press, 1997), 234.

31. Tito Boeri, Agar Brugiavini, and Lars Calmfors (eds.), *The Role of Unions in the Twenty-first Century* (Oxford, England: Oxford University Press, 2001), 81–83.

32. "The World's Wealthiest Hedge Fund Managers Add More to Their Earnings in 2004," http://www.hedgeco.net/news/05/2005/world%92s-wealthiest-hedge-fund-managers-add-more-earnings–2004.html.

33. "Recent Changes in U.S. Family Finances: Evidence from the 1998 and 2001 Survey of Consumer Finances," http://www.federalreserve.gov/pubs/bulletin/2003/0103lead.pdf.

BIBLIOGRAPHY

BOOKS

Adamic, Louis. *Dynamite: The Story of Class Violence in America.* New York: Viking Press, 1931.

AFL-CIO. *The Changing Structure of Workers and Their Unions.* Washington, DC: AFL-CIO, 1985.

Asbury, Herbert. *Gem of the Prairie.* New York: Alfred A. Knopf, 1930.

Barber, Benjamin. *Strong Democracy: Participatory Politics for a New Age.* Berkeley: University of California Press, 1984.

Bean, Walton. *Boss Ruef's San Francisco: The Story of the Union Labor Party.* Berkeley: University of California Press, 1952.

Bell, Daniel. *End of Ideology.* Cambridge, MA: Harvard University Press, 2000; originally published 1960.

Berman, Sheri. *The Social Democratic Movement.* Cambridge, MA: Harvard University Press, 1998.

Blake, Gary, and Robert W. Bly. *The "I Hate Kathie Lee Gifford" Book.* New York: Kensington Publishing, 1997.

Boeri, Tito, Agar Brugiavini, and Lars Calmfors (eds.). *The Role of Unions in the Twenty-first Century.* Oxford, England: Oxford University Press, 2001.

Bok, Derek C., and John T. Dunlop. *Labor and the American Community.* New York: Simon and Schuster, 1970.

Brandt, Charles. *I Heard You Paint Houses: Frank "The Irishman" Sheeran and the Inside Story of the Mafia, the Teamsters, and the Final Ride of Jimmy Hoffa.* Hanover, NH: Steerforth Press, 2004.

Brecher, Charles, and Raymond D. Horton, with Robert A. Cropf and Dean Michael Mead. *Power Failure.* New York: Oxford University Press, 1993.

Brill, Steven. *The Teamsters.* New York: Pocket Books, 1978.

Bronfenbrenner, Kate (ed.) et al. *Organizing to Win: New Research on Union Strategies.* Ithaca, NY: ILR Press, 1998.

Burns, William J. *The Masked Man.* New York: George H. Doran Co., 1913.

Chavez, Linda. *Betrayal.* New York: Crown Forum, 2004.

Christie, Robert A. *Empire in Wood.* Ithaca, NY: Cornell University Press, 1956.

Cohen, Rich. *Tough Jews.* New York: Vintage, 1999.

Commons, John R. *History of Labour in the United States.* New York: Macmillan, 1918–1935.

——. *Trade Unionism and Labor Problems.* New York: Augustus M. Kelley, 1967; originally published 1905.

Crowe, Kenneth C. *Collision.* New York: Charles Scribner's Sons, 1993.

Dawson, William H. *Bismarck and State Socialism: An Exposition of the Social and Economic Legislation of Germany Since 1870.* London: S. Sonnenschein & Co., 1891.

Demaris, Ovid. *Captive City.* New York: L. Stuart, 1969.

de Tocqueville, Alexis. *Democracy in America*, vol. 1. New York: Alfred A. Knopf, 1944.

Dewey, John. *David Dubinsky.* New York: Inter-allied Publications, 1951.

Dobbs, Farrell. *Teamster Power.* New York: Pathfinder Press, 1973.

Draper, Hal. *The Marx-Engels Chronicles: A Day-by-Day Chronology of Marx and Engels' Life and Activity.* New York: Schocken Books, 1985.

——. *Dictatorship of the Proletariat: From Marx to Lenin.* New York: Monthly Review Press, 1987.

Dubinsky, David, and A. H. Raskin. *David Dubinsky: A Life with Labor.* New York: Simon and Schuster, 1977.

Economic Report of the President, 1999. Washington, DC: U.S. Government Printing Office, 1999.

Ellis, Edward Robb. *Echoes of Distant Thunder: Life in the United States, 1914–1918.* New York: Coward, McCann, and Geoghegan, 1975.

Erem, Suzan. *Labor Pains.* New York: Monthly Review Press, 2001.

Esping-Anderson, Gosta. *The Three Worlds of Welfare Capitalism.* Princeton, NJ: Princeton University Press, 1990.

Farmer, James. *Lay Bare the Heart.* New York: Arbor House, 1985.

Fentress, James. *Rebels and Mafiosi.* Ithaca, NY: Cornell University Press, 2000.

Fine, Sidney. *Walter Drew, the National Erectors Association, and the Open Shop Movement, 1903–1957.* Ann Arbor: University of Michigan Press, 1995.

Foner, Philip S. *History of the Labor Movement in the United States,* multiple volumes. New York: International Publishers, 1964–1988.

Foster, William Z. *The Wrecking of the Labor Banks: The Collapse of the Labor Banks and Investment Companies of the Brotherhood of Locomotive Engineers.* Chicago: Trade Union Educational League, 1927.

Fox, Stephen. *Blood and Power.* New York: Penguin, 1990.

Franco, Joseph, with Richard Hammer. *Hoffa's Man.* New York: Prentice Hall, 1987.

Fraser, Steve, and Josh Freeman (eds.). *Audacious Democracy.* Boston: Houghton Mifflin, 1997.

Freeman, Richard B. (ed.). *Working Under Different Rules.* New York: Russell Sage Foundation, 1994.

Freeman, Richard B., and James L. Medoff. *What Do Unions Do?* New York: Basic Books, 1984.

Freeman, Richard B., and Joel Rogers. *What Workers Want.* Ithaca, NY: ILR Press, 1999.

Friedman, Samuel R. *Teamsters Rank and File: Power, Bureaucracy, and Rebellion at Work and in a Union.* New York: Columbia University Press, 1982.

Gambetta, Diego. *The Sicilian Mafia: The Business of Private Protection.* Cambridge, MA: Harvard University Press, 1993.

Ginger, Ray. *Eugene V. Debs: A Biography.* New York: Collier, 1962.

Ginsborg, Paul. *Italy and Its Discontents.* New York: Palgrave Macmillan, 2003.

Gompers, Samuel. *Labor in Europe and America.* New York: Harper & Brothers, 1910.

Gottlieb, Robert, and Irene Wolt. *Thinking Big: The Story of the Los Angeles Times.* New York: G. P. Putnam's Sons, 1977.

Gottschalk, Marie. *The Shadow Welfare State.* Ithaca, NY: ILR Press, 2000.

Gould, William B., IV. *A Primer on American Labor Law,* 3rd ed. Cambridge, MA: MIT Press, 1997.

Greene, Julie. *Pure and Simple Politics: The American Federation of Labor and Political Activism, 1881–1917.* Cambridge, England: Cambridge University Press, 1998.

Gutman, Herbert. *Work, Culture, and Society in Industrializing America: Essays in American Working Class Social History.* New York: Vintage, 1977.

Haber, William T. *Industrial Relations in the Building Industry.* Cambridge, MA: Harvard University Press, 1930.

Hall, Burton (ed.). *Autocracy and Insurgency in Organized Labor.* New Brunswick, NJ: Transaction Books, 1972.

Halpern, Rick, and Jonathan Morris (eds.). *American Exceptionalism? U.S. Working Class Formation in an International Context.* New York: St. Martin's Press, 1997.

Harrington, Michael. *Socialism.* New York: Bantam Books, 1973.

Harris, Marvin. *Cannibals and Kings.* New York: Vintage, 1977.

Heckscher, Charles. *What's Next for Organized Labor: The Report of the Century Foundation Task Force on the Future of Unions.* New York: Century Foundation Press, 1999.

Hobsbawm, Eric. *Primitive Rebels.* New York: W. W. Norton, 1965.

Hoffa, James R. *Hoffa: The Real Story as Told to Oscar Fraley.* New York: Stein and Day, 1975.

Howe, Irving. *World of Our Fathers.* New York: Harcourt Brace Jovanovich, 1976.

Hutchinson, John. *The Imperfect Union: A History of Corruption in American Trade Unions.* New York: E. P. Dutton, 1970.

Jackson, Kenneth (ed.). *The Encyclopedia of New York City.* New Haven, CT: Yale University Press, 1995.

Jacobs, James B. *The Final Report of the New York State Organized Crime Task Force.* New York: New York University Press, 1990.

———. *Gotham Unbound.* New York: New York University Press, 1999.

James, Ralph, and Estelle James. *Hoffa and the Teamsters.* Princeton, NJ: Van Nostrand, 1965.

Jefferson, Thomas. *The Portable Thomas Jefferson.* New York: Penguin Books, 1975.

Johnson, Curt. *The Wicked City: Chicago from Kenna to Capone.* New York: Da Capo Press, 1998.

Johnson, Malcolm. *Crime on the Union Front.* New York: McGraw-Hill, 1950.

Jones, Kathleen. *The Making of Social Policy in Britain, 1830–1990,* 2nd ed. London: Athlone Press, 1994.

Josephson, Matthew. *Sidney Hillman: Statesman of American Labor.* Garden City, NY: Doubleday, 1952.

——. *Union House, Union Bar.* New York: Random House, 1956.

Kazin, Michael. *Barons of Labor.* Urbana: University of Illinois Press, 1989.

Kennedy, Robert. *The Enemy Within.* New York: Da Capo Press, 1994; originally published 1960.

Kerr, Clark, and Paul D. Staudohar (eds.). *Labor Economics and Industrial Relations.* Cambridge, MA: Harvard University Press, 1994.

Kornbluh, Joyce L. (ed.). *Rebel Voices: An IWW Anthology.* Chicago: Charles H. Kerr Publishers, 1998.

Kwitny, Jonathan. *Vicious Circles.* New York: W. W. Norton, 1979.

La Botz, Dan. *Rank-and-File Rebellion.* London: Verso, 1990.

Landesco, John. *Organized Crime in Chicago*, part 3 of the Illinois Crime Survey, 1929, Midway Reprint. Chicago: University of Chicago Press, 1968.

Lapides, Kenneth (ed.). *Marx and Engels on the Trade Unions.* New York: International Publishers, 1990.

Laurie, Bruce. *Artisans into Workers.* Champaign: University of Illinois Press, 1989.

Lester, Richard. *As Unions Mature: The Evolution of American Unions.* Princeton, NJ: Princeton University Press, 1958.

Lewis, Charles. *The Buying of the President 2000.* New York: Avon, 2000.

Lichtenstein, Nelson. *State of the Union.* Princeton, NJ: Princeton University Press, 2002.

Lipset, Seymour Martin. *American Exceptionalism.* New York: W. W. Norton, 1996.

Locke, Richard, Thomas Kochan, and Michael Piore (eds.). *Employment Relations in a Changing World Economy.* Cambridge, MA: MIT Press, 1997.

London, Jack. *The Iron Heel.* Chicago: Lawrence Hill Books, 1981; originally published 1907.

Maas, Peter. *The Valachi Papers.* New York: Bantam, 1968.

——. *Underboss.* New York: HarperPaperbacks, 1997.

Machiavelli, Niccolò. *Discourses on Livy*, book 1. London: Penguin Press, 1970.

Maddison, Angus. *The World Economy: A Millennial Perspective.* Paris: Development Center of the Organization for Economic Cooperation and Development, 2001.

Mandel, Bernard. *Samuel Gompers.* Yellow Springs, OH: Antioch Press, 1963.

Marx, Karl, and Frederick Engels. *The Communist Manifesto.* London: Verso, 1998; originally published 1848.

Masters, Marick F. *Unions at the Crossroads.* Westport, CT: Quorum Books, 1997.

Matthews, Richard K. *The Radical Politics of Thomas Jefferson.* Lawrence: University Press of Kansas, 1984.

Meier, Mark. *City Unions.* New Brunswick, NJ: Rutgers University Press, 1987.

Michels, Robert. *Political Parties.* New York: Free Press, 1962.

Milkman, Ruth (ed.). *Organizing Immigrants.* Ithaca, NY: ILR Press, 2000.

Mill, John Stuart. *Utilitarianism; on Liberty, Considerations on Representative Government: Remarks on Bentham's Philosophy,* Geraint Williams (ed.). London: J. M. Dent, 1993.

Mills, C. Wright. *The New Men of Power: America's Labor Leaders.* Urbana: University of Illinois Press, 2001; originally published 1948.

Mishel, Lawrence, Jared Bernstein, and Heather Boushey. *The State of Working America, 2002/2003.* Ithaca, NY: Cornell University Press, 2003.

Mishel, Lawrence, Jared Bernstein, and Sylvia Allegretto. *The State of Working America, 2004/2005.* Ithaca, NY: Cornell University Press, 2005.

Moldea, Dan E. *The Hoffa Wars.* New York: Charter Books, 1978.

Montgomery, David. *The Fall of the House of Labor.* New York: Cambridge University Press, 1987.

Montgomery, Royal E. *Industrial Relations in the Chicago Building Trades.* Chicago: University of Chicago Press, 1927.

Morgan, Ted. *A Covert Life.* New York: Random House, 1999.

Mort, Jo-Ann (ed.). *Not Your Father's Union Movement.* New York: Verso, 1998.

Murray, R. Emmett. *The Lexicon of Labor.* New York: New Press, 1998.

Nash, Jay Robert. *World Encyclopedia of Organized Crime.* New York: Da Capo Press, 1993.

Neff, James. *Mobbed Up.* New York: Dell, 1989.

Nelli, Humbert S. *The Italians in Chicago, 1880–1930.* New York: Oxford University Press, 1970.

Nietzsche, Friedrich. *The Gay Science.* New York: Vintage, 1974.

Olasky, Marvin. *The Tragedy of Compassion.* Washington, DC: Regnery Publishing Co., 1992.

Orleck, Annelise. *Common Sense and a Little Fire: Women and Working Class Politics in the United States, 1900–1965.* Chapel Hill: University of North Carolina Press, 1995.

Parker, Mike, and Martha Gruelle. *Democracy Is Power.* Detroit: Labor Notes, 1999.

Perry, Jeffrey B. (ed.). *A Hubert Harrison Reader.* Middletown, CT: Wesleyan University Press, 2000.

Pileggi, Nicholas. *Wiseguy.* New York: Pocket Books, 1987.

Pocock, J.G.A. *The Machiavellian Moment*. Princeton, NJ: Princeton University Press, 1975.

President's Commission on Organized Crime. *The Edge: Organized Crime, Business, and Labor Unions*. Washington, DC: Government Printing Office, 1985.

Ragano, Frank, and Selwyn Raab. *Mob Lawyer*. New York: Charles Scribner's Sons, 1994.

Robertson, David Brian. *Capital, Labor, and State*. Lanham, MD: Rowman & Littlefield, 2000.

Robinson, W. W. *Bombs and Bribery*. Los Angeles: Dawson's Book Shop, 1969.

Rorty, Richard. *Achieving Our Country*. Cambridge, MA: Harvard University Press, 1998.

Ross, Andrew (ed.). *No Sweat*. New York: Verso, 1997.

Rousseau, J. J. *The Discourses and Other Early Political Writings*. Cambridge, England: Cambridge University Press, 1977.

——. *Social Contract*. Harmondsworth: Penguin, 1968.

Rudwick, Elliott M. *Race Riot at East St. Louis*. Carbondale: Southern Illinois University Press, 1964.

Russell, Thaddeus. *Out of the Jungle*. New York: Alfred A. Knopf, 2001.

St. Augustine. *The City of God*. London: Penguin Books, 1984.

Sassoon, D. (ed.). *Looking Left: European Socialism After the Cold War*. London: I. B. Tauris, in association with the Gramsci Foundation, 1997.

Saxton, Alexander. *The Indispensable Enemy*. Berkeley: University of California Press, 1975.

Seidman, Harold. *Labor Czars*. New York: Liveright Publishing Corp., 1938.

Sifakis, Carl. *The Mafia Encyclopedia*, 2nd ed. New York: Checkmark Books, 1999.

Sloan, Alfred P., Jr. *My Years With General Motors*. New York: Currency Doubleday, 1990.

Sombart, Werner. *Why Is There No Socialism in the United States?* White Plains, NY: International Arts and Sciences Press, 1976.

Steffens, Lincoln. *The Shame of the Cities*. New York: Hill and Wang, 1992; originally published 1902.

Stimson, Grace Heilman. *Rise of the Labor Movement in Los Angeles*. Berkeley: University of California Press, 1955.

Sullivan, Edward. *This Labor Union Racket*. New York: Hillman-Curl, 1936.

Sweeney, John. *America Needs a Raise*. Boston: Houghton Mifflin, 1996.

U.S. Commissioner of Labor. *Workmen's Insurance and Benefit Funds in the United States, Twenty-third Annual Report*. Washington, DC: U.S. Government Printing Office, 1908.

U.S. Senate Committee on Education and Labor. *Report of the Committee of the Senate on the Relation Between Labor and Capital*, 4 vols. Washington, DC: U.S. Government Printing Office, 1885.

Van der Linden, Marcel, and Jurgen Rojahn, *Formation of Labor Movements, 1870–1914.* Leiden: E. J. Brill, 1990.

Velie, Lester. *Desperate Bargain.* New York: Reader's Digest Press, 1977.

Von Drehle, David. *Triangle: The Fire That Changed America.* New York: Grove Press, 2003.

Waldinger, Roger. *Still The Promised Land?* Cambridge, MA: Harvard University Press, 1996.

Wall Street Journal. *A History of Organized Felony and Folly.* New York: Wall Street Journal, 1923.

Ware, Norman. *The Labor Movement in the United States, 1860–1890.* New York: D. Appleton, 1929.

Witwer, David. *Corruption and Reform in the Teamsters Union.* Urbana: University of Illinois Press, 2003.

Zausner, Philip. *Unvarnished.* New York: Brotherhood Publishers, 1941.

Zeller, F. C. Duke. *The Devil's Pact: Inside the World of the Teamsters Union.* Secaucus, NJ: Carol Publishing Group, 1996.

Zieger, Robert H. *The CIO: 1935–1955.* Chapel Hill: University of North Carolina Press, 1955.

Zinn, Howard. *A People's History of the United States.* New York: Harper Perennial, 1995.

NEWSPAPERS, MAGAZINES, & PERIODICALS

American Prospect
American Spectator
Asian Week
BNA Daily Labor Reporter
Boston Globe
Boston Herald
BusinessWeek
Capitalism Magazine
Chicago Tribune
Chief-Leader
Corriere della sera
Die Zeit
Engineering News-Record
Forbes
Fort Worth Star Telegram
Forward
Harper's Weekly
Harvard Law Review

Humanities in Society
Illinois Times
In These Times
Irish Voice
Journal of Social History
Labor History
Labor Notes
Le Monde
Los Angeles Times
McClure's
Miami Herald
Mother Jones
Nation
New England Journal of Medicine
New York Daily News
New York Magazine
New York Observer
New York Times

Newark Star-Ledger
Newsday
Organized Labor
Outlook
People's Weekly World
Philadelphia Inquirer
Providence Journal
Providence Journal-Bulletin
Quarterly Journal of Economics
Ramparts
San Francisco Chronicle
Scientific American
Slate

Socialist Worker Online
Spectator
TIE Asia
Tikkun
Time
Union Democracy Review
Utica Observer-Dispatch
Village Voice
The Villager
Wall Street Journal
Washington Times
Women's Wear Daily

INDEX

PUBLICAFFAIRS is a publishing house founded in 1997. It is a tribute to the standards, values, and flair of three persons who have served as mentors to countless reporters, writers, editors, and book people of all kinds, including me.

I. F. STONE, proprietor of *I. F. Stone's Weekly,* combined a commitment to the First Amendment with entrepreneurial zeal and reporting skill and became one of the great independent journalists in American history. At the age of eighty, Izzy published *The Trial of Socrates,* which was a national bestseller. He wrote the book after he taught himself ancient Greek.

BENJAMIN C. BRADLEE was for nearly thirty years the charismatic editorial leader of *The Washington Post.* It was Ben who gave the *Post* the range and courage to pursue such historic issues as Watergate. He supported his reporters with a tenacity that made them fearless, and it is no accident that so many became authors of influential, best-selling books.

ROBERT L. BERNSTEIN, the chief executive of Random House for more than a quarter century, guided one of the nation's premier publishing houses. Bob was personally responsible for many books of political dissent and argument that challenged tyranny around the globe. He is also the founder and was the longtime chair of Human Rights Watch, one of the most respected human rights organizations in the world.

· · ·

For fifty years, the banner of Public Affairs Press was carried by its owner Morris B. Schnapper, who published Gandhi, Nasser, Toynbee, Truman, and about 1,500 other authors. In 1983 Schnapper was described by *The Washington Post* as "a redoubtable gadfly." His legacy will endure in the books to come.

Peter Osnos, *Founder and Editor-at-Large*